PRAISE FOR *MASTERING THE C*

CW01498335

"The transition to a circular economy is a do-or-die choice facing soci-ety. More and more companies are willing to make the journey, but still lack the necessary insight, skills and tools to succeed. *Mastering the Circular Economy* is a must-have guidebook for transforming business into a proactive force for good. This vital book by Rozanne Henzen and Ed Weenk will broaden your perspective on the circular economy, deepen your knowledge and raise your aspirations to do more and better. The chapters weave together important concepts and best-practice examples, while offering helpful tools to turn ideas into reality. This book gives vital clues to how we can and must avoid overshoot and collapse in nature, society and the econ-omy. I highly recommend it."
Wayne Visser, presenter of *Closing the Loop*, the world's first feature-length documentary on the circular economy; holder of the Chair in Sustainable Transformation at Antwerp Management School; Fellow of the University of Cambridge Institute for Sustainability Leadership

"Here are my two suggestions on how to enjoy this very practical and at the same time rigorous book: either as a perfect complement to the Blue Connection business simulation game (my favourite option!) to design a whole course around these two clear and powerful teaching tools and get the most out of them, or as a source of inspiration for a multitude of mini-cases and exercises to have a hands-on learning experience on the circular economy."
Valentina Carbone, Professor, Scientific Co-director of the Circular Economy Chair, ESCP - Paris Campus, France

"Hands-on and engaging writing style with a brilliant structure where the reader is taken on the journey from idea to practice, and towards envisioning the future. Truly recommendable!"
Desirée Knoppen, Head of Academic Department. Associate Professor of Circular Economy and Supply Chain Management, EADA Business School. Barcelona, Spain

"At last: supply chain featured prominently in *Mastering the Circular Economy*! Operationalizing the circular economy poses a great challenge across our industry and profession: this book gives a solid foundation to grasping the importance of supply chain as we transition our operations, business models, and economies towards circularity."
Deborah Dull, Founder, Circular Supply Chain Network , USA

"*Mastering the Circular Economy* is a very timely and appealing book for multiple reasons. First and foremost the transition from traditional linear models to circular ones is of course a major societal and business challenge. Second, the book contains numerous relevant practical examples and exercises, with a prominent role for the Blue Connection simulation game. Third, the book provides a truly integrated learning approach, hence facilitating an experiential learning journey. And finally, this learning experience is supported by numerous inspiring illustrations. My favourite? It is difficult to make a choice, but I would opt for Figure 4.9, 'The T-shaped supply chain manager'. This picture elegantly captures the complexity of the circular economy challenge, starting already in primary education. So, in the spirit of the Blue Connection simulation: Game on!"
Bart Vos, Professor of Supply Chain Innovation and Scientific Director, Brightlands Institute for Supply Chain Innovation (BISCI), Maastricht University, Netherlands

"*Mastering the Circular Economy* is an engaging and hands-on approach to applying the concepts of circularity to business practices and developing the leadership competencies to drive organizational transformation. It gives clarity where we tend to see complexity and makes caring for our people, our organizations, and our environment accessible for managers worldwide. It is a must-read for purpose-driven people leading purposeful organizations."
David Dinwoodie, Centre for Creative Leadership, Spain, and co-author of *Becoming a Strategic Leader: Your role in your organization's enduring success*

"Our current linear approach has got to change and adapt to a more mindful approach that recognises the impact our activities are having on the world. Adopting a circular approach that seeks to reduce our impacts that benefit all stakeholders is critical. One major challenge is – How to transition existing linear supply chains and business to a more circular approach? Managers both current and future will need to develop their understanding of the different strategies to achieving this. The Blue Connection is a simulation that allows us to manage this transition for an electric bicycle manufacturer. It surfaces many of the challenges we will face in reality and allows us to test different solutions and approaches to understand the interactions and inherent complexities. The book, *Mastering the Circular Economy*, which integrates the theory with the simulation will provide a unique opportunity for circular education and training and significantly enhance the experiential learning curve."
Denyse Julien, Associate Professor, Cranfield University School of Management, UK

"Circular supply chains are getting momentum as a way to answer to the world's limited resource availability and to the trend towards more responsible consumption. However, translating the idea into practical actions has proven to be challenging

and we need to educate and train the current and next generations of leaders. *Mastering the Circular Economy* is a very useful textbook to this purpose."
Yann Bouchery, Associate Professor in Operations Management & Logistics, Head of the Centre of Excellence in Supply Chains, KEDGE Business School, France

"I have got to know Ed Weenk as an excellent scholar and outstanding executive educator. In the classroom, he leverages his academic background with his long-standing professional experience. For these qualities, he is truly appreciated by our students in the Executive and Professional MBA programmes. His substantial under-standing for the field is not only demonstrated in the classroom setting, but clearly displayed in his books. Therefore, I am happy to see that in his latest publication, co-written with Rozanne Henzen, the focus is on a timely and crucial topic – circular economy. It needs experts like Ed and Rozanne to bring these pressing issues close to students at all levels and executives to make sure such that it also transcends fast and effectively into today's business practice."
Barbara Stöttinger, Dean WU Wien Executive Academy, Associate Professor International Marketing Management, Austria

"This timely book provides a thorough overview of the different aspects of the circu-lar economy and concrete tools and exercises for implementing a circular strategy. The combination with the Blue Connection simulation game enables an experiential learning experience that will ensure that students master knowledge and skills needed in the circular economy. Both the didactical approach and the contents reso-nate very well with what TIAS stands for as School for Business and Society: transformative learning based on a combination of business modelling, sustainable innovation, collaboration and responsible leadership. The book covers these various challenges in an integrative manner."
Eric Dooms, Associate Professor of Strategy, and Mirjam Minderman, Policy Adviser & Lecturer Business and Society, TIAS School for Business and Society, Netherlands

"I have used the Blue Connection simulation in my sustainable supply chain manage-ment course. I believe the textbook *Mastering the Circular Economy* will be an excellent resource to help integrate the simulation concepts with the course content of a sustainable supply chain management course, as well as provide guidance for the students in playing the Blue Connection simulation."
Evelyn Thomchick, Associate Professor of Supply Chain Management, Department of Supply Chain & Information Systems at The Pennsylvania State University, USA

"This book offers an excellent contribution to the important topic of circular econ-omy. It is practically relevant and academically rooted, it is well-balanced and interesting and in combination with the circular business game it serves as a fun and

inspiring teaching tool that deals with the realities of today and tomorrow. It is my sincere pleasure to recommend it!"
Viktor Elliot, Senior Lecturer in Accounting and Finance at Gothenburg University and Director of Bitlab, Sweden

"The book is an impressive combination of theoretical frameworks and practical tools on Circular Economy, supported by the online game on the virtual company 'The Blue Connection' of Inchainge. A must-have for lecturers in the field of circular economy and logistics!"
Hedda van Raalte, Lecturer, Logistics Management/Supply Chain Management, thesis coordinator, Hogeschool Rotterdam, Netherlands

"*Mastering the Circular Economy* provides comprehensive insights to our new reality post Covid-19. This book offers a theoretical and practical advice to rethink, reimagine, revalue and be resilient in a new business environment. The research by Henzen and Weenk reveals how the circular economy is the responsibility of every leader. This new approach is a major step toward the new humanity era."
Mario Chong, Professor, Universidad del Pacifico, Lima, Peru

"Circular economy will most certainly be one of the top issues when companies develop strategies for the coming years. At the universities, the circular perspective will become a major topic when teaching students supply chain skills. This book, in combination with the game The Blue Connection, provides a practical and concrete tool for both top-level executives in companies and for professors at universities."
Søren Schulian, Associate Professor, cphbusiness Copenhagen, Denmark

"Great timing! Now that the concept of circular economy is embraced more and more by governments and companies around the world, more practical questions in regards to implementation start to arise. This book helps fill the knowledge gap that exists between abstract circular economy policies and plans and the most practical level of implementation."
Bas Hillerström, Head of Operations, Circo NL, Netherlands

"Henzen and Weenk have done an excellent job in *Mastering the Circular Economy*. With their book, they bridge the gap between the theoretical value chain concept and direct applications. They take the complex idea of circularity and clearly explain concepts and relationships using The Blue Connection to fully integrate different circular challenges. They also provide many examples and cases for the learner to think about how to apply data and overcome these challenges."
Wendy L Tate, William J Taylor Professor of Business, Cheryl Massengale Faculty Research Fellow at University of Tennessee, Knoxville, USA

"Mastering the circular economy: from (easy to explain) theory to (difficult to obtain) supply chain circular efficiency. The book is a combination of an extensive description of theoretical concepts and an online supply chain serious game, allowing the reader/user to recognize that the devil is in the details in order to master the circular economy and to understand that a coordinated functional strategy for the different circularity factors impacting the supply chain is necessary to succeed."
Christian van Delft, Professeur Associé, HEC Paris, France

"*Mastering the Circular Economy* is an honest and powerful resource to learn what the circular economy is and how people can master its application. The book will provide the reader with foundational knowledge, spark their curiosity, challenge their ideologies and fundamentally support the reader to take action. This is a book to not only sink your mind into but your whole being into. I am excited by what *Mastering the Circular Economy* will do for catalysing action. Our most critical need now is to move beyond theory to implementation and this book has the power to catalyse that."
Ashleigh Morris, CEO and Co-Founder of Coreo, Australia

"A hands-on approach to learn all about how to transition to a circular economy! Especially the integration of a business simulation in a textbook is refreshing. I think it allows the learner to apply the theoretical circular concepts right away in a realistic and dynamic context, making it a powerful learning experience."
Maayke Damen, CEO of Excess Materials Exchange

"For anyone keen to explore circular economy and even implementing it into practice, this is a great in-depth go-to guide. It takes you from a theoretical concept of CE through the practical challenges and considerations to an actual change in strategy and business models. All while providing insights on the market landscape, organisational lens, role of leadership, changing cashflows and value generation. This is done in an engaging way through exercises, examples and gamification. The Blue Connection game is simulating an actual business environment where you are developing circular products and services. Circular economy is crucial in the sustainability transition which is the only way to secure a liveable future for ourselves and the next generations. If you are keen to be a part of it, this book is a very good game plan to start with."
Andrea Orsag, Co-Founder of MissionC and circular economy evangelist

"Our current transition from a linear to a circular economy is fraught with many obstacles, mostly of our own making. The methods and training exercises contained in *Mastering the Circular Economy* are aimed at allowing physical design choices regarding material use and re-use to be integrated with economic design choices.

They allow students to work with fundamental concepts in a highly practical matter. *Mastering the Circular Economy* will help you reassess the value proposition of products by taking (functional) residual value into account, alongside the lesser burden on operational expenses that a flexible, future ready product design allows for. This book will help you achieve this goal, better than most."
Olaf J Blaauw, Senior Consultant on Systems Thinking-based Transition and the Circular Economy

"This comprehensive guide sets a new standard that is relevant for anyone wanting to learn how to increase the circularity of his value chain."
Julien Atgé, Head of Supply Chain Management, Weleda Switzerland

"*Mastering the Circular Economy* presents an innovative multimedia format that turns the book from an inevitable alphabet soup of concepts into a gourmet delight with true business substance. As a reader, I found myself exploring the book's concepts through various media and highlighted by a practical and robust computer simulation that gets you immersed and engaged. Don't just read this book – experience it!"
Lawrence Suda, CEO at Palatine Group/Management Worlds, Inc.

"Very comprehensive reference book on the topic of circularity. You will find the entire journey from theory into execution. Really informative and useful for your circular transformation."
Wineke Haagsma, Director of Corporate Sustainability PwC, Netherlands & EMEA

"At a time of rupture, as the Covid pandemic reveals our prevalent economic models as even less sustainable than we thought, systematizing circular economy models is seen as one of the solutions. So *Mastering the Circular Economy* is on cue, the kind of book many students, professionals and educators wanting to understand, implement and teach the subject will rejoice in: it's accessible, clear, unpretentious and includes recent thinking on circular economy as well as a comprehensive overview of the topic looking back. It will please both the 'hands-on' and the more reflective reader, student or professional, with an array of exercises and tools and an extensive bibliography. A must-read for those engaging on the topic, and a complement to the Blue Connection circular economy business game, which is also an integral part of the book. Let's build back circular!"
Phoebe Blackburn, communications and circular economy consultant

"A great book that gives the reader a tangible blue print and to start the transition toward circularity."
Ditte Lysgaard Vind, Managing Partner at Lendager, The Circular Way, and author of *A Changemaker's Guide to the Future*

"Through a business lens, the circular economy is a strategy framework allowing a company to mitigate linear risk and capture circular opportunities more effectively than its competition. *Mastering the Circular Economy* uses this perspective in equipping its readers with practical tools and replicable examples that allow them to start their circular transitions immediately."
Brendan Edgerton, Director of Circular Economy, World Business Council for Sustainable Development

"Great insights into the circular economy seen from a business perspective in this book. Taking part in the testing of the Blue Connection simulation game I found it a true eye opener into the circular decision making in companies and into the complexity of producing bicycles based on circular principles –and how great it felt, when we succeeded in making our successful change of your production to a more circular business model."
Markus Bjerre, Special Adviser at the Danish Business Authority

Mastering the Circular Economy

*A practical approach to the circular
business model transformation*

Rozanne Henzen
Ed Weenk

KoganPage

First published in Great Britain and the United States in 2021 by Kogan Page Limited

Apart from any fair dealing for the purposes of research or private study, or criticism or review, as permitted under the Copyright, Designs and Patents Act 1988, this publication may only be reproduced, stored or transmitted, in any form or by any means, with the prior permission in writing of the publishers, or in the case of reprographic reproduction in accordance with the terms and licences issued by the CLA. Enquiries concerning reproduction outside these terms should be sent to the publishers at the undermentioned addresses:

2nd Floor, 45 Gee Street	122 W 27th St, 10th Floor	4737/23 Ansari Road
London	New York, NY 10001	Daryaganj
EC1V 3RS	USA	New Delhi 110002
United Kingdom		India
www.koganpage.com		

© Ed Weenk and Rozanne Henzen 2021

ISBNs

Hardback	9781398602755
Paperback	9781398602748
Ebook	9781398602762

British Library Cataloguing-in-Publication Data

A CIP record for this book is available from the British Library.

Library of Congress Control Number

2021934580

Typeset by Integra Software Services, Pondicherry
Print production managed by Jellyfish
Printed and bound by CPI Group (UK) Ltd, Croydon CR0 4YY

CONTENTS

LIST OF FIGURES

LIST OF EXERCISES

ABOUT THE AUTHORS

Rozanne Henzen

Rozanne Henzen holds an MSc in Strategic Communication Sciences from the University of Antwerp, and received a Fellowship at the Stockholm School of Entrepreneurship during her studies, both focusing on consumer behaviour and circularity for the textile industry. Currently, Rozanne is researcher and circular economy expert within the Expertise Centre for Sustainable Transformation at Antwerp Management School (AMS).

Her research and consultancy services involve research for several national and international research projects within the field of sustainable transformation. She manages the AMS Corporate Leadership Groups, whereby companies jointly commit to public annual actions to promote the circular or well-being economy. As part of her work for AMS she gives Circular Economy 101 lectures and is part of the Global Leadership Skills faculty team.

Rozanne was previously a member of the Dutch National Think Tank focusing on Accelerating the Transition to a Circular Economy and conducted research on individual sustainability leadership. In 2020 her first book was published for the Dutch market, titled *De kleine Circulaire economie for Dummies*, being the first official *For Dummies* book on a circular economy with a clear and thorough explanation, and tips to contribute to a fully circular Netherlands. She is currently being recognized for her sustainability efforts as one of the Sustainable Young 100 of 2020 in the Netherlands.

In her spare time, she tries to make the complexity of a circular economy and other sustainability related topics accessible for everyone through her Instagram (@reduce.reuse.rznn). In doing so, she hopes that people will see the transition to a circular economy as an adventure, instead of a restriction.

Ed Weenk

Ed Weenk MSc PDEng is an experienced lecturer, corporate advisor and workshop and training facilitator. His professional passions are sustainable operations and supply chain, managers and management, projects and project management, training and teaching, and business simulations and experiential learning.

He has extensive practical experience since the mid-1990s in managing international logistics and distribution projects at strategic and operational level and is a strong believer in the principles of experiential learning. Alongside his practice as an independent professional, he is delivery partner and authorized trainer in the Inchainge business simulations in the Netherlands and the Palatine Group in New York.

Ed collaborates as a Senior Associate Professor at business schools such as EADA Barcelona (Spain), Maastricht School of Management (the Netherlands), TIAS School for Business and Society (the Netherlands), Antwerp Management School (Belgium), WU Wien Executive Academy (Austria), Rotterdam School of Management (the Netherlands) and Centrum Graduate School of Business (Lima, Peru). His specialization is on the topics of operations and supply chain management, circular economy, project management, and intra- and entrepreneurship.

Ed has previously written a management book, *The Perfect Pass: What the manager can learn from the football trainer*, published in English, Spanish and Dutch, about the importance of seeing the *big picture*, having good internal and external *alignment* and achieving *coherence* at all levels. In 2019 his second book was published, titled *Mastering the Supply Chain: Principles, practice and real-life applications*, now available in English and Dutch. Similar to *Mastering the Circular Economy*, this book combines relevant theory and frameworks with practical application through a business simulation.

Noah Schaul (contributor)

Noah, originally from Luxembourg, speaks five languages fluently (Luxembourgish, English, German, French and Dutch) and currently lives in Utrecht, the Netherlands.

From a young age, sustainability was a key interest, later on developing into his passion for sustainable business. Noah graduated *cum laude* from Utrecht University's honours programme, studying a BSc in Economics and Business Economics, with a minor in Economic Geography. His thesis about revisiting the impossibility of universal basic income was published on the Citizen's Basic Income Trust website.

After projects in sustainable food, the sharing economy and art business, Noah joined Inchainge in 2019. There, he had the opportunity to dive deep into the circular economy.

Among his first projects was the launch of the newly developed circular business simulation The Blue Connection. During the 'City Tour', key stakeholders were invited to showcase events across Europe to experience the brand-new circular strategy business simulation. This project allowed Noah to meet professionals, academics, NGOs, consultants and politicians to discuss optimal ways to transition to circularity.

Over the course of 2020, Noah has developed into a thought leader on circularity within Inchainge, establishing a reputation as 'Mr Circular' within his team. Noah is now one of the master trainers in The Blue Connection, facilitating Train the Trainer events, professional programmes, university courses and MBAs.

As a strong believer in cooperation, Noah has started to build a circular economy community for the Netherlands on LinkedIn and is growing the network of delivery partners for Inchainge.

BACKGROUND

EGGE HAAK – PARTNER AT INCHAINGE

Inchainge is a Dutch company fully dedicated to experiential learning in Value Chain Management based on business simulations. We constantly create new simulations and training programmes as well as enhancing our existing ones, so that learners around the industry and around the world can be supported in their learning journeys. Being a small and compact organization we take great care in developing and maintaining a large network of both professional trainers and educational teachers and professors around the globe.

We see around us that the volatile and uncertain world we currently live in creates enormous challenges for companies and their value chains. Change is the only certainty in everyday business and in order to adapt supply chains successfully, a thorough understanding of their dynamics and interdependencies is absolutely necessary. But just understanding the system as a whole will not be enough – constant adaptation also calls for leadership skills in collaboration and teamwork.

At Inchainge, we believe that such understanding and the corresponding skills can only be acquired through active experience. I'm referring to the full experience of managing a value chain with a team, of handling all dimensions in an integral way, of exploring how everything is connected, of working effectively together as a team. On top of this our mission is to help students and companies create alignment between strategy and execution, between departments in a company, and between business partners in the value chain.

We have designed and built all of our business simulations with these objectives in mind, starting with The Fresh Connection in 2008: to help learners understand relevant concepts, to provide them with a platform to experience these in a virtual company setting and thus acquire the necessary skills in order to better deal with the complexities of alignment in the competitive and fun setting of a game. But we don't stop there – we also have a wide diversity of materials to support teachers, trainers and learners in their usage of our simulations and to enrich their experience with meaningful content.

That is also where this book fits in, like its predecessor *Mastering the Supply Chain*. Apart from our existing simulations and supporting materials, we were looking for a way to further bridge the gap between theoretical value chain concepts and their direct application and that is precisely what you will find here. The book starts with an overview of many critical concepts around the topic of circularity, then invites you to discover their practical application using The Blue Connection as an interactive case. The third part of the book goes beyond the pure context of the simulation, providing learners with a wealth of additional circular challenges to think about. With this, I believe the book will be extremely useful to both learners and their instructors, be it in business or in the educational world.

At Inchainge, we trust that *Mastering the Circular Economy* will set a new standard and bring the integral experience of The Blue Connection to a higher level.

FOREWORD: GAME ON!

PROF DR MICHIEL STEEMAN, WINDESHEIM UNIVERSITY
OF APPLIED SCIENCES

We are fortunate that, for the good of the planet, consumers and regulators have environmental concerns much more front of mind than ever before. From carbon emissions to resource depletion to the junk that floats in our seas, we all have a far greater awareness of the need to be much more careful about how we use and dispose of all the things we buy. Manufacturers and other players in the distribution chain have, for the most part, not been slow to recognize that they have legal and moral responsibilities to society. The smarter ones have seen a business opportunity as well.

But the circular economy concept is developing further, becoming more structured and sophisticated in its approach. In its wake are coming new ideas about product ownership and use, new business models – and new financial models to support circular supply chains. From an academic research perspective there are still a lot of questions to be answered. In my own field of research, for example, we look into changing ownership models, the importance of residual value, the effects on cash flow and the need for trusted data. However, it can be said that collaboration and alignment are the keystones in these emerging paradigms. We are going to see new forms of collaboration between partners up and down the physical, financial and information supply chains, upstream and down.

Such a collaborative transition to a circular economy – for all its obvious advantages in terms of natural resources, climate change and pollution of all kinds – is not easy. Windesheim partnered with Inchainge and ING over the past several years to develop The Blue Connection, a circular business game that will entice company employees and university students to understand how to get a grip on all the conflicting challenges that a transition to a circular economy entails.

And now, with this book on *Mastering the Circular Economy*, Rozanne Henzen and Ed Weenk have achieved an integration of all the elements that professors, teachers, educators and trainers need to teach about the circular economy. A truly integrated learning approach as the authors would call it. It will take students on a journey, which starts with exploring the current theory and historical background of circular economy. Students can then apply these concepts in a realistic context using The Blue Connection and eventually imagine how the transition will unfold in the future.

The combination of the book and the circular game supports a truly blended approach to teaching: offline and online, individual and team learning, soft skills and hard skills, serious and fun. It will allow educators to really engage students with different learning styles or cultural backgrounds. I go so far as to say that this topic is actually binding this generation of students and young professionals.

What a privilege it has been to work together with these authors, game developers, professionals, researchers and teachers to develop these learning tools that can harness the intrinsic motivation of this generation. Let us now try to reach as many people as possible and engage them to support the movement to a circular economy. Game on!

FOREWORD: HANDS-ON GUIDANCE FOR FUTURE-PROOFING YOUR BUSINESS THROUGH CIRCULARITY

ALICE SCHMIDT MSC, AS CONSULTING, VIENNA UNIVERSITY OF ECONOMICS AND BUSINESS

Companies around the world are beginning to realize that future-proofing their businesses and brands will require shifting from linear approaches to circular ways of doing business. Whether large or small, the companies that come to us for advice have in common that they want to know how to do this in a way that makes business sense. To these enlightened companies, the 'why' no longer needs to be explained.

The case is clear: virgin resources are finite and hence getting harder and more costly to obtain. Regulators are waking up to the social and economic costs of pollution, requiring companies to take responsibility for their impact along the entire value chain. At the same time, tools, technologies and business models exist that help companies reduce, reuse and design their products in ways that minimize virgin resource input while allowing for repair and refurbishment, thus leaving recycling as a last resort rather than as a centrepiece of sustainability. And by the way, circularity is a key tool to address climate change as well: products are responsible for almost half of all greenhouse gas emissions!

Business models that ignore these factors or, worse, are built on planned obsolescence are not fit for the future. While we must drastically rethink the way in which we do business, it's not like we need to reinvent the wheel. Only a couple of generations ago we found it natural to treat 'waste' as a resource and have things fixed when they were broken as this simply made economic sense. Some companies and many people, particularly in developing countries, have retained this wisdom.

When teaching BA and MBA students from around the globe about Sustainable Business and Managing for Tomorrow, I am always inspired by their intense interest in sustainability, circularity and in harnessing the immense power of business to create a better world. They realize that destroying the natural environment which we all depend on for a healthy and happy life does not make economic sense.

Despite these students' interest and passion – and the fact that business demand for employees who understand sustainability and circularity is significant and growing – the offer of concrete guidance, such as practical textbooks on circularity and sustainability, has been very limited. Generations of students and hence businesses may have missed out on essential practical tools and insights to translate academic insight into concrete, circular action.

This is why *Mastering the Circular Economy: A practical approach to the circular business model transformation* is so welcome and essential. It offers comprehensive insights into anything you ever wanted to know about the circular economy and, importantly, provides a wealth of tools that help you master sustainable business model transformation in a hands-on manner.

FOREWORD: THE CORPORATE CIRCULAR IMPERATIVE, THROUGH THE LENSES OF PHILIPS AND ING

The circular economy is not only taking a new perspective in terms of how things are being set up and done, but also in terms of mindset. A key element of this mindset is collaboration, so here we have a joint view on the corporate perspective by ING and Philips.

HARALD TEPPER, SR DIRECTOR SUSTAINABILITY AND CIRCULAR ECONOMY PROGRAMME LEAD, ROYAL PHILIPS

At Philips, a leading health technology company, our purpose is to improve people's health and well-being through meaningful innovation. We aim to grow Philips responsibly and sustainably and have set ourselves ambitious environmental and social targets. For a sustainable world, we see the transition from a linear to a circular economy as a necessary boundary condition. We are fundamentally rethinking our economic model and the role of business in society.

The heart of the circular economy lies in decoupling value creation from the use of natural resources. Everyone in business should always ask: 'How can I offer value – to customers, end users, and society at large – with minimal use of materials?' You can offer products 'as a service', and reuse, repair, or refurbish them. You can extend their value by predictive maintenance, and (remote) upgrades. And, in this age of digitization, you can often design software solutions that offer greater benefits while needing less hardware.

At Philips, we find that the business benefits extend far beyond growing revenue and reducing cost: circular economy drives innovation, allows employees to live their purpose, and changes relationships with customers and suppliers into true partnerships.

To succeed on this journey, you need courageous targets, personal leadership and commitment, as well as radical collaboration – across businesses, governments, and knowledge institutions. I hope this book will help readers to better understand the topic and to gain the necessary skills to put theory into practice.

MARLOES BERGEVOET, SR MARKETEER AT ING WHOLESALE BANKING

The pathway to circularity is a road that has already existed for a long time, although we did not give it this name in the early days. When I first set foot on it, about five years ago, I realized that it is an evident route if we want to tackle the environmental challenges we face today. Luckily, more and more travelling companions are joining, which is necessary because making circular concepts successful requires collaboration across companies, industries, countries, government bodies and beyond.

This collaborative approach is something that appeals to me, as well as the obvious links the circular economy has to sustainability, innovation, economics, and customer intimacy. In my function as a marketeer at ING, I have been able to explore and connect the dots between all these pillars. The possibilities are endless, and I find it fascinating to explore how companies rethink the way they design, produce, and sell their products (as a service).

From an economic perspective it is key to understand that in the circular economy, economic growth is decoupled from resource consumption. Different ownership structures arise, the lifetime of products and materials is extended, revenue models change and as a result we as a bank have to value differently, treat risk differently and finance differently. It truly requires a shift in mindset, and ING is investing heavily in financial solutions to support the circular economy as well as the circular mindset.

At ING, I've seen the beauty of applying supply chain simulation games to boost knowledge, build relationships and spark commercial discussions. That's why ING, and I personally, have been involved from day one in the development of The Blue Connection. I've seen in practice the power of the simulation throughout the numerous sessions I've hosted with clients and colleagues around the globe. It makes complex concepts, such as the circular economy, tangible and allows people to play and experiment with it in a scenario where they need to build their own circular company. And after every session I facilitate, I hear back from the audience the need to collaborate and look beyond your own area of expertise; not only within your own company but even within your own value chain.

I'm a strong believer in experiential learning and really happy to see how this book helps to build the theoretical backbone to support the action learning in The Blue Connection. I hope that with these tools you'll pick up the energy to make change happen and look forward to connecting with you on the road to circularity.

PREFACE: THE CORPORATE CIRCULAR IMPERATIVE: NARRATIVE AND NUMBERS (1)

> Many students learn best when they are actively doing things and not only studying ideas in the abstract: when their curiosity is aroused, when they are asking questions, discovering new ideas, and feeling for themselves the excitement of these disciplines.
>
> KEN ROBINSON AND LOU ARONICA, 2015

Circularity is not just about recycling. Circularity is not just about fighting climate change. Circularity is also not just the latest hype in sustainable business. In fact, circularity isn't even new.

Check out any major city in Africa, India or South America to find large clusters of car repair shops, household appliance repair shops, clothing repair shops and so on. In Europe or the United States, for most people circularity arguably was quite a normal element of daily life until at least the 1950s. A world in which things which were broken, from household appliances to tools to clothing, would be repaired, mainly out of *economic necessity* – there simply was no money to buy something new.

In Europe and the United States, with the economies booming from the 1960s onwards, consumerism has entered over time as the *modus vivendi* and people have gotten used to throwing things away to be replaced by newer or more fashionable things. At best these items are replaced at the end of their physical lifecycle, but in many cases it is long before, and all too often even before using them at all. If other countries that are trailing in the development curve follow similar development patterns, possibly similar behaviour will be observed there in the future.[1] As much research demonstrates, we are already moving fast towards hitting resource boundaries on the planet. Thus, the economic necessity is maybe no longer the main issue; rather, *resource necessity* (read: scarcity) may become the issue.

As the saying goes, *necessity is the mother of invention* and it can be observed that more and more people, governmental institutions and companies are beginning to see that action is required and that new ways of looking and acting are needed. In short, circularity is gaining relevance, and fast.

Circularity is a highly complex, multi-faceted subject, ranging from product design to reverse logistics to fiscal regulations to international governmental policies to company ecosystems, and more. In addition, the field of circularity is developing rapidly, in terms of academic research as well as new legislation and the proliferation of circular startups.

At the same time, the topic is approached from very different angles. Many people involved in circularity have a strong ecological or even ideological drive, emphasizing that action is needed in order to save the planet from disaster and even our species from extinction. Others approach circularity from a much more technical point of view, not necessarily driven by sustainability motives at all, looking for example at how new materials or new technologies can be used. We believe that somehow, when speaking about circularity, all of these dimensions, angles and voices need to be heard in order to get a complete picture.

Having said that, however, what does this mean for individual companies? Why should a company at their micro level be involved in helping to solve macro issues like climate change? Or invest heavily in more durable product designs and/or materials, at the risk of becoming more expensive than their competitors? In other words, what's the *Corporate Circular Imperative*? Why should a company care? That's one of the central questions we raise in this book, with *narrative and numbers* as recurring key themes.[2]

And we want to do that in the spirit of the quote at the beginning of this Preface: to create a textbook with a clear and strong focus on practical application by learners. Albert Einstein allegedly used to say that instead of focusing on teaching and explaining theories and concepts, he preferred to put emphasis on providing the conditions in which students could practise and learn. In allusion to Einstein, this book wants to provide a solid basis for learners to practise and learn how to master circularity from a company perspective.

Mastering the Circular Economy is written for people studying such diverse topics as Business, Sustainability, Supply Chain Management and so on. It can be used as part of courses in schools and universities within specialized circularity or sustainability programmes, but also links well to courses within programmes of a more generalist nature, from Bachelor level up to (Executive) MBA. In addition, the book is written in such a way that it is also suitable for use by professionals, either for individual self-study or for in-company trainings.

Integrated learning approach

In the same spirit as the previous textbook, *Mastering the Supply Chain*, from the same series, this book is proposing an integrated learning approach.

Specifically, there are three main desires behind the topics chosen for the book and the strong emphasis on practical application:

1 The desire to put the increasing need for developing *21st-century skills* such as critical thinking, complex problem solving and coordinating with others into the practical context of circularity.

2 The desire to actively address the recurring theme of *simple but not easy*, i.e. to provide a way to make learners feel first-hand the many complexities of actually applying the often relatively straightforward concepts and frameworks at play in circularity.

3 The desire to combine the *multiple perspectives on circularity* into one coherent and holistic view on the topic, focusing in particular on the company perspective, the leadership perspective and perspective beyond the company frontiers.

One element related to those, however, deserves specific attention here. Since we're dealing with practical skills, experiential learning seems to be a very appropriate way of developing and training such skills. We'd like to particularly reference the work of David Kolb, whose book *Experiential Learning* is a classic on the topic. Among other important contributions, such as for example the concept of individual learning styles, Kolb is well known for what is called the learning cycle.

The main idea behind the learning cycle is that 'knowledge results from the combination of grasping and transforming experience. Grasping experience refers to the process of taking in information, and transforming experience is how individuals interpret and act on that information. [...] This process is portrayed as an idealized learning cycle or spiral where the learner "touches all the bases".'[3]

In experiential learning, the focus is on going through a first-hand experience, which allows for reflection on what happened and why, leading to forming a conceptual view on the situation, potentially reinforced by existing theories and/or frameworks. This combination will then be the basis for an improved view on the situation, which can then be applied in the next experience, either in class or other study environment, or directly in a real-world situation. In the book we will use a business

FIGURE 0.1   Integrated learning approach

Integrated learning approach

Meaningful & relevant	Needs to appeal to learner's perspective: business, society, citizenship
For now & the future	Not only the basics, but link to future changes & challenges
'Feel' the complexity!	Everything looks simple, until you're in the driving seat
Knowledge & skills	Not only '*know the concepts*', but also '*able to decide*' (trade-offs)
Individual & team activities	Individual view versus team & cross-functional alignment
Engaging & fun	Motivate: through the *content,* but also through the *methodology* ('gamification')

FIGURE 0.2   The learning cycle

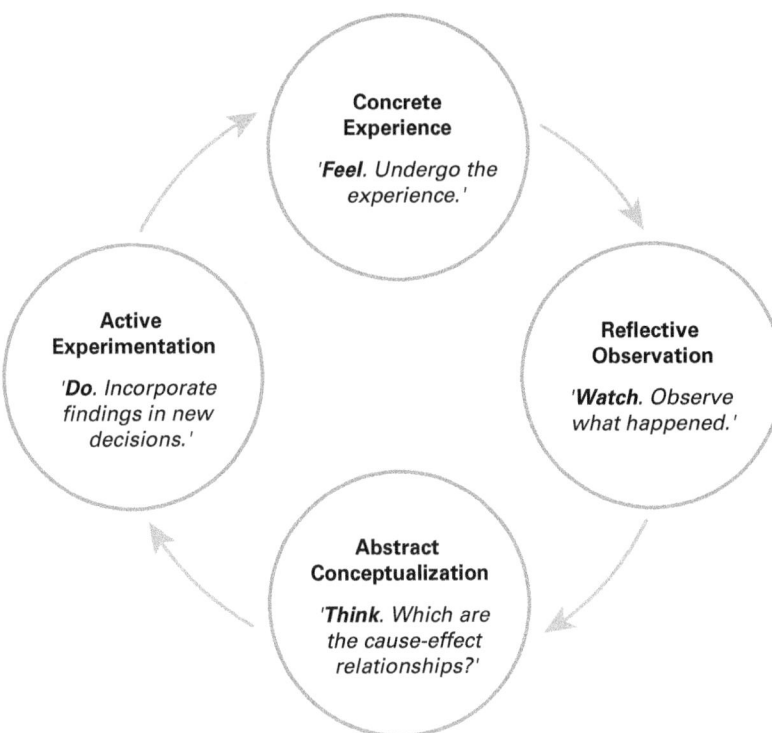

SOURCE after McLeod (2017), based on Kolb (2015)

simulation game called The Blue Connection as an important tool for facilitating this experiential learning.

The multiple perspectives on circularity

Circularity has many faces and covers a wide array of activities as far as scope is concerned. But it also has very distinct dimensions, which are very different in nature. Even if we want to focus on what circularity can mean at the (micro) company level, there are still many aspects to be addressed.

First, we need to define what circularity means from the '**company perspective**'. Why would a company engage in becoming more circular, i.e. how does it match with concepts like strategy and purpose? And what does becoming circular mean at the company level? What are the alternatives and what are their implications for the goods flows that need to be managed? And what are feasible and viable business models that go together with circular strategies? And what does that mean for the company's financials?

Second, circularity also has a clear 'perspective beyond the company boundary'. Even more than in regular business, the dependency on what governments do or do not do, which new circular ecosystems emerge, or which new educational requirements become visible, mean that companies are forced to have a clear view on what happens outside.

And third, becoming and being circular calls for a high degree of coordination and collaboration, but also of innovation and change. Therefore, circularity at the company level also has a clear 'leadership perspective'. How can circularity be measured? How do the different departments involved need to align? What does the path from linear to circular look like and how can the transformation best be managed?

Because of their importance and because of their differences as well as interdependencies, these three distinct perspectives (company, beyond the company boundary and leadership) will be dealt with explicitly and separately. In fact, together they form the backbone of the structure of the book.

As a last comment in this Preface, we want to go back to the *Corporate Circular Imperative*, mentioned earlier on. There are many opinions about why companies should or should not engage in becoming circular. And practice unfortunately shows examples of companies claiming to be very sustainable or circular when reality turns out to be much less positive about what they really do. John Elkington, a long-time advocate of sustainability and the person who coined the concept *Triple Bottom Line* of people, planet and profit, in fact did a 'concept recall' recently, because he found that too many companies were merely using the concept in order to look good, rather than do good (Elkington, 2018).

In the book, we want to stay away from imposing opinions, but we do address the many viewpoints that can be found in practice. We introduce a few (fictitious)

FIGURE 0.3   The three perspectives on circularity at the core of the book

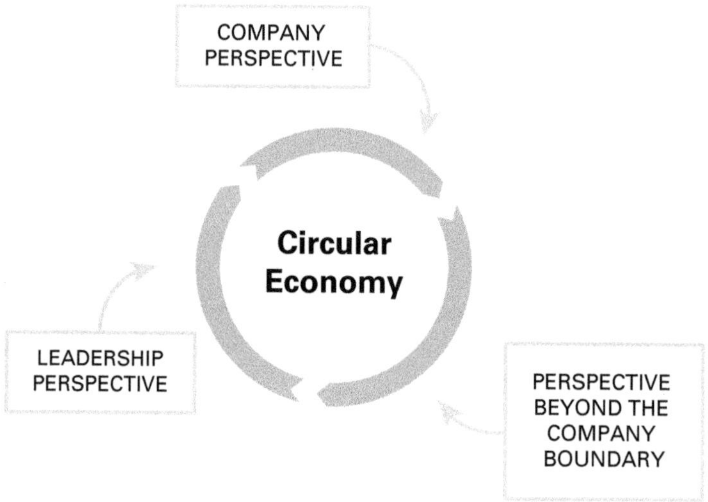

COMPANY
PERSPECTIVE

**Circular
Economy**

LEADERSHIP
PERSPECTIVE

PERSPECTIVE
BEYOND THE
COMPANY
BOUNDARY

FIGURE 0.4   The journey of narrative and numbers (the Corporate Circular Imperative)

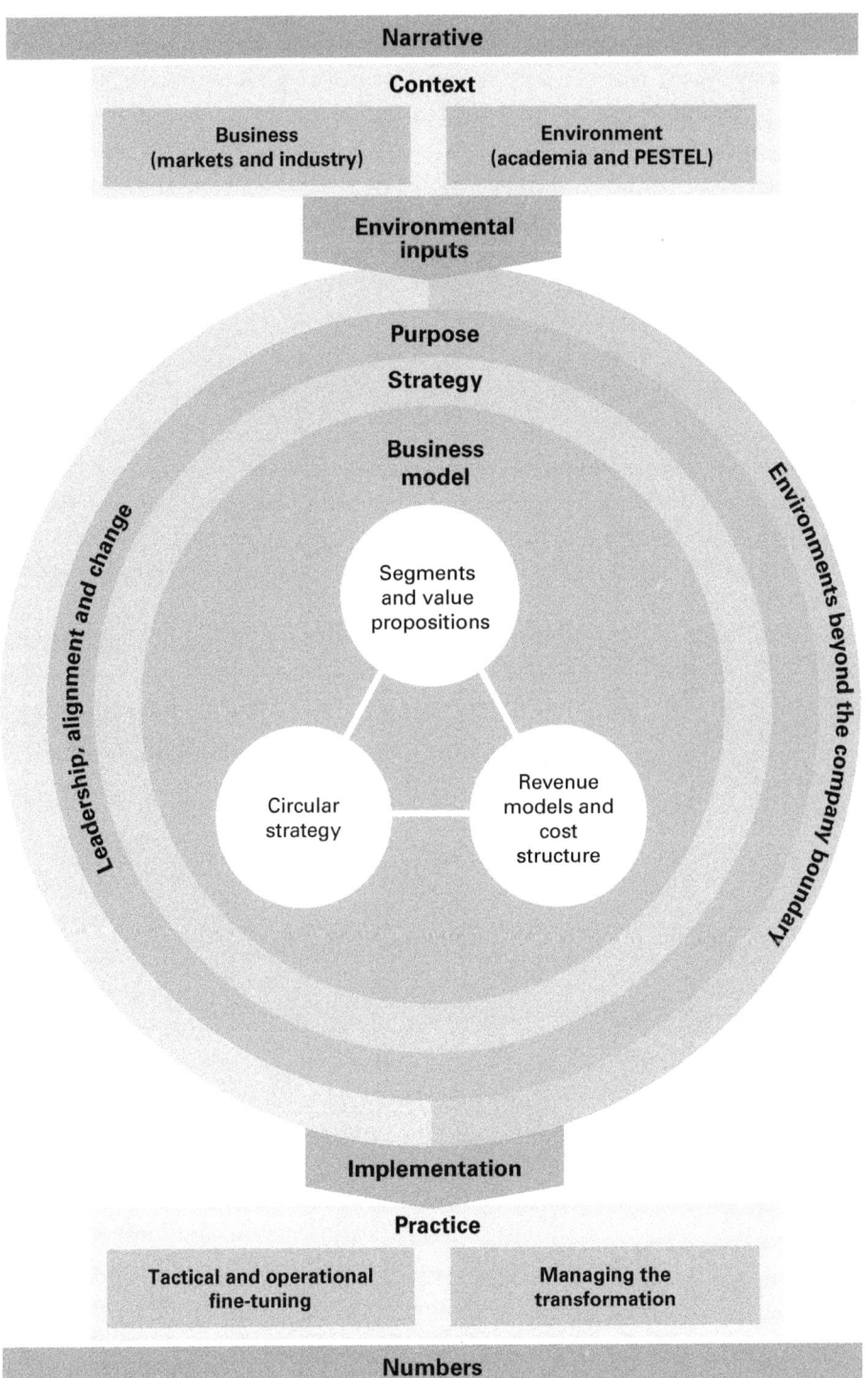

characters to accompany the learner on their circular journey, via dialogues that appear throughout the book. These characters express opinions that can be found around us, sometimes agreeing, sometimes disagreeing. Step by step, they go from context to company purpose, strategy and business models to practice, thus discovering the multitude of aspects involved in the narrative and numbers of the Corporate Circular Imperative.

We hope that this book will help the learner to better understand the topic of circularity and that these dialogues will allow the learner to make up their own mind and define what they see as the Corporate Circular Imperative and the narrative and numbers that could go with it.

Notes

1 Please do note that the simplistic distinction between 'developed nations' and 'developing nations' in practice requires a much more differentiated view, even within countries, as has been shown beautifully in Hans Rosling's work (e.g. Rosling et al, 2018).

2 The notion of 'narrative and numbers' was introduced in an article on business models by Magretta (2002).

3 McLeod, S (2017) Kolb's learning styles and experiential learning cycle, SimplyPsychology, available from: https://www.simplypsychology.org/learning-kolb.html (archived at https://perma.cc/74X7-QD8F)

STRUCTURE OF THE BOOK: A PRACTICAL APPROACH TO THE CIRCULAR BUSINESS MODEL TRANSFORMATION

In line with the desires behind the book as explained before, the objective of this book is to fully facilitate for the *learner touching all the bases*, using the principles of experiential learning, training 21st-century skills, while going through the first-hand experience of the circular economy being simple but not easy and working with the distinct perspectives of the topic.

The Blue Connection business simulation game will be at the heart of this learning experience in Parts Two and Three of the book. In subsequent steps, the business simulation serves as a vehicle for grasping experience, as well as transforming experience, by offering the possibility for the simulation of rounds of gameplay complemented by conceptual frameworks, as well as active reflecting by the learner, leading into a new round of simulation, creating a steep learning curve based on first-hand experience. In addition, fields of direct application outside the simulation tool will be touched upon, to widen the learner's perspective even further.

In Part One: Exploring the circular economy, we will be presenting a helicopter view of the main important *principles*, i.e. relevant theories, frameworks and concepts of the circular economy and the relationships between them. Although the list itself is quite extensive we want to keep it as simple as possible for this book and that is why instead of going into much detail, we will limit ourselves to brief and to-the-point introductions. Wherever relevant, reference will be made to leading textbooks and articles from the area of circularity. Most of the topics covered will be accompanied by some initial exercises to have the learner actively work with them in order to get acquainted with them. These exercises serve to *explore* the topics at hand. This first section thus sets the scene for *the practical approach to the circular business model transformation* in Parts Two and Three.

Part Two: Mastering circularity then focuses on practically applying the fundamental concepts from Part One. Here, The Blue Connection business simulation will be the main vehicle that will serve for the application of the individual concepts that were introduced in Part One. The basic set-up of the simulation used in this second section presents a relatively stable environment in which to make a wide variety of basic decisions related to circular scenarios, to make the value chain run smoothly and the company profitable. In this way, the learner will get the first-hand experience of *analysing real company data* from different functional areas in order to *make good decisions*. Reflections and exercises in this section will thus be structured in

FIGURE 0.5   Overall structure of the book

	Explore	Master	Imagine
	Part One: **Exploring the** **circular economy**	**Part Two:** **Mastering circularity**	**Part Three:** **Imagining the** **transformation from** **linear to circular**
Company	**01** Exploring the context of circularity **02** The company perspective –Purpose –Strategy –Business models –Segments and value propositions –Circular strategies –Revenue models and cost structure –Finance and financing –Selecting and capturing a circular business model	**06** Getting started with The Blue Connection: Game on! **07** Mastering the company perspective –Decisions, inputs, installed base and decision support tools –Purpose –Strategy – Business Model Canvas –Circular strategies: mapping –Segments and revenue models –Additional revenue –Savings potential –Mechanisms to monetize circularity –Cost structure –Fine-tuning the chosen business model	**11** The transformation from linear to circular **12** Imagining the transformation –Imagine the transformation: Purpose and strategy –Imagine the business model transformation: circular strategy –Imagine the business model transformation: customer relationships –Imagine the business model transformation: suppliers and partnerships –Imagine the business model transformation: revenue model, cost structure and financing
Beyond the company boundary	**03** The perspective beyond the company boundary –Legislation –Inter-firm collaboration –Ecosystems –Education	**08** Mastering the perspective beyond the company boundary –Legislation –Interfirm collaboration –Ecosystems	**13** Imagining beyond the company boundary –Imagine the transformation: legislation –Imagine the transformation: interfirm collaboration –Imagine the transformation: ecosystems –Imagine the transformation: education
Leadership	**04** The leadership perspective –Leading by leveraging polarity –Leading by spanning boundaries –Leading change –Leading by shaping culture –The (transformational) leader in the value chain **05** The Corporate Circular Imperative 2: narrative and numbers	**09** Mastering the leadership perspective –Leading by leveraging polarity –Leading by spanning boundaries: silos –Leading by shaping culture –Leading by spanning boundaries: process and stakeholders **10** The Corporate Circular Imperative 3: narrative and numbers	**14** Imagining the transformation from the leadership perspective –Imagine the transformation: objectives and scorecards –Imagine the transformation: innovation –Imagine the transformation: uncertainty –Imagine the transformation: change management **15** Conclusion: The Corporate Circular Imperative 4: narrative and numbers

steps: *analyse, develop* and *decide*. In addition, through the possibility of running the simulation, there will be a clear and visible link between cause and effect (decisions and results).

Part Three: Imagining the transformation from linear to circular value chains, then elaborates on how to achieve the transition from the current linear value chains to true circular solutions. For example, what are the implications of introducing a circular focus into the company's purpose and strategy, how are business models affected, or how should the period between the linear AS-IS and the circular TO-BE be organized? Reflections and exercises in the third section fall under the umbrella of *imagining the transformation* of certain internal corporate directions, or the anticipated response to those from external stakeholders. All aspects covered in Part Three will be related to the company at the heart of the gameplay in Part Two, so wherever possible, real company data from the simulation will be used.

In each of the three parts, the following perspectives on circularity will be addressed: the company perspective, the perspective beyond the company boundary and the perspective of leadership and change.

This gives the book the overall structure that can be seen in Figure 0.5.

GUIDED TOUR, WEB RESOURCES AND BUSINESS SIMULATION GAME

Guided tour

In order to facilitate optimal learning, chapters in the book all have the following structure besides the pure content of each of them:

- Introduction and bullet-point overview of topics at the beginning of each chapter.
- In total 90+ numbered exercises of different types, which can be done individually or as part of lecture plans:
  - o Chapters of Part One: '*explore*', for example by investigating internet resources.
  - o Chapters of Part Two: '*analyse*', '*develop*' and '*decide*', using The Blue Connection business simulation game as an interactive case, analysing detailed data from the simulation, allowing for gameplay and seeing cause and effect relationships.
  - o Chapters of Part Three: '*imagine*', using the virtual company from The Blue Connection business simulation game as a reference case – how the company should shape the period of transformation from linear to circular.
- Summary at the end of each chapter, bridging current and next chapter.

Accompanying web resources

Mastering the Circular Economy is supported by web resources for learners and for lecturers and trainers. You can visit http://www.inchainge.com/mce to see which additional resources you can have access to.

Examples of resources for lecturers and trainers

- Request a free consultative call to get advice on how to optimally integrate the book into a learning programme.
- Inspiring showcases of past learning programmes.
- Request a self-paced online Train the Trainer to gain certification with The Blue Connection and learn how to use it as an interactive learning experience in combination with the book (free of charge for university staff). After completion of the training you get access to:

- o examples of course outlines and lecture plans;
- o several supporting PowerPoint slide decks, exercises for an interactive course;
- o multimedia teaching cases;
- o and more.

Examples of resources for participants

- Reading lists.
- Supporting videos.
- Overview of relevant industry associations.

Access to The Blue Connection business simulation game

To access The Blue Connection and be able to use it as an interactive case with the book, you need to follow the steps below:

1 Add my@inchainge.com to the list of trusted email recipients in your email program.

2 Register yourself in the Inchainge portal via https://my.inchainge.com, by choosing the option 'No account yet? Register as a new user'.

3 Follow the steps indicated, including the instructions you get in the confirmation email.

4 After finalizing the registration process you can log into the Inchainge portal.

5 Enter the code MCE_WATCH_ONLY into the 'Code Entry' field and click submit.

There are several options to use The Blue Connection in combination with the book. As part of the book you can use the standard option for free. Depending on your learning objectives and budget, you can explore other options and formats (e.g. interactive version) on the website http://www.inchainge.com/mce:

- **Standard option (free)**
  Use this code MCE_WATCH_ONLY which is included in the purchase of this book and is thus free of charge. It includes full visibility of all screens and access to all elements inside the business simulation game, thus allowing you to work through all of the exercises in the book.

- **Interactive option (paid)**
  The interactive set-up of The Blue Connection allows you to use the business simulation game in a more dynamic format. Participants can split up into teams where each person takes over one department in the business simulation. Over the

course of six rounds the teams can take decisions while facing increasing complexity and seeing the impact on the company after every round of decisions. This allows for a steep learning curve, an engaging team experience and a step-by-step implementation of different circular strategies. This interactive format is being used by universities and companies across the world. Information about the usage and pricing of this package can be found by reaching out to Inchainge directly via info@inchainge.com or on the following webpage: http://www.inchainge.com/mce.

- **Interactive option diving into various learning topics (paid)**
  With the interactive set-up of The Blue Connection you also have the option to dive into several learning topics. Inchainge is continuously working on these extensions (e.g. legislation, supplier development, bank selection, market dynamics and collaboration and so on) and you can find the available ones on the website http://www.inchainge.com/mce.

ACKNOWLEDGEMENTS

There are a number of people we would like to thank for their contributions to the final result you're holding in your hands. First of all, to Egge Haak, Hans Kremer and Michiel Steeman for inviting us to take on the challenge of writing a book and for critically proofreading and reviewing the content along the journey. Also a big thank you to the rest of the team at Inchainge for helping us out with the tons of queries we had about The Blue Connection.

Secondly, a thank you to the entire team at Kogan Page for their support throughout, with special mention to Adam Cox and Amy Minshull. Thanks also to Noah Schaul, who has been of great help 'behind the scenes' in proofreading, coordinating images and preparing the simulation environment and so on. Furthermore, a big thank you to Claire Ahlborn for your help with the images in the book.

In addition, from Rozanne: I would like to express a special thanks to my parents, sister and my Antwerp family: for your continued support, encouragement, the coffees and the walks, your sympathetic ear, the happy distractions to rest my mind, and the conversations to sharpen my thinking. Thank you! To my fellow Millennials, to Gen Z: we have the fantastic opportunity to create a new system in which we will not make the same mistakes our parents' and grandparents' generations did. With the help of creativity, innovation and trust in our own capabilities we can rethink, redesign and rearrange our future and our now.

In addition, from Ed: as the saying goes, we haven't inherited this planet from our parents, but we are borrowing it from our children. So, last but not least, the biggest possible thank you to my parents and parents-in-law, as well as to Marieke. All of you have been fundamental in me now being able to thank Pau and Marc for having me borrow their planet and I promise that I will do my best to treat it in the best possible way. Thanks for giving me continuous inspiration and energy. This one is for all of you.

Exploring the circular economy

The beginning of Project 'Circularity'

'Oh, don't talk such nonsense!'

Joanna Harrison Moore heard the voice of her nephew Peter coming from the garden. Probably he was quarrelling with his cousin Maria again; they always seemed to enjoy teasing each other at every possible occasion. It was the yearly family lunch at Joanna's house and apparently her niece and nephew had found a new topic they could disagree on. In fact, Joanna sort of liked these discussions between Maria and Peter. At the heart of it they were good kids, always defending their standpoints, but fortunately with the education and decency to never really let it get out of hand.

Joanna stepped up to them. 'Hey, it's my favourite niece and nephew, how are you guys doing, having fun again together?' she said with a big smile.

Maria was the first to reply: 'I was telling Peter about this new minor I signed up for, which is about climate change, sustainability and business. But when I saw the totally bored look on Peter's face I said that probably in his super-duper business school they would never be addressing such important topics because they would be too busy making plans for turning themselves into hotshot executives driving big SUVs.'

'Yeah right,' Peter interrupted her, 'my dear cousin here was pretty much accusing me of being a superficial business student, only interested in big money and big cars. Which is obviously nonsense. It's just that I don't see how businesses at their micro level can be made responsible for solving macro problems like climate change. And why should they? In Maria's view, everything is always so simple and easy. So, I told her that she shouldn't blame me, but instead take a good look in the mirror. She calls me superficial, but it is her and her 'green friends' who buy fancy smartphones from companies they later accuse of abuse of the environment and cheap labour and then they all go on and fly around the planet in polluting aeroplanes to visit "authentic" tribes in the jungle and regain their connection with nature. Now, how sustainable is that?'

'Oh, you're so low, just like your business friends, showing off about how "environmentally friendly" you are whenever it suits you,' replied Maria, 'but actually doing nothing at all about it, what a disgrace!'

'Hold on, hold on,' Aunt Joanna interfered, 'I know you like to debate, but let's not get too excited here!'

She thought for a second and said, 'Actually that's a very interesting topic you're talking about. With the board of Harrison Moore & Co we just had our annual meeting with the external executive committee and they literally asked me, as the CEO, what my plans were in terms of getting the company to become more "sustainable". One of the committee members in fact seemed very keen on the topic of the *circular economy* and as it turned out, they want us to come up with some concrete ideas for becoming more circular. Now that I hear you discussing, I'm thinking, would you be willing to help me in figuring it out for our family company?'.

'What do you have in mind, Aunt Joanna?' asked Peter.

'Well,' Aunt Joanna said, 'why don't the two of you join the company during part of your summer break for an internship and we define the circular economy as the main topic. Let's call it Project 'Circularity' and as you apparently have very different views on the topic, we can only benefit from connecting those views, I think.'

'That sounds pretty cool, Aunt Joanna, you can count me in,' Peter answered. 'What about you, Maria, are you in as well?'

'What do you think, Peter, that I'd trust you to do a good job on your own?' Maria replied without pause, 'Of course I'm in!'

'Great! There's only one rule I'd like to establish before we start,' Aunt Joanna said. 'Everyone is obviously entitled to their own opinions, but I want the final story to be as objective as we can possibly have it, OK? I have one main interest and that is to find out what circularity means for our company.' Peter and Maria both nodded in confirmation.

'OK then! I'd like to see you in my office next Monday. I have a few phases in mind for the project,' Aunt Joanna continued, taking a beer coaster from a stack on one of the tables and starting to draw what seemingly was her plan for the project. 'Your first task is to help me *explore* circularity, from a number of very different perspectives. That will give us a good and solid basis to dive into the details of how to actually *master* circularity in practice in the second part of our project, followed by *imagining the transformation* that might be required to get there, which would be the third and last part. And you may want to do some internet research into the circular economy upfront, just as a warm-up.'

FIGURE 0.6 The beer coaster with Aunt Joanna's plan for the project

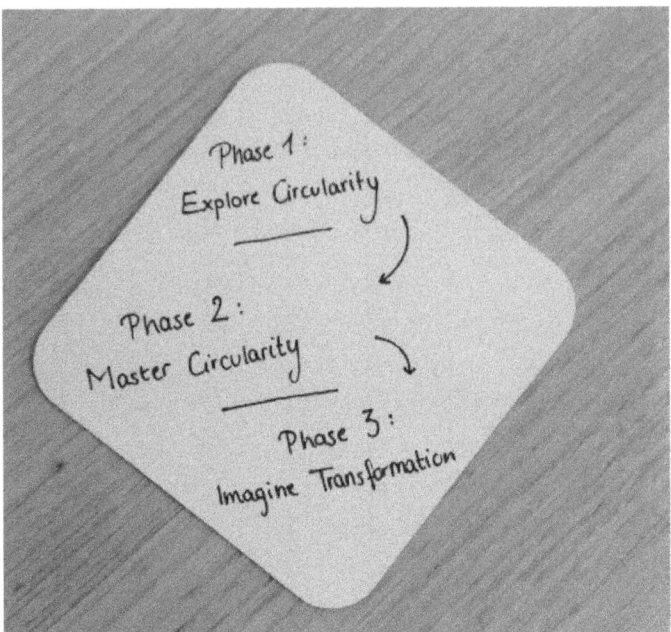

01

Exploring the context of circularity

MONDAY MORNING, AUNT JOANNA'S OFFICE: PROJECT 'CIRCULARITY' DAY 1

'Hello, good morning, my favourite niece and nephew, how great to see you here at the office!' Aunt Joanna welcomed Maria and Peter. 'Had a good remainder of the weekend after the family lunch? Energized to get to work? Why don't you join me for a coffee or a tea and I'll show you around and explain what I would like you to start with, OK?'

'Sounds like a plan, Aunt Joanna,' Maria said, 'I'm really looking forward to the project. And to working together with my monstrous cousin of course!' she added with a big smile on her face. Aunt Joanna was happy to see that Peter and Maria were in a good mood and seemed very eager to get started.

When they got back to the office after coffee and the quick tour around the company facility, Aunt Joanna invited Maria and Peter to take a seat; she grabbed a bunch of markers and stepped up to the whiteboard. 'I did a bit of thinking yesterday,' she said, while writing Project 'Circularity' in big blue letters at the top of the whiteboard. 'As I said on Saturday, I want you to help me find out what circularity can mean for our company, good or bad.'

'I once read a good article about business models and it spoke of 'narrative and numbers'.[1] That's what I think we also need here. Whatever the final conclusion, we will need a strong and coherent storyline and we will need numbers to create a compelling overall picture of our plans. With that in my pocket, I will have what I need to convince my fellow board members, our staff, our stakeholders and, of course, our executive committee.'

'In the first phase of the project, I would like us to set the scene of the story and explore the circular economy from a number of very different perspectives, starting with the general context of the topic,' she continued, 'so question number one to you is: what are those different angles that can help us sketch a broad and multidimensional view on the topic? What do you think?'

Maria was the first to respond: 'Well obviously there is the *planet*, because if we don't embrace circularity now, we will destroy it all and there will be no livable planet left for us. Then there is *society* as a dimension as well, because there is more and more pressure from people who believe that circularity is a big step in creating a better world, leaving our obsessive focus on growth and consumption behind.'

'This relates to another topic,' she continued, 'which is the *global programmes for a better world* that are being created. You know, programmes like the UN's Sustainable Development Goals and so on.'

Peter mentioned that they should probably also look at how *business and industry* had dealt with this topic in the past, if at all. 'And,' he continued, ' I would also suggest including government and policy, to know about the importance of *rules and regulations* in favour of or against circularity.'

'Very good, guys,' Aunt Joanna said enthusiastically, 'We're definitely on the right track. Keep going, what else?'

'I think we should also look at *academic research*,' Maria said, 'so what are the important schools of thought, which are the main concepts described and, very important as well, I believe, what does the academic world actually state as the *definition of circularity*?'

'And there's something else, I think,' said Peter with a teasing look on his face. 'It seems we're only looking at the circular economy so far as a clear solution to clear problems, but don't you think that some of that will actually be questionable?'

'No, really, I'm serious,' he continued when he saw disbelief on Maria's face. 'Not everybody necessarily wants this circular stuff. Simply look at how consumers behave, for example, many always going for the cheap buy... or think of those people who challenge the human factor in climate change? Or the degree to which our current supply chains have been optimized for low cost, which makes the required changes extremely costly... So, I think we should definitely look into *criticism and complexity* as well.'

'I agree, we might actually find some of those criticisms and complexities right here at Harrison Moore & Co so we need to be prepared and have our answers ready,' Aunt Joanna replied while she turned around and looked at the results of their brainstorming. On the whiteboard, the image in Figure 1.1 could now be seen.

'That looks wonderful, guys! So, you now know what you're going to be looking for in this first step of exploring circularity,' said Aunt Joanna. 'I'm really happy with this overview. Although I can see that the topics we have identified are not necessarily 100 per cent different and that connections and even overlap may exist between them, I believe that for the sake of argument and clarity we should deal with them separately. I think elaborating on these items should provide us with a good starting point for our overall narrative about the circular economy. Let's meet again in a couple of days to check out what you've found, OK?'

FIGURE 1.1 Exploring the context of the circular economy

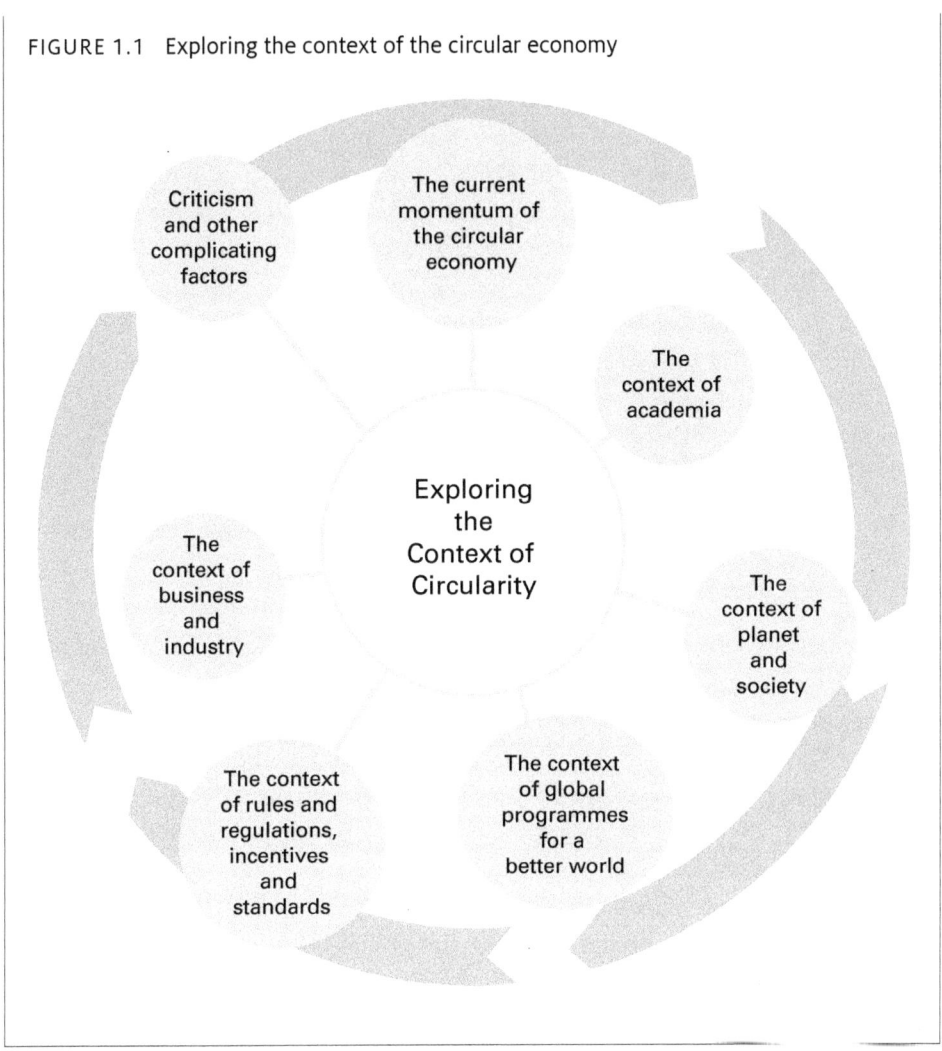

The current momentum of the circular economy

A large number of different factors can be mentioned to explain the recent boom in attention to the topic of the circular economy. Roughly speaking, they can be summarized under two headings: society pull and enabler push.[2] In a way, *society pull* reflects the underlying problems of climate change, resource scarcity and global instability being addressed more and more actively by the stakeholders in society, such as citizens, businesses, non-governmental organizations (NGOs) and governments. Through their calls for action they create the need for new solutions.

The *enabler push* reflects the side of innovative developments in terms of technologies and business models, aiming at offering effective ways forward, as well as the facilitating role of, for example, regulations and incentives. Some of these developments may in their origin have had very little to do with circularity, but due to the emerging need for solutions, they may be moving towards application in the field of circularity as well.

It is becoming very clear that due to increasing society pull, circularity is now firmly on the agendas of policy makers, academia and NGOs. On the business side of things, it can be observed that the recent increase in attention for the circular economy has led to an important increase in corporate, consultancy and entrepreneurial activity related to the topic. The remainder of this chapter will elaborate in detail on the elements of society pull and enabler push. All in all it seems fair to say that CE is here to stay.

The context of academia: research areas, concepts and definitions

Academic research has reached the age of CE 3.0

Reike et al (2018) provide a historical sequence of events, in which most of the aforementioned topics also appear in some way or another. They speak of CE 1.0, dubbed by them as the period 'dealing with waste' and assigned to the timeframe running from the 1970s to the 1990s. The focus here was mainly on the aspects related to the 'downstream' end of value chains, i.e. what happened with products at the end of their lifecycle, as well as on aspects related to what happened to any by-products from the main manufacturing process.

Reike et al continue by coining CE 2.0, running from the 1990s to 2010, and focused on 'connecting input and output in strategies for eco-efficiency', in other words connecting aspects of waste (output) to aspects of materials, design and production process (input) in one holistic view. According to them, we have now reached CE 3.0, a period starting around 2010, still ongoing and dubbed 'maximizing value retention in the age of resource depletion'. With this denomination the authors highlight the increased public attention to the urgency of resource scarcity, as well as the much more differentiated potential approaches for circularity as expressed by the 10-R framework (more about that later on in this section).

Another way that the increased attention for the subject can be noted is that for some years we have also seen the emergence of specific circularity performance indicators and reporting. Indicators at the micro (company) level will be addressed in Chapter 4. For now, we highlight a macro reporting about the circular economy at the country level and above: the *Circularity Gap Report* (CGRi, 2020).

Link to a variety of research areas

In the academic world a wide diversity of contributions to the development of concepts linked to circularity have been available for many years. The terms *closed-loop systems* and *product recovery management* were already appearing in scientific papers in the 1990s, often from an operational and logistics background and focused on mathematical modelling approaches to support decision making (e.g. Thierry et al, 1995; Flapper, 1995; Fleischmann et al, 1997). Allegedly the first international academic workshop about reuse was held at Eindhoven University of Technology in 1999 (Flapper and de Ron, 1999).

As has been exposed clearly and extensively by Reike et al (2018), other 'clusters' of academic publications are *waste management and environmental sciences*, *product design and cleaner production* and *industrial ecology*. While the first two can be understood relatively easily by looking at their names, industrial ecology refers to the 'discipline that traces the flow of energy and materials from their natural resources through manufacture, the use of products, and their final recycling or disposal.' The term 'circular economy' (CE) only gains attention in academic publications from 2010 onwards; in other words, it has been introduced only very recently.

In addition to the above-mentioned clusters of academic publications, the following concepts are frequently mentioned as the main schools of thought related to circularity, each typically connected to their intellectual founders, as described in e.g. Webster (2017) and Weetman (2020):

- *performance economy*, based on the work by Walter Stahel;
- *biomimicry*, based on the work by Janine Benyus;
- *blue economy*, based on the work by Günter Pauli;
- *regenerative design*, based on the work by John Lyle;
- *cradle-to-cradle*, based on the work by Michael Braungart and Bill McDonough. It has been cradle-to-cradle in particular that is seen by many as a conceptual breakthrough in the maturity of circularity. It has been the main inspiration for the famous butterfly model of circularity as popularized by the Ellen MacArthur Foundation.

Furthermore, also in academia, clear links exist between the topics of circularity and sustainability. Geissdoerfer et al (2017), on the basis of an extensive literature review, have highlighted the differences and similarities/overlaps between the two concepts. In addition, the notion of footprints (carbon, water, energy and so on) as used often in connection to sustainability is now appearing within the context of circularity (e.g. Wang et al, 2019; Porcelijn, n.d.).

THE BUTTERFLY DIAGRAM: BIOLOGICAL AND TECHNICAL CYCLES

The Butterfly diagram illustrates a system of continuous flow in a value chain, in which two cycles are distinguished, each centred around different types of materials: the *biological cycle* (on the left-hand side, focused on biological materials) and the *technical cycle* (on the right-hand side, focused on technical materials). The biological and technical materials are in need of different reuse processes. In order to reuse the biological and technical materials correctly, it is essential to collect them separately after use.

Technical cycle: circular strategies and the R-ladder

Products such as washing machines, refrigerators or mobile phones are not biodegradable, they are synthetic, produced from man-made materials, typically based on resources with limited availability. Within the technical cycle we look for ways to reuse these valuable metals, polymers (various types of plastic) or other raw materials. Here, products are designed in such a way that they can be reused. Within this cycle, the management of finite material stocks is therefore very important. After use, the technical materials are restored and flow back into the technical cycle, meaning that materials are recovered from waste and restored to their original or even higher value, for example by refurbishing, remanufacturing or repairing them. Since the technical cycle is receiving much attention, we will come back extensively to these so-called circular strategies and the R-ladder in Chapter 2 and in Part Two you will have the opportunity to apply them yourself through gameplay in the Blue Connection business simulation game.

Biological cycle: bio-inspired and bio-based loop strategies

In a circular economy, biological materials such as wood or food re-enter the biosphere to be composted or are organic nutrients that, at the end of their use, can be safely returned to the bio-cycle as 'food' for other forms of life and without generating waste, meaning that the waste of one 'product' is reused in another. For example, compostable packaging that can be safely deposited with organic waste after use or oyster mushrooms grown on coffee grounds, which is normally a waste product (check out companies like GRO, Rotterzwam en Zwamburg). Or the example of the company PeelPioneers, who offer a circular solution for companies that have to dispose of peels, such as supermarkets, restaurants and hotels. They collect the peels and extract essential oils from them to be used in the cosmetics industry.

Although in most companies the (circular) focus seems to be on the technical cycle, the value of 'Design for a Biological Cycle' can also be highlighted. It represents design solutions inspired by (or occurring in) the natural ecosystems: 'Its biological nature represents a level of efficiency close to the intrinsic perfection of the efficiency of nature's closed-loop ecosystem, as opposed to the impact-minimizing technical cycle'

FIGURE 1.2 Butterfly diagram

RENEWABLES FLOW MANAGEMENT

RENEWABLES

FINITE MATERIALS

STOCK MANAGEMENT

FARMING/COLLECTION[1]

REGENERATION   BIOSPHERE

BIOCHEMICAL
FEEDSTOCK

PARTS MANUFACTURER

PRODUCT MANUFACTURER

SERVICE PROVIDER

RECYCLE

REFURBISH/
REMANUFACTURE

REUSE/REDISTRIBUTE

MAINTAIN/PROLONG

SHARE

USER

CONSUMER

COLLECTION

COLLECTION

CASCADES

BIOGAS

ANAEROBIC
DIGESTION

EXTRACTION OF
BIOCHEMICAL
FEEDSTOCK[2]

MINIMIZE SYSTEMATIC
LEAKAGE AND NEGATIVE
EXTERNALITIES

ELLEN MACARTHUR
FOUNDATION

1 Hunting and fishing
2 Can take both post-harvest and post-consumer waste as an input

SOURCE
Ellen MacArthur Foundation
Circular economy systems diagram (February 2019)
www.ellenmacarthurfoundation.org
Drawing based on Braungart & McDonough,
Cradle to Cradle (C2C)

(Mestre and Cooper, 2017). Design for the bio-cycle consists of bio-inspired and bio-based loop strategies. The bio-inspired strategies draw upon the science of bionics (the study of natural systems to address human engineering problems), such as Leonardo da Vinci's study of birds' wing structure for the design of flying objects. The bio-based strategies aim to utilize biological materials which, at the end of their lifecycles, can be returned safely to the biosphere in order to provide nutrients to other biological life (e.g. the bio-based C2C coffee cup, reusing (biological) coffee waste to construct a short-lived disposable product). You can find more information on lifecycle design strategies for bio-inspired and bio-based loop in Mestre's and Cooper's (2017) paper on circular product design. This also links, for example, to organic recycling, which will also be touched upon in Chapter 2.

Main important concepts

Before addressing a workable definition of circularity later on in this section and diving deep into the details in Chapter 2, it is interesting here and now to briefly cover some of the most relevant terminology and concepts related to circularity:

- The notion of *value retention* in products and materials after they are sold.

- Value retention goes hand in hand with the notion of *loops*, i.e. ways to organize the return flows of products and materials.

- The notion of the critical indicator of *virgin material*, or *linear inflow*, defined as raw material that has not been subjected to use or processing, other than that for its original manufacture (Gooch, 2011). Virgin material is used as so-called feedstock into the production process and thus seen as an input to be minimized, for example as expressed in the Material Circularity Indicator – MCI (EMF, n.d. b) or the Circular Transition Indicators – CTI (WBCSD, 2018; 2020a).

- The relevance of two different cycles, the product *concept and design* cycle and the product *produce and use* cycle (Reike et al, 2018), similar to the concepts of Development Chain and Supply Chain (Simchi-Levi et al, 2009).

- The notion of *designing out waste* in the above-mentioned concept and design cycle; in other words, enabling future options of loops by designing them into the products, thus avoiding waste throughout the lifecycle.

- In terms of strategies, there are the concepts of *closing, narrowing and slowing loops*, which directly connect to the concept of waste hierarchy and the 10-R framework, built on the foundation of Lansink's Ladder (which will be briefly touched upon later on in this chapter).

- The notion of *sustainable business models* and the innovation taking place in these, aiming at incorporating sustainability into the development of new business models (e.g. Bocken and Boons, 2017; Bocken et al, 2019; Bocken and Geradts, 2020).

Definitions of the circular economy

The recent dramatic increase in scientific production around the topic of circularity has shown the proliferation of concepts and has, above all, demonstrated a lack of standardized definitions and terminology (e.g. Kirchherr et al, 2017; Reike et al, 2018; Geissdoerfer et al, 2017).

Since it's not our objective here to extensively debate the many potential definitions of circular economy and reinforced by the notion that academics also have not agreed yet between themselves on one clear definition, we propose the use of two explanations as a *practical backbone* for the remainder of this book. The first one, cited often in relevant literature, expresses a more generic definition, whereas the second one links to a more tangible framework, suitable for application in companies:

Circular economy: an industrial system that is restorative and regenerative by intention and design. It replaces the 'end-of-life' concept with restoration, shifts towards the use of renewable energy, eliminates the use of toxic chemicals, which impair reuse, and aims for the elimination of waste through the superior design of materials, products, systems and, within this, business models (EMF, 2015a).

Circularity: the different practical strategies for achieving circular flows, applicable in a practical way by companies, captured by the 10-R framework, specifying hierarchical levels R0 to R9, applied to both the concept and design cycle, as well as the Produce and Use cycle (Reike et al, 2018).

So, in the remainder of the book, we will refer to the circular economy as a wider, more global and more generic concept, whereas we will use the term circularity when referring to the more specific (micro) context of a single company.

The context of planet and society

The attention that can be seen nowadays towards the topic of the circular economy in relation to planet and society is the culmination of many different initiatives over time, some from very different origins. Some have circularity as their main focus, some cover a wider scope.

Climate change

Without a doubt one of the major issues related to planet and society is *climate change*. Nowadays, a wide range of publications, indicators and rankings are making sure that the subject is never far away. Examples of such indicators are:

- *The great acceleration* by the Stockholm Resilience Centre. Probably the first of its kind, first published in 2004, updated in 2015 (Stockholm Resilience, 2015).

- *Earth overshoot day*, also called 'ecological debt day', by the Global Footprint Network, updated yearly (Global Footprint, n.d.).
- *Living planet index (LPI)* by World Wildlife Fund and the Zoological Society of London, with a specific focus on biodiversity, updated every two years (LPI, n.d.).

What these indicators have in common is that they try to capture the state of the planet, although in slightly different ways. What they also have in common is that in their message they all establish a direct link between the trends they indicate and human (economic) behaviour as the main driver of these trends taking place. This phenomenon has been dubbed 'The Anthropocene' (e.g. Steffen et al, 2015; Weetman, 2020; Raworth, 2017; Elkington, 2020) and it is cited often in relation to the circular economy. As a direct consequence of the concept of the Anthropocene and its implications, there is the conclusion that 'if human behaviour is the main cause of the problem, then human behaviour should also be a main part of the solution.'

In relation to climate change, circularity is considered a possible part of the solution: circularity leads to less new production, therefore less energy consumption and less pollution, both of great help in reducing the emission of greenhouse gasses.

Although there is an overwhelming quantity of scientific literature aimed at factually proving climate change, it seems that the topic is only recently also making it to corporate agendas. For example, the World Economic Forum states in their 2020 Global Risk Report that 'for the first time in the history of the Global Risks Perception Survey, environmental concerns dominate the top long-term risks by likelihood among members of the World Economic Forum's multi-stakeholder community; three of the top five risks by impact are also environmental' (WEF, 2020b).

Decreasing resource availability

Another often-mentioned reason to engage in circularity is the issue of *decreasing resource availability* due to an increasing world population and the corresponding increasing levels of consumption on planet Earth. Probably the three most often cited and well-known references for the wide recognition of this resource issue are Malthus's 1798 (!) 'An Essay on the principle of population' (Malthus, 1798), the 1966 essay 'The economics of the coming Spaceship Earth' (Boulding, 1966)[3] and the famous report 'The limits to growth' (Club of Rome, 1972). All three works hold a similar message: the planet will not be able to sustain the expected levels of growth.

In fact, the project behind the Club of Rome report was started by a team of researchers from the Massachusetts Institute of Technology (MIT) and the initiative sought to create a computer model for predicting as accurately as possible the limitations of growth on earth. Five interacting factors were identified: population increase, agricultural production, non-renewable resource depletion, industrial output and pollution generation.

Their conclusion: 'The earth's interlocking resources – the global system of nature in which we all live – probably cannot support present rates of economic and population growth much beyond the year 2100, if that long, even with advanced technology' (Club of Rome, 1972).

Almost two decades ago the United Nations published a study called the 'Millennium Ecosystem Assessment' (2005), which revealed that 15 of the 24 ecosystems studied were being degraded (or used unsustainably). This means that we consume more than the productivity of our ecosystems can cope with. The conclusion of the study: the earth's natural capital is being depleted by human activity. Human beings are burdening the environment to such an extent that the ability of these ecosystems to sustain future generations can no longer be taken for granted. Fortunately, the study also had some hopeful news at the time: with appropriate measures it would be possible to reverse the decline of many ecosystems over the next 50 years (counting from the publication of the report in 2005).

Global instability and resilience

Parallel to increased attention for climate change and resource scarcity, recent history has also shown that people have become more aware of the interdependencies between countries and the associated degrees of vulnerability this brings. Geopolitical tensions and the Covid-19 pandemic are examples of the effects these interdependencies can have, causing fear to citizens and government leaders alike and stimulating the drive to look for solutions.

It can even be argued that climate change has a direct impact on global instability, for example by the fact that climate change leaves certain areas in the world almost without reasonable options for agriculture and therefore food production, ultimately causing people to migrate to other regions, which is a cause for tension. Likewise, scarcity of resources can contribute to instability, for example causing disruption of material flows into critical industries or even leading to political tensions (Guardian, 2019; IRTC, 2020).

More and more voices can be heard asserting that circular solutions offer more resilience against such vulnerability, for example because they lead to less need for resources, but also because they tend to be more local, thus reducing the dependency on others (e.g. WEF, 2020a; Circular Flanders and VITO, 2020).

Need for a new economic paradigm

Another angle in which problems for planet and society are signalled is formed by schools of thought related to the conclusion that we have a *failing dominant economic paradigm*. Roughly speaking, the line of thinking of these schools of thought is that the current dominant economic paradigm of (neoliberal) capitalism is centred too much around capital and growth as critical indicators for economic health and individual prosperity. This is valid for the macro level, meaning growth of GDP of nations, as well as for the micro level, meaning growth of revenue and profit of companies.

It is argued that such growth in combination with a growing population cannot be sustained. It will ultimately lead to extreme inequality in society and depletion of resources on the planet; therefore a new capitalism should be defined. Also here, circularity is addressed as part of possible solutions to the problem (e.g. Raworth, 2017; Piketty, 2017, Elkington, 2020).

Some even take a much wider view and actually see the *circular economy* as the main alternative economic paradigm, beyond the perspective of an individual company. For example, the vision of the Ellen MacArthur Foundation about the circular economy is 'a new economic system that delivers better outcomes for people and the environment. Business models, products, and materials are designed to increase use and reuse, replicating the balance of the natural world, where nothing becomes waste and everything has value. A circular economy, increasingly built on renewable energy and materials, is distributed, diverse, and inclusive' (EMF, n.d. a, 2015b).

EXERCISE 1.1
Explore the context of planet and society

Explore

Explore climate change, resource scarcity, global instability and resilience, new economic paradigm:

- Do some (internet) desk research into the topics, for example by looking into the mentioned references and related sources.
- What's your opinion about these issues?
- How exactly do you think they are related to circularity?

The context of global programmes for a better world

Supranational programmes and multilateral country agreements

In the year 2000, the United Nations under the leadership of Kofi Annan launched the UN Global Compact as 'the world's largest corporate sustainability initiative: a call to align strategies and operations with universal principles on human rights, labor, environment and anti-corruption, and take actions that advance societal goals.' It has taken considerable time for these measures to materialize, but finally in 2015, the Agenda 2030 was presented and signed by all 193 member states of the United Nations.

The central elements in Agenda 2030 are the 17 so-called Sustainable Development Goals (SDGs), a term widely used today by governments, businesses and in education. Circularity is directly as well as indirectly related to a number of these SDGs.

In 2019, 47 years after the publication of their famous report and in the light of the perceived slow speed of change, the Club of Rome issued an additional statement 'proposing nations declare a planetary emergency for climate and nature in 2020'. In the corresponding Planetary Emergency Plan, 10 commitments are proposed, clustered into three main themes (Club of Rome, 2019):

- transforming energy systems;
- shifting to a circular economy;
- creating a just and equitable society founded in human and ecological well-being.

As can be appreciated, 'shifting to a circular economy' is explicitly mentioned as one of the three main themes.

Concerns about planet and climate have also been the spark for setting objectives between countries, in the form of *multilateral country agreements*. The two larger initiatives here are the Paris Climate Agreement, also originating from the United Nations, but in this case not the Global Compact, but the UN Framework Convention on Climate Change (UNFCCC). In December 2015, 'parties to the UNFCCC reached a landmark agreement to combat climate change and to accelerate and intensify the actions and investments needed for a sustainable low carbon future' UNFCCC (n.d.). Important to mention is that the main line of action behind the agreement is that the global goals for carbon emission reduction are to be translated by the individual countries into 'nationally determined contributions'. In some countries this may lead to projects promoting circularity.

In 2020, the European Union presented their Green Deal and Circular Economy Action Plan: 'Climate change and environmental degradation are an existential threat to Europe and the world. To overcome these challenges, Europe needs a new growth strategy that will transform the Union into a modern, resource-efficient and competitive economy, where:

1 there are no net emissions of greenhouse gases by 2050;

2 economic growth is decoupled from resource use;

3 no person and no place is left behind.

The European Green Deal is our plan to make the EU's economy sustainable. We can do this by turning climate and environmental challenges into opportunities, and making the transition just and inclusive for all' (EU, 2019, 2020). Points 1 and 2 in particular have direct connections to circularity and are likely to be a driving force behind circular initiatives.

Private initiatives

In addition to governmentally initiated programmes like the ones mentioned before, private initiatives were also started with the aim of helping to shape a better world and do good for planet and society. Probably the best-known example when it comes to circularity is the Ellen MacArthur Foundation. Founded in 2010, their aim is to accelerate the transition to a circular economy, developing visions for learning, business, institutions, governments and cities (EMF, n.d.).

Also a private initiative, Singularity University, have formulated their own version of objectives to make the world a better place. They call them the '12 Global Grand Challenges' (GGCs). In addressing each GGC, they aim to solve for the following three perspectives: ensuring basic needs are met for all people, sustaining and improving quality of life, and mitigating future risks (Singularity University, n.d.). Two categories are distinguished: resources needs and societal needs. In some way, they can be considered Singularity's version of the UN's SDGs.

From the side of businesses and in line with the corporate stakeholder approach and the concept of corporate social responsibility, a large number of initiatives can also be observed. For example, the foundation in 1995 of the World Business Council for Sustainable Development, 'a global, CEO-led organization of over 200 leading businesses working together to accelerate the transition to a sustainable world.' In 2010 the WBCSD launched their Vision 2050, in which circularity plays a role as part of the solution, particularly through their Factor 10 project (WBCSD n.d. a, 2018, 2020a).

Another example from the business side is the Business Roundtable, an organization in the United States, which published a declaration in 2019 distancing itself formally from the shareholder doctrine and embracing attention for other stakeholders such as society, personnel and, indirectly, the planet. With a similar spirit, the World Economic Forum published its 'Davos Manifesto 2020: The universal purpose of a company in the Fourth Industrial Revolution' (BRT, 2019; WEF, 2019).

EXERCISE 1.2

Explore the context of global programmes for a better world

Explore

Explore the Planetary Emergency Plan, SDGs, the Paris Climate Agreement, the EU Green Deal, the EMF visions, the Singularity Grand Global Challenges, the Business Roundtable and World Economic Forum declarations, the World Business Council for Sustainable Development's Vision 2050:

- Do some (internet) desk research into the topics, for example by looking into the mentioned references and related sources.
- What's your opinion about these examples?
- What do you think in terms of their practical applicability?

The context of rules and regulations, incentives and standards

Levels of government

One step beyond global programmes for a better world, which normally are not embedded in national or local laws, there is the topic of government and policy. Companies typically have to deal with different levels of government. In the best of cases these levels are aligned, but in many cases it is not that easy. One dimension is *geographical scope*, with local government at the bottom level, followed by the regional (provincial) and national levels within a country and then the supranational level (e.g. the European Union) and finally the global level.

Another dimension is the *degree of autonomy* that each of these geographical levels has regarding certain issues. In some cases, local governments can decide whatever they feel appropriate, in other cases there may be regional or national decisions overruling them. In some cases governments can impose, in some cases they can only recommend, facilitate and/or stimulate. In addition, of course no two countries are the same, so the overall context is very complex, especially for companies with activities that span the borders between two or more countries.

In the following sections a number of the most important items regarding government and policy in relation to circularity are described.

Regulation: restrictions and fiscal incentives

The first and probably most important topic related to government is related to restrictive regulations. In simple terms, first defining in the law what is allowed and what is not allowed and then putting the resources in place to enforce those laws (e.g. the police), accompanied by systems of appropriate penalties as a (negative) incentive for people and companies to respect the rules.

Examples related to circularity are laws around the topic of waste, which on the one hand are aimed at reducing the public burden of waste by making sure the

FIGURE 1.3   The Ladder of Lansink

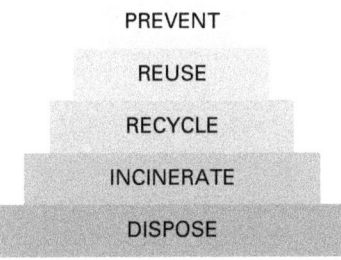

'polluter pays', and on the other hand aim at those penalties becoming an incentive for polluters, such as companies, to find innovative solutions to effectively reduce the amounts of waste produced.

In 1975, the European Commission (the predecessor of the European Union) published the Waste Framework Directive (EEC, 1975), which later on also came to include the so-called 'Ladder of Lansink', a diagram expressing a hierarchical classification of waste, from more desirable to less desirable: prevent waste, reuse waste, recycle waste, burn and recover energy from waste, bury waste (Lansink, n.d.). In some ways it could be considered to be one of the foundations of what nowadays is known as the R-ladder (more about that in Chapter 2).

As a consequence of such waste-related regulations and the increasing attention towards reduction of waste streams, another area of regulation has emerged. These other regulations not only focused on waste in terms of undesired by-products of manufacturing, but included the main products themselves and what happened to those until the very end of their lifecycle. Such legislation is known under the umbrella name of End-of-Life responsibility (EOL) and take-back legislation (Toffel, 2003).

In the European Union, one of the most well-known regulations in this respect is the so-called WEEE directive, which stands for the Waste of Electrical and Electronic Equipment. According to the EC, 'The first WEEE Directive (Directive 2002/96/EC) entered into force in February 2003. The Directive provided for the creation of collection schemes where consumers return their WEEE free of charge. These schemes aim to increase the recycling of WEEE and/or re-use' (EC, n.d.).

Financial and fiscal incentives

As the WEEE example already shows by mentioning 'free of charge' return schemes, not all legislation or regulations are about imposing rules and putting law enforcement in place. Governments can also stimulate certain behaviour by offering fiscal or other incentives to businesses or to citizens. Examples related to climate change are fiscal incentives on the installation of solar panels or on the use of electric bikes for commuting between home and work. Related to circularity and waste, there is the well-known example from Germany where a deposit system ('Pfand') exists on one-way bottles and cans in which the deposit will be returned to the consumer upon return of the bottles and/or cans to the retailer or accredited recycling centres.[4]

Such fiscal incentives typically have very strong effects, as was demonstrated in a very peculiar way in the Netherlands where Tesla sold some 11,000 Model 3 cars in December 2019 alone, which represented half of their total European sales in that month. The main reason for the strong increase in sales was the fact that specific fiscal regulations to stimulate the adoption of electric cars in the country were about to come to an end on 31 December of the same year.

Industry initiatives: standardization and codes of conduct

Regulatory pressure is not necessarily always government-imposed; it can also originate within industry and the impact in some cases is pretty much the same as in the case of government regulations. An interesting example of non-government-imposed industry-wide collaboration, but almost equalling the impact of formal government policy, can be seen in the beer industry in the Netherlands.

In the 1980s, an industry-wide agreement was made to standardize the material, colour, form and shape of beer bottles with the introduction of the Brown Dutch Return bottle (Bruine Nederlandse Retourfles – BNR). In addition to this, there was the already existing system of deposits on crates and beer bottles, which has made the return of used bottles a common and accepted practice among consumers. Both of these elements have facilitated an enormous boost in standardization of bottle re-collection, leading to an increase in scale and efficiency in the global system for reuse of beer bottles and crates. This was a big step forward in the attractiveness of the concept, leading to wider adoption in industry and a great example of effectively and efficiently 'closing the loop' (Nederlandse Brouwers, n.d.).[5]

Another type of industry-driven initiative is the development of so-called industry standards, for example the British Standards (BS). Formally, this may be considered to be different from government policy, because the BS standards are created and maintained by a commercial institution, the BSI Group (European Standards, n.d.). This also implies that the use of these standards cannot be enforced by law, meaning that in principle they are voluntary.

Arguably, the development and spread of British Standards related to 'environmental management' and the corresponding system of accreditations and audits have played an important role regarding moving companies towards more sustainable practices (McKinnon, 1995a). For example, for some companies such accreditations are now among the 'must-comply' criteria used when selecting suppliers.

As documented by Hopkinson et al (2018) in their paper about Japanese printer, imaging and document original equipment manufacturer (OEM) Ricoh, the British Standards have even contributed towards higher acceptance of refurbished and remanufactured products in the market. Since the BS stipulated that manufacturers of such products had to guarantee the original specification, therefore the refurbished and remanufactured products had to be equal in quality to the original, as well as from a customer perspective ('it is essentially impossible to differentiate the two products'). Allegedly, this has contributed a lot towards taking away customers' potential reluctance and doubts about the quality of refurbished and remanufactured products, thus effectively taking away a barrier to buying them. As the Ricoh example shows, such measures can have an enormous positive boost for remanufactured products, thus stimulating companies to engage in circular approaches.

Something similar is envisioned in the case of so-called 'codes of conduct', many of which are not as explicit and detailed as standards, but serve as a framework to guide behaviour. Examples of standards and codes of conduct with various degrees of adoption and acceptance in industry around the world are (Lawrence and Weber, 2017):

- *ISO 14000 (environmental management)*, developed by the ISO Group, a set of voluntary standards specifically related to environmental aspects, complemented by accreditation and audits. Contains guidelines for minimizing a company's negative impact on the environment, e.g. through reduction of the use of energy, or improving processes that pollute air, water or land (ISO, n.d.).

- *The Greenhouse Gas Protocol*, developed by the World Resources Institute in collaboration with the World Business Council for Sustainable Development. According to their website, 'GHG Protocol establishes comprehensive global standardized frameworks to measure and manage greenhouse gas (GHG) emissions from private and public sector operations, value chains and mitigation actions' (Greenhouse Gas Protocol, n.d.).

- *Forest Stewardship Council Principles*, developed by the non-profit organization the Forest Stewardship Council and widely accepted in many paper-based industries, ranging from books to packaging materials. Certifies forest management that 'confirms that the forest is being managed in a way that preserves biological diversity and benefits the lives of local people and workers, while ensuring it sustains economic viability' (FSC, n.d.).

- *Leadership in Energy and Environmental Design (LEED) Standards*, developed originally by the US Green Building Council. As they state on their website: 'Available for virtually all building types, LEED provides a framework for healthy, highly efficient, and cost-saving green buildings' (USGBC, n.d.).

- *B Corp Certification*, developed by the B Corp Movement, a community of companies, based on their Declaration of Interdependence and supported by their B Impact Assessment. It claims to be 'the only certification that measures a company's entire social and environmental performance. The B Impact Assessment evaluates how your company's operations and business model impacts your workers, community, environment, and customers.' (B Corporation, n.d.).

It is important to note that since industry standards, codes of conduct and declarations of intentions are not regulated by government, legal enforcement of their use is impossible. Much depends on peer pressure in the industry itself, pressure from the customers in the market, and/or on (mainly large) companies taking the lead in the industry, almost literally setting the standard and thus making it nearly impossible for other industry incumbents not to follow suit.

Ecosystems

Another contribution from government to the development of circular solutions is through active stimulation of the creation of 'circular ecosystems' in a way very much related to the wider topic of so-called public-private partnerships (PPP, or 3P, or P3). These are initiatives in which different stakeholders collaborate, ultimately seeking benefit for society (OECD, 2012). In the specific case of partnerships aimed at innovation, PPP has been the foundation for the development of the concept of the Triple Helix, in which academia has been added to the equation as a collaboration partner (Etzkowitz and Leydesdorff, 1995).

At the more local or national level, circular ecosystems can be seen as similar to the recent rise in the number of more generic 'startup' ecosystems, in which typically government, academia and entrepreneurs join forces in so-called *incubators*, in many cases around specific topics and/or industries and backed by funding from government and sometimes also industry. More about ecosystems will follow in Chapter 3.

You may want to explore this geographical dimension of rules, regulations and standards through the following exercise:

EXERCISE 1.3
Explore the context of rules, regulations and industry standards

Explore

For a country of your choice, explore relevant government policies related to circularity (from local to national level):

- What's the situation in terms of legislation related to circularity?
- What's the situation in terms of fiscal policies related to circularity?
- What's the situation in terms of ecosystems related to circularity?
- To what extent do specific industry standards exist and which ones are they?
- If you have the opportunity to do so, you may want to compare your findings with colleagues/teammates. What are the differences/similarities between the policies in different countries and/or regions?

The context of business and industry

Business: circular approaches from before the term was coined

Independent from circular initiatives related to planet and society or government and policy, businesses have also already been exploring circularity for quite a number of years, in many cases with academia following in their slipstream and aiming at developing supporting concepts and frameworks. These initiatives can be considered *circular approaches 'avant-la-lettre'* because interestingly enough, no one used the term 'circularity' at the time, even though the solutions that emerged would nowadays definitely receive that label.

Being consumers ourselves, most of us know that markets for second-hand goods have been around for a very long time. These markets give a second chance to products that would otherwise have ended up not being used, being burnt as part of waste disposal or transported to a landfill as its final destination. In connection to the second-hand market, there is the activity of refurbishment, sometimes taken care of by the retailer of the second-hand product, sometimes by specific companies dedicated to repair and refurbishment. Examples are cars, clothing, mobile phones or office (IT) equipment, but even age-old concepts like the pawn shop are basically circular in nature.

A similar example is the age-old existence of maintenance and repair services, for example for cars, household appliances or shoes. In many countries such services have been steadily disappearing, particularly for those products whose prices have become so low that repair would in fact be more expensive, because of hourly wages, than buying a new one altogether.

Another interesting development can be found in the markets of relatively expensive asset-based products like large copying machines for offices: in the 1990s Xerox were already offering the pay-per-page option, as opposed to the customer purchasing the device as well as the consumables and separate repair services. Xerox changed this approach and worked to turn its product into a service, including supply of devices, consumables and maintenance, a concept that nowadays is seen as an innovative type of business model very close to the heart of circularity.

Another example from the same industry is Ricoh, who, also in the 1990s, started their journey into the possibilities of remanufacturing, leading to the formal development in 1994 of their Ricoh Remanufacturing and Asset Recovery Framework, expressed by what they called the Comet Circle™, a graphical representation of the various steps, hierarchies and parties involved in product recovery, component recovery and material recovery (Hopkinson et al, 2018).

Business: 'non-CE' concepts with a circular impact

Although strictly speaking developed outside of the scope and objectives of circularity, there are other concepts developed in business which could be favourable to its implementation. For example, basic concepts like transportation route optimization or the widely applied principles of Lean Management, in which seven types of waste are identified and sought to be reduced, fit very well with the objectives of the circular economy. The same goes for the design principles of product modularity, design for logistics and design for disassembly (which can favour effective transportation and disassembly), design for serviceability (which favours repair and maintenance) and, following in the same line, but applied to materials, concepts on design for durability, for refurbishability or for remanufacturing.

Similarly, operational concepts exist such as reverse logistics and Value-Added Logistics (VAL), in which products are being re-collected from the customer and checked for quality, sorted and sometimes even disassembled by the logistics service provider. Although initially developed mainly as an additional service from a customer satisfaction viewpoint, for example offering customers the flexibility to send back products if they didn't like them, these concepts are well developed and fit for wider application as part of more holistic circular approaches.

Corporate social responsibility (CSR)

Maybe somewhat less directly related to circularity only, but certainly of influence, is the increasing pressure from society on companies to behave responsibly: *corporate social responsibility (CSR)*. At its heart, CSR is very closely related to the topics of the role of companies in society and business ethics, which is a highly debated arena in which very opposing views tend to clash (Vaccaro and Kusyk, 2011).

Until well into the 21st century, the so-called 'Friedman doctrine' was the dominant logic for companies. It was named after economist Milton Friedman, who wrote a famous article titled 'The social responsibility of business is to increase its profits', in which he described a company management's obligation to focus totally on delivering returns to the owners, i.e. the shareholders of the company (Friedman, 1970).

Over time, this way of looking has started receiving criticism and pressure from society, ultimately leading to an opposing view called the *stakeholder approach*. Freeman (please note: not to be confused with the *Friedman* mentioned a moment ago!) was allegedly the first to write extensively about this in the early 1980s (see, e.g. Freeman and Parmar, 2017). Also here, circularity can be seen as part of the solution, i.e. one of the actions that companies can take in order to become more socially responsible.

With the increased awareness about the state of the planet and the increased pressure from society towards business to do something about it, Elkington developed his famous concept of the Triple Bottom Line (TBL) in which he argues that company performance should be defined as a well-balanced mix of financial, environmental and social parameters (Elkington, 1997). Nowadays, in many corporate annual reports the TBL is referred to as the triangle of People, Planet and Profit.

In the slipstream of the ongoing acceptance of TBL, the concept of Shared or Integrated Value has emerged, which will be addressed more extensively in Chapter 2. In addition, a number of rankings have started appearing on the scene in which company performance on more than just financial parameters is taken into consideration. Some examples are the *Dow Jones Sustainability World Index (DJSI)* by Standard & Poor's, updated continuously (SP Global, n.d.), the *Sustainable Brand*

Index™ by Swedish company SB Insight, updated annually (SB Insight, n.d.) and the *Business Sustainability Risk and Performance Index* by Ecovadis, updated frequently (Ecovadis, n.d.).

What is clear from the appearance of the TBL in the corporate world and the development of corporate sustainability rankings, is that corporate sustainability performance is watched more and more by the general public.

Circular innovation as a business opportunity

Companies' interest in the topic of circularity has also been generated simply because circularity offers new business opportunities, as described for example in the article 'Saving the planet from ecological disaster is a \$12 trillion opportunity' by John Elkington (2017a), as well as in the work of Stahel, who speaks of 'CE leading to a wealth of opportunity' (e.g. Stahel, 2019).

Independent from the circular economy, we are hearing more and more that we are entering into the Sixth Industrial Revolution, much linked to the concept of Industry 4.0 (e.g. Schwab, 2016; Culey, 2019), in which a large quantity of new technologies emerge in a seemingly relatively short timeframe. On the one hand this leads to much uncertainty, since many of these innovations will need time to prove themselves while others may even disappear without flourishing at all. On the other hand, this wave of innovation will without doubt lead to what Schumpeter already coined in the 1930s as 'creative destruction': the emergence of new technological paradigms that replace the existing ones. The area of circularity will surely be affected by this wave of innovation, while it can also be argued at the same time that the increasing drive for circularity will in itself spark new innovations.

Examples of some of the advancements being made in research and development leading to innovation in materials, products, processes and business models and with a direct or indirect relation to circularity are:

- New material developments, such as vegetable-based materials, recyclable and bio-degradable materials and so on enable new and more circular product designs.
- Technologies aimed at creating transparency and analysing movements in value chains, such as the Internet of Things (IoT), Blockchain, RFID, Artificial Intelligence (AI) and Big Data enable tracking of the installed product base, e.g. leading to increased insights into where products go, into material behaviour and into more effective maintenance schemes (Accenture, 2018b; IBM, 2020).
- Technologies and concepts such as 3D printing, robotics, modularization and design for disassembly enable more efficient production, refurbishment and remanufacturing (Accenture, 2018b; IBM, 2020).
- New concepts such as materiality passports create clarity and enable better decision making about product design, material usage and return flows (Heinrich and Lang, 2019).

- Developments in renewable energy enable the lowering of products' entire energy footprint.
- Development and proliferation of new business models such as 'product-as-a-service' and 'shared-user models' enable higher degrees of circularity.

As this section shows, the relation of business and industry to circularity goes back a long way, even before the term was used at all. It also shows that the links of business to circularity can have diverse backgrounds, from stakeholder pressure to the search for efficiency to innovation as part of exploring new business opportunities.

Since the largest part of this book will be dedicated to circularity from a company perspective, for now it may be sufficient to explore the topic of corporate social responsibility a little bit further.

EXERCISE 1.4

Explore the context of the shareholder and stakeholder approaches

Explore

- Do some more desk research into the shareholder view of business ('Friedman doctrine').
- Do some more desk research into the stakeholder view of business (e.g. Freeman).
- What do you see as the main arguments in favour of and against each of the two approaches?
- What is your own preference regarding these two schools of thought and why?

The context of criticism and other complicating factors

In order to avoid an unbalanced image, it is good to dedicate some words to the fact that not everything around the topic of the circular economy is free of controversy, nor are the various initiatives associated with it. A few examples of such controversial topics are described below.

Climate sceptics

Even though most people seem to agree that (man-made) climate change is real, it cannot be ignored that there are influential scientists who do not necessarily deny climate change, but at least put in certain important question marks. Such question marks can be about the degree of climate change itself, but also for example about the measures that are taken to fight it. In addition to these leading scientists, scepticism and indifference can still be found among the general population (e.g. Dunlap, 2013; Business Insider, 2009).

Population growth

According to research, the world's population is indeed still growing but this growth has been steadily slowing down since the end of the 1960s and is expected to have its turning point around 2064, when population is expected to start decreasing (Vollset et al, 2020). Critics are highlighting that this expected decline of the world population is not getting sufficient attention in the discussions around, for example, resource scarcity.

Resource scarcity

Common wisdom has it that more people means more use of resources. However, there are voices claiming that this is not necessarily true. For example, economist Julian Simon has developed his 'Simon Abundance Index', which shows that raw materials become more abundant as well as cheaper as the population grows. Allegedly this is because more people also means more creativity and more solutions being developed for solving critical issues (HumanProgress, 2020; Boudry, 2020).

Corporate social responsibility and the stakeholder doctrine

Criticism from another source is aimed at companies involved in CSR-related activities or those embracing the stakeholder doctrine over the shareholder doctrine. Even though companies claim to be actively involved in CSR-related activities, research shows that concrete actions and practical results are often difficult to find and that shareholder pressure still seems to be the overwhelming force at play (Bebchuk and Tallarita, 2020; NRC, 2020a).

One way of looking at this is that in such cases the company would probably be in the early stages of CSR maturity and still learning about its true implications (e.g. Visser, 2014; Gluszek, 2018). Critics, however, would in fact question whether these companies really have the intention to mature at all or if they would simply be 'greenwashing': trying to look good but without really trying to do good. It was Elkington who in 2018 did an unprecedented 'concept recall' of his own Triple Bottom Line concept, stating that it was merely used as an accounting tool rather than an instrument for pursuing its real goal of system change geared towards the transformation of capitalism (Elkington, 2018).

Consumerism and our human bi-polarity

Businesses try to develop products and services that meet with the expectations of consumers, because in the end, that's where the revenues come from. So what if a company wants to become circular but the consumer doesn't seem to care? Changing the behaviour of consumers may be a hard nut to crack.

To begin with, we are all *citizens*. Each one of us as a member of society has opinions about how we would like this society to be. The same goes for our economy and the planet on which we live. Probably very few citizens would argue against the main objectives of circularity: to create a situation in which fewer resources and energy are required for the same level of industrial production. This objective in itself is fairly uncontroversial – who could be against it?

But besides being citizens we are also *consumers*; we also express ourselves through our consumption patterns. Throughout our lifetime, we spend our money on food, on clothing, on housing, on leisure and so on. As a direct consequence of the enormous growth of wealth since World War II, in many countries there is now a dominance of so-called consumerism in which traditional media, social media, influencers and our peers put constant pressure on us by telling us what to buy and use, and to share our experiences with others.

Apparently, the way we behave as consumers often doesn't match our desires as citizens. It's almost as if all of us suffer from some degree of *bi-polarity*; what we (say we) like or don't like as citizens is often not supported by how we behave as consumers.

We complain about climate change, but we still keep flying around the planet on cheap airline flights. We complain about child labour and unfair salaries and working conditions for factory workers, but we keep buying cheap fashion in gigantic quantities. We complain about companies crossing the boundaries of privacy law, but our use of social media platforms keeps growing like never before. We complain about companies including 'planned obsolescence' in the designs of their products, but still we keep queueing up at the stores when the latest model smartphone is launched.

Consumerism and the constant desire for buying new 'stuff' doesn't logically match with the desire to become more circular; in many cases it's quite the opposite. But since it's the consumers who drive demand, ultimately we require the mass market to take a big step in the circular direction. For the moment, it remains to be seen if we will really put our consumer money where our citizen mouth is.[6]

Optimized supply networks

As we've said, consumerism has become part of normal life in many countries. Low-cost products, special offers and discounts are pushing consumption to even higher levels. To support our high levels of consumption we now find ourselves with the situation that many of the supply chains we have built over the years are built on the premise of being able to supply large quantities of reasonably priced (read: cheap) products. In most cases, complex worldwide supply networks have emerged. Changing this set-up around will be an enormously complex and time-consuming task.

A complicating factor is that the efficiency in these supply chains has been optimized to an extreme extent nowadays, resulting in very low prices for the consumer. These extremely low prices for new products mean that alternatives for return and recycling of products at a competitive price level are virtually impossible. For example, new plastic products are just so cheap that most manufacturers would not see any incentive for setting up circular systems or turning to more expensive recycled raw materials. And how many people would pay €60 for repairing a four-year-old device, waiting three weeks for it to be finished, if a brand new one can be purchased online and delivered to your doorstep within two days for €70?

Complexity of worldwide regulation

The topic of rules and regulation was addressed earlier on in this chapter. Since some of the problems that circularity can help address, such as climate change or resource scarcity, are worldwide, worldwide legislation would definitely favour the implementation of circular initiatives around the world. Companies interested in exploring circular opportunities would benefit from having a so-called level playing field in which market and legal conditions are the same or at least similar for all competitors.

However, international legislation is a very complex affair. Not only do countries have very different legal systems, but they may also have very different priorities. Much depends on the current state of the national economy, on their international position, but also for example on the main dominant national industries.

Being realistic about criticism and complicating factors

The above-mentioned criticisms and complicating factors are very relevant, because it shows that whichever company wants to embark on a journey to become circular, to justify its action it will most likely also have to deal with these critical voices, either within the company or among its external stakeholders.

EXERCISE 1.5

Explore the context of criticism and other complicating factors

Explore

Explore the criticism around climate change, about population growth, about resource scarcity and about CSR and the complicating factors of consumerism, optimized supply networks and worldwide regulation:

- Do some more (internet) desk research into each of these criticisms and complicating factors.

- What's your own opinion about these criticisms and complicating factors and why?

- What do you see as the main implications for an individual company?

Discussions in circular economy discourse and practice

As this chapter so far has hopefully shown, there is still a lot of ambiguity around the topic of circularity. The discourse on the circular economy has been led by players such as NGOs, consultancies, governments, academics, the European Commission and multinationals. The principles of a circular economy are more often celebrated than critically examined. However, as we have seen, there is not one single definition and understanding of what a circular economy precisely entails. In practice, the circular economy principles might be interpreted differently depending on the school of thought. This may lead to circularity being an idea or ideal for most, while its enactment might be fragile and limited (Gregson et al, 2015). For some legislators, a company achieving a product that is recyclable at all, can already be considered 'circular'. For others, just achieving 'recyclability' can hardly be considered true circularity yet.

A circular economy relies on a systems-wide innovation, not just of one product or one company, and aims to 'redefine products and services to design out waste and pollution, while minimizing negative impacts. Underpinned by a transition to renewable energy sources, the circular model builds economic, natural and social capital' (EMF, n.d. c). The emphasis on the recycling of materials and the redesign of processes contributes to more sustainable business models, but it also encapsulates limitations and tensions. For example, some products are just too complex to recycle. As we have seen, the idea of a circular economy is not new: people have been turning waste into resources for centuries. However, the difference is that the materials we use now are far more complex. A 2018 study on the Fairphone 2 (a modular smartphone designed to be repairable, recyclable and with a longer lifespan) shows that the use of complex man-made materials, such as batteries and microchips, makes closing the loop impossible (Reuter et al, 2018). They found that only 30 per cent of the materials used in Fairphone 2 can be recuperated.

Another topic of discussion is that the input of materials exceeds the output. Global resource use increases year by year. This growth makes a circular economy impossible. Because, simply put, even if 100 per cent of materials were recycled, but our global resource use keeps increasing year by year, the amount of recycled material will always be smaller than the material needed for growth. Thus, we have to continuously extract more resources. Here, one of the most important aspects – to some scholars – is overlooked: the refuse and reduce strategies on the production *and* the consumption side. To be sustainable and circular, it is essential that the circular economy principles, in discourse and in practice, focus on reducing the ever-growing demand for new products and materials and refuse overconsumption (Van Poppel, 2020).

In addition, the absence of a social dimension in most definitions, which is inherent in sustainable development, limits the circular economy's ethical dimensions. Therefore, some scholars propose that social objectives such as human well-being, participative democratic decision-making, the SDGs or socioeconomics should be included in the circular economy concepts, metrics and tools (Gregson et al, 2015; Geissdoerfer et al, 2017; Murray et al, 2017; Korhonen et al, 2018; Padilla-Rivera et al, 2020).

But what does all of this mean for an individual company? To what extent can an individual company be made responsible for taking on activities considered beyond their scope, such as competitors, consumerism and so on? In practice, much discussion takes place here and it seems that the debate is far from settled (e.g. Van Poppel, 2020).

Summary

THE FINDINGS OF PHASE 1, STEP 1 OF PROJECT 'CIRCULARITY': EXPLORING THE CONTEXT OF THE CIRCULAR ECONOMY

Some days after the kick-off of Project 'Circularity', Aunt Joanna, Peter and Maria got together again to talk about the findings of their research. The picture was impressive, but quite complex at the same time. 'I really didn't imagine that there were so many different angles to circularity,' Peter said. 'No, me neither,' Maria responded, 'and I actually had no idea that the topic goes back such a long way; I thought it was something much more recent.'

'I agree, but let's get to the point and try and summarize where we stand,' Aunt Joanna said. 'We now have a pretty clear picture about the general context of circularity. It seems clear that there is a pull from society, a call for action to deal with a number of problems related to the planet. In addition, there is the push from a number of relevant enablers. These two factors together explain why the circular economy has actually gained so much attention lately.'

'Furthermore,' she continued, 'we now have a clear picture showing that circularity is a very diverse topic which has a wide diversity of angles, but also has to deal with criticism and other complicating factors. This means that people from very diverse areas in academia, business and government as well as the general public are somehow involved in it, which in turn probably makes it unlikely that everyone agrees on which direction should be taken. That's important to keep in mind for our own storyline, I think.'

Aunt Joanna continued, 'OK, let's park these results for the moment and move on and *explore the company perspective* in more detail in the next step. I'm interested to find out *why* companies should engage in circularity at all and *what* circularity actually looks like in detail at the company level in terms of activities, goods flows, business models and so on.'

FIGURE 1.4   Exploring the complexity of the context of circularity (detailed)

Notes

1   The notion of 'narrative and numbers' was introduced in an article on business models by Magretta (2002).

2   We are paraphrasing the terms *market pull* and *technology push* from basic innovation literature here (e.g. Rothwell, 1994).

3   The famous Buckminster Fuller, architect and inventor, but also often cited in the context of the circular economy, built on the Spaceship Earth metaphor in his 1969 book *Operating Manual for Spaceship Earth*, which undoubtedly has contributed to the popularization of the metaphor (Fuller, 1969).

4   In Germany there is also a deposit on reusable bottles and cans, but interestingly enough that one is not regulated by law, but left up to individual chain partners such as producers, distributors and retailers.

5 The examples of the German 'Pfand' systems (operationally very different for one-way and for reusable packaging) and the industry-wide initiatives in the Dutch beer industry also highlight the need to look into the details at the national level, because such differences can be observed in many cases. More about this later on in this chapter as well as in Chapter 3.

6 Maybe it is appropriate to add a shade of nuance here. Even in countries where consumerism seems the current dominant *modus vivendi*, there are also consumers who possibly don't have much choice due to their budget constraints and who are therefore pushed towards the cheaper options of buying, rather than the more sustainable options.

02

Exploring the company perspective of circularity

PROJECT 'CIRCULARITY', PHASE 1, STEP 2, AUNT JOANNA'S OFFICE[1]

'Whoa, what's with the sad face?' Peter said to Maria, while coming into their aunt's office, where he found his cousin already seated at the table. 'Had a bad start to the week?'

'I don't know,' Maria answered, 'I was listening to this podcast about sustainability on the way here and they were talking about "greenwashing". You know, companies pretending to do the "green thing" when they really don't do anything at all? It seems "green marketing" is even an official course you can take at some schools, where you can learn how to make stuff look greener than it is, so that others will buy it.'

Maria continued: 'They had this talking point on companies who design obsolescence into their products so that after a given time they don't work anymore and you have to throw the old one away and buy a new one. And to top it off, they were talking about our government leaders denying climate change and saying don't worry, things will cool down in time... I mean, how sick is all of that?'

'Wow, you're really on a roll already at this hour,' said Peter with a teasing look on his face, 'and what podcast was that? Are you sure it was a well-informed and objective one? Or was it one of those podcasts done by your activist friends who are always trying to make companies and governments look like they're the evil enemies?' Peter was clearly trying to provoke his cousin into one of their legendary verbal clashes.

'No, you wish.' Maria wasn't in for teasing and responded in a serious way, 'Don't you think I get all of my information only from my friends. You may not believe it, but I do look around me sometimes, you know. This was actually a podcast from a well-known journalist and she clearly had put a lot of research into it.'[2]

'Alright, alright,' Peter said, 'I already believe you, don't worry, just checking....'

'Well, maybe I can cheer you up,' he continued, 'because I actually brought a story to share of a company where they have done this really great circular initiative. I thought it would demonstrate to you that not all companies are evil but that they can in fact contribute to a greener world and some actually do.'

Peter continued: 'I guess you just can't generalize. Of course there are always some bad guys around, but don't let that distort your view because there are also a lot of good people and companies around, same as that there are ecologists who mainly shout and who are not very constructive or practical either. Anyway, let me share this circular company initiative with you...'

'Hello, good morning! Did I just hear my favourite niece and nephew mention the words 'company' and 'circular' in one phrase?' said Aunt Joanna with a big smile as she entered the room, 'because that was exactly the next topic on our list of Project 'Circularity' wasn't it?'

And with the typical whirlwind of energy around her, she came directly to the point and continued: 'Look, I'm interested to find out the following:

- First of all, **why** companies should engage in circularity at all, so that's related to *purpose*.

- Then we should get a clear picture on **what** circularity actually looks like and **how** it works in detail at the company level in terms of *business models*. You know, *segments and value propositions, circular strategies, revenue models* and so on.

- And of course, I would like to understand **how much** a company's financials would be affected, so what the *profit & loss statement, the balance sheet* and the *financing* could look like.

'My feeling is that this next step is an important one for us,' she said, 'in order to get a real and thorough understanding of circularity at the company level.'

'Sounds cool, Aunt Joanna,' said Maria, who was clearly cheering up, inspired by the energy of Peter and her aunt this morning. 'Peter and I will get started right away. Come on, dear cousin, don't be lazy, we have a lot of work to do. And you can start by sharing that beautiful circular company example you said you found....'

Purpose (why?)

We as humans have always strived to find meaning and purpose in life. This long-standing struggle has now crept into our businesses and organizations. The Purpose Economy, coined by Aaron Hurst in 2014, suggests that businesses will be most

FIGURE 2.1   Exploring the company perspective on circularity

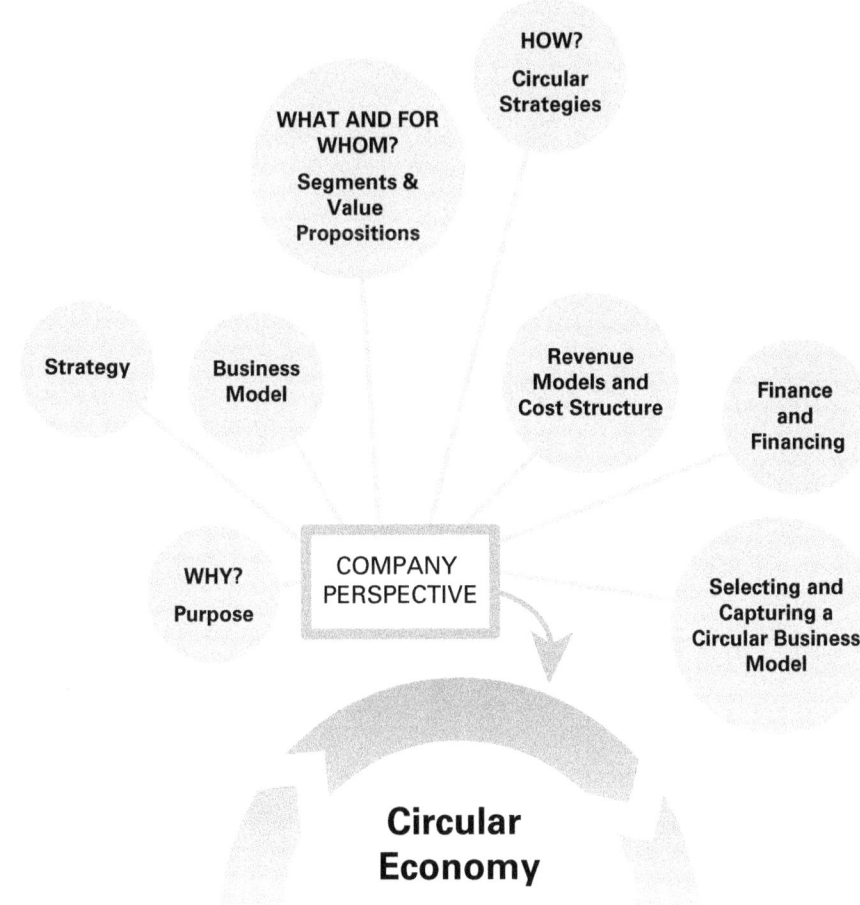

successful in the long term if they have a very clear sense of their purpose, with which employees can closely identify. There are three types of purpose central to this line of thought (Hurst, 2014):

- **Personal purpose:** what we love doing, our passion.
- **Social purpose:** share the meaningful work that you do, relationships matter to humans more than anything else.
- **Societal purpose:** strive to contribute to the well-being of the world around us, to society and ourselves.

FIGURE 2.2   Three types of purpose

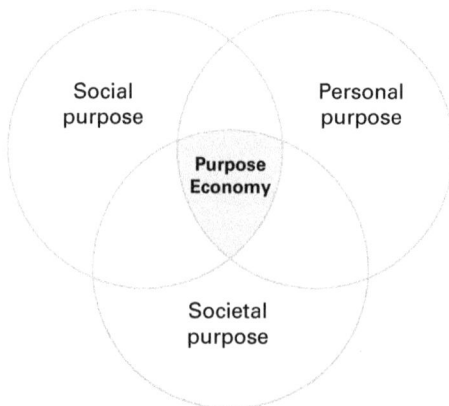

To sum up, the Purpose Economy serves the need for people to develop themselves (personal purpose), be part of a community (social purpose), and affect something greater than themselves (societal purpose).

Way back at the beginning of the 20th century, Ford Motor Company was already putting purpose alongside profit, by offering to double their workers' wages, cut the work day to eight hours and share profits with their workers. As a result, the company became one of the most popular employers in the industry, and continued to profit throughout the rest of the century.

Taking a jump forward to the beginning of the 21st century, the emergence of purpose-led businesses points to a paradigm shift in the world of businesses. To Simon Sinek, bestselling author of the book *Start With Why* (2009) – and presenter of the third most popular TED video of all time – central to this paradigm shift in the world of business is the 'why' behind doing business: 'People do business with those who believe what they believe. People don't buy what you do; they buy why you do it.' Existing for profit, cutting costs and increasing output is not enough. It is the why, the purpose of a business's existence, that can stand the test of time.

To solidify their purpose, in recent years more and more businesses have published 'purpose statements' in addition to their 'mission statements'. A mission statement is the *what* they're trying to accomplish, and a purpose statement is the *why*. Back in the day, Apple's mission was becoming the leading computer company, but Steve Jobs' purpose was to design innovative, robust and beautiful products that delighted customers. Apple was not focused on shareholders or taking short-cuts or short-term actions to maximize shareholder value; instead they focused on their customers. Their success and, in turn, value to their shareholders has been a long process of product design, introduction and product excellence (Heineman, 2011).

Among the biggest and best known for their purpose is Unilever with its *Unilever Sustainable Living Plan* (USLP), launched in 2010 to deliver short-term and long-term benefits for their shareholders and society (Unilever, n.d.). USLP is a blueprint for a sustainable future in which everyone can live well within the natural limits of the planet, which transcends the original notion of purpose. With its USLP the company also takes a leadership role on social and political issues. It aims to decouple business growth from environmental impact by focusing for example on sustainable sourcing, fairness in the workplace, opportunities for women and rethinking plastic packaging, towards a circular economy, so that while the company increases in size it will reduce its total environmental footprint across the value chain.

EXERCISE 2.1
Explore purpose and mission

Explore

Explore purpose statements, mission statements:

- Do some (internet) desk research to find more examples of purpose and mission statements. For example, look at your favourite companies and see what their purpose and mission are.
- If they did not define their purpose, what do you think their purpose could be?
- Define in one sentence their why and their what.

Due to fundamental economic change and the failure of governments to provide lasting solutions for social, economic and political issues, society is increasingly looking to both public and private businesses to address these issues. Given the magnitude of the global challenges that we face today, it is no surprise that the stakeholders in society, such as citizens, businesses, non-governmental organizations (NGOs) and governments, are all pressing business to stop being so much of the problem and to start becoming more of the solution (in Chapter 1 we described this as *society pull*).

Just like in Unilever's Sustainable Living Plan, these issues range from gender and racial inequality to protecting the environment to retirement, among others. In his 2019 annual letter to CEOs, investment company BlackRock's CEO Larry Fink called on other CEOs to not only ensure their organizations have a purpose and deliver more than financial returns to stakeholders (as he had done in his 2018 letter) but to also take a leadership role on social and political issues (BlackRock, 2018, 2019).

It's no longer enough for companies to just create a good product. Larry Fink wrote in 2019: 'Purpose is not a mere tagline or marketing campaign; it is a company's fundamental reason for being – what it does every day to create value for its stakeholders. Purpose is not the sole pursuit of profits but the animating force for achieving them.' People want to support businesses that have a purpose, with values that align with their own values, and that really act on those principles — not only use them for greenwashing purposes.

In order to counter the suspicions of greenwashing, businesses are under increasing pressure to measure and monitor their environmental, social and governance (ESG) activities to arrive at a more precise assessment of their purpose-driven actions. Many businesses follow the Global Reporting Initiative (GRI) principles, and the World Economic Forum – together with Big Four firms – have developed a set of metrics for the disclosure of non-financial ESG factors. It covers key measures, such as greenhouse gas emissions, nature loss, resource circularity, and gender and ethnicity pay gaps (WEF, 2020c).

It goes without saying that businesses need purpose. In today's competitive market a well-defined purpose enables a company to thrive. The old notion that purpose-driven businesses require a non-profit status has shifted. One third-party certification standard to balance profit and purpose is called B Corporation. B Corp requires companies to meet social and environmental performance, legal accountability and public transparency (B Corporation, n.d.). As society's most challenging problems cannot be solved by government and non-profits alone, the B Corp community works toward reduced inequality, lower levels of poverty, a healthier environment, stronger communities, and the creation of more high-quality jobs with dignity and purpose. As of April 2020, there are over 3,300 certified B Corporations across 150 industries in 71 countries.

The Sustainable Development Goals (SDGs), already briefly introduced in Chapter 1, provide a compass and guidance for businesses on how they can align their strategies with the massive economic, environmental and social challenges our planet is facing. The guiding principles of sustainable development which led to the development of the SDGs are the 5 Ps (United Nations Foundation, 2019):

1 *People*: end poverty and hunger in all forms and ensure dignity and equality.

2 *Planet*: protect our planet's natural resources and climate for future generations.

3 *Prosperity*: ensure prosperous and fulfilling lives in harmony with nature.

4 *Peace*: foster peaceful, just and inclusive societies.

5 *Partnership*: implement the agenda through a solid global partnership.

GRI, the UN Global Compact and the World Business Council for Sustainable Development created an SDG Compass to help businesses to operationalize the goals (SDG Compass, n.d.).

FIGURE 2.3   SDG Compass

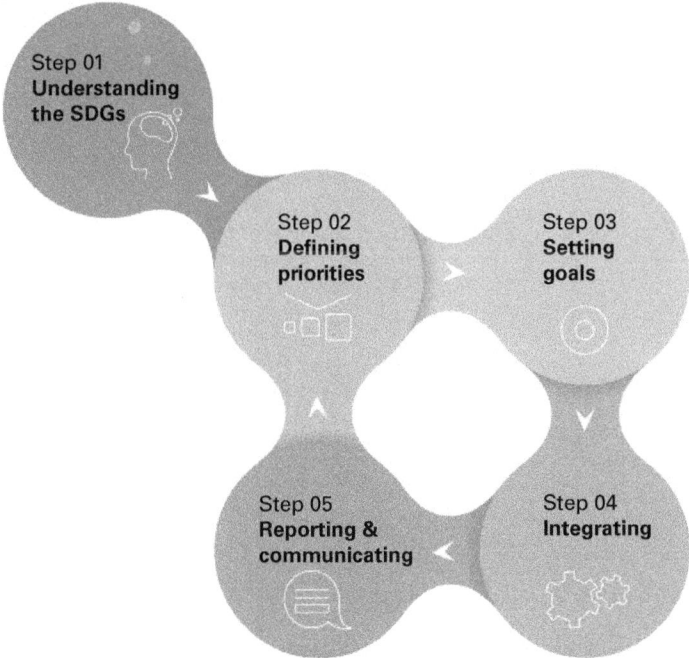

Step 01
Understanding
the SDGs

Step 02
Defining
priorities

Step 03
Setting
goals

Step 05
Reporting &
communicating

Step 04
Integrating

EXERCISE 2.2
Explore the Sustainable Development Goals and the circular economy

Explore

Explore Sustainable Development Goals, circular economy:

- Do some (internet) desk research into the circular economy and the SDGs – which SDGs strongly and directly benefit from the circular economy?
- Can you also find SDGs that facilitate the uptake of circular economy practices?

The purpose of purpose

Both trade press and academic literature indicate that purpose-led businesses are not just better able to attract and retain employees and customers, but also catalyse innovation and boost revenue growth and shareholder value. Cranfield University (2014) conducted research with two generations of leaders – more than 50 CEOs and 150 future leaders – on the topic of business purpose. They found that the two generations have very different views on the purpose of business and how well companies are delivering this:

- They both overwhelmingly believe that businesses should have a social purpose, but only 19 per cent of future leaders think businesses currently have a clear social purpose, compared to 86 per cent of CEOs.

- They also both agree that profitability and shareholder value are the key indicators of business success today. But while current leaders believe these will remain the most important indicators, future leaders believe that other factors such as the development of future talent, societal and environmental impacts, and innovation will define the successful business of the future.

A 2019 survey by Deloitte states that 42 per cent of Millennials have initiated or deepened a business relationship because they perceive the company's products or services to have a positive environmental and societal impact. In addition, around 37 per cent say they've decreased or stopped dealing with a company because of its ethical behaviour (Deloitte, 2019). Besides, Millennials represent 35 per cent of the workforce. They have new and more exacting expectations of the companies they work for, buy from and invest in, writes Larry Fink in his 2019 CEO Letter. Employees, rather than just shareholders, are likely to have a great say in defining a company's priorities and purpose. The beginnings of this shift can already be seen, Fink suggests, in recent walkouts of 'skilled employees' over the past year. Given this, companies that wish to attract and retain talent will need to adapt to these new expectations.

But it is not only a concern for young people: nearly two-thirds across all age groups want businesses to take a stand on issues like fair labour practices, transparency and sustainability (Accenture, 2018c).

The employee benefits of purpose-led business

Nowadays, purpose-driven businesses focus on identifying societal needs and working to fill those needs; they mobilize people and resources instead of managing them. It drives ethical behaviour, guides culture and provides a framework for consistent decision-making. Purpose-driven work makes employees prouder, more productive and more successful.

The purpose-led business focus often resonates with employees' personal values. This creates a healthy balance, because employees are able to do their job without experiencing any conflict with their personal feelings and values. Purpose is an employee motivator regardless of culture, language, region and occupation. It turns employees into ambassadors for the organization.

A LinkedIn study found that 73 per cent of purpose-oriented employees are satisfied with their job (LinkedIn & Imperative, 2016). People want to be proud of what their organization is doing. They want to feel like their work matters and to contribute to something bigger than themselves, in terms of business, social and environmental impact. This is exactly what a purpose-led business does: it creates a positive impact and value for society, without compromising its business focus. Working for a purpose-led business gives employees personal fulfilment. This leads to an increase in productivity and a decrease in absenteeism. Since proud and purpose-oriented employees stay longer with the organization, purpose is a key ingredient for a sustainable, scalable and strong organizational culture.

Redefining value

Central to redefining value is the incorporation of natural, human and social capital in organizational decision making, to manage risk and seize new opportunities (WBCSD, n.d. b). Finding the balance between natural, human and social capital and managing the corresponding stakeholder expectations, which change over time, is a constant dilemma for businesses. However, if there is a change in what society values, then there is always an opportunity to generate new value in response to that change. Conversely, if an organization does not generate sufficient value for society, they are losing their social licence to operate. Businesses should be able to look at these developments and spot the opportunities to support the change, while creating value for society and their own organization.

Redefining value and the corresponding sustainable transformation, including the transition to a circular economy, entails a systemic transformation of entire value chains, covering design, production and consumption phases, increasing material productivity, etc. Such a profound transformation is unlikely to happen suddenly.

FIGURE 2.4 Leading value creation concepts

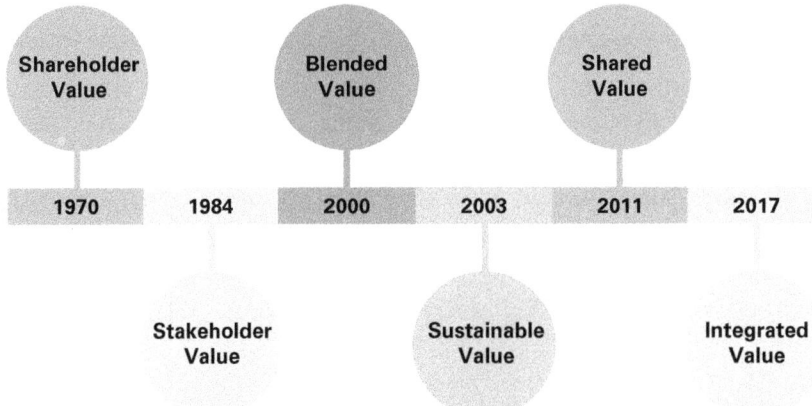

Option 1

Various models have been developed by academic experts and businesses to steer business's contribution to society, and while a sustainable transformation is underway, challenges and resistances remain. Understanding, in a critical and thoughtful way, the existing theoretical concepts, methodologies and practical applications and their implications for people, organizations and society, will be important for the further development and adoption of value creation approaches. There are currently five leading value creation concepts that reconceive business's value to society (Figure 2.4).

1 *Stakeholder Value*. Central to this concept is how stakeholders (e.g. customers, suppliers, employees, financiers, communities and management) work cooperatively to create value. This means that business is a 'set of value-creating relationships among groups that have a legitimate interest in the activities and outcomes of the business and upon whom the business depends to achieve its objectives' (Phillips et al, 2019).

2 *Blended Value*. In this conceptual framework – also known as mission-related investing, impact investing, aligned capital and social investments – businesses, investments and non-profit organizations are evaluated based on their ability to generate a blend of social, environmental and financial value (Emerson, 2000). This holistic approach is sometimes used interchangeably with the triple bottom line's people, planet and profit.

3 *Shared Value*. Creating Shared Value already has an acronym, CSV, and it's a framework in which a business's success and social progress are interdependent. It enhances the competitiveness of a business while 'simultaneously advancing the economic and social conditions in the communities in which it operates. Shared Value creation focuses on identifying and expanding the connections between societal and economic progress' (Porter and Kramer, 2011).

4 *Sustainable Value*. The framework views global sustainability challenges through the business lens, which helps to identify the right strategies and practices that contribute to a more sustainable world while simultaneously driving shareholder value. This win-win approach is defined as the creation of sustainable value (Hart and Milstein, 2003).

5 *Integrated Value*. Creating integrated value is the simultaneous building of multiple 'non-financial' capitals (such as human, ecological, social, technological and infrastructural capital) through synergistic innovation across the nexus economy (including the circular, well-being, access, exponential and resilience economies) that result in net-positive effects, thus making our world more satisfying, sustainable, shared, smart and secure (Visser, 2017a).

EXERCISE 2.3
Explore redefining value

Explore

Explore Stakeholder Value, Blended Value, Shared Value, Sustainable Value, Integrated Value:

- Do some (internet) desk research into the topics, for example by looking into the references and related sources mentioned.
- Create value propositions for each of the conceptual value frameworks.
- What's your opinion about these examples?
- What do you think in terms of their practical applicability? Also elaborate on the criticism towards these approaches; what do you think of these criticisms? What is your own view?

Critiquing the WHY dimension of the company's business: potential downsides to purpose

In this first part of the chapter, we have discussed the positive impact of purpose-led businesses and redefining value. However, it must be mentioned that there are also downsides to a purpose-led workplace that tie our identities, self-worth and emotional security to our jobs. Purpose-led businesses become more than just offices to their employees: they encourage people to spend more time working towards company goals, cultivate friendships and help them find their life's purpose. But for example, the round after round of layoffs during the Covid-19 pandemic show the downside of the purpose-led work culture (Griffith, 2020). People lose more than just their income: they lose things that are less tangible but potentially more costly, such as their self-worth, identity, emotional security and their life's purpose connected to their job. This leads us to the following question: do we need a new type of value that prioritizes the individual in the workplace, giving employees greater agency over their own work, and allowing them to find balance – and meaning – in other parts of their lives as well?

Critiquing the WHY dimension of the company's business: potential flaws in CSR

There is a broad global consensus about the fact that corporate social responsibility is an incremental element of the core business of a company, instead of a supplement to business activities. It is not about how to spend profit, it is about how it is made in the first place. In the shift from *responsibility* to creating *value* this notion is sometimes missing (Beschorner and Hajduk, 2017).

If we look at CSV it reinforces the idea that businesses meet 'societal needs' while they are generating profits. However, here societal needs are seen as a means to an end, allowing the business to discover new market opportunities and invest profitably when there is a win-win situation. Only when opportunities are identified to create economic (one win) *and* social value (two wins) should the business act.

However, when there are win-lose cases (the business profits, but society doesn't) or lose-win cases (society profits, but at a cost to business) the focus comes back to generating profit. It shows that this framework only caters to relevant stakeholders, instead of society as a whole (de los Reyes et al, 2017). Pretending that businesses above all concentrate on creating economic value is untrue and can be seen as a flaw in the shared value framework.

When businesses act as corporate citizens, such as in the framework of stakeholder value or sustainable value, they get involved in their communities and help shape their societal environments. They become more than just economic agents; they go beyond generating economic value and show that they can operate in different roles within society.

When even John Elkington calls to rethink his triple bottom line, because it is used as a balancing act adopting a trade-off mentality, instead of provoking deeper thinking about the future of capitalism, we can argue a case against blended value as well. As businesses 'move heaven and earth to ensure that they hit their profit targets, the same is very rarely true of their people and planet targets,' states Elkington (2018). We need value creation frameworks with the necessary radical intent that stop us overshooting our planetary boundaries.

Redefining value and creating purpose is a hot topic for businesses, partially also because of pressure from society, as addressed in Chapter 1 and once more at the beginning of this chapter. Many scholars are dealing with the (further) development and adoption of value creation approaches, their practical applications and implications for people, businesses and society. A business needs to decide what their position is, because it will ultimately guide their competitive strategy.

EXERCISE 2.4
Explore the link between purpose and circularity

Explore

On the basis of your current understanding about what a company's purpose could be and how it can be phrased, now explore how the concept of circularity fits in with purpose. How can the steps that a company takes on the path towards circularity positively contribute to fulfilling their purpose?

Strategy

After extensively elaborating the concept of purpose in the previous section and connecting purpose to the topic of circularity, let's now take a look at translating the principles of 'why?' to tangible business strategies, i.e. 'Where do we want to go?', 'What will we offer and to whom (commercially)?', 'How will we do it (operationally)?' and 'How much will it bring (financially)?' (Figure 2.5).[3]

Once a company has clarity on its purpose, it needs to break this down into actionable practical objectives and define 'where it wants to go to'. Thus, the more generic purpose statement will have to be translated into concrete objectives, plans and actions. As Douma et al (2020) state:

- 'a strategy is nothing more than a plan;
- the plan relates to the long term;
- the strategy relates to the function of a company in society;
- the strategy contains which objectives a company wants to achieve;
- the strategy indicates how the company wants to achieve the objectives.'

The process of strategy formulation has been and still is under intense debate and various schools of thought exist. Mintzberg already distinguished 10 such schools of thought in 1990 and the academic discussion in a series of articles on the topic in which Mintzberg and Ansoff exchange views, concepts and critiques is famous (De Wit and Meyer, 1994). In a slightly simplified view, on the one hand there is the notion of strategy as an outcome of a series of steps of structured investigation and analysis, e.g. environmental analysis, industry analysis, market analysis and so on are the

FIGURE 2.5   Purpose, strategy, business model

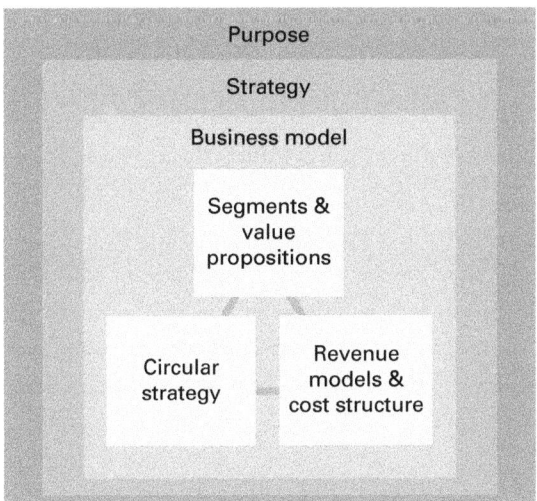

inputs for specifying a detailed strategic plan (the 'design school', based on thinking before acting). On the other hand there are the schools of thought that see strategy much more as something which emerges over time and is adapted continuously, although based on the so-called Strategic Intent, which gives general direction and prevents the company from changing direction every week (the 'learning school', based on learning while acting).

It is beyond the scope of this book to dive into much more detail about the strategy formulation process itself. Instead, we focus on the business model of a company and its specific building blocks, and placing these into the context of circularity.

Business models: an introduction

One element that sets the circular economy apart from its predecessors, such as eco-design, industrial ecology, eco-efficiency, cleaner production or the 'pollution prevention pays' motto, is the combined thinking in business models (Reike et al, 2018). This means that the transition to a circular economy, and the implementation of circularity and preventive measures in a value chain, not only rely on technical matters, but also heavily rely on organizational aspects, as well as on how to monetize the circularity. This is also where business models come into the picture.

Every business model has two parts (Magretta, 2002). One part includes activities associated with making something (designing, purchasing materials, manufacturing and so on), and the other part includes activities focused on selling something to the right customer (sales, distribution, delivering the service, revenue and so on).

According to Teece (2010), an organization's business model defines the way a company persuades customers to be willing to pay for the offered value (create value), the way a company actually makes the offered value into a reality (deliver value), and the way it converts payments into profit (capture value). It reflects the assumptions about what customers want, how they want to get it, and what the organization will do to satisfy those needs. The essence is to summarize how value is created, delivered, captured and distributed among all the parties involved.

Please note that there is a difference between a business model and a revenue model. Although both have similarities, they are two outlines that serve a different purpose: the revenue model is a subset component of the business model. The revenue model addresses the question of how an organization creates added value, such as money, while the business model describes all facets that influence the creation of this added value. We will come back to revenue models towards the end of this chapter. The term 'business model' therefore has a much broader meaning, which we will cover first, using the so-called Business Model Canvas as a simple tool to visualize a business model.

The Business Model Canvas

Osterwalder and Pigneur (2010) have developed nine building blocks that combine the revenue and business model. Together these building blocks form a simple one-page template called the Business Model Canvas, describing nine fundamental elements that give a good overview of how a company's business model is formed (Figure 2.6).

As you can see from Figure 2.6, the upper right-hand side of the canvas focuses on external factors, such as the customer and the market, which are mostly out of a business's control (focusing on answering the question '*for whom* will we do it?'):

1 **Customer relationships**: the type of relationship established with the specific customer segments.

2 **Customer segments**: defines the groups of people or organizations the business aims to reach or serve.

3 **Distribution channels**: describes how to communicate with and reach the customer segments to deliver the value proposition.

The upper left-hand side of the Business Model Canvas focuses on the business and its internal factors, which are mostly under their control (focusing on the question '*how* will we do it?'):

4 **Key partners**: the relationships with other businesses such as suppliers and manu-facturers, governmental or non-consumer entities that help realize the business model.

5 **Key activities**: the most important activities in executing the value proposition.

6 **Key resources**: the most important assets required to create and offer the value proposition, reach markets, maintain relationships with the customer segments and earn revenues.

The middle building block focuses on the value proposition, which represents the value exchange between the business and its customers (thus addressing the question '*what* do we offer?'):

7 **Value propositions**: the business offer, both product and service, that creates value for a specific customer segment.

The bottom parts of the canvas then reflect the monetary implications of the business model choices in terms of the financials (focusing on the question '*how* much will it bring?'):

8 **Revenue streams**: the way in which the business creates added value, or the answer to the question 'how does the business create revenue?'

9 **Cost structure**: all the costs and expenses that will be incurred while operating the business model.

FIGURE 2.6   The Business Model Canvas

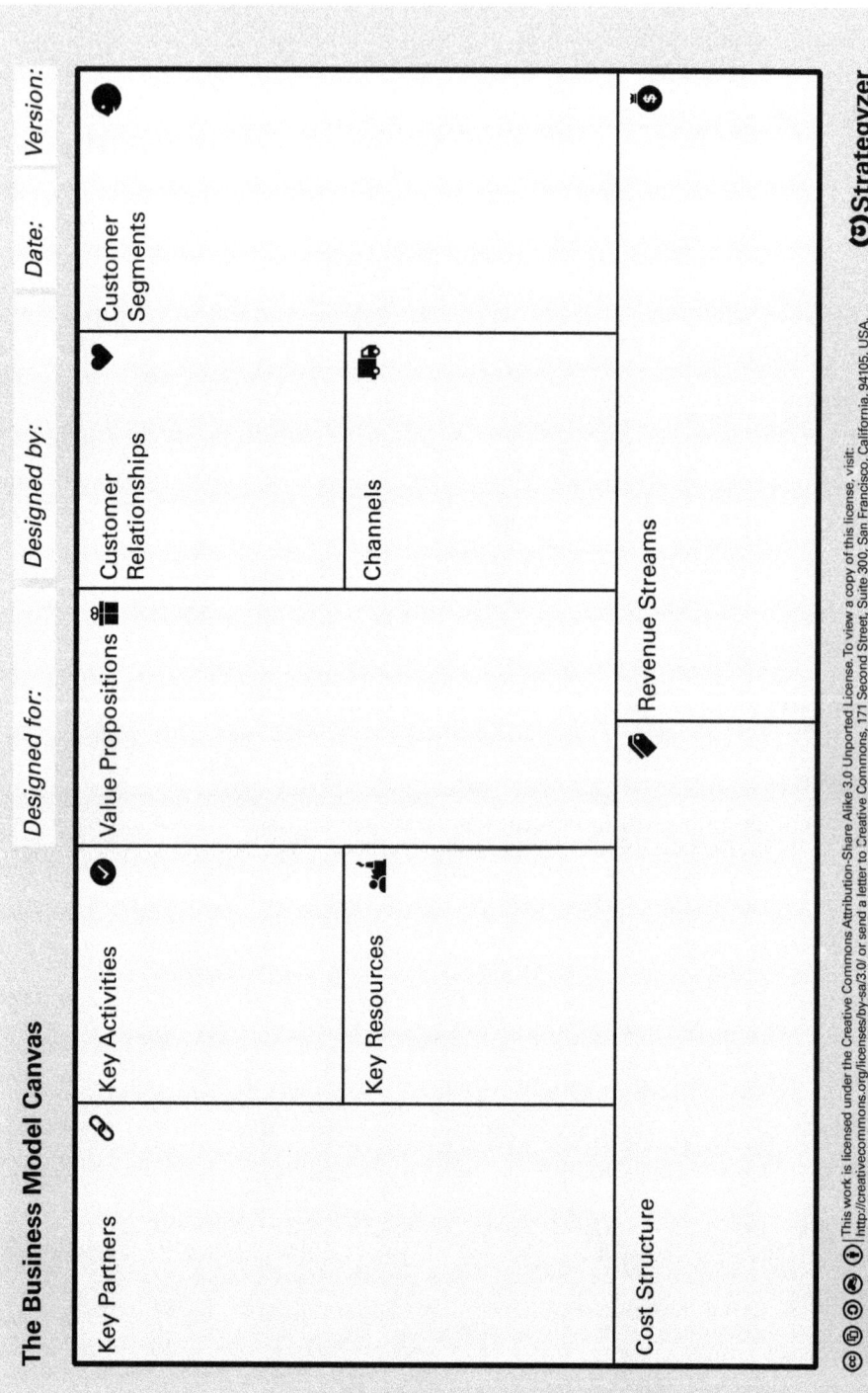

The Business Model Canvas

Designed for: Designed by: Date: Version:

Key Partners 🔗	Key Activities ⊘	Value Propositions 🎁	Customer Relationships ❤	Customer Segments 👥
	Key Resources		Channels 🚚	
Cost Structure		Revenue Streams		

Ⓢ **Strategyzer**
Strategyzer.com

Inspired by the big success of the Business Model Canvas, other frameworks that capture a company's business model have emerged, such as the Lean Canvas (Maurya, 2012), which in effect is an adaptation of the Business Model Canvas, or the Strategy Sketch by Kraaijenbrink (2015), used to describe the overall strategy, adding elements such as 'competition', 'goals' and 'values'.

Specific variations have also been developed in relation to 'sustainable business models', incorporating elements to highlight environmental and societal impacts in addition to the commercial business aspect. First of all, the Ellen MacArthur Foundation has provided an add-on to the basic Business Model Canvas, with specific prompts and questions related to circularity (EMF, 2016a). Other examples are the Triple Layered Business Model Canvas, which extends the original canvas by adding a social layer based on stakeholder perspective, and an environmental layer based on lifecycle thinking, aimed at combining economic, environmental and social value (Joyce and Paquin, 2016) and the Circular Business Model Canvas (Circulab, n.d.).

EXERCISE 2.5
Explore the different Business Model Canvasses and circularity

Explore

Explore the different Business Model Canvasses and circularity:

- Do some (internet) desk research to find the original Business Model Canvas by Osterwalder and Pigneur (2010) and the one addressed by the Ellen MacArthur Foundation (see EMF, 2016a for more details).

- What are the biggest differences between the prompts and questions by Osterwalder and Pigneur, and the ones addressed by the Ellen MacArthur Foundation?

- Do some (internet) desk research to find the other canvasses mentioned. Which canvas would you use when setting up your own circular startup?

- Describe and be prepared to discuss.

In the following sections, we will zoom in on the different elements of the business model, clustered into three logical blocks, thus covering the most relevant parts of the canvasses mentioned above: segments and value propositions (*what and for whom?*), circular strategies (*how?*) and revenue models and cost structure (*how much?*).

Segments and value propositions (what and for whom?)

As the first building block of the company's business model, let's look into the topic of segments and value propositions.

The concept of value propositions: why would they buy from me?

A company generates revenue by selling to its customers. In this context, the term 'value proposition' is also often used. A company must give its customers something they value and that they are willing to pay for. We would call that the 'what?' of the company; in other words, what is it that we promise to our customers that they perceive as valuable?

In academic literature about marketing there are a wealth of references and frameworks about the concept of value, for example in the famous work of Kotler and Lane (2015). A generally accepted expression is that value is a function of the benefits perceived by a customer, in relation to the price paid for the product or service. In a way, this refers to the term 'price-and-quality relationship' that we are all used to in our daily lives.

So where are these perceived benefits coming from, or which are the elements of the 'value proposition'? In marketing literature there are plenty of frameworks and concepts dealing with the definition of value propositions, from the 'product levels' of Kotler (2015), to the Value Proposition Canvas (Osterwalder et al, 2014) and the five value attributes and corresponding 5-4-3-3-3 strategies as proposed by Crawford and Mathews (2003). DeSmet (2018) combines the latter framework of Crawford and Mathews in a very original way with the basic strategies of product leadership,

FIGURE 2.7   Segments and value propositions

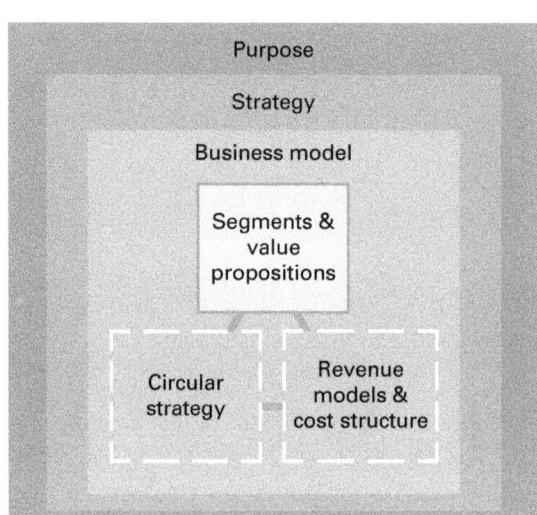

customer intimacy and operational excellence (Treacy and Wiersema, 1995). Christopher (2016) and Rushton et al (2017), take a rather more simplified yet powerful view: they start with the core product at the heart of its value. Some people would refer to this as the basic or core benefits of the product. Aspects like the product quality, functionality, product features and durability come to mind: an umbrella should effectively protect you from the rain, a medicine cure a disease and mineral water relieve your thirst.

But in some markets, especially mature ones where products from different companies are very similar to one another, those basic benefits might just not be enough to differentiate you in the eyes of the customers, unless you successfully pursue a cost leadership or operational excellence strategy. For the other companies, differentiation could take place at what Christopher and Rushton call the 'service surround' or 'product surround'. In this additional layer, aspects beyond the pure physical product come into the play, like for example delivery speed, delivery reliability, flexibility to change an order before delivery, after-sales or maintenance service, a buyback service, choice of packaging variety, or the possibility of adding customized labelling.

So where do aspects of circularity come into play? That's an easy question to ask, but the answer may be less straightforward. For example, do consumers buy a more durable circular product because it's durable or because it's circular, or because of both? The answer may in fact be different from person to person. However, for the company selling the product the difference may be significant, especially when looking at the implications for customer segmentation, publicity, branding, but even seemingly unrelated issues like waste treatment or environmental reporting.

FIGURE 2.8   Value, core product, service surround

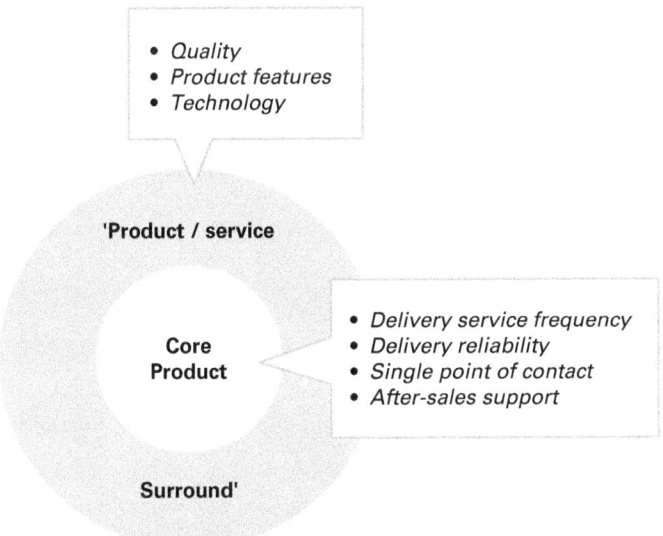

SOURCE After Christopher (2016) and Rushton et al (2017)

Being everything to everyone versus one size fits all: smart customer segmentation

Please note that most companies do not only attend one single customer segment; they normally deal with various segments. In marketing literature many references can be found about customer segmentation, but the basic thought behind it is that customers are not all 100 per cent identical and that 'one size fits all' might be very efficient, but results in hardly anyone receiving exactly what they want. The opposite would be to give every individual customer exactly what they ask for, but the downside of that approach would be that efficiency and therefore prices and/or margins would be at stake.

That is where the art and science of smart customer segmentation comes on to the scene: how to determine as many useful segments as necessary while at the same time keeping the number as low as possible, thus optimizing between customization and efficiency. The exact concepts, methods and tools of customer segmentation are a bit beyond the focus of this book, but for the moment it is sufficient to understand that most companies work for multiple segments and that each of these segments might call for different value propositions (even though more or less overlap might exist, they would not be 100 per cent identical). And in turn, those different value propositions might require different operational (circular) solutions, each playing with the same tension between customization and efficiency.

Customer and consumer: not (always) one and the same

It was briefly hinted at already earlier on, but in any given company situation there might be a difference between characteristics that are important to the direct paying customer of a company and those characteristics that are important to the (final) consumer. When considering a local convenience store owner in the city centre of town, their customers in most cases would be the same as the end consumers, so there is no need for me to differentiate between customer and consumer.

But, for example, in the case of a pharmaceutical company, the final consumer is the patient and they are obviously interested in what a medicine will do inside their body, referring to the core benefit of the product caused by the so-called 'active ingredient(s)' it contains. However, the pharmacy that is buying the medicine from the pharmaceutical company is probably not interested in the core benefit because in the end they will not use the medicine themselves. For them the core benefit of the product is mainly important because they know it will represent a potential sales volume to patients looking, for example, for a medicine for headaches. In addition to that, the pharmacy will most likely be very interested in delivery-related aspects, like delivery lead time, flexibility, packaging types, product availability, etc.

So even though it is tempting to focus only on why a consumer might want to buy a certain product from a company, it's crucial not to forget the aspects that provide value to the ones who directly pay us, our customers, especially in case they are not the same. From a value chain perspective, we need to make this distinction explicit and include both points of view, since they might have different implications for the different supply chain building blocks. In literature about industry types, business models and marketing, the distinction is commonly made between business-to-consumer (B2C) and business-to-business (B2B). However, even a B2B company selling to other businesses will ultimately have a consumer at the end of the chain, so it might be tempting to mix up the concepts of customer and consumer.

EXERCISE 2.6
Explore circular value propositions

Explore

- Explore circular value propositions by doing some (internet) desk research into product offerings that you would consider 'circular'.

- To what extent is the circular dimension of the offering centred around circularity?

- To what extent do you think that the circular dimension would be relevant for all customers/consumers interested in the product?

Circular strategies (how?)

Now that segments and value propositions have become clearer, let's look into the second building block of business models and focus that mostly on circularity: so-called circular strategies (Figure 2.9).

FIGURE 2.9 Circular strategies

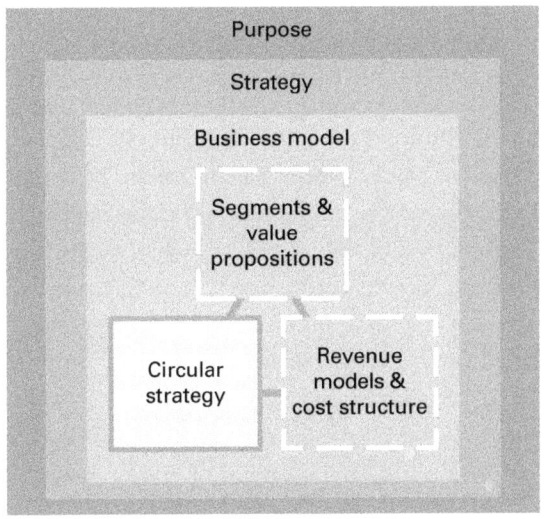

Linear supply chains as the starting point

Traditionally, a (linear) supply chain is the sequence of events and actors that move a commodity from manufacturing to market. Every industry has one and for most existing companies this is still the dominant model. The way these linear supply chains are managed has a strong effect on a business's competitiveness. Traditionally you could see a supply chain as a straight-line model, where various actors work together to acquire raw materials, convert them into final products and deliver them to end users:

Raw materials → supplier → manufacturer → shipping → end user

However, due to our global economy a value chain isn't this simple anymore – it looks more like a web crossing the globe, especially when we take circularity into account, which means that closed loops and cycles are introduced into the value chain to organize the return flows of products and materials, for the purpose of recycling, remanufacturing, reuse or other value retention strategies that we will discuss later in this chapter.

Supply chain strategy, as a logical consequence of overall company strategy, defines a connection of activities and a sequence of events throughout the value chain to fulfil the value proposition to customers, while operational efficiency focuses on achieving excellence in the individual activities (Porter, 1980). There are six generic supply chain models, which you can divide into two groups (Perez, 2013): the efficiency-oriented and the responsiveness-oriented models:

1 *Efficiency-oriented models*: within these models the value proposition is oriented towards low cost, asset utilization and end-to-end efficiency. The three supply chain models are the efficient, fast and continuous-flow models.

2 *Responsiveness-oriented models*: these models are characterized by high demand, market mediation costs and uncertainty. The three supply chain models are the agile, custom-configured and flexible models.

Once a business has made the choice of which supply chain strategy best aligns with its value proposition, it is important to evaluate supply chain management for reliability, responsiveness, costs, agility and asset efficiency. The Supply Chain Operations Reference (SCOR) model could be used (APICS, n.d.) to benchmark the supply chain performance and track improvements. SCOR is a process framework that organizes the supply chain processes into six categories: plan (what, when and where to make); source (buy the materials needed); make (manufacture your product); deliver (sell and get products to customers); return (reverse logistics); and enable (everything else needed that does not belong in the other categories).

As said, for most companies, such linear supply chains and strategies are still the norm. In itself, this makes the transformation to a circular supply chain more

FIGURE 2.10 The Value Hill

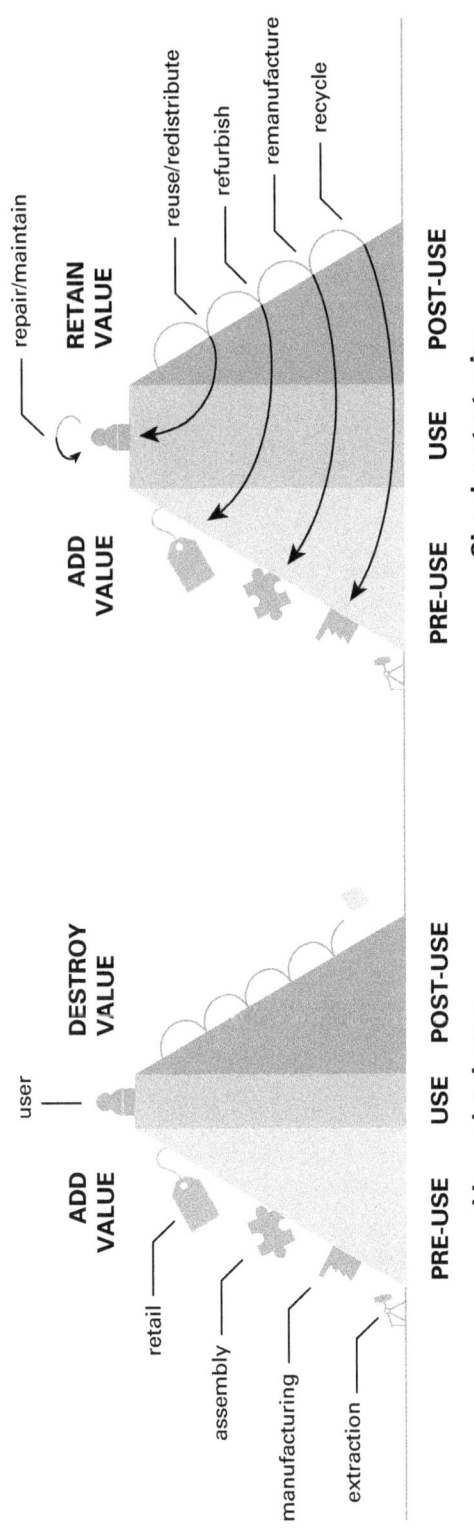

SOURCE Achterberg et al (2016)

complex, since there is an existing supply chain infrastructure to take into consideration as a starting point. We will come back to this aspect in Part Three.

Circularity in the supply chain

As you know from Chapter 1, there is a lack of standardized definitions and terminology for a circular economy. On top of that, new circular business models are still being developed. To provide you with a clear and visually appealing overview of the most important business models and their strategies, we will use the Value Hill (Achterberg et al, 2016).

The Value Hill is a strategy framework that equips businesses with the right concepts to position their business, its strategy and their value chain in a circular context. The aim is to keep products for as long as possible at their highest value on top of the Value Hill.

As you can see from Figure 2.10, the Value Hill is an actual hill. While travelling up the hill we start at the pre-use phase, covering mining, production and distribution. When a product moves up the hill, value is added in every step. Once the product has arrived at the top it begins its in-use phase. Central in the pre-use and in-use phases is *narrowing the loop*, where circular strategies minimize the use of materials and products, and keep the product at its highest value for as long as possible. As we discussed in Chapter 1, products can be designed to last and to be suitable for repair and maintenance.

When the current owner is done with the product, it can start its way downhill. Starting at the top of the hill and travelling down, circular strategies focus on *slowing the loop* to ensure that the product and its components are maintained at their highest utility. The journey downhill depicts the post-usage phase, where with every step a product loses value. However, on its way down a product, its components or materials, can be taken back up the hill into previous stages on the left of the hillside. In this way, they flow directly back into the use phase and their value is not lost, but in fact retained. When materials finally reach their end-of-life stage, *closed loops* focus on material recycling and thus creating further value out of the remaining materials.

Circular strategies and the R-ladder

Value retention refers to the idea of resources carrying an intrinsic value, opposed to the economic notions of value. In terms of finished goods this means retaining their state or reusing them with as little change as possible to ensure consecutive lives, and in the case of the conservation of resources retaining them closest to their original state (Reike et al, 2018). In practice today, incineration and recycling – which are lower forms of value retention of materials – still dominate policies. Besides, data on resource input reduction or reuse is difficult to obtain.

As you can observe, most concepts related to circular strategies have 're-' in their name: retain, reuse, refurbish, recycle and so on. 'Re-' in Latin means 'again', 'back', but also 'afresh', 'anew', which all point to the essence of a circular economy (Sihvonen and Ritola, 2015). This is normally referred to as the R-ladder or the R-imperatives. Reike et al (2018) have analysed 69 academic articles on the conceptualization of R-imperatives, or strategies, and created a single systemic typology of 10 resource value retention options (ROs), as most commonly found in the literature. In Chapter 1 we briefly mentioned the R-ladder, founded on the hierarchical classification of waste – the so-called 'Ladder of Lansink' – and the Waste Framework Directive. For those who are already a little familiar with the circular economy, the letter 'R' must indeed already sound familiar.

The R-strategies all have different implications for resource use, design, manufacturing, consumer usage and the afterlife stage. There are 10 strategies that start with 'R' and some you probably have heard of: refuse, reduce, resell/reuse, repair, refurbish, remanufacture, repurpose, recycle materials, recover (energy) and re-mine. The first two strategies are the preventive options, the other eight are the reutilization options. The 10Rs can be divided into three stages:

- *Stage 1*: short loops aimed at smarter production and use of products by refusing, reducing or reselling/reusing. We also call this *narrowing the loop*, contributing to minimizing the use of products and materials, maintaining value as long as possible (Bocken et al, 2016).

- *Stage 2*: medium-long loops aimed at extending the lifespan by repairing, refurbishing, remanufacturing or repurposing products and components. We also call this *slowing the loop*, contributing to maintaining products and materials at their highest utility.

- *Stage 3*: long loops focused on useful application of materials by material recycling, (energy) recovery and re-mining. We also call this *closing the loop* to use materials again when they reach the end-of-life stage, creating further value.

The rule of thumb for the R-ladder is the higher up the ladder you go, the more resources are used, thus the higher the environmental burden. Important to remember is that these strategies can be implemented by businesses and within value chains simultaneously.

FIGURE 2.11 The R-ladder

Lifecycle & stages on the R-ladder
(Reike et al, 2018)

Circular Strategies on the R-ladder

Narrowing, slowing & closing the loop
(Bocken et al, 2016)

Product *concept and design* lifecycle (R0 & R1)

R0–R2: *short loops* aimed at smarter production and use of products

R0 = Refuse	(consume less)	
R1 = Reduce	(use less materials)	
R2 = Resell, Reuse	(Second-hand market)	

R0–R2: *narrowing the loop* to minimize the use of products and materials, maintaining value as long as possible

R3–R6: *medium-long loops* aimed at extending the life of products and components

R3 = Repair	(extend lifetime, same user)
R4 = Refurbish	(extend lifetime, new user)
R5 = Remanufacture	(of components in new, similar product)
R6 = Repurpose	(of components, in other function)

R3–R6: *slowing the loop* to maintaining products and materials at their highest utility

Product *produce and use* lifecycle (R2–R9)

R7–R9: *long loops* aimed at useful application of materials

R7 = Recycle materials	(downcycle, recycle, upcycle)
R8 = Recover energy	(incinerate, but store/use energy)
R9 = Re-mine	(mining of landfills and waste plants)

R7–R9: *closing the loop* to use materials again when they reach the end-of-life stage, creating further value

TWO THEORETICAL LIFECYCLES

Within a circular economy we can identify two theoretical lifecycles: the product *produce and use* cycle and the product *concept and design* cycle (Kuik et al, 2011; Reike et al, 2018).[4]

The product *produce and use* cycle focuses on material flow from pre-use to use and to the post-use stage. This cycle is linked to the circular strategies R2 up to and including R9 on the R-ladder: resell/reuse, repair, refurbish, remanufacture, repurpose, recycle, recover and re-mine (see Figure 2.11). These are the strategies that improve product utilization and keep a product at its highest value for as long as possible (keep products on top of the hill), and the strategies that ensure that a product, its components or materials flow back into the produce and use phase so that their value is retained (bring products, components or materials back up the hill) and product disposal is reduced.

The product *concept and design* cycle is the overarching framework taking the role of (re)designing the lifespan of a product concept, taking into account the strategies of the *produce and use* cycle. Central to the *concept and design* cycle are circular strategy R0 (refuse) and R1 (reduce) on the R-ladder and five core activities: policy (strategy formulation), idea generation (using creativity), designing (product design and cleaner production including other preventive and design approaches), realization of the idea (which is the timespan up to producing the product) and evaluation and reconsideration.

Rethinking the *concept and design* lifecycle is crucial in the transition to a circular economy, as pollution and waste should be designed out, and a product's consecutive lives should be taken into consideration from the design stage on. Bakker et al (2015) distinguish six different design strategies in the function of the circular strategies, which can be implemented as stand-alone design strategies or combined within one product: design for attachment and trust, design for reliability and durability, design for ease of maintenance and repair, design for upgradability and adaptability, design for standardization and compatibility, and design for dis- and reassembly.

Stage 1: Short loops aimed at smarter production and use of products

The first strategy – R0 on the R-ladder – is **refuse**.[5] As we pointed out in Chapter 1, our current linear economic model is driven by production and consumption, where the take-make-use-waste principle is central. This means that we take an excessive amount of primary raw materials and fossil energy sources, make products as cheaply as possible, use these products briefly and waste them immediately after usage. The refuse strategy aims to be a response to the 'take-make-use-dispose' way of doing things, for example by refusing the use of hazardous materials and chemicals in the design stage; refusing planned obsolescence – the design method in which products

FIGURE 2.12   The Value Hill, stage 1: refuse, reduce and resell/reuse

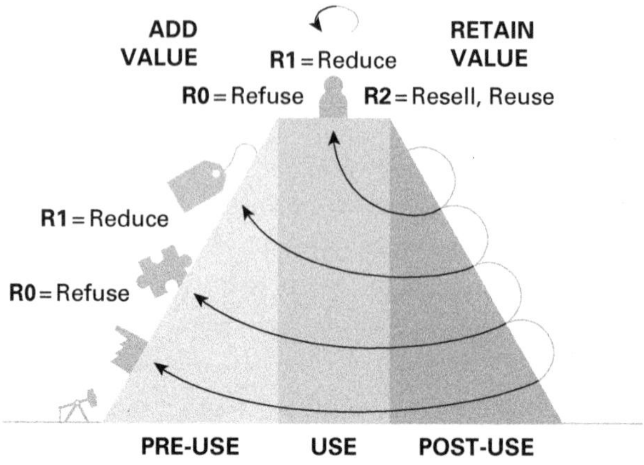

are deliberately designed with a limited lifespan or poor recoverability; refusing packaging waste by rethinking design; or completely refusing the production of certain products because within a circular economy context they don't make sense anymore (e.g. single-use plastics). Besides, they choose to create better alternatives.

The second strategy of this section – R1 on the R-ladder – is **reduce**.[6] This strategy focuses for example on reducing the number of raw materials used in a product by producing them either with fewer materials (e.g. less plastic in a plastic bottle), by switching to mono-materials (i.e. materials that only consist of one material or fibre) or by using secondary raw materials (i.e. recycled materials). In addition, the reduce strategy focuses on eliminating waste and pollution from the design stage by making better choices that lead to less waste and less pollution, as 80 per cent of a product's environmental impact is determined at this stage (EU, 2014b). For businesses this means, for example, adopting zero-waste design techniques, optimizing transportation and distribution or becoming carbon neutral by, for example, switching to renewable energy and fuel sources.

The third strategy – R2 on the R-ladder – is **resell/reuse**. This strategy entails the reuse of products as a whole, in the same function and hardly needing any adaptation, by another user. In a consumer-to-consumer (C2C) environment this is done by reselling unused products on websites such as eBay, Vinted, Facebook Marketplace or even TicketSwap, by swapping clothes or by giving certain products away. Research by ABN Amro (2018) shows that almost 60 per cent of consumers buy second-hand products, and 67 per cent are willing to do so. This points to a big potential for businesses to diversify their current strategies to adopt resell/reuse tactics for their existing products, such as IKEA's furniture buy-back and resell programme or Patagonia's Worn Wear.

THE ADVANTAGES OF THE STAGE 1 STRATEGIES OF REFUSE, REDUCE
AND RESELL/REUSE

By refusing our current linear economic model and the reduction of material usage, the Ellen MacArthur Foundation (EMF, 2012) has calculated that US \$340 to \$380 billion per year can be saved in net material costs in the European Union in a 'transition scenario' for a circular economy. In an 'advanced scenario', it saves US \$520 to \$630 billion a year by closing material loops and introducing cycles into the economy. Additional advantages of these three strategies are:

- By designing out waste and pollution, and refusing linear product categories, business can positively influence the environment instead of harming it.

- Demand for primary raw materials will decrease, resulting in net material savings that reduce costs for various raw materials.

- As planned obsolescence is no longer used, the total cost of ownership will be significantly reduced.

- When products are designed for reuse, warranty costs for consumers will be reduced.

- By reselling products businesses create extra financial value, and consumers save on the costs of buying a new version of a product.

EXERCISE 2.7
Explore refuse, reduce and resell/reuse

Explore

Explore the first stage on the R-ladder, combining circular strategies, your environment – what do you see?

- Look around and pick a product that you see: something that you are wearing, that you are sitting on, working at, travel with, etc.

- What would you reduce, what would you choose to refuse, how would you resell/ reuse the product?

Stage 2: Medium-long loops aimed at extending the lifespan

The strategies at the centre of the R-ladder are aimed at extending the lifespan of products and parts in medium-long loops. Instead of the dispose and replacement culture, this creates a culture of return and reuse, leveraging activities such as repair, refurbishment, remanufacturing or repurposing, where product utilization is maximized, the

FIGURE 2.13 The Value Hill, stage 2: repair, refurbish, remanufacture and repurpose

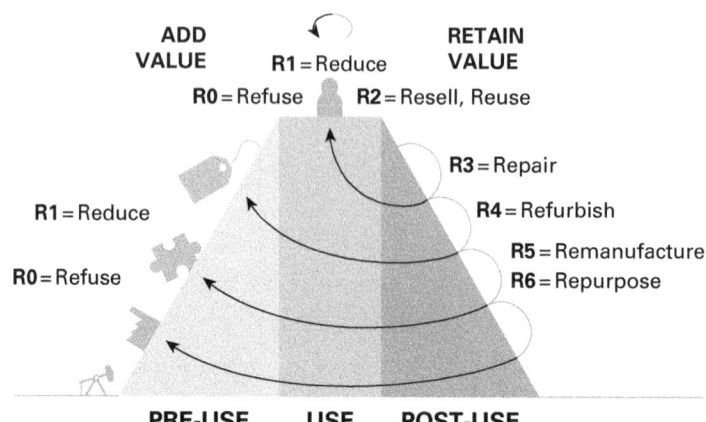

lifespan of products is extended and waste is avoided. But that's not all: value is retained or even added. Here, concepts like lifecycle thinking, reverse logistics, closed-loop supply chains and efficiency through the reduction of residuals and resource input become principles for action.

The fourth strategy – R3 on the R-ladder – is **repair**. As you know by now, within a circular economy it is very important to use our existing products for as long as possible and to their fullest potential. By repairing original parts in the original product, the quality upon first purchase (or production) is preserved. This ensures prolonging the lifespan of the original product. Aside from peer-to-peer repair workshops, businesses may re-collect their products in their own manufacturer-controlled repair centres or partner up with repair and maintenance companies. Research by the European Commission for the Environment (EU, 2014a) has shown that 77 per cent of EU citizens would rather repair their belongings than buy new ones. Yet they do not. They are discouraged by the cost of repairs or the level of service. However, as part of the Circular Economy Action Plan (EU, 2020) – one of the main blocks of the European Green Deal – the Commission will work towards establishing the 'right to repair' for consumers, meaning a higher availability of spare parts, access to repair, and upgrading services.

The fifth strategy – R4 on the R-ladder – is **refurbishment**. By means of refurbishment, an existing product is rebuilt using reused, repaired and new parts or a combination thereof. In short, refurbishment requires the repair or replacement of worn and obsolete parts of the original product by the manufacturer. The products used for refurbishment may be new products, for example unsold products that could use an upgrade or of which a newer version has been launched, but they may also be defective products that have been returned to the manufacturer or retailer under their warranty.

The sixth strategy – R5 on the R-ladder – is **remanufacturing**. 'Remanufacture' means to revise. The focus is on maintaining the original parts of products as much as possible. Remanufacturing is the production of new products, using the remanufactured parts of the original product. This is done by the manufacturer of the product. Upgraded parts from the original product form the basis for making a new, similar product, which is often put back on the market with a warranty. The economic incentives for remanufacturing consist of lower production costs through the use of existing parts, lower prices for the consumer, and offering affordable alternatives for new products. In addition, remanufacturing reduces the risks associated with the international supply of materials and parts and creates stronger relationships within the value chain.

The seventh strategy – R6 on the R-ladder – is **repurposing**, which is finding a new use for something with a purpose other than its original use. Components are reallocated or modified to fit a new, functional product. This extends the lifespan of the product or components by giving it a different purpose than it was originally produced (or built) for.

THE ADVANTAGES OF THE STAGE 2 STRATEGIES OF REPAIR, REFURBISH, REMANUFACTURE AND REPURPOSE

With circularity, innovation and entrepreneurship are often central. This combination triggers and accelerates the transition to a circular economy. Without technological innovation the realization of a circular economy is far away; however, the maintenance and repair of these new innovative products and services is necessary to guarantee their longevity and maximize their usage. Therefore, the repair sector has enormous potential within a circular economy.

Research by WRAP (2015) has shown that there is a direct and positive relationship between the efficient use of our primary (and secondary) resources and job creation. By reusing products and parts through repurposing, remanufacturing, refurbishing, repairing and reuse, about 8 to 20 jobs can be created per 1,000 tons of unwanted products. For comparison, energy recovery and recycling can create about 5 to 10 jobs per 1,000 tons of unwanted products, and landfilling 1,000 tons of unwanted products creates only 0.1 jobs. Other advantages of these five strategies are:

- prolonging the life of a product or components;
- by refurbishment and repairing, value is added to an original product, because its quality and functionality are as good as or even better than those of a new product;
- the (unnecessary) recycling, incineration or landfilling of products and materials is prevented;
- minimizing the use of primary raw materials for the production of new products and in turn saving on the associated costs;
- reducing the amount of waste generated.

These strategies contribute to the objectives of the Paris Climate Agreement mentioned in Chapter 1, by reducing CO_2 emissions and being less harmful to the environment than the production and usage of new products and components.

EXERCISE 2.8

Explore repair, refurbish, remanufacture and repurpose

Explore

Explore the second stage on the R-ladder; combining circular strategies; your environment – what do you see?

- Look around and pick a product that you see: something that you are wearing, that you are sitting on, working at, travel with, etc.
- What could you repair, refurbish, remanufacture or repurpose?

Stage 3: Long loops aimed at useful application of materials

As you read in the first chapter, the preference in a circular economy is to design out waste and pollution from the design stage on. Ideally, the entire product, including all its components and materials, is reused. When this is not possible, products or components can be reused in any form, including modifications, by any user, aimed at extending the lifespan of products and components. And lastly, when waste does arise, we focus on the recovery of materials and their useful application. This stage on the R-ladder focuses on 'dealing with waste', i.e. what happens with products at the end of their lifecycle?

FIGURE 2.14 The Value Hill, stage 3: material recycling, energy recovery and re-mining

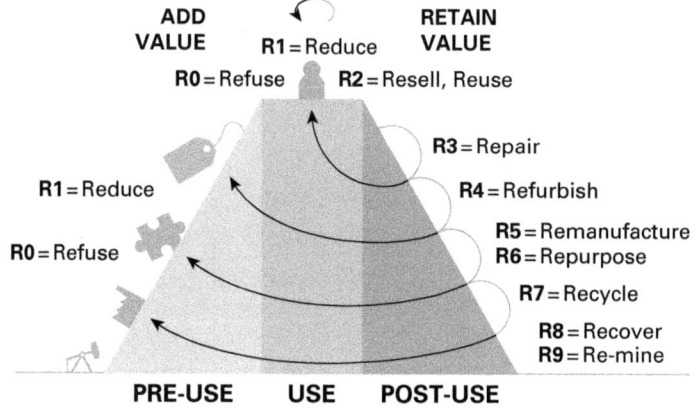

Long loops are introduced focusing on traditional waste management activities where products lose their original function. Material recycling, energy recovery and re-mining are strategies aiming at the useful application of materials as an alternative to incineration without energy recovery or the landfilling of residual waste, for which there is no place in a circular economy. If we look at the Value Hill, these three strategies are placed in the bottom right downhill corner.

The eighth strategy – R7 on the R-ladder – is **recycling**. This is a broad term for the processing of used materials into the same, higher or lower quality. Recycling clearly differs from reuse, as the raw materials are separated and processed instead of reusing components or products as a whole. Often when people hear about a circular economy, they think about recycling on steroids. But as you can see in Figure 2.14, material recycling only becomes an option in this last stage, when all other strategies aiming at smarter production and usage, and lifespan extension are no longer possible (Rood and Kishna, 2019). A prerequisite for recycling is the pre-sorting and separation of waste. There are different types of recycling, such as mechanical, chemical and organic recycling.

In the case of mechanical recycling, the returned materials are manipulated mechanically (e.g. shredded), so that they can be used as an input for new products. In other words, the chemical composition of the materials remains the same. In the case of chemical recycling, the returned materials are treated chemically, i.e. the chemical composition of the materials may be changed or even brought back into the original molecules of the plastic and then used as an input to new materials. Linking back to the Butterfly diagram as seen in Chapter 1, mechanical and chemical recycling are part of the technical cycle. Organic recycling is a bit different, and belongs to the biological cycle.

ORGANIC RECYCLING

A large part of our waste consists of biological materials such as vegetables, fruit, grass, leaves or pruning waste. It is desirable for this type of waste (i.e. vegetable garden fruit – VGF – and green waste) to be collected separately, but this is not yet the case everywhere. In the Netherlands, for example, one-third of residual waste consists of biological materials. This is a pity, because if collected separately, the materials can be turned into biogas or compost. Approximately two-thirds could be composted directly. In turn, the compost is reused by horticulturists, farmers, municipalities or private individuals as a soil improver, fertilizer or potting soil. The remaining one-third must first be fermented. By composting or fermenting biological waste, in the end the waste material gets reabsorbed by the soil and is reused within the biological cycle.

In addition to compost, this process also produces biogas. Biogas is used to generate heat and electricity. The burning of residual waste, or composting/fermenting biological waste, releases a great deal of energy (e.g. circular strategy Recover). The energy is released as electricity, heat or steam. What remains is a sandy, black material that can be reused in the construction of new roads instead of sand or gravel. If the released energy is captured properly, the heat or steam can be connected to the heat grid to heat buildings or the generated (green) electricity can be used, for example, to light houses or street lamps.

Dutch waste processor Meerlanden processes VGF waste into compost in a special fermentation plant. In their process five new (by)products are created: CO_2, biogas, compost, heat and water. As a result, the company's sweeping trucks are powered by the water created in this process, and all of Meerlanden's garbage trucks run on biogas, making them climate-neutral.

Within recycling there are three differentiations:

- the downcycling of raw materials into a lower raw material, after which reuse in any shape or form is no longer possible;
- the recycling of raw materials into the same material, for example a glass bottle becomes a glass bottle again;
- the upcycling of raw materials where value is added, so that the end material is of higher quality than in its original state.

EXERCISE 2.9
Explore downcycling, upcycling and recycling

Explore

Explore downcycling, upcycling, recycling, mechanical recycling, chemical recycling and organic recycling:

- Do some (internet) desk research to find examples of downcycling, upcycling and recycling within a circular economy.
- What do each of these recycling categories mean for a supply chain? Try to illustrate this using the Value Hill and the businesses that you have found for each recycling type.
- Do some (internet) desk research to find the difference between mechanical, chemical and organic recycling. Which type of recycling do you think has the most potential in a circular economy?

FIGURE 2.15 The difference between downcycling, recycling and upcycling visualized

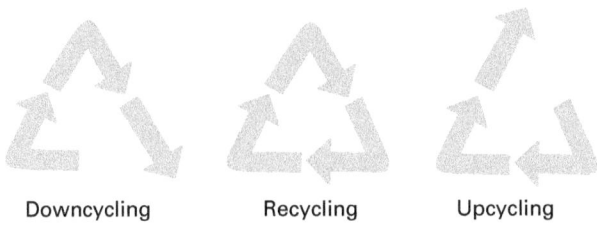

Downcycling   Recycling   Upcycling

The ninth and least circular strategy – R8 on the R-ladder – is the **recovery** of energy from the incineration of our residual waste. This energy is put forward as green energy. However, it must be noted that, for example, in the Netherlands only 58 per cent of waste is collected separately, meaning that the residual waste still consists of valuable materials that are lost due to this way of waste processing (Milieu Centraal, n.d.). Globally, less than 20 per cent of waste gets recycled or composted (World Bank, 2018).

The tenth strategy – R9 on the R-ladder – is **re-mining**. This strategy is often overlooked, as it is aimed at retrieving materials after the landfilling phase. In developing countries, obtaining valuable parts from disposed products is a more or less informal sector in which people try to earn a living by finding existing materials and waste stock that is currently lost as untreated waste. In these countries, where controlled landfilling is the norm, organizations start to focus on 'urban mining' and 'landfill mining' to obtain valuable resources stored in waste plants and old landfills (Reike et al, 2018).

THE ADVANTAGES OF THE STAGE 3 STRATEGIES OF MATERIAL RECYCLING, RECOVERY AND RE-MINING[7]

Energy recovery is a valuable alternative to the residual waste that cannot be recycled. It contributes to a circular economy because even though residual waste still consists of valuable materials, by recovering energy from their incineration, fewer primary raw materials are needed for the production of heat or energy. Besides, it provides energy that can be used as an alternative fuel, heat or green energy, and even the by-product, a black sand-like substance, can be reused in the construction of new roads. The recycling and re-mining of used materials also has several advantages:

- fewer primary raw materials and less agricultural land (e.g. for wood or cotton production) is needed;
- our CO_2 emissions are reduced, because the use of recycled materials needs less energy than the production of new materials, which creates a reduction in emissions;
- it reduces the amount of incinerated residual waste;
- it creates opportunities for employment and innovation.

Interrelationship between the strategies in the three stages

In the previous sections, the 10R circular strategies have been presented one after the other. However, in reality they overlap, are connected and can be applied together. For example, you can imagine that during the refurbishing of a product (the fifth strategy, or R4) not all of the product may be successfully refurbished; in other words, there is a waste stream as a consequence of the refurbishment activity. This waste stream can obviously be the input for one of the other circular strategies, and the company can opt to apply more than one circular strategy at a time, effectively one or more of those being applied as a complement to the chosen dominant circular strategy. We will come back to this concept of **dominant circular strategy** at the end of this chapter as well as in Parts Two and Three of the book in relation to The Blue Connection simulation game.

Material characteristics and the link to emerging Industry 4.0 technologies

To reduce waste, recover materials after usage and in essence *slow* and *close* the loop, we like to highlight the importance of material characteristics. Some materials are more easily reused than others, so it is of the utmost importance to have maximum clarity on the materials used in a certain product. Besides, complex circular practices drive the need for better collaboration and data sharing among all actors in a supply chain (Gupta et al, 2019). According to the European Commission (EU, 2020), 'Insights provided through open data can improve the decision-making of the efficient use of resources as data can predict certain trends (e.g. market, weather, demographics) of future supply and demand.' By using open data, actors in a specific value chain can, for example, solve logistical issues, improve recycling and waste collection processes, optimize inventory levels or improve strategic decision-making by having biodiversity logged and deforestation mapped. An example of this is SmartChain, which stimulates demand-driven innovation in short food supply chains using a multi-actor approach. Another great example of the usage of data is Blockchain initiatives such as Provenance, a startup that uses Blockchain to track tuna from line to store, authenticating the fishermen with verified social sustainability claims.

Important to remember is that '*to measure is to know*'. Using new technologies related to Big Data and the Internet of Things, enhancing circularity could improve the shift from selling products to providing services with an emphasis on use rather than on possession; making underused products, services or assets available to third parties (paid or not); and leveraging urban spaces with the use of technology focused on improving the living conditions of citizens or inhabitants (Nobre and Tavares, 2020). Information is at the heart of ensuring that companies around the world can make the right decisions to eradicate waste and use resources effectively. According to the Ellen MacArthur Foundation:

The Internet of Things, with its smart sensors and connected technologies, can play a key role in providing valuable data about things like energy use, under-utilized assets, and material flows to help make businesses more efficient… Looking forward, the Internet of Things will provide information about what resources we have and what we are losing. With objects becoming increasingly self-aware, the sharing platform of the future could have assets making themselves available for use in real-time. Enhanced tagging and tracking capabilities, such as insect-inspired swarm intelligence, present enormous economic opportunities to plug leaks and make use of materials previously considered to be waste (EMF, 2016b).

A truly circular economy arguably cannot exist without the Internet of Things and the usage of Big Data. To be sustainable, a system must be responsive: behaviours and actions must be connected via knowledge and data.

In that context we would like to introduce you to the concept of **material passports**, initiated by architect Thomas Rau. Rau is of the opinion that waste is material that has fallen into anonymity. Only proof of identity, in the form of a material passport, can prevent this (Rau and Oberhuber, 2016). If all material data of a finished good is recorded in a material passport, then all these materials can be recovered after the in-use stage in order to be reused. Doing so prevents their value being wasted by burning or landfilling. A finished good thus becomes storage for useful materials. The material passports initiated by Thomas Rau are registered on Madaster, an online one-stop access point that provides information for the registration of products, components and material used in construction objects. An interesting overview of the application of material passports for the construction industry can be found in Heinrich and Lang (2019).

EXERCISE 2.10
Explore a product: 'deconstruction workshop'

Explore

After zooming in on the different circular strategies in the previous sections, in this 'deconstruction workshop' you will explore the characteristics of a certain product from different angles, the same way the producer would need to do in the case of considering moving into circularity.

As a starting point, take a product you know from your own household, for example a drill, roller skates, a Bluetooth audio set, the mixing faucet from your shower or bathtub, a flatscreen TV, a microwave oven, or the dishwasher.

Step 1: Create a basic product factsheet of the chosen product (see partially elaborated example below for a washing machine). For inputs you may want to consult, for example, manufacturer websites, product manual websites, YouTube videos on 'how to disassemble…' or 'what's inside…'. If possible, you can of course also check your own devices at home (physical device, product manual and so on).[8]

FIGURE 2.16 Product factsheet of a washing machine (example, not fully elaborated)

NAME:

PRODUCT AND IMAGE:
- Washing machine

TYPICAL CUSTOMER / USER:
- Households

AVERAGE PRICE:
- 400–800 EUR

AVERAGE COMMERCIAL LIFESPAN:
- 5 Years

AVERAGE TECHNICAL LIFESPAN:
- 7–13 Years

BILL OF COMPONENTS:

WASHING MACHINE PARTS IDENTIFICATION

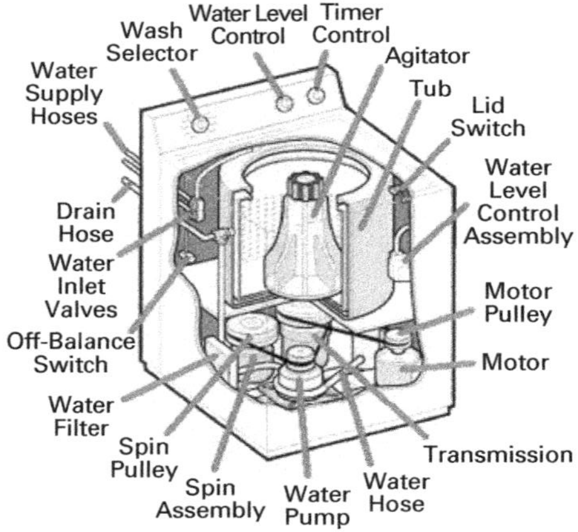

Water Supply Hoses · Wash Selector · Water Level Control · Timer Control · Agitator · Tub · Lid Switch · Water Level Control Assembly · Drain Hose · Water Inlet Valves · Off-Balance Switch · Water Filter · Spin Pulley · Spin Assembly · Water Pump · Water Hose · Motor Pulley · Motor · Transmission

BILL OF MATERIALS:
- Cover: sheet steel, coated with zinc
- Cover: porcelain coating

- PCB: copper foil
- PCB: glass
- PCB: resin

- …
- …

SOURCES: www.coolblue.nl, https://www.ariel.in/en-in/washing-machine-101/your-guide-to-washing-machines/anatomy-and-parts-explained, https://www.manualslib.com/manual/738779/Electrolux-Washing-Machine.html?page=54#manual, https://www.youtube.com/watch?v=j8_TzIoPCwY

FIGURE 2.17 Circular strategy template: repair and maintain

NAME:

PRODUCT AND IMAGE:
- Washing machine

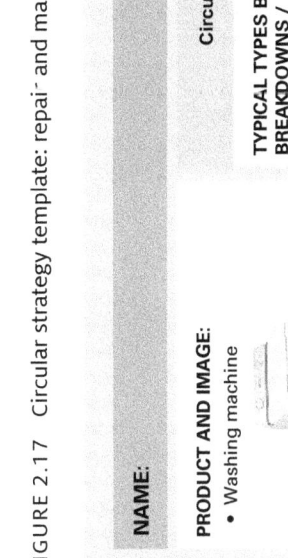

TYPICAL CUSTOMER/USER:
- Households

AVERAGE PRICE:
- 400–800 EUR

AVERAGE COMMERCIAL LIFESPAN:
- 5 Years

AVERAGE TECHNICAL LIFESPAN:
- 7–13 Years

SOURCES:

Circular strategy: 'SLOW THE LOOP' → Repair and maintain

TYPICAL TYPES BREAKDOWNS / FAILURES & FREQUENCY OF BREAKDOWNS / FAILURES?

TECHNICAL EASE OF REPAIR / MAINTENANCE? EASE OF (DIS-)ASSEMBLY?

REQUIRED MAINTENANCE INFRASTRUCTURE (WHERE? WHO? RESOURCES?)

COST OF MAINTENANCE/REPAIR vs COST OF PRODUCT

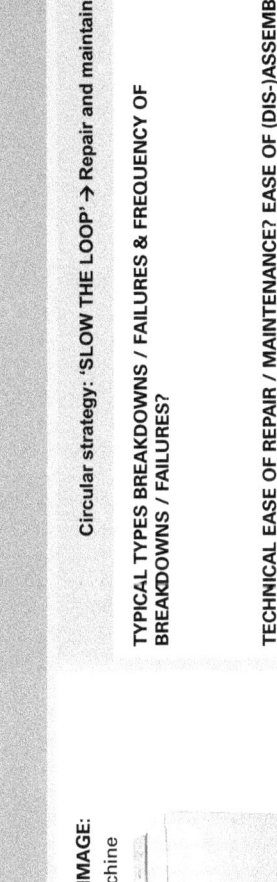

Component production

→

End product manufacturing

→

Retailing

→

Consumer/ User

Repair/ Maintain

FIGURE 2.18 Circular strategy template: refurbish and redistribute

TEAM NAME:

Circular strategy: 'SLOW THE LOOP' → Refurbishment and redistribution

PRODUCT AND IMAGE:

- Washing machine

TECHNICAL EASE OF REFURBISHING?

COMMERCIAL ATTRACTIVENESS AND ACCESSIBILITY OF SECOND-HAND MARKET FOR REFURBISHED PRODUCT?

TYPICAL CUSTOMER/USER:

- Households

AVERAGE PRICE:

- 400–800 EUR

AVERAGE COMMERCIAL LIFESPAN:

- 5 Years

AVERAGE TECHNICAL LIFESPAN:

- 7–13 Years

REQUIRED REFURBISHING AND REDISTRIBUTION INFRASTRUCTURE (WHERE? WHO? RESOURCES?)

COST OF REFURBISHING AND REDISTRIBUTION vs COST OF PRODUCT

SOURCES:

Component production → End product manufacturing → Retailing → Consumer/User

Refurbish and Redistribute

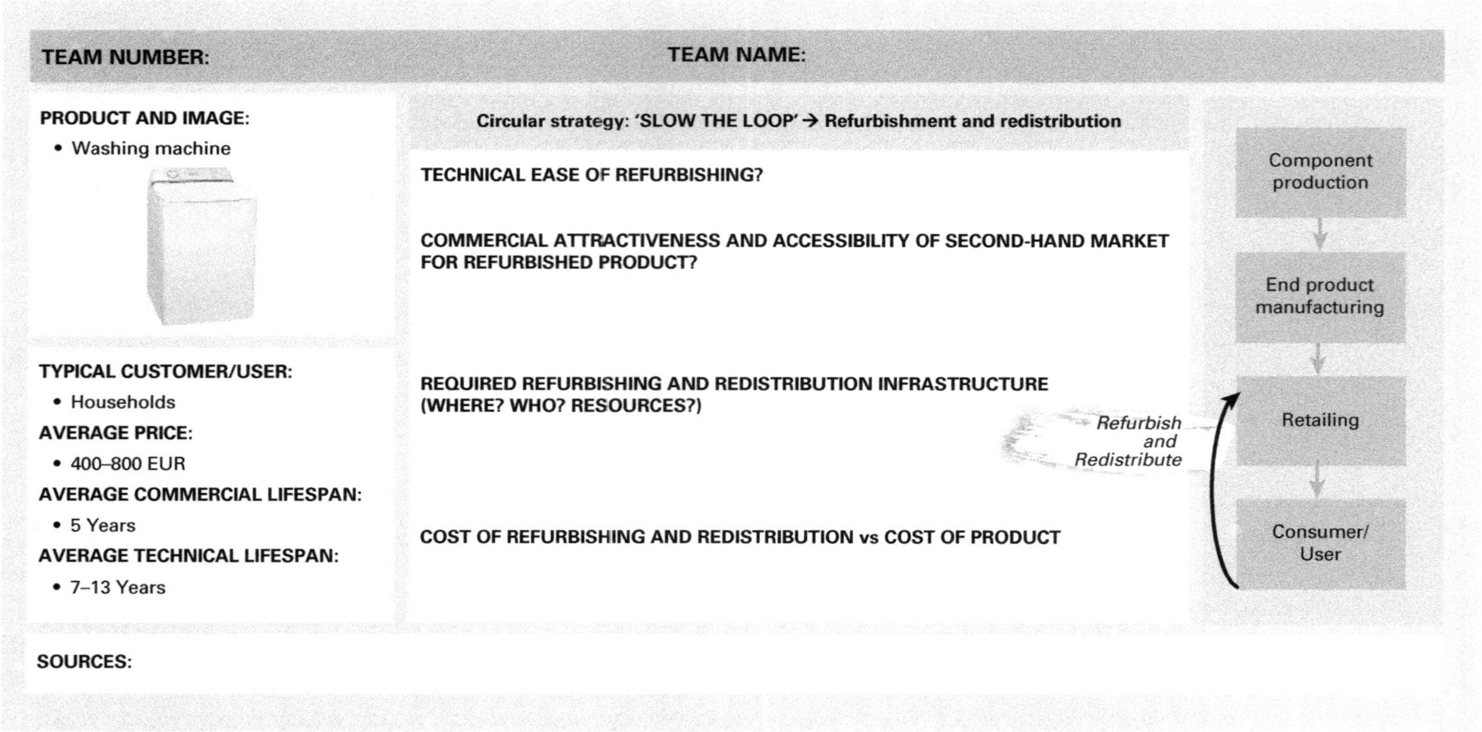

FIGURE 2.19 Circular strategy template: remanufacturing of components

TEAM NUMBER:

TEAM NAME:

Circular strategy: 'CLOSE THE LOOP' → Remanufacturing of components

WHICH COMPONENTS WOULD BE WORTH REMANUFACTURING? WHY?

TECHNICAL EASE OF DISASSEMBLY? TECHNICAL EASE OF REMANUFACTURING?

REQUIRED REMANUFACTURING INFRASTRUCTURE (WHERE? WHO? RESOURCES?)

Component production → End product manufacturing → Retailing → Consumer/User

Remanufacture components

PRODUCT AND IMAGE:

- Washing machine

TYPICAL CUSTOMER/USER:

- Households

AVERAGE PRICE:

- 400–800 EUR

AVERAGE COMMERCIAL LIFESPAN:

- 5 Years

AVERAGE TECHNICAL LIFESPAN:

- 7–13 Years

SOURCES:

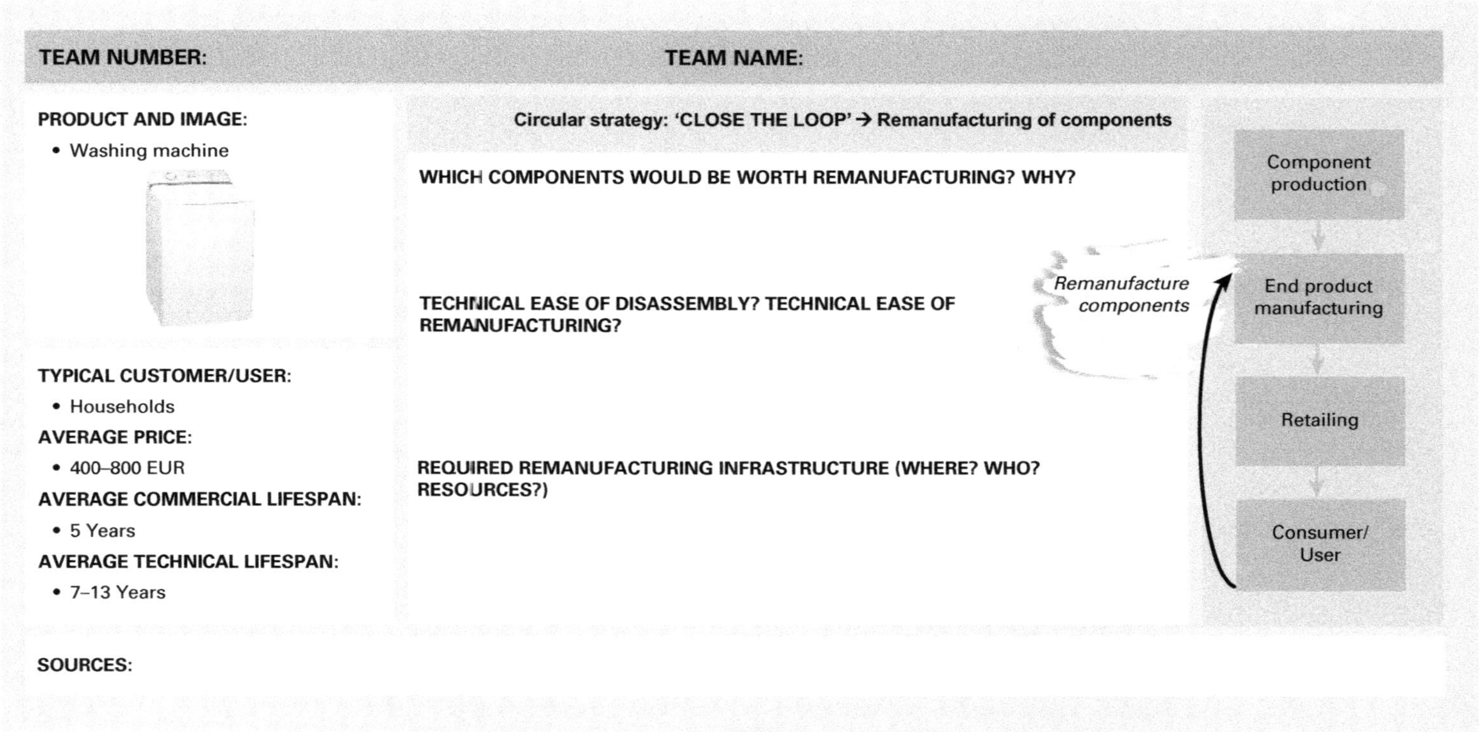

FIGURE 2.20 Circular strategy template: recycling of materials

TEAM NUMBER:

TEAM NAME:

Circular strategy: 'CLOSE THE LOOP' → recycling of materials

Component production → End product manufacturing → Retailing → Consumer/User

Recycle materials

WHICH MATERIALS WOULD BE WORTH RECYCLING? WHY?

TECHNICAL EASE OF DISASSEMBLY? TECHNICAL EASE OF RECYCLING?

REQUIRED RECYCLING INFRASTRUCTURE (WHERE? WHO? RESOURCES?)

PRODUCT AND IMAGE:
- Washing machine

TYPICAL CUSTOMER/USER:
- Households

AVERAGE PRICE:
- 400–800 EUR

AVERAGE COMMERCIAL LIFESPAN:
- 5 Years

AVERAGE TECHNICAL LIFESPAN:
- 7–13 Years

SOURCES:

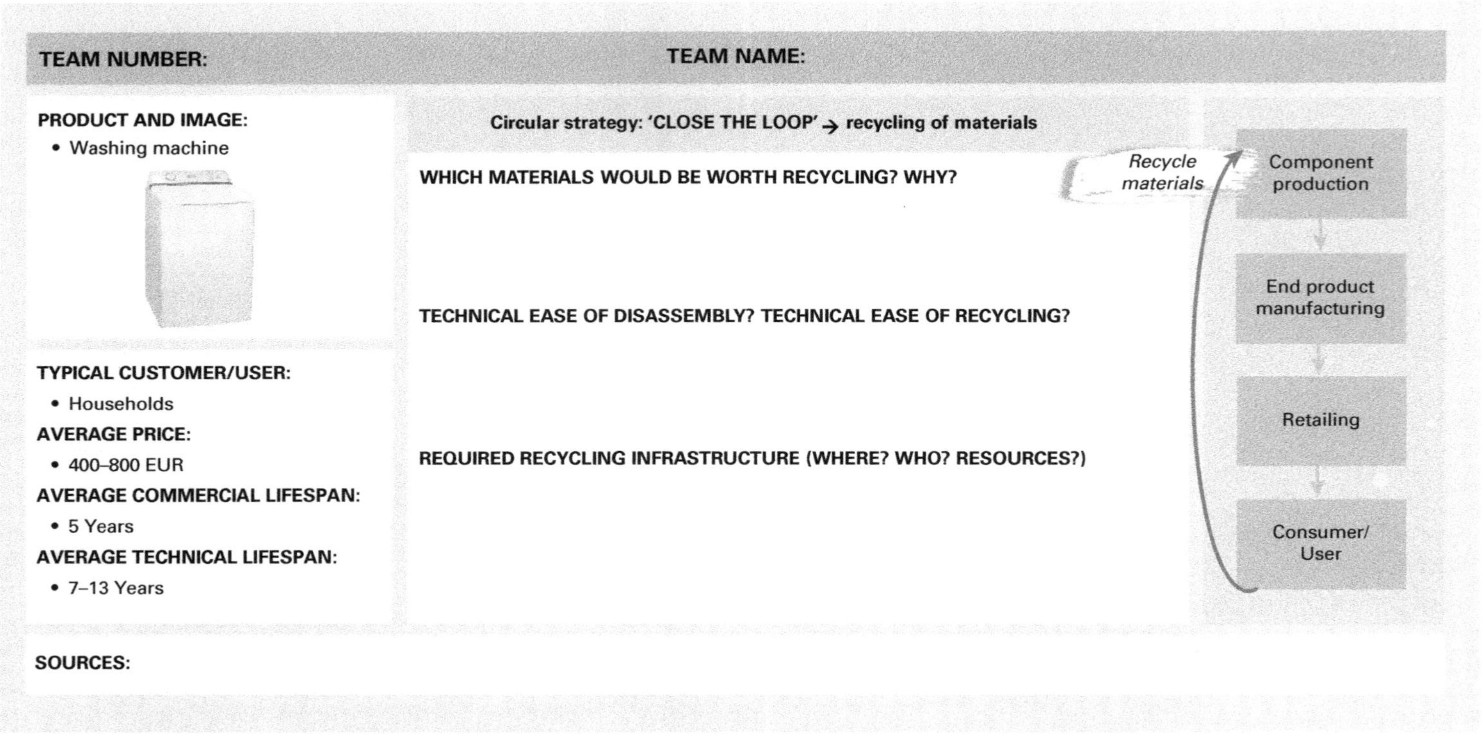

FIGURE 2.21 Circular strategy template: overall evaluation

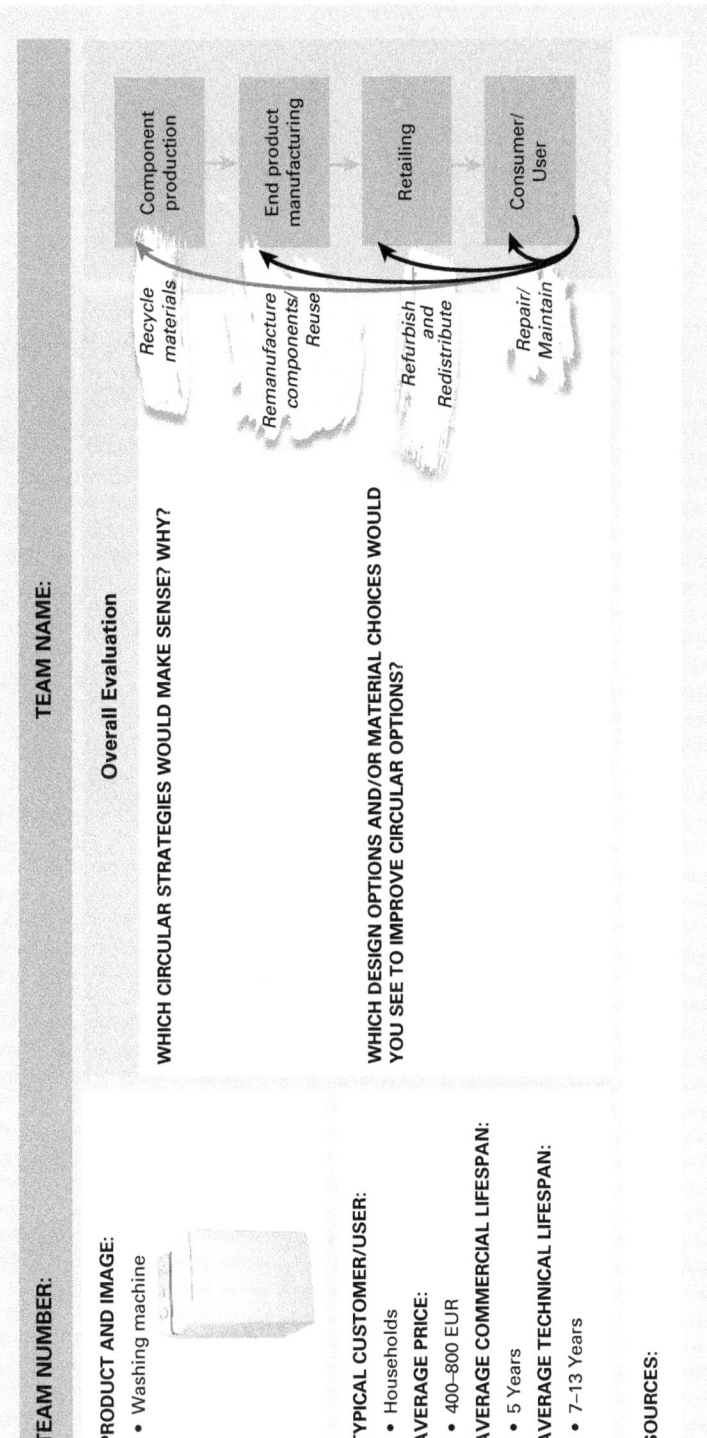

TEAM NUMBER:

TEAM NAME:

PRODUCT AND IMAGE:
- Washing machine

Overall Evaluation

WHICH CIRCULAR STRATEGIES WOULD MAKE SENSE? WHY?

WHICH DESIGN OPTIONS AND/OR MATERIAL CHOICES WOULD YOU SEE TO IMPROVE CIRCULAR OPTIONS?

TYPICAL CUSTOMER/USER:
- Households

AVERAGE PRICE:
- 400–800 EUR

AVERAGE COMMERCIAL LIFESPAN:
- 5 Years

AVERAGE TECHNICAL LIFESPAN:
- 7–13 Years

SOURCES:

Component production → End product manufacturing → Retailing → Consumer/User

Recycle materials

Remanufacture components/Reuse

Refurbish and Redistribute

Repair/Maintain

Step 2: Elaborate the templates in Figures 2.17–2.20, each representing a different circular strategy.

Step 3: On the basis of the template in Figure 2.21, make an overall evaluation about which circular strategy/strategies you see as most favourable for the chosen product and which design options and/or materials choices you would see to increase the feasibility and viability for circularity.

Revenue models and cost structure (how much?)

As a last element of a company's business model, let's zoom in on the topic of revenue models and cost structure, which is where the *mechanisms to monetize circularity* should be specified and which should give an important indication as to whether circularity can be achieved in a profitable way.

Circularity as a framework for change stimulates innovation and creative solutions. This requires a new way of thinking and doing business, which also applies to the field of business models. For example, Pieroni et al (2020) and Lacy et al (2020) have provided frameworks that capture such circular business models. In a way, they build on the work by Bocken et al (2016), who distinguish six different business model innovations that focus on either slowing or closing the loop, and place those into the context of revenue models.

Four business model strategies and their revenue models were identified by Bocken et al (2016), for *slowing resource loops* that encourage extending the lifespan of products and reuse:

FIGURE 2.22   Revenue models and cost structure

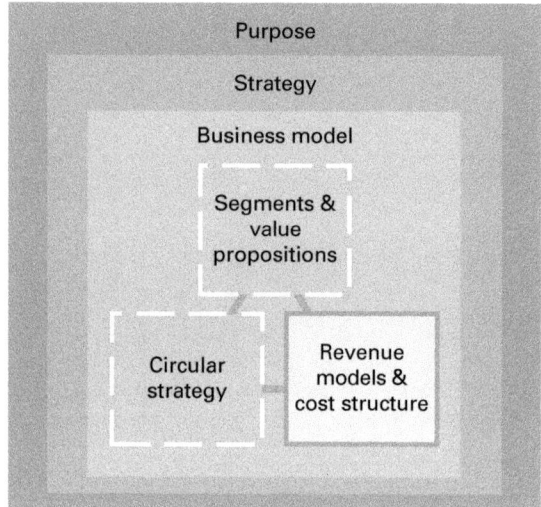

1 **The access and performance model**: satisfies users' needs without them actually owning a product, by providing the product's functionalities or services (e.g. car sharing, leasing phones, clothing libraries). In turn, maintenance is done by the manufacturer or retailer, so the user can just enjoy the benefits of the product or service.

   o **Revenue model**: the user pays per service or unit, for example through a subscription, lease or as-a-service model.[9] Besides, 'additional costs for life extension are offset by additional revenues, because the company can use the product longer' (Bocken et al, 2016).

2 **Extending product value model**: capitalizing on residual value of products and components, for example by pushing Extended Producer Responsibilities, remanufacturing parts, installing take-back systems (H&M return initiative) or offering consumers cash for used phones.

   o **Revenue model**: Bocken et al (2016) mention that entrepreneurs obtaining the extending product value model 'can offer a platform to allow customers to exploit the residual value of their products (e.g. eBay)'. Additional costs for installing take-back or deposit systems, installing collection points or applying reversed logistics will be offset by capturing new forms of value through reduced material costs, the reuse of residual materials and through second-hand sales/refurbished product sales.

3 **Classic long-life model**: aimed at high-quality, long-lasting products through design for durability and high levels of repair and maintenance service such as Patek Philippe's luxury watches with its slogan 'You never actually own a Patek Philippe. You merely look after it for the next generation'.

   o **Revenue model**: the product price is high and paid by the consumer through direct sales, often including a lifetime warranty. The warranty and long-term service costs are absorbed by the manufacturer.

4 **Encourage sufficiency model**: also focuses on long-lasting, high-quality products through direct sales; however, state Bocken et al (2016), 'The main principle of "encourage sufficiency" is to make products that last and allow users to hold on to them as long as possible through high levels of service'. This entails a non-consumerist approach, such as Patagonia's 'Don't buy this jacket' ad, and products often including a lifetime warranty.

   o **Revenue model**: these products are high end with a 'premium' price and premium margins for the business. The service offered creates long-term loyal customers, and extra revenue is created by offering maintenance and repair.

Bocken et al (2016) also identified two business model strategies and revenue models for *closing resource loops*, which capture the value of – what is regarded in a linear economy as – waste:

1 **Extending resource value model:** aimed at the sourcing or collecting of end-of-life materials, and turning them into new forms of value (e.g. secondary raw materials). It is essential to set up partnerships and collaborations to ensure the sourcing, collection and processing of the end-of-life materials.

   o **Revenue model:** using secondary raw materials reduces the overall material costs and product price. In addition, say Bocken et al (2016), 'Value is captured by turning otherwise wasted resources into new forms of value' for the business. This also makes the finished goods more appealing to green consumers.

2 **Industrial symbiosis model:** similar to the 'extending resource value model', industrial symbiosis focuses on turning waste from one process (or business) into feedstock for another product or process (often for another business). Industrial symbiosis benefits from local collaborations, for example on one industrial site.

   o **Revenue model:** revenue is created through potential new business lines or products made of former waste streams, and shared cost reductions.

EXERCISE 2.11
Explore circular revenue models and strategies on the R-ladder

Explore

Explore the circular business models and the strategies on the R-ladder:

- Look around and pick a product that you see: something that you are wearing, that you are sitting on, working at, travel with, etc.

- Which revenue model would you use to make the product circular? Also include the strategies on the R-ladder.

- Describe and be prepared to discuss.

Finance and financing

It's clear that to survive, all businesses need to make a profit, so spend less than they earn, at least in the long run. At the same time, there needs to be a healthy balance between the profits generated and the investments made in order to achieve them. If, even though only temporarily, ongoing operational costs cannot be paid from the available cash, then the need for financing becomes evident. In the following sections

FIGURE 2.23   Items on the income statement (profit & loss or P&L)

Revenues	
–/–	Costs of goods sold (COGS)
Gross profit	
–/–	Operating expenses
	Selling expenses
	Research & development expenses
	General administration expenses
+/–	Other operating income/expenses
Earnings before interest and taxes (EBIT)	
–/–	Interest and taxes
Net income	

we will deal with the income statement, the financial position and the topic of (sustainable or green) financing.

Receive and spend: the income statement

The first important financial statement in the annual report of a company is the income statement, or profit and loss statement (P&L). It shows if a company has made a profit or a loss and shows the details of how it's built up, starting with the revenue and subtracting all expenses.

As can be seen in the overview above, there are plenty of direct links between the activities in the (circular) value chain and the income statement. Firstly, it can be argued that superior circular performance in terms of durability or service package will lead to sustainable revenue, or might even very well lead to additional sales or a premium price if performance is better than the competition. Furthermore, there are obviously very clear links between the value chain and the money spent, as expressed in the costs of goods sold, for example purchasing of raw materials, inbound transportation, energy and labour costs for manufacturing and warehousing, remanufacturing, maintenance, refurbishment or the costs for getting product back from the market (refunds, buyback). In addition, there are the costs for distribution to customers, which are normally to be found as part of the sales expenses.

All in all, the income statement gives us a clear view on what is called the top line (revenue), and the bottom line (profit). From this statement it can also be deduced that a market strategy aimed at top-line growth is not necessarily the same as one aimed at bottom-line improvement.

EXERCISE 2.12
Explore top line and bottom line

Explore

- Strategically speaking, in which cases do you think that the focus of a company might be on 'top-line growth'?
- And in which cases on 'bottom-line improvement'?
- Which specific actions can you think of that would fit well with a top-line growth focus? And with a bottom-line improvement focus?
- How are these two strategies different and/or similar?

Now that we can see what earnings and expenditures have been like, let's look at the investments that have been made and the financial structure that has been set up in order to make the ongoing business happen.

Own and owe: the balance sheet

The second important financial statement in the annual report of a company is the balance sheet, also sometimes called 'financial position'. It shows the assets, liabilities and equity of the company, in other words, the resources that the company owns, as well as the money it still owes to others.

FIGURE 2.24   Items on the balance sheet (financial position)

Current assets		Current liabilities	
	Cash and cash equivalents		Accounts payable (A/P)
	Accounts receivable (A/R)		Notes payable
	Inventory		Accrued expenses
	Other		Deferred revenue
Total current assets		*Total current liabilities*	
Property, plant and equipment (PPE)		**Noncurrent liabilities**	
	Land		Long-term provisions
	Buildings and improvements		Long-term debt
	Equipment	**Equity**	
	Less accumulated depreciation		Capital stock
Other assets			Capital and other reserves
	Intangible assets		Retained earnings
	Less accumulated amortization		
Total noncurrent assets		*Total noncurrent liabilities and equity*	
Total assets		**Total liabilities and shareholders' equity**	

Although the financial position includes more than just value-chain-related items, the main important ones from an operational value chain point of view are the snap-shots of inventories, trade accounts receivable (A/R) and property, plant and equipment (PPE) on the part of the assets, and the trade accounts payable (A/P) on the part of the liabilities. One could potentially also add cash as related to value chain, when thinking about the relationship between deliveries done, delivery relia-bility and even invoice accuracy. A/R and A/P have direct links with topics like payment terms, order sizes and so on. Inventories are relatively straightforward to understand, and together with the accounts receivable and accounts payable they make up the working capital of a company (see next section). Property, plant and equipment have a direct link with the supply chain infrastructure and production and logistics technologies and equipment applied.

Another important part related to the company's choices in terms of business model is the assets in terms of the products it makes. For example, from a financial position point of view, it is very different to sell those products to customers, where the asset moves to the customer, than to offer them 'as a service' (an increasingly popular circular business model). In the latter case, the products are for example leased to the customer, or offered on a subscription or 'per use' basis, so they stay as assets on the company's balance sheet and need to be financed somehow.

Alternatively, the company could choose an off-balance 'vendor lease' with a bank, in which the assets move to the balance sheet of the bank and the company would pay a fee to the bank for that service. Three different possibilities, each with different implications for the P&L and balance sheet.

Financing: where does the money actually come from?

Obviously, a healthy business's prime source for financing is the profit it generates from its own operations. Having profits avoids having to go to external parties to ask for money. However, it's also clear that sometimes profits are not enough, for example in the situation of investments that need to be made into new products, new processes or technologies, or into market expansion. In these cases, external sources of finance are needed. Lacy et al (2020) distinguish four such external sources of finance from the particular context of sustainability:

- *Banks and lenders*, who can issue bonds or loans that link outcomes to the cost of lending, for example offering lower interest rates if sustainability improves.
- *Commercial investors*, such as specialized private equity firms, looking particularly for sustainability-related investment opportunities.
- *Non-commercial capital providers*, such as development institutions or private philanthropies, aiming at providing (co-)funding through grants, public capital or government-backed loans, which typically have less strict requirements than commercial loans.
- *Corporate venturing*, such as larger corporations investing in innovative startups.

Shifting towards a circular economy will not only deliver social, environmental, governance and climate benefits, it could for example also offer annual benefits of €1.8 trillion (US $2.1 trillion) in 2030 if adopted in the mobility, food and built environment sectors in Europe. In addition, activities such as recycling, remanufacturing and resale could create over half a million jobs in Britain alone by 2030 (EMF, 2020).

Besides being increasingly recognized as part of the solution to climate change and other environmental, social and governance issues, the circular economy also offers opportunities for better and new growth. The question asked within the financial sector is no longer whether these issues matter, but rather how the sector will address them. Although 'sustainable' or 'circular' funding is still in the early stages, interesting movements can be observed and the circular economy finance market is taking off (EMF, 2020).

Since 2016, there has been a ten-fold increase in the number of private market funds investing in the circular economy, including private equity, private debt and venture capital funds. Banks are issuing so-called 'green bonds', but interestingly enough, initiatives in this same direction have also been launched by companies. As of 2020, there are 10 global public equity funds with sole or partial circular economy investment focus (BlackRock, BNP Paribas, Candriam, Cornerstone Capital Group, Credit Suisse (two funds), Decalia, Goldman Sachs, NN Investment Partners and RobecoSAM), when in 2017 none yet existed. Within the first 10 months of 2020, assets managed through these public equity funds have increased six-fold, from US $0.3 billion to over US $2 billion. In addition, in the 1.5 years leading up to 2020, 10 outstanding global corporate bonds with a circular economy focus were issued (Alphabet, BASF, Daiken Corporation, Henkel, Intesa Sanpaolo, Kaneka Corporation, MOWI, Owens Corning, PepsiCo and Philips).

Investment powerhouses are introducing sustainability into their policies, like BlackRock's investment stewardship report, Morgan Stanley's plastic waste resolution, AXA's solutions to peer-to-peer sharing models, or the activities by ex-JPMorgan top executive John Fullerton's Capital Institute (BlackRock, 2020; Morgan Stanley, n.d.; EMF, 2020; Capital Institute, n.d.).

In other words, 'shareholders are getting serious about sustainability', as could be read in a *Harvard Business Review* article titled 'The investor revolution' (Eccles and Klimenko, 2019). Terms like green investment, impact investing, regenerative finance, financial citizenship and even 'shactivism' (shareholder activism) appear more and more, indicating that sustainable companies might indeed get a lower cost of capital in the future (Bernick, 2019, as referred to in Elkington, 2020). All finance aspects play an important role in accelerating the transition to a circular economy. Crucial in the upcoming years is for financial services to not only invest in specific and perfectly circular businesses, but to encourage businesses from all industries to make this essential transition.

EXERCISE 2.13
Explore 'green' financing

Explore

On the basis of the examples mentioned above, explore new ways of 'green' financing by doing some (internet) desk research:

- What concrete financial products and services can you find as new or innovative 'green offerings'?
- At whom are they aiming?
- How do they work in practice?
- Which concrete examples of successful implementations can you find?
- What do you think could be the 'business rationale' for banks and financial institutions to offer better conditions when financing CE-related initiatives?
- Which specific dimensions of CE-related projects can you identify that lead to either higher returns or decreased risks, thus forming the foundation for the better conditions?

Selecting and capturing a circular business model

Choose a dominant circular strategy

So, now that we know about the different circular strategies we have at our disposal, how do we actually decide on which way to go? The choice can be made on the basis of many different criteria, such as:

- suitability of the existing (linear) product for circular strategies, in terms of design, materials and/or components, as seen in the 'deconstruction' workshop;
- degree of change, as seen as feasible and reasonable by the company's leadership team;
- preference for big-bang or gradual implementation through pilot projects;
- current relationship with potential circular value chain partners;
- estimated market potential;
- and so on.

In addition to the above, we want to bring back a topic that was briefly touched upon earlier in this chapter, which is that some of the circular strategies can be applied simultaneously. In any case, there will most likely always have to be a choice for **one dominant circular strategy** as the central strategy. Other circular strategies can then be applied as complementary, in the case that they indeed are compatible with the chosen dominant strategy and can, for example, provide a second option for waste streams coming out.

EXERCISE 2.14

Explore dominant and compatible supporting circular strategies

Explore

On the basis of the template in Figure 2.25, which dominant circular strategies could potentially (technically) fit with which supporting circular strategies, i.e. which ones are potentially compatible? For the moment you don't have to worry about the financial viability, just look at the technical feasibility and coherence between the strategies, from component design all the way down to the consumer and back into the value chain.

FIGURE 2.25   Dominant and supporting circular strategies

	POTENTIAL SUPPORTING STRATEGIES									
	R0	R1	R2	R3	R4	R5	R6	R7	R8	R9
R0 = Refuse	/									
R1 = Reduce		/								
R2 = Resell, Reuse			/							
R3 = Repair				/						
R4 = Refurbish					/					
R5 = Remanufacture						/				
R6 = Repurpose							/			
R7 = Recycle materials								/		
R8 = Recover energy									/	
R9 = Re-mine										/

DOMINANT STRATEGY

FIGURE 2.26 Example of items to be included for capturing a circular business model

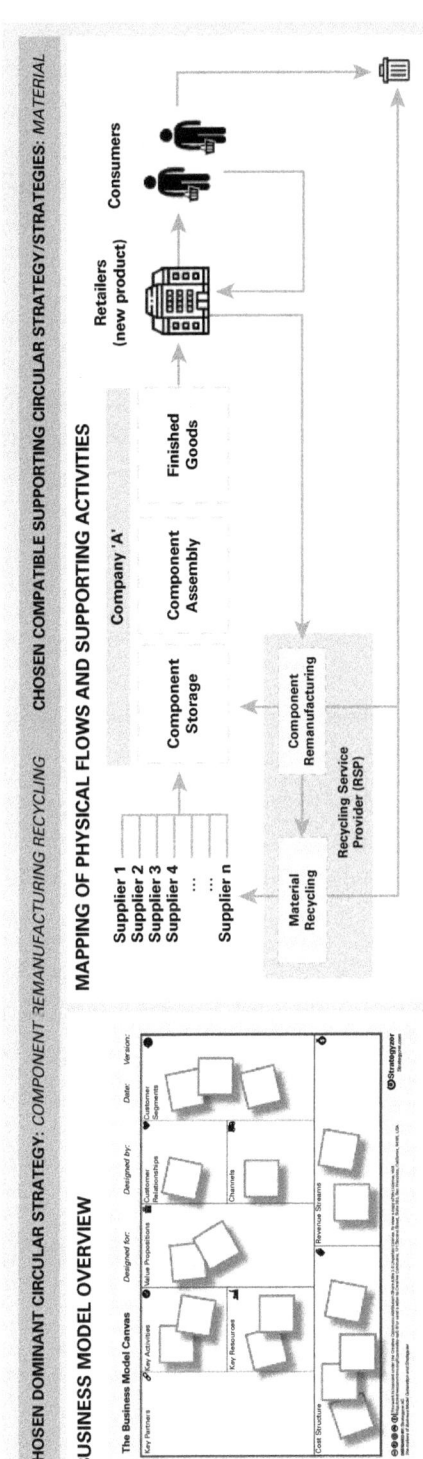

Capture the business model of the chosen dominant circular strategy

Another topic, apart from the choice for a dominant circular strategy, is how to capture a circular business model. Which items will need to be described in order to get a good understanding of a certain circular scenario, thus providing a profound understanding? Returning to some of the subjects touched upon in this chapter, we suggest the following items should be on the list (Figure 2.26), on the basis of the chosen dominant circular strategy:

- *Integrated conceptual view* of the business model, for example through the use of a Business Model Canvas.
- A *mapping of the physical flows*, showing the stages in the value chain, including any envisioned return loops and/or required supporting activities (e.g. maintenance and repair, refurbishment and so on). This mapping can be enriched by adding volume in terms of number of items, number of kilograms, amounts of money corresponding to the different flows. The mapping should preferably include three types of flow: materials, components and finished goods (sales as well as returns).
- An overview of the *revenue model* per customer segment, including corresponding figures.
- An overview of the *mechanisms to monetize circularity*, e.g. through sales in the second-hand market, or sales of recycled materials to suppliers.
- An overview of *additional and/or reduced costs*, such as costs associated with refurbishing or remanufacturing, or capital costs related to off-balance financing in the case of leasing or subscription, or savings due to the reuse of remanufactured components, leading to less purchasing of new components.

Please note that in Parts Two and Three of the book we will come back extensively to the concepts of dominant and supporting circular strategies and the ways of capturing a circular business model, then specifically apply them to The Blue Connection business simulation game.

Summary

THE FINDINGS OF PHASE 1, STEP 2 CIRCULARITY: EXPLORING THE COMPANY PERSPECTIVE

'What a tremendous deep dive this was! After this, who of you still thinks that circularity is only about recycling...?' said Aunt Joanna, 'It's so clear now that it all starts with our

FIGURE 2.27 Exploring the company perspective on circularity (detailed)

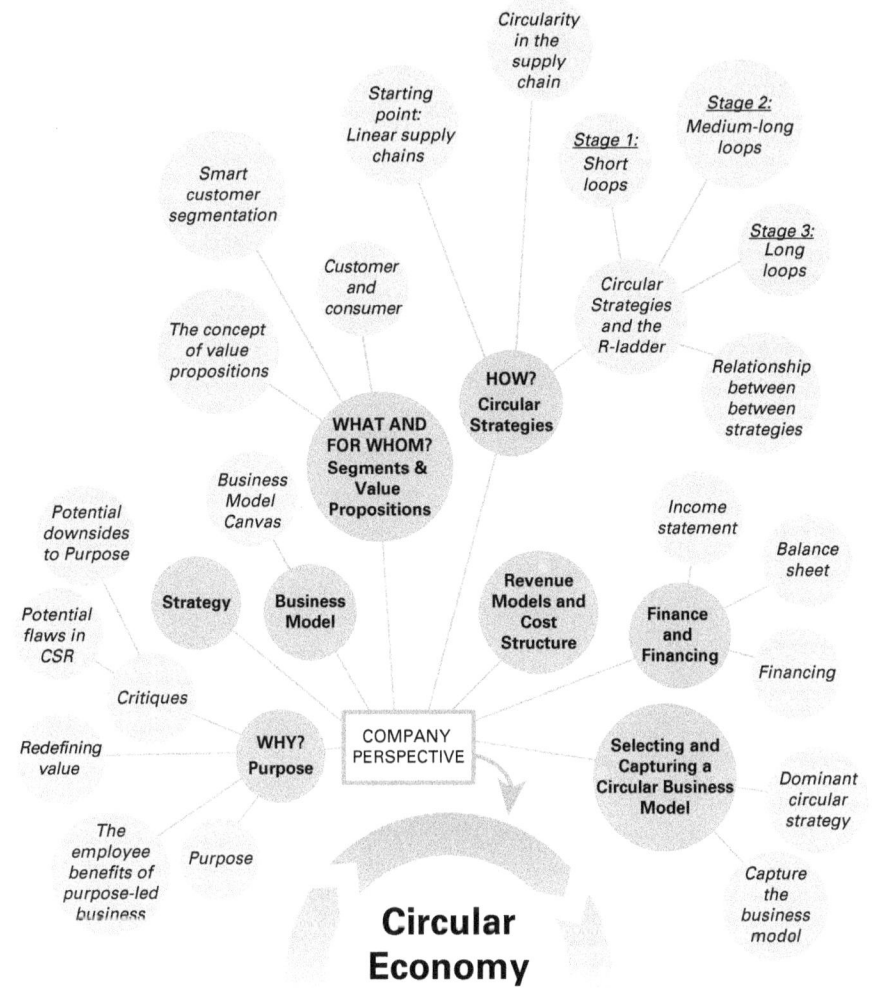

company's purpose and the potential motivations behind choosing to become more circular. The question of "why". I definitely need to put some thinking into that.'

'I also see much clearer now,' she continued, 'how purpose gives guidance to strategy and how circularity could fit in. And I've also learned that if we want to pursue circularity, we should do that on the basis of one dominant circular strategy, potentially complemented by one or more other compatible supporting circular strategies. Once defined, we should figure out which revenue models fit with our existing customers, because obviously we would need to monetize the circularity. Next step would then be to see other impacts on costs, either additional costs, for example for maintenance or refurbishment activities, but also potential savings, for example by recuperating remanufactured components which reduces the need for purchasing new components. And the Value Hill and the 10Rs are the basis here. Quite a complex picture, guys, but at least it's clear now!'

'Complex indeed, but you know what, Aunt Joanna?' Maria said, 'I was thinking that you may want to consider doing this "deconstruction workshop" with some people at the company. For sure it will give some great additional insights!'

'That's a very good idea!' Aunt Joanna responded enthusiastically. 'The overall picture I get is that circularity is indeed a very wide and diverse topic and that if we really want to move on with it in our company, we will have a very big task ahead of us, so we'd better start mobilizing some other people here at the company now.'

Aunt Joanna paused for a moment, as if she was concerned about something. 'I have the feeling, though, that there is something else we still have to look into before we can really make up our minds,' she moved on, 'and to be honest I'm not sure if I'm looking forward to the findings, because there is a risk that we will find that the influence of us as a company is much smaller than we sometimes like to think. Or let me phrase it differently: that we depend much more on certain external forces than we might like.'

'What could make *you* nervous, Aunt Joanna?' Maria asked.

'Well,' Aunt Joanna responded, 'based on our previous steps, my intuition tells me that circularity is a topic that is much wider than just our company. We can have all the drive and the energy and the projects we want, but I suspect that that's not necessarily going to be enough – we simply cannot be in control of everything. I think that we should also explore what is there beyond the company boundary. You know, take a look at the importance of what governments do or do not do, look at legal aspects, both national and international, check out the impact of circularity on education and, last but not least, see the relevance of circular ecosystems.'

'Great news, Aunt Joanna,' Peter said with a smile, 'I almost feared we were done already with the project, but luckily you found some more work for us to do!' All three laughed and Maria said 'OK, so when do we meet again?'

Notes

1 References alluded to in the dialogues of Chapter 2: Hollender (2010), Business Insider (2018), Chua (2018, 2020).

2 In the web resources that go with this book you can find an overview of a number of interesting podcasts about circularity.

3 Please note that the three elements shown as part of the business model cover in a simplified way the most critical parts of business models as expressed in the canvasses we will see later on in this chapter.

4 Please note that something similar, although focused on linear value chains, can be found in traditional supply chain literature under the names of the supply chain and the development chain (Simchi-Levi et al, 2009).

5 In the text we will focus on the business perspective, but of course there is also a consumer perspective. Consumers may refuse cheap bargains, buy and use less, aiming at minimizing waste creation, and they may rethink their consumption patterns. Here, the concept of the sharing economy and products-as-a-service are introduced by rethinking ownership. From a sustainability point of view, refusing is the best thing to do in a circular economy, because by refusing we consume nothing.

6 This strategy seen from the consumer perspective would centre around using products longer and with more care, in turn also reducing waste and their own environmental impact.

7 Please do note that critical voices can also be heard: some people claim that the creation of extensive recycling and incineration infrastructure will ultimately lead to creating demand for it, in order to earn back the investments made, almost like a self-fulfilling prophecy. This demand creation for recycling and incineration would then stand in the way of designing out waste from the beginning (e.g. Guardian, 2013).

8 Please note: even though this activity is called 'deconstruction workshop', it is not necessary to actually physically take the device apart. In case you do want to perform a true deconstruction, please keep required safety measures in mind, especially in the case of electrical devices and/or items with sharp (metal) parts. And be sure to ask the owner of the device if they agree with the activity!

9 Although sometimes all considered part of the 'product-as-a-service' revenue model, there are some differences between the options. In the case of leasing, typically an agreement is made upfront for a fixed period, e.g. a four-year lease, on the basis of a monthly lease fee. In the case of subscription there is typically no end date; it is an agreement for an indefinite time period, with a condition of a minimum timespan for cancellation and a fixed monthly subscription fee. In the case of as-a-service, the agreement is typically on a per-service basis, e.g. in the case of sharing models. In all of these cases ownership remains with the manufacturer, retailer or service company, which means that the product is appearing either on the balance sheet as an asset, with the corresponding source(s) of financing also on the balance sheet, or the company may choose off-balance financing, for example through a vendor lease agreement, in which the products go to the balance sheet of the financial institution and an interest rate is paid to have the desired loan amount available.

03

Exploring the perspective beyond the company boundary

PROJECT 'CIRCULARITY', PHASE 1, STEP 3, AUNT JOANNA'S OFFICE

'Hello Maria and Peter, good morning, good to see you,' Aunt Joanna said. She obviously was in quite a rush and on her way out. 'I really wanted to be with you this morning, but I do need to take care of this other matter now. Our main plastics supplier wants to discuss an investment proposal for expanding capacity and supporting future growth. They apparently have a delegation from their headquarters visiting them, so they want us to come over today. And since they are a critical supplier to us, I really have to go. I wrote the topics we discussed for the next step of our circular journey on the whiteboard for you, so you have a checklist and can get started. See you later!' And off she went.

'How can she do that?' Maria cried out, after aunt Joanna had left the room. 'We set this meeting with her days ago and now she just leaves to visit a *plastics* supplier?' She spoke the word 'plastics' as if it was some sort of very dirty or evil thing. 'Those are one of the most polluting industries of all! They shouldn't invest in growth, they should invest in reduction!'

'Well, my dear cousin,' Peter replied, 'business goes on, you know, whether you like it or not. Even though our Aunt Joanna is eager to know about circularity and what that means for her company, she still has a business to run today, with responsibility towards her customers, her own personnel and their families and so on. Don't make any mistake about it: there's little point in becoming circular if your company goes bankrupt in the meantime. By the way, plastics are still an essential material for many products and in many cases it's even relatively easy to recycle if you compare it to other materials, so don't be too negative. It might be one of the more promising alternatives as a first step in becoming more circular.'

'In any case,' he continued, 'shall we get to work and get some of these things from Aunt Joanna's list done?'

FIGURE 3.1 Exploring the perspective of circularity beyond the company boundary

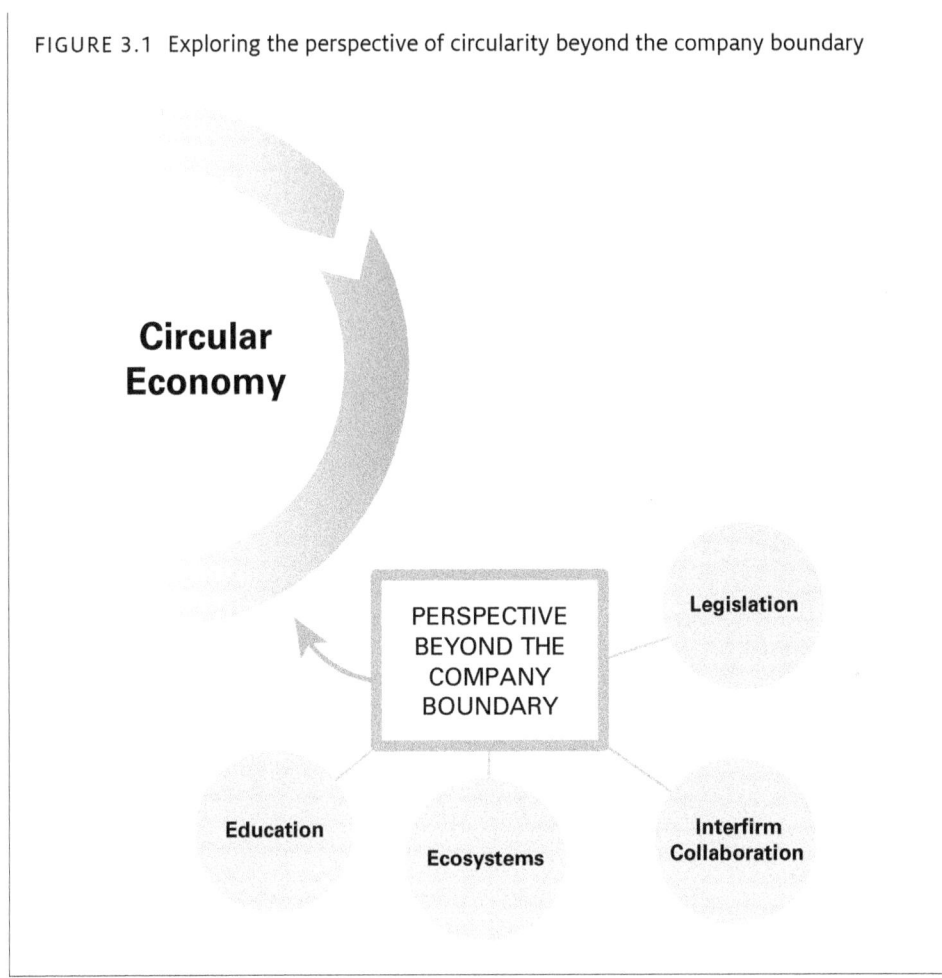

Despite the fact that more and more companies are committing to a circular transition, there are many instruments beyond the company boundary that hinder this transition. In this chapter we will go into detail about how legislation, interfirm collaboration, ecosystems and education can hinder or accelerate the transition to a circular economy.

Legislation

To foster a circular economy, all steps of the product's lifecycle have to be taken into account: design, sourcing, production, sales, use and reuse. This touches upon a great many legal questions, for example around the topics of waste laws, warranty periods, EU eco-design policies, tax law, extended producer responsibility or even competition law (Backes, 2017).

Policies and legislation in support of the transition to a circular economy work as an *enabler push*, as described in Chapter 1, meaning that they facilitate an effective way forward. But before we continue this part of the chapter, you might be asking yourself, 'What is the difference between policies and legislation?' A policy is a document that outlines what a government, or any entity, wants to achieve, oriented towards a long-term purpose, what they are going to do and using which methods, regulations (the rules made to comply and behave in a certain manner), and the principles they follow in executing its directive. Legislation for that matter points to a law, or a set of laws, enacted by the governing body of a country, or part of a country. The key difference is that policies set out goals and activities, whereas legislation might be needed to enable the necessary legal and institutional frameworks to achieve the policy's purpose.

Legislative and policy barriers

Aside from the fact that the combined pull from society and push from enablers is resulting in growing attention for the circular economy, current legislation and policies are generally in support of a linear economy. They could even slow down the circular transition and could cause four types of barriers (Steward et al, 2016):

1 they could provide unclear or fuzzy messages;

2 there are multiple policies, they are complex and have changing regulations;

3 policies have low legislative pressure and there is a lack of control;

4 sometimes legislation or policies hinder innovation and become an obstacle in the transition to a circular economy.

An example of how legislation and policies can hinder the transition to a circular economy on a supranational level, is the current legislation around waste and the trade in secondary resources. The European Waste Shipment Regulation (EU, 2006) is a bottleneck in the international trade in waste as a valuable secondary resource. Here, waste is not regarded as a resource or input for circular innovation and production, but as an unusable or unwanted material. Therefore, the collection and cross-border transportation of homogeneous waste streams for circular use is hindered. Besides, the legislation also focuses on quantity, instead of the quality of the recycled material. Without specific legislation, many possible secondary resources end up as mixed waste streams, where high-quality recycling costs are higher than the income generated by the recycled materials, such is the case with plastic packaging (EU, 2016). This is also the case with designing for strategies on the R-ladder: there is a lack of enforceable and concrete requirements for product design. However, change is coming. As part of the EU's new agenda for sustainable growth, the Commission is assessing options to review the Waste Shipment Regulation, which is foreseen in the Spring of 2021.

In addition, there are inconsistencies between existing legislation and regulation: for example, the use of recycled materials as input for production processes is undermined by aspects of health and consumer protection raised in the current legislation, while this is covered in existing regulations such as the EU's End-of-Waste criteria or REACH (EU, 2016).

In a lot of cases the policy (long-term purpose) is there, but following the directive is hindered by unclear, fuzzy or lack of legislation; such is the case with food hygiene legislation with regard to food donations or using foods after the estimated expiration date. The advertising, presentation and labelling of food products is also a very important cause of food waste originating from fuzzy and unclear legislation. Aside from legislation and policy barriers on a supranational level, which also count on a national level, there are additional barriers specifically on local, regional or national levels (Het Groene Brein, n.d.), such as:

- the legal interpretation of ownership could hinder lease or rental agreements;
- regulations on renting and buying products stipulate depreciation without residual value, while in a circular economy these products may represent economic value;
- competition policy could be a barrier to cooperation between businesses for the optimal usage of waste streams;
- incentivizing the use of biological materials as biofuels (including food);
- stimulating measures that lead to an increase in consumption and a decrease in circularity, such as a lower VAT, while a higher VAT would stimulate a circular economy;
- the high taxation of labour costs makes labour-intensive circular activities, such as repairing, often too expensive; and
- by not internalizing a product's externalities (cost or benefit of an economic activity experienced by an unrelated third party, such as environmental or social costs) through policy, the 'true' costs of products are not paid – this does not give the economic signal to use resources efficiently or to switch to a circular model.

EXERCISE 3.1
Explore the context of policy and legislation barriers related to circularity

Explore

For your country of origin or a business of your choice, explore relevant government or business policies related to circularity and compare to the current legislation (local to supranational level):

- Is there a 'circularity gap' between the policy and what is possible on a legislative level?

- If you have the opportunity to do so, you may want to compare your findings with those of your colleagues/teammates. What are differences/similarities between the policies in different countries or businesses in relation to legislation?

Positive and negative externalities

When talking about the concept of a circular economy, we often talk about 'externalities'. Production, investment and consumption decisions regularly affect people who are not directly involved in the specific transaction (Helbling, 2010). When these indirect effects become too big, they become problematic: the negative effect on society is bigger than the individual benefit to the company. Such is the case with pollution: the polluter makes their decisions based on the direct costs and profit they make, and does not take into account the indirect costs for society of those harmed by the pollution. Although sometimes difficult to establish, those indirect costs for society may include higher health costs, decreased quality of life or forgone business opportunities. The 'true' price of the polluter's product is therefore much higher than the price for which the product is offered. Positive externalities occur when production, investment or consumption benefit a third party that was not involved in the specific transaction. Here, the benefit to society is bigger than the personal benefit to the company. An example of a positive externality is the benefit to the environment of switching from conventional farming to organic farming, as fewer chemicals are being used.

Complexity of international legislation and the 'Brussels Effect'

As already mentioned in Chapter 1, international legislation such as the EU legislation is a very complex affair. Although companies would really benefit from a level playing field where legal and market conditions are the same or similar for all competitors, countries have different legal systems, different priorities and are at very different stages in the transition towards a circular economy. As reported in the *World Guide to Sustainable Enterprise*, many differences between countries also exist in terms of the state of development of sustainable practices (Visser, 2017b). This image is confirmed in the *Circular Economy Handbook*, where a short section is dedicated to the different continents (Lacy et al, 2020). For example, recycling rates for municipal waste in mid- and north-western European countries like Belgium, the Netherlands, Austria, Germany and Switzerland are beyond the EU's 50 per cent target (with some regions even reaching 80–90 per cent), while countries like Turkey,

Romania and Bulgaria are close to a 0 per cent recycling rate. The landfilling rate in those countries is 80–100 per cent, while the landfilling rate in Switzerland and the Netherlands, for example, is close to 0 per cent (Reike et al, 2018). This European divide is a double challenge, a balancing act, for EU policymaking in terms of feasibility and ambition: challenging the frontrunners to go even further (and move beyond EU targets), and supporting the laggards to catch up.

There are two legislative dimensions companies have to take into account: the geographical level (local, regional, national, supranational and global) and the degree of autonomy each of these geographical levels have. The EU legislation is an example of legislation on the supranational level, with a limited amount of autonomy. Allegedly, history demonstrates that the European Union has often played a leading role when it comes to setting standards for new legislation, which is later on also adopted by other regions of the world, a phenomenon coined 'the Brussels Effect' by Bradford (2020). This highlights the importance of adding the geographical dimension to the point of government, policy and standards. What happens in one place may ultimately reach another place, but as long as it's not there yet, it may be of little practical use to the people and companies who are there (except for those who may want to anticipate the future and be the first ones, while taking the risk of being too early).

Legislative and policy enablers

There are several policy and legislative measures that stimulate the transition to a circular economy, both at the national and European level, such as the end-of-life responsibility (EOL), take-back legislation or fiscal incentives on the installation of solar panels, already mentioned in Chapter 1. Below, we will give a non-exhaustive overview of other policies and legislations.

In order to switch to a circular economy, countries like Austria, Cambodia, China, Finland, France, Germany, Italy, Japan, the Netherlands, Portugal and Slovenia, or regions like Flanders, Scotland and Ontario, have developed national or regional circular economy strategies (Backes, 2017; Iles, 2018; EEA, 2020; UNDP, 2020). Due to these strategies, various measures have been implemented such as the Versnellingshuis Nederland Circulair (Acceleration House Circular Netherlands), Scotland's Revolve Reuse Standard aimed at making reuse a key part of their economy, and Extended Producer Responsibility (EPR) for specific product groups. There are even measures on a city level, such as the cradle-to-cradle carpets for city buildings in San Francisco, meeting environmental and material health goals within city buildings, or the city of Amsterdam's Sharing Economy Action Plan. You can find more examples of regional and national examples of circular economy implementation and promotion in the 'Institutions, Governments & Cities' database of the Ellen MacArthur Foundation.

Besides governments on a regional or national level, the European Commission also adopted an action plan to stimulate Europe's transition to a circular economy on a supranational level (EU, 2019). Policy measures cover, for example, a Plastic Pact aimed at changing the way plastics and plastic products are designed, produced, used and reused; a circular economy funding support platform; and an eco-design working plan.

Another way to give society's innovative, sustainable initiatives room to manoeuvre is Green Deals, which are voluntary agreements between (private) partners and governmental agencies (Departement Omgeving, n.d.). In doing so, environmental objectives are pursued that go hand in hand with increased competitiveness and good business management. The mutual agreement contains a clear division of roles and responsibilities, a description of the expected results, related actions and a time schedule. Examples of Green Deals are Circular Procurement Deals focusing on scaling up pilot projects to create a strong demand for circular products and services or the European Green Deal aiming to be climate neutral by 2050.

In addition to the current legislative and policy measures mentioned above, there are extra measures necessary to speed up the transition to a circular economy. Such measures involve more drastic legislation, such as a shift in taxes based on the principles of sustainability. Here, the 'polluter pays' principle is followed. Legislative measures are put into place that, for example, tax non-renewable resources and pollution instead of taxing renewable resources, and use the revenues to lower the high tax burden on labour. Taxing energy and materials promotes low-resource and low-carbon solutions, which, as you know by now, implies moving towards a circular economy. Besides, a tax shift like that creates an inclusive circular economy, enables job creation, greenhouse gas emission reductions, and preserves our environment (Ex'tax, n.d.; Stahel, 2013; Wijkman and Skanberg, 2020).

Another example linked to the polluter pays principle is Extended Producer Responsibility (EPR) or Extended Producer Liability (EPL), which creates a strong financial incentive for producers to prevent waste and liability costs from end-of-service-life objects (Stahel, 2019). Stahel also calls this 'closing the liability loop': products with no value at the end of their service life are returned to their producer, who is the Ultimate Liable Owner (ULO). This will give producers the incentive needed to prevent future liabilities by designing products for maximum end-of-service-life value and minimum liability. EPR/EPL might therefore be one of the most powerful tools for policymakers to promote the transition to a circular economy, and make it the default option for individuals, economic actors and policymakers.

EXERCISE 3.2

Explore the context of policy and legislation enablers related to circularity

Explore

For your country of origin or a business of your choice, you have already explored relevant government or business policies related to circularity and compared them to the current legislation (local to supranational level):

- Are there any current policies or legislation that enable the transition to a circular model in your country of origin or the business that you chose?

- Are there any future policies or legislation that could accelerate the transition to a circular model in your country of origin or the business that you chose?

- If you have the opportunity to do so, you may want to compare your findings with colleagues/teammates. What are differences/similarities between the policies in different countries or businesses in relation to legislation?

Interfirm collaboration

Multi-stakeholder interfirm collaboration is pertinent in implementing circularity, as it leads to transparency, technology transfer, organizational learning and the right partner connections necessary for clean technology and resource efficiency in a circular economy (Mishra et al, 2019). Essential for multi-stakeholder interfirm collaboration is systems thinking, meaning that we look at the value chain as a whole in which all systems and stakeholders are connected.

A great example, given in Chapter 1, is the industry-wide collaboration of the beer industry in the Netherlands. Think of the beer industry as a game of Jenga: if you remove or replace one block and disrupt the whole, it will influence all the other blocks. For example, if one company decides to introduce their own model of bottle again, thus going against the industry agreement of using standardized bottles to favour closed-loop bottle re-collection and reuse, then that affects the entire system. Taking that influence into account is systems thinking. This requires cooperation within and between producers, suppliers, other organizations and end users in the entire system, as they depend on each other for the success of the circular cooperation. For example, involving suppliers in cross-functional teams at the early stages of new product development (e.g. Early Supplier Involvement), from idea generation to post-launch review.

Organizations not only work for their own (financial) gain, but focus on improving and making the entire system in which they operate more sustainable. Within a circular economy, this means that the various players in a value chain work together to narrow, slow and close the loop. This was exactly the aim of Royal KPN's Circular Manifesto, in which they call on all networking equipment suppliers to make their equipment longer lasting and more durable, while using fewer virgin materials, with the aim of close to 100 per cent of components and parts being reused by 2025 (KPN, 2017).

The importance of working together in the value chain is paramount here. If a certain resource in the chain loses its value, all players in the chain suffer. An example of this is the carpet manufacturer Interface. They work together with Aquafil, which recycles discarded fishing nets into new yarn under the brand name ECONYL. Interface uses this yarn to make carpet tiles. If the quality or quantity of the collected fishing nets is not in order, Aquafil cannot make its yarn and does not comply with the delivery agreements to Interface. It is therefore essential that the collaborative risks, costs and benefits are properly discussed by all parties involved.

Realizing successful interfirm collaboration: transparency

As the need for collaboration in the circular economy is clear, in practice it is often a challenge for all parties involved. To ensure collaboration, upstream to downstream, certain steps need to be taken as the different actors in the value chain have different perspectives and dependencies. Transparency and the willingness and openness to share sensitive information is extremely important. Transparency in a production process and honesty in collaboration create trust and make it possible to exchange information, take each other's perspectives into account, find the right partners for improvements and implement them.

Making a certain value chain transparent sounds easier than it actually is. In large organizations it is often difficult to chart all internal and external supply flows objectively and correctly. This is especially the case when these supply flows cross national borders and continents. Besides, stakeholders are not keen on openly sharing information and/or trusting a central party, as it may pose a risk to their competitive advantage.

Dutch startup Circularise helps stakeholders across supply chains with this issue, as they help to trace raw materials from source, into parts and ultimately to end products, utilizing a combination of Blockchain, peer-to-peer technology and cryptographic techniques like Zero-Knowledge Proofs (a method by which Blockchain is made truly private by verifying things without sharing or revealing underlying sensitive data) to build a decentralized information storage and communication platform for all participants in a value chain.

Next to transparency, a fundamental basis for informed decision-making is the usage of data, specifically Big Data, in interfirm collaboration throughout the value chain (Gupta et al, 2019; Nobre and Tavares, 2020). Big Data could, for example, provide smart cities with the right data to better understand and thus better manage resources, waste and pollution in real time.

EXERCISE 3.3
Explore Blockchain and Big Data in the circular economy

Explore

Blockchain and Big Data application in a circular economy:

- Do some (internet) desk research to become more familiar with the concepts of Blockchain and Big Data.
- Can you think of some examples of how Blockchain and Big Data can enable circularity?
- What is needed from an interfirm collaboration perspective?
- Describe and be prepared to discuss.

To guide businesses in multi-stakeholder collaborations, Circle Economy (2020b) identified nine steps for successful collaboration, including four collaboration types, fourteen roles and nine characteristics to identify suitable and attractive partners (Figure 3.2): first recognize the need to collaborate, as collaboration is an enabler in a circular economy; understand the local market and material flows, including the four collaboration types; create and align on the project's vision; assess internal resources and existing gaps, including the 14 roles (see Exercise 3.4); form an internal team; reach out to potential partners; evaluate and select the right partners using the nine partner characteristics; formulate agreements; and start the collaboration. You can find more information about the collaboration types, roles and partner characteristics in the Appendix.

EXERCISE 3.4
Explore the 14 roles in a circular collaboration

Explore

The 14 roles in the Circle Economy (2020b) report 'Will you be my partner?' are: initiator, financier, internal educator, circularity expert, market expert, piloter, impact extender, use-phase supporter, end-of-life supporter, mediator, knowledge broker, external educator, enabler and promoter.

Look up what these roles mean. Which role would you aspire to take on at your current or future job, and why?

FIGURE 3.2 Overview: the ecosystem collaboration set-up steps

OVERVIEW: THE COLLABORATION SET-UP STEPS

1 Recognize the need to collaborate

Zoom in Step 1: Collaborate as enabler in a circular economy

2 Understand the local market and material flows

Zoom in Step 2: The circularity network and collaboration types

3 Create and align on the project's vision

4 Assess internal resources and existing gaps

Zoom in Step 4: 14 roles in a circular economy

5 Form an internal team

6 Reach out to potential partners

7 Evaluate and select partners

Zoom in Step 7: Nine partner characteristics in a circular economy

8 Formulate agreements

9 Start the collaboration

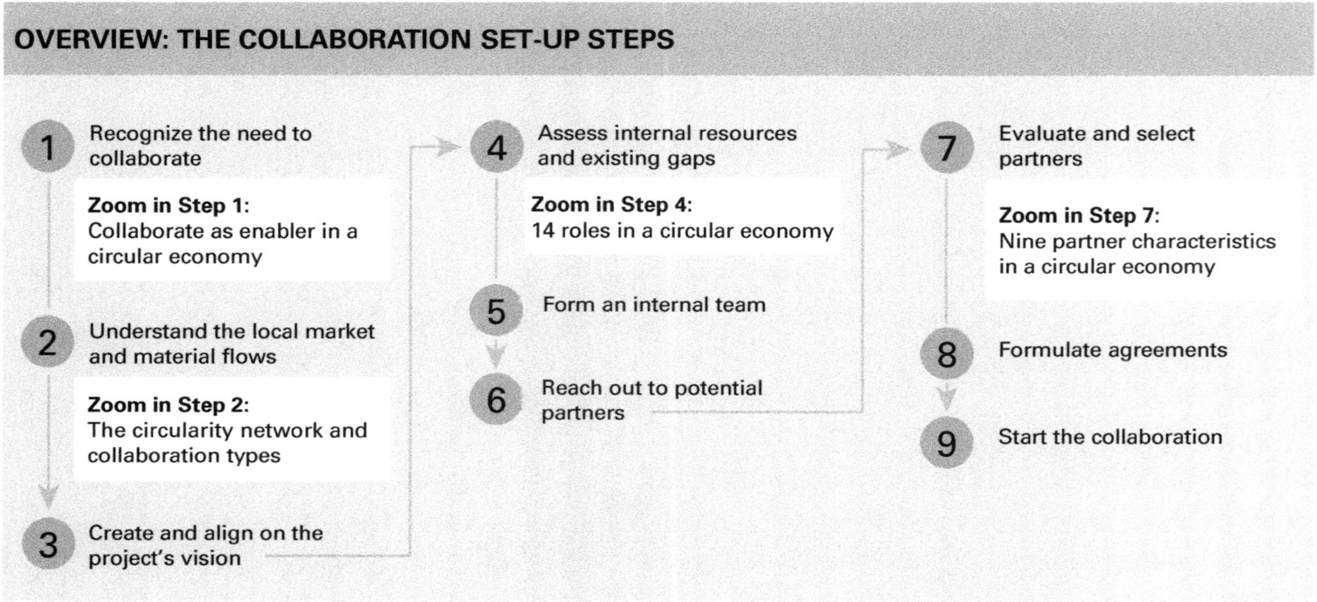

Another form of interfirm collaboration is corporate accelerators, in which companies collaborate with startups to insource external innovation capabilities (Weiblein and Chesbrough, 2015). Established corporations tend to focus on their core business due to their standardized systems and rigid organizational structures; this could limit the innovation capabilities needed to transition to a more circular model. In order to compensate and strengthen their own innovation capabilities, companies insource these capabilities by collaborating with startups, resulting in access to new technologies, industries, markets and customers. The startups get resources and expertise in exchange. Great examples are Dutch retailer Albert Heijn and food waste prevention restaurant Instock, which serves food made from unsold products from (among others) Albert Heijn.

EXERCISE 3.5
Explore interfirm collaboration for a circular economy

Explore

Explore interfirm collaboration for a circular economy:

- Do some (internet) desk research to find more examples of interfirm collaboration. For example, look at your favourite sustainable companies. Are they involved in any interfirm collaborative networks?
- If they are not involved in such collaborations, can you make any recommendations as to who they should set up an interfirm collaboration with?
- Describe and be prepared to discuss.

Ecosystems

You are probably familiar with the word 'ecosystem' as part of the natural world, used to describe a geographic area where animals, plants and other organisms, as well as landscapes and weather, work together as a system, where every element of that system depends on every other element, either directly or indirectly. The term 'business ecosystem' was introduced in 1993 and is defined as:

An economic community supported by a foundation of interacting organizations and individuals – the organisms of the business world. In a business ecosystem, companies co-evolve capabilities around a new innovation: they work cooperatively and competitively to support new products, satisfy customer needs, and eventually incorporate the next round of innovations (Moore, 1993).

In Chapter 2 we discussed circular business models and as you know by now, one individual business cannot reach a 'circular product', which fully exploits the opportunities of one or more circular strategies, on its own. A systemic approach is needed to implement circularity along all lifecycle phases of a product (Takacs et al, 2020). All the multi-stakeholders – each with their own circular business model – collaborating in the same value chain are part of an ecosystem. As we mentioned in Chapter 1, even academia and governmental institutions can be added to the equation as collaboration partners following the concept of the Triple Helix. All parties together enable a circular flow of resources along a specific system. An example of an ecosystem collaborating to drive sustainable transformation is the EU Horizon 2020 'Zero Brine' project (www.zerobrine.eu), in which an international consortium formed by over 20 partners is collaborating to redesign the value and supply chain of water and minerals in the process industry (Baldassarre et al, 2020).

In this type of co-creation, *collaborative innovation* is essential, meaning that cross-sectoral and multidisciplinary collaboration is required to inspire innovative solutions (Bocken and Geradts, 2020). Besides, when a broad range of external stakeholders are involved this enables transformation. Within a circular ecosystem, multi-stakeholder interfirm collaboration takes place to create a sustainable value proposition with narrowed, slowed and closed resource loops.

Balancing economic, social and ecological sustainability requires an approach that builds on the assumption that each of these three sub-systems must be healthy and viable if the ecosystem is to flourish. Here, a circular value chain can be seen as the interplay of complementing business models along all lifecycle phases in a circular ecosystem (Takacs et al, 2020). The value creation is collaborative: ecosystems create more value as a whole than the sum of individual participants acting independently. It is therefore essential that businesses create these ecosystems to make a circular economy work.

(Virtual) Open Source Circular Economy

Currently, most organizations and businesses promoting a circular economy tend to focus on their own in-house solutions, but it is unlikely that individual businesses can construct perfect circular processes. They could be a lot more effective in the transition to a circular economy with more cross-industry collaboration, more open standards and more transparency across industries and countries.

When good solutions are developed, we need to be able to use them, to build upon them, and to improve them. To do so, Muirhead (2016) and Raworth (2017) argue, we need an Open Source Circular Economy (OSCE) to unleash the full potential of circular manufacturing through a worldwide network of designers, innovators and activists:

> Open source is a methodology which enables people to work effectively and invite collaboration with unknown others – whomever and wherever they are in the world.

It provides a system wherein organizations and individuals can all autonomously contribute to and benefit from a shared ecosystem, tackling different parts of a larger problem without wasting time on redundant replication of work (Muirhead, 2016).

In practice, this means publishing how circular goods or processes are created (e.g. software codes, design files, production data or design files) so that anyone can study, use and build upon this information. This often occurs through decentralized and distributed online collaboration: prototyping solutions, giving feedback, diverse groups discussing project ideas, fixing bugs and building customizable and useful software, hardware, tools and culture.

Data enabling circular economy

In both Chapter 1 and Chapter 2 we have touched upon the subject of technologies aimed at creating transparency and analysing movements in value chains, such as the Internet of Things (IoT), Blockchain (see transparency, as previously discussed), RFID, Artificial Intelligence (AI) and Big Data – all enable tracking of the installed product base. When we discussed how to successfully realize interfirm collaboration, we talked about transparency and Blockchain's role in it.

The IoT and intelligent assets can sense, communicate and store information about themselves (EMF, 2016b). If we take the circular reuse and repair strategies as an example, IoT will enable the fusion of digital and manufacturing technologies, creating products that can signal any problem, determine when they need to be repaired, and schedule their own maintenance. Inexpensive sensors could be installed in everything from coffee makers to drills, and from vacuum cleaners to washing machines, and help to extend their lifespans by keeping them in perfect working condition for longer. Besides, IoT-enabled products could help eliminate waste if they are also manufactured to be shared: apps could be used to share rarely used equipment and charge a small price per use, such as the Dutch sharing platform Peerby, where you can actually reserve, locate, and rent tools and equipment. For businesses this poses new opportunities. If, for example, a tools manufacturer produces a durable lawnmower, equipped with sensors to charge people per minute of use and indicate when a component needs to be replaced, it could make thousands instead of milions every year and collect usage fees.

RFID tags – short for Radio Frequency Identification – are a type of tracking system that uses smart barcodes in order to, for example, identify items, measure quantity or monitor stock (Condemi et al, 2019). RFID tags are used for multiple purposes, such as monitoring waste containers, tracking the real-time availability of goods or enhancing take-back systems for e-waste. Intelligent RFID waste containers, such as the waste bin tag by Intellhydro used by many commercial waste management companies in Italy, can measure data such as humidity, weight, volume and temperature at specifically timed events such as disposal time, or on demand.

Within a circular economy, this knowledge can optimize waste collection and sorting, and increase the reuse of those materials into additional cycles (EMF, 2016).

AI is a subset of the technologies enabling the emergent 'Fourth Industrial Revolution' era and could play an important role in enabling the transition to a circular economy (McKinsey & Company, 2019). AI deals with systems and models that focus on function associated with human intelligence, such as learning and reasoning. It allows us to learn faster from feedback, expand our human capabilities, deal more effectively with complexity, complement people's skills, and make better sense of missing data. In a circular economy this could enhance the development of new products by iterative machine-learning-assisted design processes, improve reverse logistics required to close the loop, and increase product circulation and utilization. The Excess Materials Exchange uses AI to match materials to a new high-value reuse option. They use material passports, or, as they call them, *Resources Passports*, to give an insight into the composition, origin, toxicity or deconstructability of the material or product. In addition, they track and trace these resources throughout their lifecycles, using barcodes, QR codes and chips. Their goal is to unlock the maximum potential of a company's materials, products and waste streams by matching them to a new high-value reuse option across industries, using a combination of AI and human expertise.

EXERCISE 3.6
Collaborations, networks and ecosystems: what are the differences?

Explore

It could be confusing, all these terms about businesses collaborating, in a network or together in an ecosystem. Do you know what the differences are?

- Do some (internet) desk research to find out what the differences are between collaborations, networks and ecosystems.
- Describe and be prepared to discuss

Elements of a circular ecosystem

A circular ecosystem is compiled of multiple elements (Rabello et al, 2015):

1 **Actors:** academia, industry, governments, supporting institutions, financial systems, topic experts, entrepreneurs, customers and civil society, and their economic and social relationship, playing various roles throughout the circular ecosystem.

2 Culture: the mindset of the organizations and people involved combined to support circular innovations and solve related problems.

3 Infrastructure: technical and physical conditions and general resources to support the development of circular innovations and the ecosystem itself.

4 Regulation and legislation: rules, goals and laws that frame the innovation environment and the ecosystem's functioning.

5 Interface: the channels that support the interaction within the ecosystem, and outside the ecosystem with external actors.

6 Knowledge: specialized knowledge and supporting theoretical foundations used, generated and eventually organized and managed, made available and learned along the circular value chain.

7 Ideas: intentional thoughts that trigger circular innovation actions around which the whole circular ecosystem works.

8 Capital: financial assets provided by all the actors, or a part thereof.

9 Architectural principles: the way the circular ecosystem's elements are orchestrated and combined.

FIGURE 3.3 A circular business ecosystem

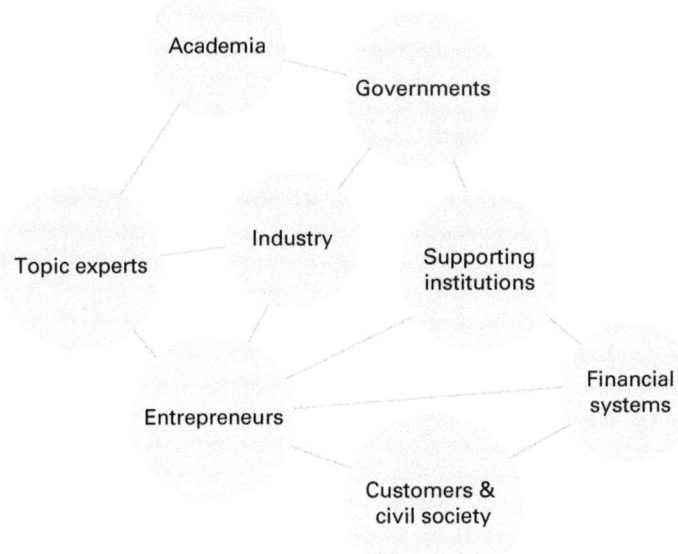

Circular ecosystems and resilience

The Covid-19 crisis affected millions of citizens globally, leading to countrywide social distancing, restrictions and lockdowns. Future crises are likely to happen around the topic of climate change. The word 'resilience' has been used frequently throughout the Covid-19 crisis. Circular Flanders and VITO (2020) conducted a resilience survey among various organizations, going into detail about how they experienced the crisis and how they look to the future. The resilience survey highlights three success factors that make companies more resilient to disruption:

1 renewed focus on local and connected business;

2 creativity;

3 cooperation.

All three success factors are fundamental for the transition to, and in, a circular economy. During the Covid-19 crisis circular companies experienced fewer shortages than other companies: 34 per cent of circular companies experienced shortage compared to 98 per cent of 'business-as-usual' companies. The circular strategies that led to fewer shortages appear to focus mainly on local, short supply chains, and less material use. It shows that circular ecosystems not only make businesses more sustainable, they also make them more resilient.

Realizing a successful ecosystem

Even though it is widely recognized that collaboration beyond the company boundary is an essential element to the success of the (wider) implementation of circular principles, in practice, collaboration proves to be a very complex affair. In order to collaborate successfully, companies and other involved stakeholders need to be aligned on many different aspects. As the research of Velter indicates, 'The complexity for alignment emerges through different understandings of value, diverging interests, division of risks and responsibilities, and existing processes and activities that limit actors' openness to align' (Velter et al, 2020). As traditional linear supply chain collaboration practice has also shown over the years, the point of collaboration is reasonably clear, as are the areas in which collaboration may make sense. But getting it done can be a totally different story.

Research points out that technical barriers in the transition to a circular economy are relatively small or non-existent (Takacs et al, 2020). The most critical obstacles are corporate culture and attitudes towards change. In addition, within a circular economy there is a shift from individualistic thinking to we-thinking. It is one of the first times in our recent history that we have questioned the notion of competition, and it is no longer a choice whether to engage with stakeholders or not. In order to realize a balanced and integrated ecosystem, the challenge is rather how to engage successfully. Deliberate interaction, networking, partnering and learning from multiple-stakeholder interfirm collaboration is critical. Trust, stakeholder engagement and business model innovation are among the biggest challenges organizations have to overcome. Besides, it is essential to make specific propositions that create value for all participants in the system, as all the participants have different roles and different needs (Evans et al, 2017).

Education

As you know, the transition to a circular economy requires knowledge development, knowledge dissemination and innovation. If these are insufficient, this can impede the transition. Since structural cooperation between companies, knowledge institutions and governments is currently not guaranteed, this raises the question of how knowledge development for a circular economy can be organized and how acquired knowledge can be effectively marketed (Rli, 2015).

In addition to a lack of circular knowledge, businesses also have a poor dissemination of knowledge. A lack of trust between companies and the confidentiality of information hinder the exchange of knowledge and thus transparency. Besides, knowledge development in the field of circular design and eco-design is still in its infancy – despite the growing interest in the field of design.

Moreover, a coherent approach to education and to the development of circular competences is currently lacking. Knowledge development is necessary for the transition to a circular economy. To date, however, linear approaches still appear to be deeply ingrained.

Opportunities in education, skilling and reskilling

Research by Janssens and Kuppens (2018) shows that 63 per cent of their respondents feel that current education does not focus enough on basic technical competences. However, even more strikingly, 70 per cent feel that transversal competences are not getting sufficient attention and 77 per cent perceive a lack of attention for valorization competences. This gives an indication that the respondents generally feel that more should be done in education on valorization competences and transversal competences, while technical competences also remain important. This in itself is independent from circularity, but it can be argued that all of these three types of competences are also very relevant for circularity, as we will address later in this chapter.

National and international accelerators such as Circular Flanders, Sitra or the Ellen MacArthur Foundation have created resource packages to build knowledge, provide guidance, insights and relevant resources, and stimulate dialogue around the circular economy.

A circular labour market

As a result of the transition to a circular economy, a number of jobs are expected to disappear, for example jobs in the fossil fuel industry, but in other sectors an increase in the number of jobs is expected. National governments should have a major interest in accelerating the transition towards a circular economy, as in total, there will be a net job gain whereby the share of new jobs will exceed the share of lost jobs (according to Wijkman and Skanberg (2016)).

This creates potential for local job creation, reskilling of 'silver workers' (older-generation workers) and vocational training opportunities for the unskilled or people who have lost their jobs due to the emergence of new technologies (Stahel, 2019). As mentioned in Chapter 2, by reusing products and parts, about 8 to 20 jobs can be created per 1,000 tons of unwanted products. For comparison, energy recovery and recycling can create about 5 to 10 jobs per 1,000 tons of unwanted products, and landfilling 1,000 tons of unwanted products creates only 0.1 jobs (WRAP, 2015).

The circular job market consists of jobs in all kinds of sectors, ranging from resource management and manufacturing, to waste management and creative industries. These jobs involve a combination of traditional skills, such as manual labour, and novel circular skills, such as material composition analyst or modular designer. But in short, all circular jobs contribute to one of the strategies on the R-ladder. Circle Economy (2020a) has identified three types of jobs:

- *Core circular jobs*: the name reveals it already – these jobs are the core of a circular economy, as they ensure that raw material loops are closed and cycles are introduced in the economy. This includes jobs in the waste and resource management sectors, renewable energy, and repair, such as appliance technicians, process operators or agronomic advisors.

- *Enabling circular jobs*: these jobs form the supporting shell of a circular economy, as they enable the upscaling and acceleration of core circular activities. This includes jobs in digital technology, engineering, design or leasing, such as circular equipment engineers, building information managers, demand planners or procurement professionals.

- *Indirect circular jobs*: the jobs in this category provide services to the core and enabling circular activities above. This includes jobs in logistics, the public sector or education, such as teachers or couriers.

A transition to a circular workforce must be underpinned by three core pillars, according to Circle Economy (2020a): skilling and reskilling the workforce; good-quality jobs that are secure, carry social value and are fairly paid; and an inclusive labour market that provides opportunities for all. Below we will zoom in on the *skilling and reskilling of the future and current workforce*.

Research by Bocken and Geradts (2020) emphasizes the importance of training (skilling and reskilling) and education of employees when introducing a new sustainable (or circular) business model. For businesses this means that investments in people capability development are needed, related to training and development programmes that provide employees with the competences needed for a circular economy, and the recruitment of sustainability-minded employees for the purpose of transforming,

Competences for a circular labour market

For these new circular jobs, as well as for the transition, specific knowledge and competences are needed. Integration of circularity into the education and training of the future workforce, and into the skilling and reskilling of the current workforce, must ensure that there are enough people with the right competences for a circular labour market. Support from governments, such as creating policies that promote circular competences, should enable access for everyone.

Important in the transition to a circular economy is to create a common language, definitions, metrics and standards for skills, which, as you know from Chapter 1, is still lacking (Circle Economy, 2020a).

Coming back to the research mentioned at the beginning of this section about education, competences within a circular economy can be divided into three categories (Janssens and Kuppens, 2018):

1 *Technical competences*: the competences specifically related to the workings of a circular economy (what is the circular economy about and how does it work?).

2 *Valorization competences*: all competences needed to effectively transform technical and content-related knowledge into value (how to make circularity happen).

3 *Transversal competences*: important key competences for lifelong learning, civic competences, creativity, collaboration, sense of responsibility and initiative and so on (e.g. how to spot and leverage circular opportunities, how to work together, how to engage with stakeholders).

TECHNICAL COMPETENCES

When it comes to technical competences, professional knowledge and accuracy are considered important. Current education is already strong in the transfer of professional knowledge and provides the necessary accuracy, but this should be supplemented with education on sustainability topics and the principles of a circular economy, which is rather limited so far. In addition, professional knowledge differs from sector to sector; for this reason, it is important to have general STEM skills (Science, Technology, Engineering and Maths), although an A is often added for the Arts (STEAM), meaning that there must also be a place for creativity and out-of-the-box thinking within the technical domain. Another relevant competence is 'eco-design' or a more general attention to ecology during product design.

VALORIZATION COMPETENCES

If we look at the competences needed to effectively transform technical and content-related knowledge into value, critical competences are contextualization of knowledge, the ability to implement a project or idea, and the identification of interrelations between social, economic and environmental problems. In addition, a positive attitude towards sustainability, the will to learn about circularity or the application of circular principles on a professional and personal level are also essential. Other important competences in a transition are economic, financial or legal knowledge, for example with regard to the environment, ecology, ownership or competition.

TRANSVERSAL COMPETENCES

Creative thinking, being innovative and open-minded, entrepreneurship, problem solving and skills around cooperation are important transversal competences. Here entrepreneurship is not only about working as a self-employed person or starting your own business, it is about the fact that people are given the opportunity to be entrepreneurial in their job, which is called intrapreneurship. Proactiveness, risk-taking, innovativeness, opportunity recognition and exploitation, and internal and external networking are important behavioural dimensions of intrapreneurship (Neessen, 2020).

In a circular economy, knowledge and information are shared with others and cooperation is stimulated: one of the success factors in doing so is the ability to connect the right knowledge and competency partners to build networks. In addition, flexibility and creativity were also mentioned as transversal competences. Employees must be flexible towards the future and also able to think and act flexibly. A project can suddenly look different from one day to the next. Creativity is needed to deal with the rapidly changing circumstances and the challenging problems that arise within the transition to a circular economy.

EXERCISE 3.7
Self-assessment circular competences

Self-assessment

How do you score yourself on each of the three types of circular competences?

- Use the template in Figure 3.5 and score yourself on each of the competences from 'not at all' to 'extremely'.

- Compare your results to the circular role you chose in Exercise 3.4: do your competences match the role you aspire to take on?

FIGURE 3.4 Technical, valorization and transversal competences for a circular economy

Technical competences	Valorization competences	Transversal competences
• Professional knowledge	• Contextualization of knowledge	• Creative thinking
• Accuracy	• Ability to implement a project or idea	• Innovativeness and open-mindedness
• Knowledge on sustainability topics and the principles of a circular economy	• Identification of interrelations between social, economic and environmental problems	• Entrepreneurship and intrapreneurship (including proactiveness, risk-taking, innovativeness, opportunity recognition and exploitation, and internal and external networking)
• STE(A)M skills	• Positive attitude towards sustainability and willingness to learn about circular principles	• Problem solving
• Eco-design and attention to ecology	• Economic, financial or legal knowledge	• Cooperation skills and network building
		• Flexibility

FIGURE 3.5 Self-assessment tool for Exercise 3.7: how do you score yourself on each of the three types of circular competences?

Self-assessment on circular competences

1. Technical competences

1	2	3	4	5
Not at all		Moderately		Extremely

2. Valorization competences

1	2	3	4	5
Not at all		Moderately		Extremely

3. Transversal competences

1	2	3	4	5
Not at all		Moderately		Extremely

FIGURE 3.6 Circles of Concern, Influence and Control

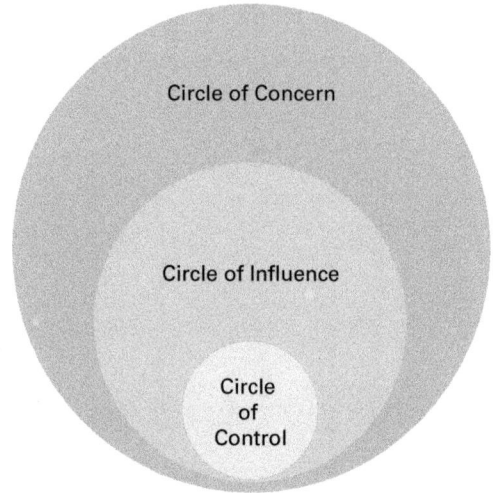

Circle of Concern

Circle of Influence

Circle of Control

SOURCE After Covey, 1987

A business's Circles of Concern, Influence and Control

Every business, as well as every individual, has a Circle of Concern and a Circle of Influence, terms coined by Stephen R Covey in 1987, and over the years a third circle was added: the Circle of Control. In this chapter we focused on four topics that are outside the company boundary: legislation, interfirm collaboration, ecosystems and education. Within these topics there are multiple elements in a business's Circles of Concern, Influence and Control.

The circles represent three areas where a business can focus their time and energy:

- **Circle of Concern:** everything that might affect a business and is of concern to the employees.

- **Circle of Influence:** elements that a business can actually influence to improve these concerns.

- **Circle of Control:** elements that a business can control, solve or change.

Proactive businesses will focus their efforts on the elements in their Circle of Influence and their Circle of Control. In doing so, they work on things they can affect and create positive outcomes. Within a Circle of Influence you can think about lobbying for a shift in taxes or Extended Producer Liability. For the Circle of Control, examples are reskilling employees or actively looking for interfirm collaboration to accelerate the transition to a circular economy. This leads to less stress and proactive behaviour, resulting in shrinking the Circle of Concern.

Reactive businesses focus their efforts on dealing with the elements in their Circle of Concern. The more energy a business and its employees spend on worrying about and working on pressures over which they (perceive to) have no control – such as an economic crisis, European policies (for which they can lobby in their Circle of Influence) or the lack of specific education on their circular needs – the more reactive and stressed they become. This results in reactive language and actions, often blaming others for their circumstances and neglecting the areas that they can affect, leading to their Circle of Concern expanding.

EXERCISE 3.8
Explore the Circles of Concern, Influence and Control

Explore

We would like you to help out Maria, Peter and Aunt Joanna at Harrison Moore & Co. Can you think of specific elements – which we have discussed in this chapter – that are in the Circles of Concern, Influence and Control of Harrison Moore & Co?

Describe and be prepared to discuss.

The topics of legislation, interfirm collaboration, ecosystems and education, as addressed in this chapter, will also come back extensively in Parts Two and Three of the book, then in direct application to The Blue Connection business simulation game.

Summary

THE FINDINGS OF PHASE 1, STEP 3, CIRCULARITY: EXPLORING THE PERSPECTIVE BEYOND THE COMPANY BOUNDARY

Towards the end of the afternoon, Aunt Joanna got back to the office, where Maria and Peter were still working. 'I'm so sorry, guys,' she said as she entered the room, 'but I couldn't refuse the invitation to go and see our plastics supplier. In fact, and both of you will surely like this,' she said with a mysterious smile. 'I took advantage of the opportunity and asked *them* about circularity and how they could help us in our journey. I even told them that we could maybe make that into a condition for helping them with their investment, but I'll tell you about that later. First, show me what you've found out today.'

'That is really impressive,' said Aunt Joanna, when Maria and Peter had finished sharing their findings with her. 'It confirms that many of the aspects of circularity are in fact beyond the company boundary. I can envision that it's going to be a very serious challenge for us to manage all of it properly, with the limited resources we have as a medium-sized company. Even keeping track of everything that's going on already seems quite a task!'

'But let's first look at what's within our own span of control and see if we could maybe establish some kind of pilot project with our plastics supplier, whether it be in joint material development or product design or recycling – it would be an interesting test to find out more in detail. Besides, it would be a good showcase if it works. Still, I'd like to set that aside until the end of our own journey, because I don't think we're there yet.'

Aunt Joanna continued: 'I'm also starting to see the enormous impact that moving into such circular scenarios can have on a company and the requirements that it will pose to company management. On the bright side, as a medium-sized family business this is definitely something that we can influence and have control over! Let's park our current results for the moment and move on to find out what circularity actually means for myself and my fellow board members as the leadership team at Harrison Moore & Co. I'd like us to *explore the leadership perspective* in more detail in the next step.'

'I think we should spend some time on finding out how to *measure circularity* and progress moving into circularity,' she continued, 'as well as specific aspects of *alignment* between the different corporate departments, and with external stakeholders, just to see if that will be different from alignment in our current linear value chain. Also, I would like

FIGURE 3.7 Exploring the perspective on circularity beyond the company boundary (detailed)

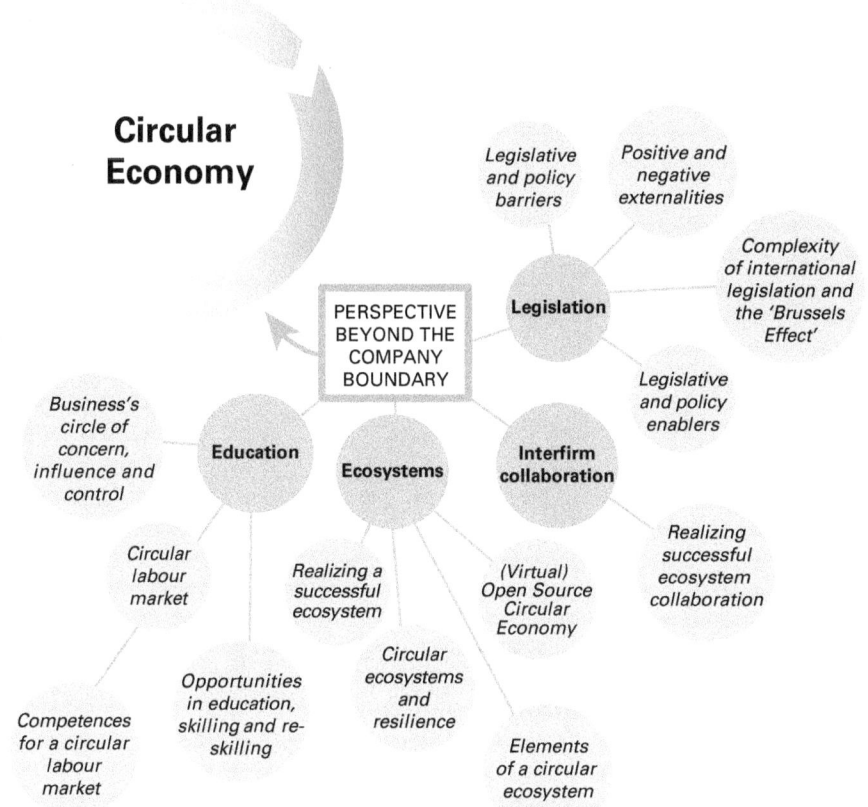

you to look at *innovation, uncertainty and transformation* in general. I know, some of these are less tangible topics, but my feeling somehow is that they will become critical once we decide to really take some serious steps in becoming circular.'

'Once again, this has been a great day – we have made pretty good progress, I think. Let me invite you for a drink before we move on with the project next week, OK?'

04

Circularity: the leadership perspective

PROJECT 'CIRCULARITY', PHASE 1, STEP 4, AN EMAIL FROM AUNT JOANNA

FIGURE 4.1   Email from Aunt Joanna

---

joanna.harrison.moore <jhm@harrisonmoore.com>   07-Dec 07:28AM
Project 'Circularity' – interesting info

To: O maria@intern.harrisonmoore.com ;   O peter@intern.harrisonmoore.com

---

Hello my dearest niece and nephew, hope this email finds you well!

I know that we will see each other in a few days anyway, but I came across this article, which I thought I'd share with you. It's about the company Unilever and their 'clean future' initiative:

https://www.theguardian.com/business/2020/sep/02/unilever-plans-to-remove-oil-based-ingredients-from-all-cleaning-products.

Of course, the article doesn't contain all of the details of Unilever's initiative, but I thought it could be an interesting example. Moreover, and that's why I think it fits nicely to where we are in the project, it triggered my thinking about a number of leadership-related topics. In other words, not so much what Unilever (in this case) is planning to achieve, i.e. the end point they're looking at, but what requirements this would pose on **leadership** to make it happen. I was thinking in particular about the following topics, which we discussed earlier:

- How do you actually **measure** circularity in order to know if you're making progress at all?

- What does circularity mean for **alignment** between our company's functional departments? We just implemented an improved alignment process called Sales & Operations Planning (S&OP), but I'm thinking if this would also work for circularity-related issues.

- What are the implications for moving towards a more circular future in terms of **innovation, change management** and **transformational leadership**?

It would be great if you could start looking into this already,

Talk soon, big hug from your Aunt Joanna!

FIGURE 4.2   Exploring the leadership perspective of circularity

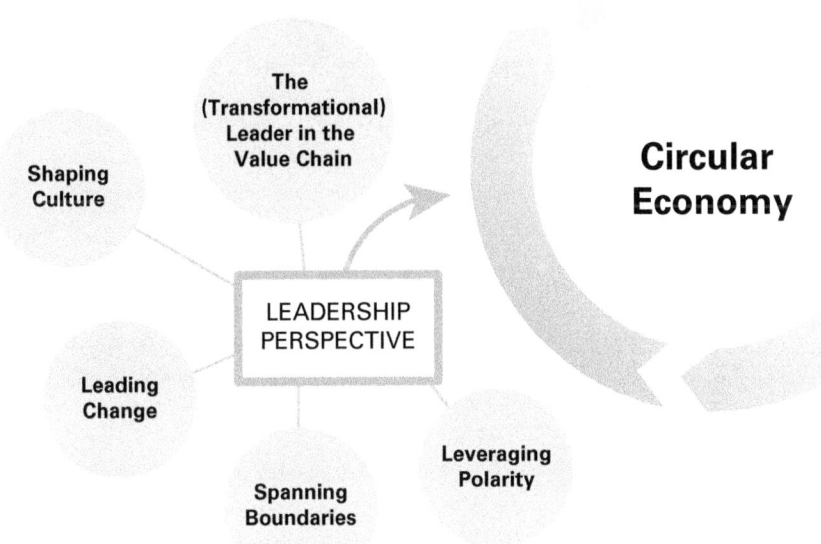

Even if it is understood what circularity can mean for the overall business of a company, and once the corresponding circular strategy, value proposition, and revenue streams and cost structure have been worked out in detail, then there is still another perspective that cannot be ignored: the perspective of leadership. Many process designs seem perfect. Until people appear. Because people come with moods, opinions, irrationality, motivations, backgrounds, family situations, health complexes and many etceteras that simply cannot be denied. This leadership and people dimension poses additional challenges on successful execution of a value chain's operations, even more so if it needs to be transformed from linear to circular.

And who needs to lead the transformation anyway? Will we see the figure of the Chief Sustainability and Circularity Officer (CSCO) emerge in the future? Or should CSR teams take the lead and 'reposition themselves as expert collaborators, not just as data consumers as part of their reporting activities' (Future-Fit CEO and co-founder Geoff Kendall, as cited in Elkington, 2020). Or should the marketing people lead, because in the end circular business is also business? Probably it's still too early to tell if new dominant patterns are indeed emerging.[1] Companies will still need time to try things out and experience first-hand what works and what doesn't.

But it's clear that whoever it will be, someone will need to take the lead in order to make things happen.

In their article 'Barriers and drivers to sustainable business model innovation: organization design and dynamic capabilities', Bocken and Geradts highlight the importance of so-called 'dynamic capabilities'. Building also on the work of others, they state that:

> dynamic capabilities govern how a firm's ordinary capabilities (e.g. effective marketing tactics; efficient manufacturing processes) are developed, augmented and combined and include competences to: (1) sense and evaluate opportunities and threats; (2) seize opportunities, mitigate threats and capture value from doing so; and (3), reconfigure a firm's tangible and intangible assets to remain competitive [...], it is argued that the dynamic capabilities of sensing, seizing, and transforming, are the ones on which top management should be most focused as they are deemed critical for the innovation and selection of business models.

In addition, they identify a number of institutional, strategic and operational barriers as well as drivers for developing such dynamic capabilities in order to achieve what they call sustainable business model innovation – SBMI (Bocken and Geradts, 2020). Many of the factors identified by Bocken and Geradts have a clear link to leadership, once more illustrating the importance of the topic in the context of circularity.

Hughes et al (2014) suggest that ultimately:

> achieving the enduring performance potential of the organization requires the hearts, minds and hands of all to be engaged. It is one thing to have that sense of engagement yourself. It is totally another thing to create, engender, and fuel that engagement with others [...] That is, leadership is engaging others to create shared direction, alignment and commitment (DAC).

They indicate four critical organizational as well as individual leadership capabilities for creating DAC (see Figure 4.3):

- leveraging polarities;
- spanning boundaries;
- leading change;
- shaping culture.

In the following sections, we will take these four suggested capabilities as an inspiration for diving a bit more into the details of leadership, while also referring to other relevant sources in literature.

FIGURE 4.3 Critical organizational and leadership capabilities

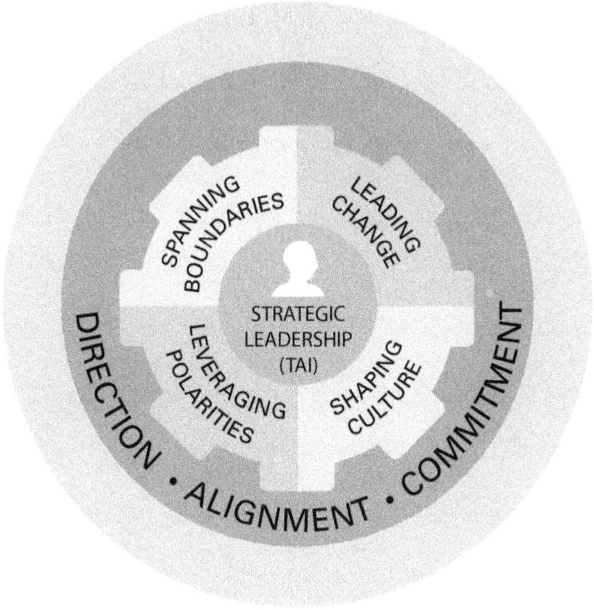

SOURCE Reproduced with kind permission of CCL

Leading by leveraging polarity: balanced objectives and scorecard(s)[2]

Value chains are full of trade-offs: many upsides have downsides as well. Reducing inventory may reduce costs, but may at the same time increase the risk of lost sales due to lack of product. Using more durable components may extend lifetime and therefore lead to more sustainable products. However, more durable components may be more expensive and therefore increase the sales price of the product, which may have a negative impact on the amount of product sold. Or pursuing long-term goals may sometimes be difficult to unite with guaranteeing maximum short-term financial benefits.

On top of the 'objective' side of trade-offs, it is likely that many different opinions exist about where to put priorities. The inventory manager may look at the decision in a different way than the sales manager. The corporate sustainability officer may have a different view from the marketeers. But that doesn't mean that either one is more right or more wrong. As Hughes et al (2014) argue, it's not either-or, it's both-and. The leadership challenge is to develop competencies for finding a positive, productive as well as practical balance in such situations, in other words to *leverage the polarities*. This is where a balanced compass could be very helpful, in order to create a multidimensional view as a starting point for decision-making.

In the end, companies are made of people, and the value chain as part of that is obviously no exception. Since just the corporate purpose and mission statements are in most cases not enough to have people move in the 'right' direction, companies put in place certain performance measurements and targets in order to set a goal to be reached within a certain timeframe. Sometimes these targets form part of individual yearly plans, sometimes they are also connected to (financial) incentives. Although performance indicators and target setting are considered by many as more of a 'technical' topic (like in the case of measuring outcomes of operational process as a starting point for defining potential process improvements), we deal with the targets under the umbrella of the leadership dimension.

This is because in our opinion, the decision of how to go about performance measurement and target setting is a leadership decision. The role and importance a leader gives to KPIs and targets defines how they are going to work with their people; it will be an important and visible part of the working climate that will be created. The manager in question has an impact on whether these performance indicators are creating a healthy challenge to make things happen or putting intense pressure on people, leading to a stressful situation. This is particularly the case when such indicators and targets are connected to individual (financial) bonuses.

A widely used concept in the context of KPI development is that of 'SMART' KPIs, alluding to the fact that the KPIs should be intelligently chosen; each letter of the word SMART represents a specific aspect to be taken into consideration (see the Appendix for an explanation). In addition, Kaplan and Norton (1992) already came up with their concept of the balanced scorecard long ago and nowadays in practice we see more and more *KPI dashboards* appearing, presenting a 'balanced' collection of KPIs, together creating a multidimensional view about the status for the user in question. Within the context of shared value or integrated value, as addressed extensively in Chapter 2, these dashboards are more likely to also include sustainability-oriented indicators.

An element to keep in mind when developing meaningful KPI dashboards is to distinguish between KPIs that measure final desirable results, and KPIs that measure in some way the path to getting to the final result. For example, if I want to lose weight, my individual KPI for measuring the desirable final result could be my actual weight. The KPI expressing the path could be to express the number of steps I have walked in a given period. Obviously, to be able to define both types of KPIs supposes a good understanding of cause and effect relationships between parameters (in the example, the assumption would be that walking a certain number of steps helps to achieve a certain weight).

Obviously, a company that wants to move into the direction of circularity will first of all need to decide how to measure its degree of circularity. At the same time, it will also need to maintain certain indicators it was already using in the linear situation, for example financial indicators like margin or profitability. Particularly complex may be the specific polarity that appears during the transition period: the company is not yet fully circular but cannot ignore the part(s) of the business that are still more linear as well as profitable.

FIGURE 4.4 The six capitals framework

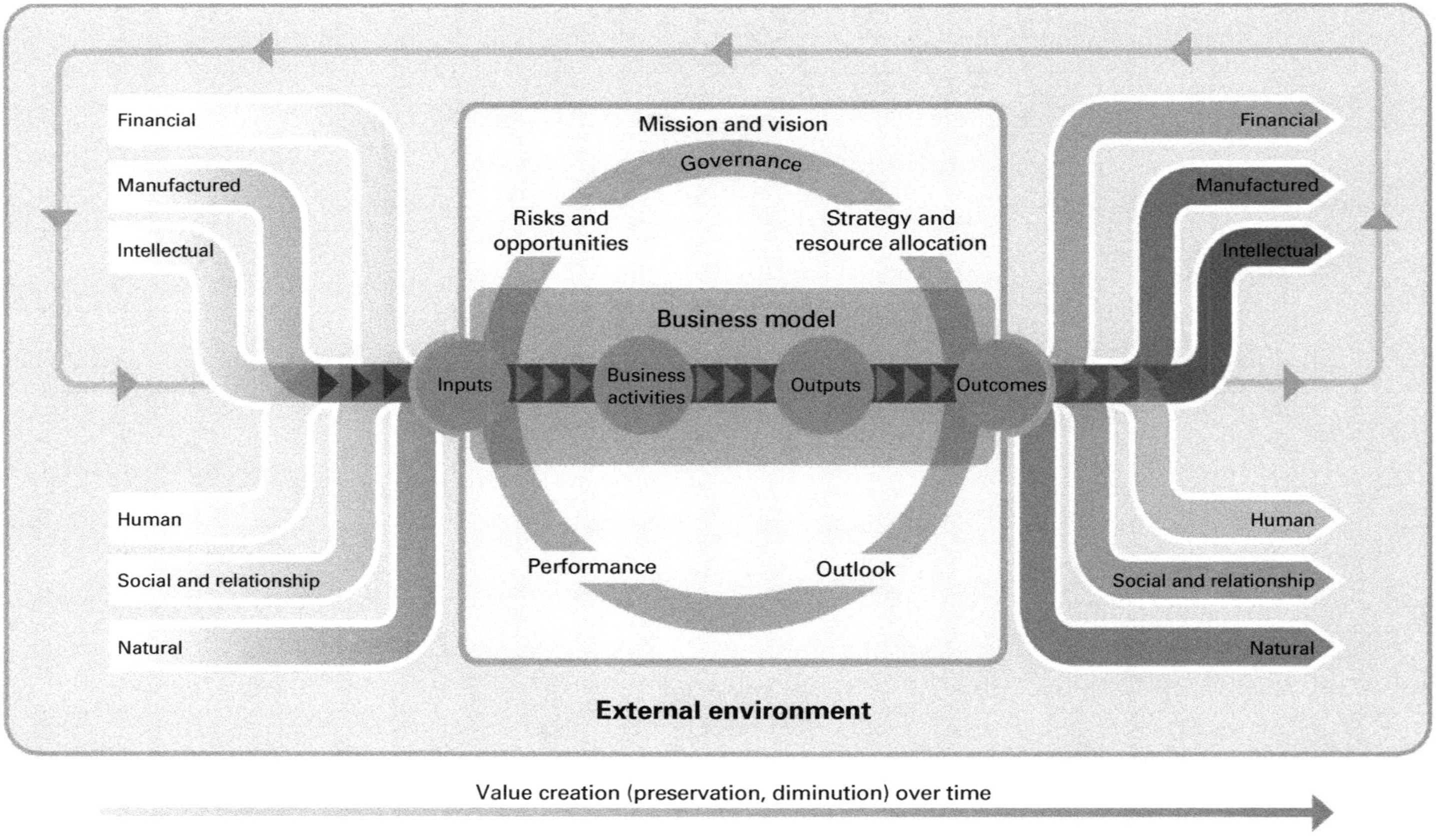

Financial
Manufactured
Intellectual
Human
Social and relationship
Natural
Mission and vision
Governance
Risks and opportunities
Strategy and resource allocation
Business model
Inputs
Business activities
Outputs
Outcomes
Performance
Outlook
Financial
Manufactured
Intellectual
Human
Social and relationship
Natural
External environment
Value creation (preservation, diminution) over time

There have been many initiatives over time to include sustainability in general and circularity in particular into the world of dashboards. First of all at the conceptual level there is the overarching concept of Elkington's Triple Bottom Line (Elkington, 1997), even though it doesn't specify which particular indicators should be used. Another very interesting multidimensional view can be found in the six capitals framework (IIRC, 2013a, 2013b), which as the name indicates distinguishes six different types of capital together in one integrated reporting concept (Figure 4.4).

EXERCISE 4.1

Explore the six capitals framework

Explore

Go on to the internet and find out more about the IIRC's six capitals framework. Which of the six capitals do you think would be directly or indirectly impacted by a company's transformation from linear to circular? In which way would they be impacted? To what extent do you think the model provides a useful basis for identifying and leveraging polarities in an organization, for example between the different internal departments?

More specifically connected to the topic of circularity, there have been many initiatives already to create meaningful indicators for the purpose. One of the first was the Materials Circularity Indicator (MCI), developed by the Ellen MacArthur Foundation (EMF, n.d. b). Its prime focus, as the name suggests, is measuring the use of materials. The MCI combines two different points of view: first of all, it looks at the amount of materials used and recuperated, i.e. the quantity of virgin material as an input, versus the amount of unrecoverable waste as an output. This is called the 'linear flow index'. Secondly, there is the lifespan and usage of the product, expressed by measuring the relationship between the lifespan of the product versus the market standard lifespan and the usage of the product versus the market standard usage (Figure 4.5).

EXERCISE 4.2

Explore the MCI

Explore

Taking the formula for calculating the MCI as a starting point, now elaborate on how the following circular strategies would impact the MCI, i.e. which of the parameters of the MCI would be mainly affected: product and/or material redesign (narrow the loop), lifetime extension strategy (slow the loop), component remanufacturing (slow the loop), material recycling (close the loop). To what extent do you think the MCI provides a useful basis for identifying and leveraging polarities in an organization, for example between the different internal departments?

FIGURE 4.5   Material Circularity Indicator (MCI)

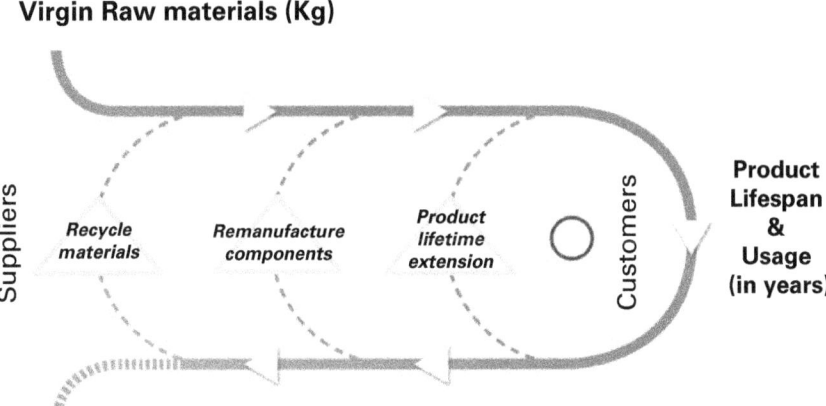

Virgin Raw materials (Kg)

Suppliers

Recycle
materials

Remanufacture
components

Product
lifetime
extension

Customers

Product
Lifespan
&
Usage
(in years)

Unrecoverable Waste (Kg)

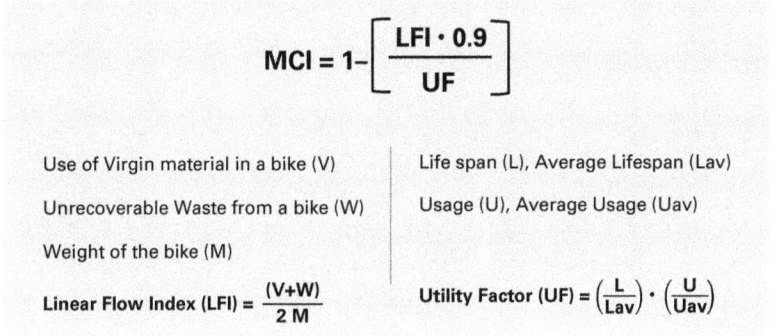

$$MCI = 1 - \left[\frac{LFI \cdot 0.9}{UF} \right]$$

Use of Virgin material in a bike (V)

Unrecoverable Waste from a bike (W)

Weight of the bike (M)

Linear Flow Index (LFI) = $\frac{(V+W)}{2\,M}$

Life span (L), Average Lifespan (Lav)

Usage (U), Average Usage (Uav)

Utility Factor (UF) = $\left(\frac{L}{Lav}\right) \cdot \left(\frac{U}{Uav}\right)$

FIGURE 4.6   Circular Transition Indicators (CTI)

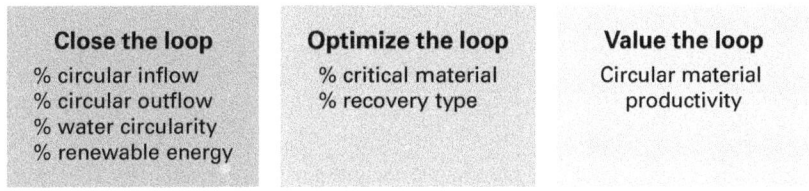

Close the loop	Optimize the loop	Value the loop
% circular inflow % circular outflow % water circularity % renewable energy	% critical material % recovery type	Circular material productivity

The Ellen MacArthur Foundation has since gone on to develop wider sets of indicators for tracking circularity. The main result of this so far is the launch of the Circulytics® framework, which 'supports a company's transition towards the circular economy, regardless of industry, complexity, and size. Going beyond assessing products and material flows, this company-level measuring tool reveals the extent to which a company has achieved circularity across its entire operations' (EMF, n.d. d).

In another interesting initiative for creating more clarity on the topic and also trying to set a standard for measuring circularity, the World Business Council for

Sustainable Development has made an extensive study into ways for measuring circularity and has now also developed a wider set of indicators for measuring the transition to circularity: Circular Transition Indicators – CTI (WBCSD, 2018, 2020a). Indicators are distinguished as 'close the loop', 'optimize the loop' and 'value the loop' (Figure 4.6), thus presenting a balanced view on different aspects of circularity, for example also including the use of water and renewable energy.

Some of the indicators of the CTI set are also used in The Blue Connection business simulation game, so we will come back to those in Part Two of the book.

Independent of the final choices a company makes in selecting indicators, creating KPIs and corresponding targets that provoke and stimulate internal collaboration and therefore an instrument to manage the aforementioned polarities, is quite difficult. Unfortunately, some of most widely used targets in (linear) value chains, defined in most instances by functional department, do quite the opposite: they seem to lead to polarization (either-or discussions) between departments instead of synthesis (both-and discussions). So having targets in place can be a great starting point but be aware that it doesn't necessarily guarantee great outcomes – that's where effective leadership comes into the play.

Leading by spanning boundaries: silos and stakeholders[3]

Independent of whether 'circularity' is managed from a separate department created for the purpose or not, the activities within the scope of circularity touch many departments in the company. Decisions related to circularity will in many cases have an impact on more than one department, which immediately implies the need for alignment and managing stakeholders. On top of that, there is the notion of the importance of stakeholders beyond the company boundary, as we have seen in Chapter 3.

Spanning boundaries within the organization

Typical organizational structures are still in most cases centred around functional departments (sales, finance, human resources, etc) and while it might be totally understandable from a specialization point of view to put functional experts together, it might also have a slightly trickier side-effect. Ashkenas (2015) notes that:

> Many organizations still have hierarchical, siloed, and fragmented processes and cultures. In fact, having to cope with a fast-changing global economy has led many companies to create even more complex matrix organizations, where it's actually harder to get the right people together for fast decision-making.

Strong organizational silos reinforce an 'us versus them' feeling between departments, which is obviously a barrier in the way of cross-functional alignment. Ashkenas goes on to argue that Jack Welch's approach, when he was still CEO of GE, would still be recommendable: create cross-functional forums 'bringing people together across levels, functions, and geographies to solve problems and make decisions in real time.' Apparently, this has proven less easy for most companies than it looked. GE had already started doing it in the 1990s, but seems to be one of the few to have figured it out. Or can it be that others just don't see it as important and haven't even tried?

Whichever way it is, apparently functional silos are going to be around for some time and having more institutionalized cross-functional platforms and mechanisms still seems rather far away in most cases. Which implies that anything related to circularity will require active cross-functional stakeholder management as well, thus breaking the silo thinking (Bocken and Geradts, 2020). This calls for strong characters not afraid of functional borders and who have other traits like a sense of empathy, negotiation skills and so on, to which Neessen adds an entrepreneurial mindset (Neessen, 2020).

At the time of writing this book during the final months of 2020, there doesn't seem to be a dominant, nor even an emerging approach to such cross-functional stakeholder management in the context of circularity, but maybe we can take some inspiration from the world of linear value chains. Here, the process of Sales & Operations Planning (S&OP) has been developed over time to give a response to precisely such internal alignment challenges. According to Tom Wallace, one of the leading people behind the important initial development of S&OP, 'Sales & Operation Planning (S&OP) is a set of decision-making processes to balance demand and supply, to integrate financial planning and operational planning, and to provide a forum for establishing and linking high-level strategic plans with day-to-day operations' (Wallace, 2009).

Nowadays, S&OP has made it into the top-level agenda of most leading firms around the planet, even though many companies still struggle to get it right. On the one hand this might be surprising, since the process steps are really not that complicated (see Figure 4.6). On the other hand, S&OP also reflects the combination of the business, technical and leadership dimensions of supply chain, so maybe we shouldn't be that surprised by the difficulties with its implementation after all.

FIGURE 4.7   S&OP process: sequential monthly steps

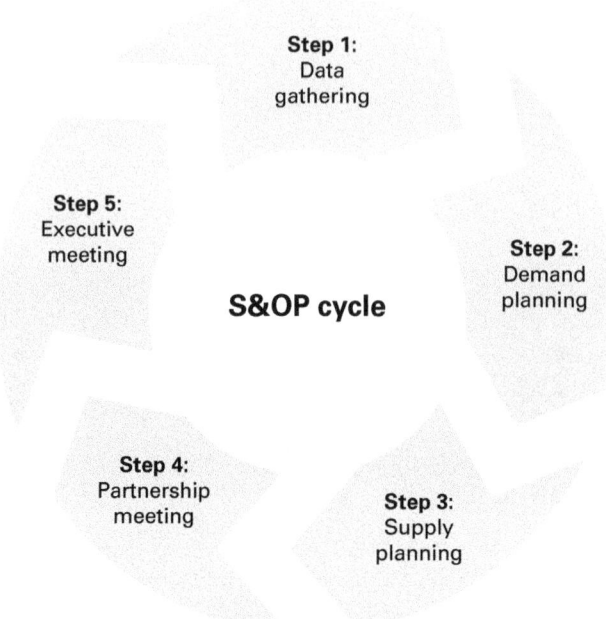

SOURCE After Stahl (2009) and Dougherty and Gray (2006)

EXERCISE 4.3
Explore S&OP/IBP and the potential application to circularity

Explore

Using the means you have at your disposal, such as the internet, libraries, databases, magazines and so on, explore the topics of Sales and Operations Planning/Integrated Business Planning. What can you pick up from these publications? To what extent do you think such a process could be applicable and/or fine-tuned to the needs of circularity in a company? What name would you give the circular version of S&OP/IBP?

Spanning boundaries beyond the organization

You can probably imagine that if spanning boundaries within an organization can already be very challenging, outside the company boundaries it becomes even more complex. At this stage, we'll phrase this topic as an exercise (Exercise 4.4):

EXERCISE 4.4

Explore spanning the external boundaries

Explore

Take a company you are interested in and envision them on the path to achieving circularity:

- Identify the main external stakeholders relevant for achieving, maintaining and improving circularity.

- Identify how each of these external stakeholders can have an influence on the company's current and/or future circularity.

- Think of the people or departments in the company who should be in the lead to liaise with these external stakeholders.

- Think of how to best establish and maintain an effective relationship with each of these external stakeholders.

- Assess how time- and resource-intensive the effective maintenance of these stakeholder relationships would be.

Leading change: innovation, uncertainty and transformation[4]

Transformation implies change. The same is therefore valid for the transformation from linear to circular. It will require innovation and it will come with uncertainty. To manage such changes successfully calls for high doses of leadership skills.

Innovation

Although in conversations we have it seems that many people still tend to think that innovation is mainly about new product development, the notion that innovation is in fact about a much broader set of areas is actually not new. Markides (1997) already noted that a company can innovate in the who (customers), the what (offerings) and the how (processes). Sawhney et al (2006) in their article 'The 12 different ways for companies to innovate' added the dimension of where (presence) to the equation, thus arriving at their concept of the innovation radar, a spiderweb-type graph with each of the 12 ways to innovate visualized, in relation to a company's performance in each.

Also by following the basic elements of a company's business model, one can see that innovation can in fact take place in all of the areas. On the customer-facing end of the company there can be innovation in the product and services portfolio, in the value propositions, in the channels and in the way customer relationship management

(CRM) is approached. Innovation can also take place in the 'production' side of the company: process innovation, innovation in key resources and/or innovative partnership models. Lastly, innovation can also take place in the way the so-called 'profit formula' of the business is defined: the revenue models and the cost structures (Johnson et al, 2008; Osterwalder et al, 2020). Chapter 2 provided extensive insights into these different types of innovation in relation to segments and value propositions, circular strategies and revenue models that might be required.

None of the above is new nor is it exclusive to circularity, but since most companies are still in the beginning of their journeys into becoming more circular, they will have to innovate to move forward. The implication is that learnings from 'basic' innovation literature and methodologies also apply in the circular context. For example, there is the concept of the innovation process that goes from the generation of ideas, sometimes also called 'ideation', to the conversion of ideas into workable solutions ('development and validation') to the diffusion of ideas to establish their wide acceptance and successful incorporation into daily practice ('implementation'). In relation to the innovation process there is the notion of the innovation funnel, implying that many ideas will need to be generated before coming to the successful implementation of one or more of them (Figure 4.8).

In addition to the above-mentioned innovation process and the funnel, Hansen and Birkinshaw argued that each of the stages in the innovation process calls for different organizational capabilities, which is why they speak about the innovation value chain (Hansen and Birkinshaw, 2007). Leadership will have to secure the presence of all required competences at the right moment.

FIGURE 4.8   The innovation process and the concept of a funnel

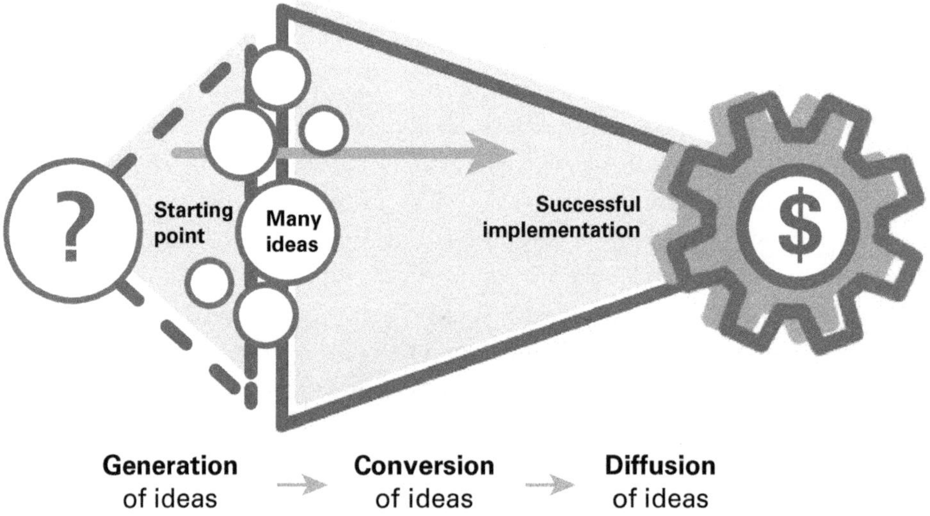

Generation of ideas → Conversion of ideas → Diffusion of ideas

From a practical point of view, methodologies such as Agile/Scrum and Lean Startup have evolved over time, aiming at achieving the conversion of ideas to workable solutions in short iterative cycles of innovation (often called 'sprints'), through building prototypes and mock-ups, so-called Minimum Viable Products or MVPs already in their early stages, and taking these to potential future customers or users to obtain feedback for improvement (Blank, 2013; Rigby et al, 2016). These methodologies are also mentioned in academic articles related to circularity, particularly in the context of sustainable business model innovation (see for example Antikainen and Valkokari, 2016; Bocken and Snihur, 2020).

Recent academic work by Velter indicates that experimentation into sustainable business models also takes place on the boundaries between different stakeholders, exploring new ways of collaboration in which past customers now become partners or companies previously focused on operational execution evolve into system integrators (Velter et al, 2020). Since circular solutions seem to provoke more holistic ways of looking at a company's business, markets and industries, existing linear supplier-buyer relationships may no longer be sufficient in order to truly become circular. It is likely that in the coming years we will see many attempts to (re-)shape relationships between companies and their external stakeholders.

A central element to be taken from the above, also when it comes to circularity, is that *innovation requires experimentation*. Experimentation has one big disadvantage, however, that causes an enormous challenge to leadership: experiments can fail. If the outcome could have been known upfront, then the experiment wouldn't have been necessary to begin with. Paradoxically enough, in corporate situations such failures are sometimes explicitly encouraged in the official R&D and innovation policies, but implicitly not easily accepted by the management accountable for the corresponding budgets and outcomes. This is another good example of the polarities mentioned earlier in this chapter.

Uncertainty and risk

If experiments can fail, then the consequence is that in such environments there will always be a certain degree of uncertainty ('we will not really know until we try'). In fact, one of the drivers behind the lean startup methodology is precisely to manage this uncertainty better and to try and reduce it through fast and short development iterations rather than taking large steps aiming for the big bang solution all at once (Bocken and Snihur, 2020).

However, uncertainty doesn't only arise from experimentation or the innovation process in general. There can also be uncertainty due to many other reasons, including 'normal' business risks such as the announcement of new legislation, the discovery of competitor movements or the appearance of new technologies. In addition, there is of course uncertainty due to plain (bad) luck or ongoing discovery over time about the initial assumptions of your business that couldn't really be tested in the design phase.

For example, imagine that you based your business model for shared electric scooters on a technical lifespan of 2.5 years based on the lifespan of the battery as one of the critical components of the e-scooter, but in practice it turns out that these e-scooters in a shared environment only last for 7.5 months because most people perceive them as rather cheap and don't treat them well ('don't be gentle, it's a rental'), then you may have a serious business issue at hand. Or that you were counting on getting 60 per cent of your products back from the market by offering a buyback price, so that you can refurbish them and sell them to the second-hand market, but it turns out that the percentage is much higher. Or much lower. Or that the acceptance in the second-hand market is much higher/lower than expected. Or that the second-hand market cannibalizes the sales of new product. In literature, Thierry et al (1995) and Hopkinson (2018), for example, addressed such issues.

Another specific uncertainty connected to innovation is with respect to the various learning curves that may be involved, for example learning about market acceptance of circular products, learning about using new materials, learning to use new technologies, learning about optimizing new revenue models, learning to work with new recycling partners and so on. Particularly important is to think about how fast you could be going through those learning curves as well as what could be the learning costs associated to going through these learning curves (cost of mistakes, of non-performance, of searching or switching value chain partners and so on).

We will come back more extensively to the topic of uncertainty and how to deal with it in Part 3. We will then use a number of the examples mentioned above and place those in the specific context of transformation based on the company in business simulation game, The Blue Connection.

Transformation and change management

As said before, the transformation from linear to circular implies change, which will undoubtedly involve uncertainty and therefore risk. These aspects put a challenge on leadership, because first of all they will need to deal with uncertainty and risk themselves. In addition, they will need to create a team of people that can effectively deal with the same uncertainty and risk as well as create an environment in which the transformation can flourish. The process to achieve that is often referred to as change management or transformational leadership and many approaches exist. Although using different terminology, at the heart of it most contain very similar elements identified as the critical ones to address for successful change or transformation. Below is probably the first extensive framework for change, as developed by Kotter, who proposed his famous eight-step process for leading change (Kotter, n.d.). As can be read on his website:

'The 8-step process for leading change:

1 Create a sense of urgency. Help others see the need for change through a bold, aspirational opportunity statement that communicates the importance of acting immediately.

2 Build a guiding coalition. A volunteer army needs a coalition of effective people – born of its own ranks – to guide it, coordinate it, and communicate its activities.

3 Form a strategic vision and initiatives. Clarify how the future will be different from the past and how you can make that future a reality through initiatives linked directly to the vision.

4 Enlist a volunteer army. Large-scale change can only occur when massive numbers of people rally around a common opportunity. They must be bought-in and urgent to drive change – moving in the same direction.

5 Enable action by removing barriers. Removing barriers such as inefficient processes and hierarchies provides the freedom necessary to work across silos and generate real impact.

6 Generate short-term wins. Wins are the molecules of results. They must be recognized, collected and communicated – early and often – to track progress and energize volunteers to persist.

7 Sustain acceleration. Press harder after the first successes. Your increasing credibility can improve systems, structures and policies. Be relentless with initiating change after change until the vision is a reality.

8 Institute change. Articulate the connections between the new behaviours and organizational success, making sure they continue until they become strong enough to replace old habits.'

As said, most other change management approaches contain similar elements. All of those, in some form or shape, emphasize the importance of (employee) participation, involvement and engagement. Peter Lacy, on the basis of work by his colleagues at Accenture, also sees these elements as critical for achieving what they call the 'wise pivot' from an existing situation to a desired new situation. Not coincidentally, this is addressed in their chapter on 'Culture and organization' (Lacy et al, 2020).

Although the above-mentioned critical factors for change management may seem straightforward, practice demonstrates that apparently this is not the case. As Ashkenas (2013) states:

As a recognized discipline, change management has been in existence for over half a century. Yet despite the huge investment that companies have made in tools, training, and thousands of books (over 83,000 on Amazon), most studies still show a 60–70 per cent failure rate for organizational change projects – a statistic that has stayed constant from the 1970s to the present.

But according to Askhenas this is not because the frameworks, theories and approaches for change management are wrong or contain important flaws. Instead, he argues, 'While it might be plausible to conclude that we should rethink the basics, let me suggest an alternative explanation: the content of change management is reasonably correct, but the managerial capacity to implement it has been woefully underdeveloped.' In other words, making a change management plan according to the chosen framework is just a first step, nothing less, but also nothing more. The actual management skills required for really making it happen cannot be underestimated.

Project and programme management

Whereas change management approaches like Kotter's in the naming of the different steps mainly focus on the outcome ('create a sense of urgency', 'build a guiding coalition' and so on), the methodologies do go beyond just that. The chosen naming sets the required spirit, but after that all needs to be put into practice, translating the objectives to concrete actions. In fact, we're talking then about the fundamentals of project and programme management (where programmes are understood as a broader set of connected projects).

Many frameworks for project and programme management exist, such as the ones by the Project Management Institute (PMI) or Prince2®. As with the many existing approaches to change management, the different approaches for project and programme management at their core are relatively similar in terms of the critical building blocks they describe. It's not the purpose of this book to discuss this extensively, but for now, let's identify what these building blocks are (see also the Appendix for an overview of relevant project management phases and tools):

- The notion of a *project lifecycle*. Most methodologies coincide in that a project passes through different stages, from the initiation phase to the planning phase, on to the execution and control phase, and finishing with the phase of project closure. Each phase has a different focus and calls for different skills, from planning to team and people management.

- *Project management areas* to be addressed. Most methodologies also coincide in that during each of the phases in the lifecycle of a project, the same management topics need to be addressed (the PMI calls these Knowledge Areas). Examples of such topics are: project scope, time (planning and scheduling), cost (budgeting and cost management), quality (performance measurement and control), team (recruitment, people management and team building), procurement (purchasing of goods and services), risk (risk identification and mitigations), communication (information and communication strategy) and stakeholders (internal and external).

In defining your project approach, think about what business process redesign thought leader Michael Hammer wrote when addressing implementation of changes in processes. He stated that 'two principles are critical to success [...]. The first is "think big, start small, move fast". [...] The second principle is "communicate relentlessly"' (Hammer, 2001).

When making the transformation from linear to circular value chains, probably the transformation itself will need to be managed through projects and/or a larger programme. We will further address this topic in Part Three of the book, applying it to the context of The Blue Connection business simulation.

Leading by shaping culture: organization and team dynamics[5]

Culture plays a fundamental role in company effectiveness, from the macro level of the entire company to the micro level of team and individual behaviour. Shaping the desired company culture is therefore a fundamental capability, even more so if the company has chosen to go into a transformation process, for example the transformation from linear to circular.

Corporate culture

At the macro level, *corporate culture* enters the equation. If people across a company share the same (strong) corporate culture, then cross-functional boundaries become less relevant, because there is another and joint 'us' that might be stronger than the 'us' of the functional departments. As stated by Campbell (2011), citing James L Heskett, a famous Harvard professor on Service and Logistics, 'Effective culture can account for 20–30 per cent of the differential in corporate performance when compared with "culturally unremarkable" competitors'.

Corporate culture can be guided very strongly by the sense of purpose, as covered extensively in Chapter 2. Purpose is then defined as a set of core beliefs on which company strategy is built. The leadership challenge is to make sure that the people on board share those core beliefs, so that they will also effectively move in the desired direction. This is obviously easier to achieve in situations where the purpose is clear from the beginning, so that shared beliefs can also be made part of the recruitment and onboarding of new staff. More complicated is the situation in which the company wants to transform, i.e. make adjustments to the purpose, for example when a company's management decides to incorporate more elements regarding sustainability into its purpose, or when it decides to make changes in priority settings within its purpose. In those cases, not all current staff at that moment might be convinced of the newly chosen purpose; they may not share the underlying beliefs, which makes motivation much more difficult to manage.

The reality is that certainly not all companies have 'effective' cultures in which corporate and individual beliefs are perfectly aligned. In those cases cross-functional alignment might be more up to the individual manager's talents for stakeholder management.

Team attributes: what successful teams seem to have in common

Even in cases when effective corporate culture is in place, that is still no more than a lower barrier for establishing communication and alignment in a company at large or, at the micro level, in the team involved in specific decision-making processes. Recent research by MIT and RSM/Delft University of Technology based on the gameplay of students with The Fresh Connection,[6] a simulation game with a dynamic very similar to The Blue Connection, in fact highlights two very interesting and important aspects of team characteristics and behaviour:

- *Trust between team members* seems to have a significant impact on team performance. Teams in which the individual team members independently of one another indicate high levels of perceived trust between them create good a working atmosphere leading to better results. The MIT research also indicates 'the fragile nature of trust' and, in the case of virtual working teams with individual team members located in physically different places, 'the sharp improvement after the team members had met face to face', suggesting that team members who did not know each other previously and who until then had only communicated via email, telephone, videoconference or the like, started working together much more productively after actually having met in person. According to the research, meeting face to face gave an important boost to mutual interpersonal trust between the team members (Phadnis et al, 2013).

- *High levels of reflexivity* also seem to have a positive impact on team performance: 'Team reflexivity is a team's ability to consciously and reflexively react to changing and fluid situations and adapt accordingly'. According to the research at RSM/ Delft University of Technology, this ability plays particularly to the benefit of teams whose mix of team members tends to favour seeking 'accomplishment and attaining positive outcomes, and where individuals are more inclined to explore all possible means [to achieve] the goals they desire'. This is in contrast to teams in which team members tend to focus mainly on avoiding negative outcomes rather than on attaining positive outcomes (Schippers et al, 2011).

So, what can we pick up from this? Because even if one said that the above-mentioned conclusions can be relatively easily understood conceptually, unfortunately, trust and reflexivity cannot really be designed, and can certainly not be imposed. However, such traits are definitely needed, also in the context of circular innovation, in which uncertainty and ambiguity are very present and need to be dealt with properly at the institutional (company) level (Bocken and Geradts, 2020). In a specific team trust needs to be earned, it needs to be developed over time, and the same might go for reflexivity. There seem to be very few shortcuts, if any. So, what do these factors depend on? In the following paragraphs we'll try to shed a light on some of them.

Characters and personalities: team composition, team roles and team dynamics

Before going on, it's important to mention that the composition of a 'team' in a company, whether a formal team put together for a specific purpose, or 'just' the accidental mix of people from different departments involved in a specific decision-making process, is in practice hardly ever the consequence of a thorough analysis of candidates based on technical knowledge and skills, nor of character traits and mindsets. In our experience, in most cases the 'team' is simply the mix of available people at a moment in time.

First, there is the mix of technical skills and experience that people bring to the table, which has an impact on the dynamic that will follow. The MIT research into team performance also highlights in this context that 'the ability of the individual team members, namely the analytical reasoning skills and overall intellectual competence [...] also attribute to team performance' (Phadnis et al, 2013). However, there are more dimensions at play. Five relatively unexperienced junior people meeting with a senior colleague who's been around for 20 years might generate a certain ambience that is quite different from six senior managers meeting to discuss an important decision. By the way, in our own experience neither the first nor the second team would be a guarantee of better results.

Another factor at play here is that of the character and personality that each of us carries. We are who we are, and we're not all the same. That might work out fine if personalities are more complementary but might also cause conflicts if personalities match to a lesser extent.

There are plenty of frameworks to describe an individual's team roles, for example the one proposed by Belbin (2010). By putting different individuals' team roles together, the overall strengths and weaknesses of the team can be assessed. Or the Thinking Hats approach as developed by de Bono (1999), which also exploits the topic of team roles. The key message here is that each team, whether a formal team in a project, or an informal team of colleagues meeting to agree on some important topics, is a mix of personalities that is to a certain extent totally random, and independent from process design. And this mix of personalities can perfectly play an important role in the outcome of the team process.

In addition to the aforementioned aspects of corporate culture, team attributes, and characters and personalities, there are some other relevant elements, which we consider to be slightly outside the scope of this book. We refer to aspects such as stages in the lifecycle of teams, motivation and communication. Readers interested to know more about these are referred to the Appendix.

Overall team performance: tasks and relationships

The fact that circularity is full of such potentially conflictive issues within and between different functional areas is what makes leadership such a relevant aspect to be looked into. So, after all the previous paragraphs talking about elements of team performance, now we're coming back to evaluation of the leadership dimension: how well are we doing in this respect?

To measure the outcomes of the team process and understand how the 'leadership', implicitly or explicitly, has worked, we can on the one hand look at how the team actually achieved the results and on the other hand at how team atmosphere has actually been. We can use a methodology as proposed by Management Worlds, Inc, who developed questionnaires for mapping two interesting dimensions of team performance: one oriented to the *tasks* (are we getting things done?) and one oriented to *relationships* (are we OK as a team?). In a way, all dimensions like the technical and intellectual skills of the individuals, their characters and personalities and social skills, the trust in the team, and the degree of reflexivity, the implicit and explicit manifestations of leadership, all come together in this analysis. These questionnaires will come back later in Part Two, connected to The Blue Connection gameplay and applied to your own team.

EXERCISE 4.5
Explore team performance

Explore

Go back into your own practical experience. This could be work experience in a company, an internship, workgroups at school, teams in sports or other hobbies and so on. Try to recall to what extent you have noticed the influence of the topics discussed before, such as functional silos, 'corporate' culture, team roles, communication, team performance in terms of tasks and relationships. What are your observations? How could these observations be useful to you when gameplay starts?

Please note that the aforementioned aspects of organizational culture and team dynamics may seem distant from the topic of circularity. But don't be fooled – change in an organization typically causes much turmoil and leads to a lot of stress among employees as well as management. A strong culture and strong teams will not be a guarantee, but are for sure an important ingredient to successfully making the transformation.

The (transformational) leader in the value chain

As the topics in the chapter so far have hopefully illustrated, the transformation from linear to circular calls for a very high dose of leadership from a number of different angles. So what does this mean for the figure of the leader?

Many different frameworks exist which try to capture the traits of a 'leader'. Sometimes these frameworks take the form of (self-)assessment questionnaires. For example, Hughes et al (2014) base their assessments on the critical leadership skills of 'building trust, managing the political landscape, spanning boundaries, involving others, connecting at an emotional level and building and sustaining momentum', not surprisingly connecting to the topics dealt with in this entire chapter.

Gattorna (2015) builds on the well-known framework of Myers–Briggs's individual leadership styles, linking the different styles to different value chain strategies, a concept which in our opinion can also be applied to circular value chains and strategies.

Wilms (2020) highlights two 'extremes' of the spectrum of leadership styles: managerial (top-down) leadership on one side and connective (participative) leadership on the other side. In some way this also resonates with the concept of situational leadership, which stresses the importance of adapting leadership style according to the circumstances. Poelmans (2020) states that:

> successful managers are capable of balancing many paradoxes, while engaging in complex human interactions that involve solving problems and building relationships. In order to balance paradoxical behaviours, leaders need 'brain flexibility', the capacity to effortlessly switch between different brain states or mindsets, and 'brain resilience', which is the capability to bounce back from cognitive overload or emotional turmoil.

Another view is the concept of the T-shaped manager, which was allegedly first coined by David Guest (1991), possibly after certain principles as applied at the time by McKinsey and Company. These principles have been promoted a lot since then by famous design firm IDEO, the company behind much of the 'Design Thinking' school of thought. The central idea of the T-shaped manager is that they combine the benefits of deep (technical) knowledge and problem-solving skills in a particular functional or business area, with broad communication skills across different areas, within or across firms.

Interestingly enough, in an article in the *Harvard Business Review*, Hansen and von Oetinger (2001) give a slightly different, and in our opinion compatible interpretation of the T-shaped manager. For them it's not so much about the mix of deep functional and wide cross-functional skills, but about the mix of moving oneself and spreading knowledge and experience vertically within one unit of the firm, and doing the same horizontally between units of the firm, a concept that can be expanded to places outside the firm in order to reach more of the supply chain's end-to-end way of looking. In other words, they focus a bit more on behaviour rather than on pure skills. From our point of view, both views are very relevant to the nature and character of what's going on in the end-to-end supply chain.

Christopher (2016) places the T-shape in the context of the value chain from a very high-level perspective and supply chain recruitment company Inspired-Search has taken the concept of the T-shaped manager a big step further, actually creating a detailed value chain-specific version of it (Figure 4.9).

EXERCISE 4.6

Explore the knowledge and skills of the circularity transformation manager

Explore

Take a good look at the diagram of the T-shaped supply chain manager in Figure 4.9. As was explained in the text, it was initially developed for the environment of 'traditional and linear' supply chains. Which elements in the figure would you see as less relevant for the case of the T-shaped circularity transformation manager? Which additions would you see for the case of the T-shaped circularity transformation manager?

You may want to park the outcomes of the previous exercise for a moment until gameplay with The Blue Connection business simulation starts in Part Two. There you can see how your views apply there, either for the CEO of your team or in the case of self-steering teams.

Finally in this chapter we would like to go back to Jack Welch, former long-time CEO of General Electric. There is a wonderful video of him speaking about the role of a leader, focusing particularly on the people aspects of that role. According to Welch, there are four vital angles to leadership. As a leader you have to be the Chief Meaning Officer, not only explaining to people where you want to go, but also showing clearly what's in it for them if they join you on the journey. Furthermore, you need to be the Chief Broom Officer, getting rid of the organizational clutter, removing the silos. Then, you also need to be the Chief Generosity Officer, enjoy your colleagues' successes, not focusing only on yourself. Finally, Welch distinguishes the role of the Chief Fun Officer, celebrating small victories with the team and making them into big victories, having fun at the job every single day (JWMI, 2015).

Linking back to the central principle of the learning cycle of experiential learning, we would invite you to track the way you apply the skills mentioned in this chapter, for example during the gameplay. This will help you first of all to identify their appearance and their importance, as well as enable you to assess your own performance in each of them.

FIGURE 4.9 The T-shaped supply chain manager

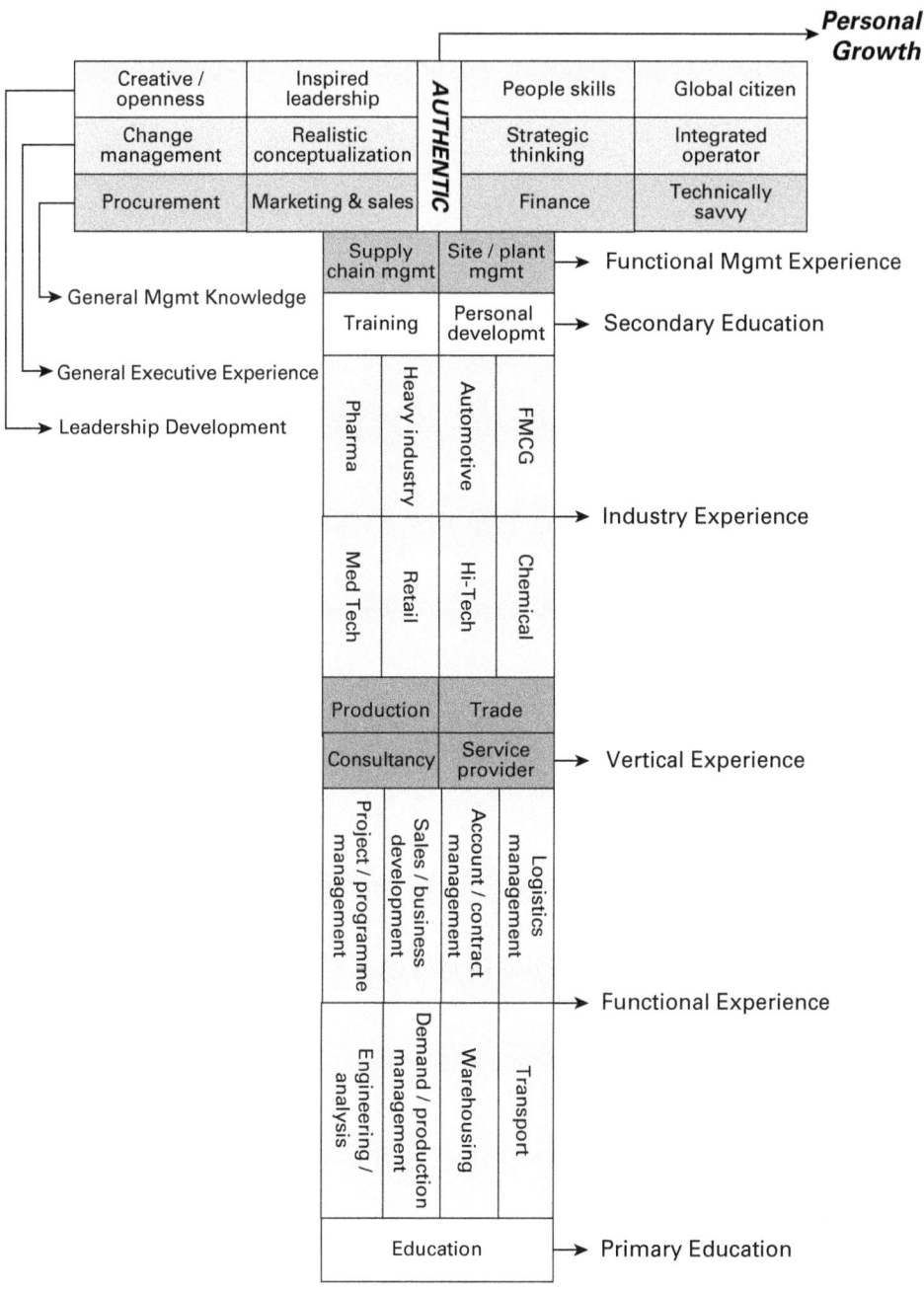

SOURCE © Inspired-Search

Summary

THE FINDINGS OF PHASE 1, STEP 4, CIRCULARITY: EXPLORING THE LEADERSHIP PERSPECTIVE

'You know what?' Aunt Joanna said to Maria and Peter, when they had finished going through the results of the past week. 'Since the beginning of our Project 'Circularity' we have dealt with so many things already, I'm quite satisfied with all of the things we have found out so far! First, we established an overview of the historical perspective of circularity, then we investigated the company perspective with details about circular strategies and goods flows and finance and so on. After that we moved on to look beyond the company boundaries and just now we finished our reporting about what the transformation means for leadership, by looking at measuring circularity, the complexities of circular alignment and issues related to innovation, change management and leadership.'

'I know it's getting late already, but if you can spare me just a little bit more of your time today,' Aunt Joanna continued, 'I'll order some food and then we take a step back and see in more detail what we've got so far and maybe draw some preliminary conclusions about the Corporate Circular Imperative, what do you think?'

FIGURE 4.10   Exploring the leadership perspective on circularity (detailed)

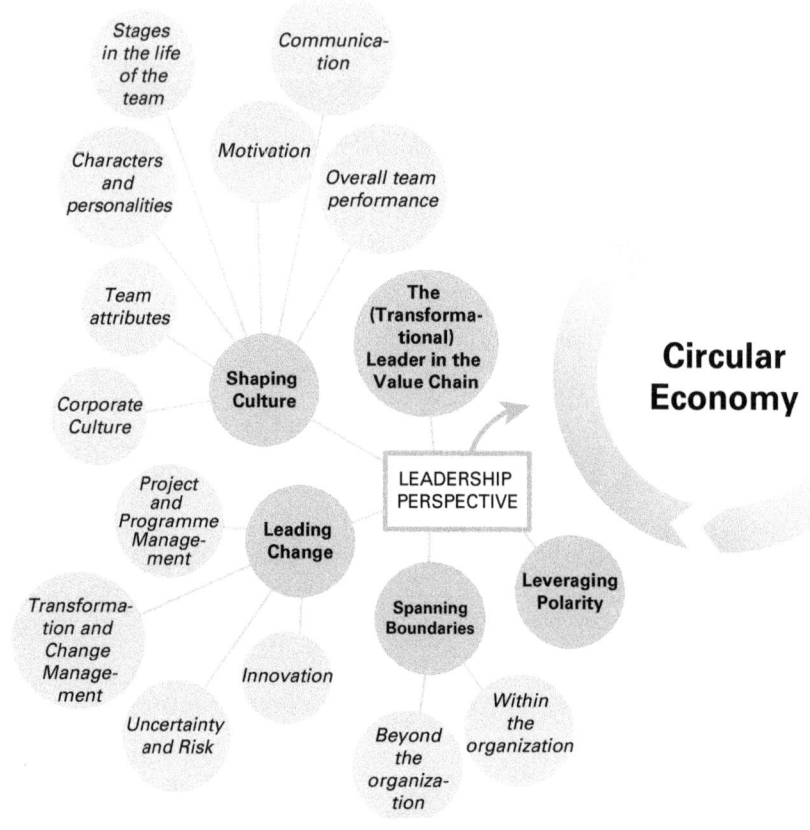

Notes

1 At the time of writing this book (September–December 2020).

2 Bocken and Geradts (2020) identify performance metrics and incentive systems as potential operational drivers or barriers in the context of sustainable business model innovation.

3 Bocken and Geradts (2020) identify functional strategy and collaborative innovation as potential strategic drivers or barriers in the context of sustainable business model innovation.

4 Bocken and Geradts (2020) identify uncertainty avoidance and embracing ambiguity as potential institutional drivers or barriers and patient investments as strategic drivers in the context of sustainable business model innovation.

5 Bocken and Geradts (2020) identify functional excellence/people capability development and standard versus more flexible structures as potential operational drivers or barriers in the context of sustainable business model innovation.

6 The Fresh Connection (TFC) is another simulation game from the same company that has also created The Blue Connection, which we will use in Parts Two and Three. The focus of The Fresh Connection is on managing complex physical and information flows in value chains. The book *Mastering the Supply Chain* (Weenk, 2019) has TFC at the heart of it, linking it directly to relevant theory in the field.

05

The Corporate Circular Imperative: narrative and numbers (2)

Wrapping-up Phase 1 of Project 'Circularity'[1]

'Food has been ordered,' Aunt Joanna said with a smile, 'it'll be here in no time. Now tell me, what have you learned so far in our Project 'Circularity'?'

Peter was the first to respond: 'Well, first of all, Aunt Joanna, I'd like to thank you once more for the opportunity to work on this project with you. So far, for me it's been an incredible journey. I've seen so many aspects of circularity that I wasn't aware of before. Having said that, I think I'm actually not ready to have a final picture, it's still a bit fuzzy to me.'

'OK', said Aunt Joanna, 'so, what's the puzzle you're struggling with?'

'Well, on the one hand,' Peter continued, 'I think we have clearly seen what the context of circularity is and why there is so much more attention for it now. Also, it is much clearer to me now how it works at the company level, with the link to purpose, then the business model with segments and value propositions, circular strategies which are visualized through the R-ladder or the Value Hill, the different possible revenue streams and cost structure, the financials and so on. Conceptually it all seems to make a lot of sense so far.'

'But on the other hand, it seems to me that in the field of circularity things are still developing extremely fast. I mean, you only have to look at how many definitions of circularity there are around, or how many different systems exist for measuring circular progress. Same goes in a certain way for legislation that poses or relieves barriers, but which is evolving rapidly in some places and can change almost without warning. And, by the way, legislation on which companies on their own have very little influence.'

'So I guess that what I'm wondering about is to what extent we are looking at a "final" picture here or just at an intermediate step of something which might be totally different in a few years? I'm thinking that it's maybe still too early to draw firm final conclusions and that maybe you should be careful with taking big steps now.'

'Hm, that's very interesting, thanks, Peter,' said Aunt Joanna. 'And Maria, what do you think? Do you agree with Peter that maybe it's still too early to tell what the best way for us to deal with circularity is?'

'No, I actually don't agree with Peter!' Maria said energetically. 'For me the urgency is really clear. We have a climate emergency on this planet and we are running into resource issues, so doing nothing is not an option anymore, not even for companies. For me taking action is the only way forward. And there is uncertainty about certain things, for sure, but that cannot stop us from moving on!'

'Yes, but listen, Maria,' Peter interrupted his cousin, 'at many moments so far during the project I wasn't sure how one single company could possibly deal with all of this uncertainty and complexity and successfully become circular in a reasonable timeframe and, given this complex context, I keep asking myself something I think is even more important, which is "why should they bother in the first place?" I mean, what's the point for a company to enter into such a complex and risky environment with the ambition to become circular?' Peter concluded, shrugging his shoulders.

'But it's so clear,' Maria responded, jumping up from her seat. 'Companies also have a moral obligation to contribute to a better world, like every citizen has, that's why they invented corporate social responsibility in the first place, didn't they? And becoming circular is one of the ways they can do just that!'

'Yes,' Peter replied, 'but how do you define circularity then? Because as we have seen, according to legislators in some countries, making your products "recyclable" is already circular, whereas if you place it on the R-ladder you can only consider that as not more than a very tiny first step and still quite far removed from truly slowing or closing loops. It's all still really very ambiguous.'

'And don't you see, Maria,' Peter continued, 'don't you see that what you say is simply only one way of looking at it? I read this interview the other day with a CEO who just brought his third company within 10 years to a successful launch on the stock exchange. It made the guy a multibillionaire. And in the interview they asked him what his "secret sauce" was for these successful IPOs. You know what he answered? He said, "There is no secret, we just have extreme discipline and don't get distracted by all of the stuff which is wrong in society. We are only interested in building a successful company, not in what's going on in the world. Just focus, no distraction." That's what he said, plain and simple. You as an individual may not like it, but does that make his standpoint less valid?'

'Yes, that's exactly what I mean,' Maria raised her voice, upset. 'I find that an unethical standpoint. Such people will ultimately destroy the planet while making themselves into billionaires, that's precisely the issue. I don't understand it, why would you want to be a billionaire anyway if there is no planet anymore where you can spend your money? Why don't these people get the point that we should truly move towards a more responsible way of organizing business and society?'

'By the way, that's also what more and more economists are claiming,' she continued. 'You remember that during our research we found the work of Picketty and Raworth and some others? And they're all saying that the current drivers behind capitalism and relentless growth will ultimately not be sustainable for the planet and the people living on it. So then unbelievably there are CEOs like the one you mention who simply don't seem to care. I mean, aren't these people at least a little bit worried about the futures of their own kids?'

There was no way to stop Maria now as she continued: 'And then to make things even worse there are other companies who on the outside do seem to take it seriously and promise solemnly that they will contribute actively to sustainability and then it turns out that some of those CEOs who do this in many cases simply lie. You remember the declaration of intentions of the Business Roundtable and everybody was so happy that these people pledged to do their best to become more responsible? Turns out that these companies have hardly done anything since then. Most of the CEOs didn't even ask their executive committees if they could even sign the declaration in the first place, which normally is compulsory for anything which is really strategic. Apparently, the signature wasn't strategic enough for them…'

'Why is it that too many companies just don't seem to truly care?' Maria said, while shaking her head. 'You both remember how happy we were when we found out about Elkington and his Triple Bottom Line concept precisely to address the unbalanced company focus on just the money? And that later on TBL was followed by other initiatives like Creating Shared Value, Integrated Value and so on. And we were happy, because this seemed to be exactly the framework we were looking for, bringing together sustainability and finance. But what has gone wrong in practice since these concepts were developed? What has happened since then?'

'All true,' said Peter, 'but don't forget that companies make money because they respond to what customers want. So, isn't the problem more with us the consumers, then, instead of with the companies? Because if we prefer to keep buying cheap stuff that cannot be repaired or recycled so we need to throw it away and buy something new, then why should companies give us something else? Can you really blame companies for that, especially if you think about the competitive environment they are in? And can you really expect companies to put so much money into educating all of their consumers into circularity? Isn't that a bit too much to ask from a single business?'

'Don't get me started on companies being so worried about their customers, Peter, we have had that conversation before, you remember? As you know, it sometimes seems that companies making money is as much about making customers happy as it is about creating bubbles or avoiding the law,' Maria said, with a sarcastic tone in her voice. 'You know the stories about money-losing pricing as a business model in order to reach monopolistic power, or the way media are used to inflate expectations in order to attract investors or the way tax havens are employed.'

'Let's not deviate from the real issue at hand here,' she continued. 'Isn't it a fact that there are more and more consumers interested in circular products and sharing models or product-as-a-service business models? And that more and more banks and even companies are willing to provide more favourable financing conditions for circular projects and businesses? And that due to, for example, the European Green Deal there is more and more legislation in favour of circularity underway?'

Peter thought for a moment: 'Hm, maybe. I just wonder if it will be big enough and come fast enough for many companies to make a move now. I don't see the business case for circularity that clearly yet.'

'But does there always have to be a business case?' said Maria. 'Isn't that the whole point of entrepreneurship? You know, that you have to deal with uncertainty all the time, spotting an opportunity and then jumping into it before many others do?'

'OK, fair comment,' said Peter, 'I'll give that to you; entrepreneurship is indeed also about risk taking and experimentation into the unknown. So, for sure some entrepreneurs will dare to jump with the desire to be the first ones and willing to take the risk of failure. But again, I'm not sure if it will be big enough and fast enough. And I'm also wondering if it is realistic to assume that established companies will be able to do this. Maybe the smaller ones or the startups should go first? And then one of the 64-million-dollar questions is whether it will reach mainstream business or stay within the startup/entrepreneurial bubble?'

'By the way,' he continued, 'to one of your previous points about a more responsible society, Piketty and Raworth indeed have many good elements in their work, I think, but they do talk a lot about the macro level, of society or countries in general, which I still find difficult to link to individual company behaviour. I don't know, the examples you mention of what you consider as bad practices, are they just about plain and simple greenwashing by companies with bad intentions, or is shareholder pressure for better short-term financial results in practice just still too big for CEOs? Because if that's still the case, for them there really will have to be a business case in favour of circularity.'

'And you also mentioned the Triple Bottom Line,' Peter went on, 'but don't forget, Elkington in fact recently recalled his own TBL concept, because he felt that companies were abusing it, trying to make themselves look good rather than really doing good. In the same line of reasoning, others have also been critical with the Creating Shared Value concept. You know, shared value is great and in fact a no-brainer if there is a win-win situation, for example when increased circularity leads to direct cost savings. No one will be against that, not even die-hard capitalists. But what to do when there is no clear win-win? If more value for the planet or the people means less profit or more financial risk for the company? Or the other way around? Apparently, it's just very difficult to do it really well.'

'Wow, guys,' Aunt Joanna said, 'I'm really impressed with all of your thoughts and observations. In fact, I'm sharing many of your doubts, especially if I think about it from our own company perspective. I think we could keep talking for hours and hours, but let me give you something to think about and we'll discuss it next time we meet, OK?'

She continued, 'When we started out, I told you about this concept of "narrative and numbers". From the context of sustainability in general, the same John Elkington you mentioned wrote an interesting article about it some time ago, called "The 6 ways business leaders talk about sustainability". He talks about the different frames, or "storylines", that executives use when they try to put sustainability on their corporate agenda. So, he's saying for example that some executives focus on resource shortage as the main driver for justifying their corporate sustainability initiatives. Others prefer to emphasize "value", meaning sustainability as a business opportunity for delivering new value to certain market segments. Yet others prefer to focus on the moral frame, highlighting that they do the "right" thing.'

'Elkington has a few more examples of possible frames,[2] and of course, they could even be combined, but my main question to you at this stage is what the two of you think. What could be the narrative for us, what could be our story about why we should engage in circularity and which will make our customers and our own staff accept it and buy into it?'

'We know that our stakeholders are not one homogeneous group and we have to deal with many different people with different opinions, so preferably, the narrative should somehow satisfy most of those at the same time. However, even more importantly I think it's absolutely crucial that our narrative should convince ourselves, we should be the first ones to really believe in it! After that we can then start looking for the numbers to support our narrative. I have one more little exercise for you and then we'll call it a day, OK?'

Final reflection on Part One

EXERCISE 5.1

The narrative to support the Corporate Circular Imperative

Going back to the topics as covered in Part One and visualized in Figure 5.1, now reflect on the narrative for circularity from a company standpoint: the Corporate Circular Imperative. Develop a convincing pitch of a maximum of 10 phrases that you yourself firmly believe in and that would also convince others to join you on the journey towards circularity.

After delivering their pitches for the one-person audience of Aunt Joanna, Maria and Peter had thanked her for the wonderful evening and were walking towards the door to go home. Just when she was about to jump on her bike, Maria received a message on her phone and after reading it she said, 'Hey, that's interesting! Listen, I just got a

FIGURE 5.1   Overview of topics covered in Part One: exploring the circular economy

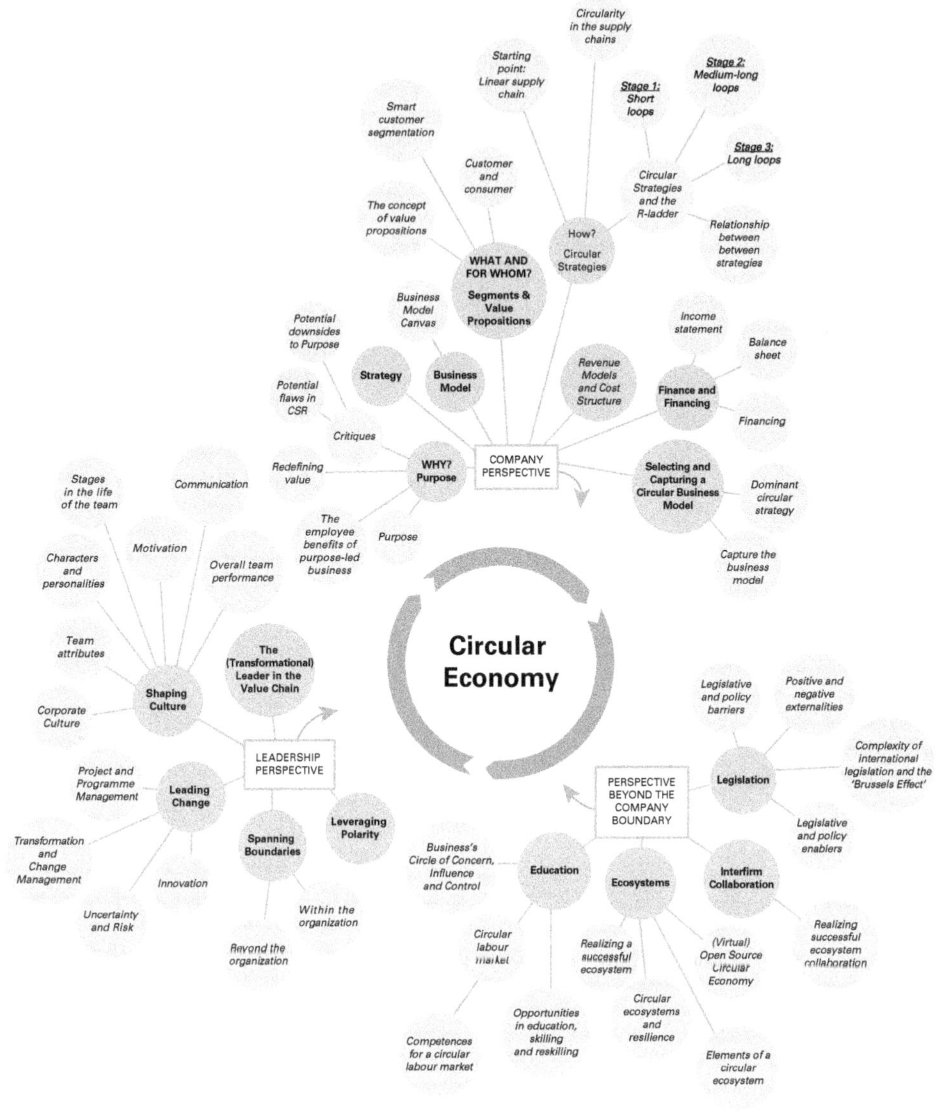

message from my friend Sarah. She's telling me that she saw this announcement for a university challenge with a business simulation game about circularity. It's played in teams and because she knows we're doing this project for Aunt Joanna, she's asking if we want to join her in the challenge. What do you think, shall we sign up?'

'You're kidding me, aren't you?' said Aunt Joanna. 'So much coincidence cannot be true.... Well anyway, if I may suggest something,' she said with a big smile on her face, 'why don't you sign up. Just let me know if you need anything from me to support you, OK? This game sounds like a great opportunity to experience first-hand how all of these topics we have explored so far actually work out and how easy or difficult it is to apply them in practice. So, what do you say?'

Notes

1 References alluded to in this dialogue: Piketty (2017), Raworth (2017), Elkington (2018), Mikulka (2018), BRT (2019), Doctorow (2019), Bebchuk and Tallarita (2020), NRC (2020a, 2020b), Van Poppel (2020)

2 Particularly: the 'time' frame, highlighting on the one hand that many developments are seemingly accelerating and we're arriving at a critical point in time (extinction of species, global warning, pollution), whereas on the other hand a transformation to more sustainable approaches requires time; the 'design' frame, highlighting that more sustainable solutions start from redesigning existing solutions (products, processes, materials); and the 'abundance' frame, which focuses on technological development and the mobilization of ever greater innovation potential in a connected world.

PART TWO

Mastering circularity

Project 'Circularity', Phase 2: Let's play a business simulation about circularity!

FIGURE 6.0 The business simulation challenge is about to begin

Project 'Circularity'
Maria, Peter, Aunt Joanna

Maria
Morning! I just received the confirmation from my friend Sarah that we have been allowed into the business simulation game competition. She has found another friend, called Matthew, who will also join us, I think you've met him once before, Peter.
08:11AM

Peter
Hey Maria, that's indeed great news! When do we start?
08:43PM ✓✓

Aunt Joanna
Good news, Maria, way to go!
You know what would be great? If during gameplay you can keep the points that we looked at during our first part of Project 'Circularity' at hand as a reference. You know, the company perspective, outside the company boundary and leadership.
And then we discuss those as you go along with the game? That way we can connect the dots between theory and practice. What do you think?
08:52PM ✓✓

Aunt Joanna
Ah, and remember the '*narrative and numbers*' we spoke about? I'm hoping that playing the game would help us understand much more about the numbers, in addition to what we've already discovered about possible narratives.
Besides, after first *exploring circularity* in our project, I would imagine that playing the game is a great way to truly start *mastering circularity*!
Good luck, guys!
08:56PM ✓✓

Type message

06

Getting started with The Blue Connection: game on!

PROJECT 'CIRCULARITY', PHASE 2: DAY 1 OF THE BUSINESS SIMULATION GAME CHALLENGE

'Oh, guys, this is so exciting!' Maria shouted out. 'Look how many teams there are, this is really cool!' 'Wow, indeed,' said Peter, 'I didn't expect so many people to participate, great that we can join as well, many thanks for the opportunity, Sarah!'

'Nothing to thank me for,' replied Sarah, 'I'm happy you could join, especially since I found out that you're becoming such circularity experts, we're definitely going to need you... By the way, anyone have a suggestion for the name of our team?'

'Hm, I read that we're going to be in charge of an e-Bike company,' Peter replied, 'so what about *Team SuperBike*?' 'Yeah, I like that one, go Team SuperBike!' Maria yelled out. 'Let's go for that number one spot!'

'Look, there's our table,' said Sarah's friend Matthew, who was also going to be part of their team. 'Let's get our laptops out and get familiar with the game.' They took their seats and started going through the instructions about The Blue Connection.

The Blue Connection business simulation game (TBC)

The Blue Connection (TBC) business simulation game has been developed by Dutch company Inchainge. The company already had an important track record using a variety of board games in their training and consultancy activities, when finally in 2008 their first simulation game The Fresh Connection was launched, bringing 'serious gaming' to another level. The Blue Connection is the company's third business simulation game, launched early 2019.

At the heart of The Blue Connection is a *lossmaking producer of electric bicycles (e-Bikes)*, located in the Netherlands, that needs to be turned profitable again by making strategic and tactical decisions over the course of a number of rounds of gameplay, each round representing one year of the life of the company. The attractiveness of such business simulation games is that participants can play in a fun, competitive, risk-free, yet realistic environment in which a direct relationship between cause and consequence (decisions and results) can be experienced.

What makes The Blue Connection stand out in comparison to other business simulation games is that it has a clear focus on the entire value chain and the flow of materials from upstream suppliers to downstream customers and the various possible return loops to become circular. Furthermore, by splitting the decisions to be made into the clear functional areas of Sales, Design/Purchasing, Supply Chain and Finance, and with a different team member responsible for each area, the experience gets very close to real corporate life, in which a functional split of responsibilities is the norm, rather than the exception.

Beyond the pure functional decision-making, this leads to the need to find effective and efficient mechanisms to ensure *cross-functional alignment*. Then add a little bit of time pressure into the pressure cooker and we have a combination of all the required ingredients for a wonderful learning experience.

The Blue Connection business simulation game has a modular set-up, each module bringing additional complexity into the experience. Typically a game set-up would start with a slightly lower level of complexity in the beginning of the game (round 1), followed by increasing complexity as the gameplay advances in subsequent rounds. In the context of educational programmes, the decision about which configuration to use would normally be taken by the lecturer or trainer in charge of the course, taking into consideration the specific content and learning objectives of the course. In the case of professionals it would normally be the trainer who would do this. The key points to keep in mind at this stage are:

- The Blue Connection is an e-Bike manufacturer that is currently making a loss and has the ambition to go on a journey to circularity.
- Gameplay is in teams, each team member taking charge of a different functional role.
- Gameplay will be in rounds of decision-making, each round representing one year of the life of the company.
- Game set-up, timings and so on will normally be defined and communicated by the course lecturer, the corporate trainer or challenge leader.

In the remainder of this chapter we will get started with the game by:

- exploring the simulation;
- analysing the starting point in which you find the company;
- starting to think about an action plan for round 1 of gameplay.

Please note that Part Two and, to a lesser extent, Part Three of the book, are based on a game configuration that corresponds to what most schools, universities and companies are using in practice. This goes for the configuration of complexity in the game, as well as the number of entities and their respective names that you will find. So, it might be that the specific configuration you will be playing in your own course is a bit different from what you will find in the book. If this is indeed the case, then don't worry, because the topics, exercises and reflections are equally valid and applicable for any configuration of the game.[1]

Introducing: Team Superbike!

You already briefly met Team SuperBike. Here you can see the team in action preparing their first round of gameplay.

Throughout Part Two you will find bits and pieces of the work done by Team SuperBike that can serve as an inspiration for your own work.

Introducing: Catherine McLaren!

Catherine McLaren had always loved the complex combination of sustainability and business. After graduating with a major in Sustainable Business she had

FIGURE 6.1 Team SuperBike

FIGURE 6.2 Introducing the company's Circular Turnaround Manager

been very active at a startup incubator in the local sustainable business ecosystem, where local government, academia and entrepreneurs worked together in creating sustainable businesses. A few successful journeys at circular startups later, she had been looking at making a move into larger and more established companies, just like her two older brothers had done before her.

Catherine's brother Bob had made it to become a well-respected CEO of a group of brands in the drinks industry, and Anthony had made a career as a crisis manager specializing in turning lossmaking companies around. Catherine had always been greatly inspired by her brothers and had always dreamt of stepping into their footsteps someday. That's probably why she was so excited when the opportunity at The Blue Connection came along. She saw this as the perfect playing field to demonstrate what she was capable of achieving. Catherine was hired to shape and lead the circular transition at The Blue Connection. And now she was looking for a team to help her make it happen.

Catherine McLaren has facilitated a few videos for your information. Please go and watch the videos, which you can find on the web portal connected to the game. These videos will give you a brief overview of The Blue Connection and its current state of affairs.

After watching the videos, please continue reading the description below.

The Blue Connection: the company, the mission, the experience

Company and retail customers. The Blue Connection manufactures and assembles bicycles. The Blue Connection delivers its products to a variety of retailers, located all over the world. It delivers to its retailers from stock, meaning that the delivery is made the day after the retailer places an order.

The Blue Connection delivers its products to three main retailers:

- *Cheetah.* A powerful retailer in France, very strong in delivery of high-quality bikes for a good price. Their consumers are trusting Cheetah to deliver durable bikes that last a lifetime, and are willing to pay for it. Unfortunately Cheetah has been bought and sold several times by private equity. This has resulted in high debts and high financial burden. The credit rating of the company reflects this.

- *HBS.* A Dutch retailer successful in a very interesting and growing market niche. Their focus is on persuading daily work commuters to switch from their car to an e-Bike. Their story of climate change and sustainability resonates stronger and stronger. Their consumers are very environmentally sensitive, trying to reduce their carbon footprint. They are also willing to pay a premium price for a circular product. But of course greenwashing is not acceptable; the claim must be real and trustworthy.

- *Gearshift.* A UK-based retailer, focused on consumers looking for a hassle-free bike experience. And the good news is, this convenience can create a profitable business when offered to the right people, at the right moment in the right format. Gearshift is a very stable and trustworthy retailer with a long track record.

Product storage. The Blue Connection's products are stored in the finished goods warehouse. The products remain there until delivery to the retailer is made.

Production process. The Blue Connection assembles all bikes itself. The production and assembly lines are part of The Blue Connection's equipment. In addition, The Blue Connection also prides itself for having a refurbishment line that is capable of refurbishing the products that have been returned by consumers. After the refurbishment the e-Bikes can be sold on the second-hand market for the going price at that moment.

Components. An extensive bill of components specifies which quantity of which component is required for a finished product. Components can include the frame, wheels, battery, etc. Each component has its own characteristics for remanufacturability, recyclability and repairability.

Materials. Each component has a bill of materials that specifies which materials the suppliers have used to produce the various components. This can include a variety of materials such as plastic, steel, paper, etc. Each material will have its own characteristics for recycling.

Suppliers. Components are purchased from suppliers. Both local and global suppliers can be candidates to supply these components to The Blue Connection.

Component storage. Components cannot always be immediately used for production. Therefore, the company owns a components warehouse to store them.

Maintenance. The Blue Connection has the possibility to offer a maintenance service directly to the end consumers, of course in collaboration with the retailer. This service enhances the consumer experience and the lifetime of the products.

Recycling Service Provider (RSP). The Blue Connection has decided to outsource all activities regarding the disassembly of the returned bikes, remanufacturing of the components and recycling the components to their original materials. A specialized service provider is contracted by The Blue Connection for those activities.

Team, roles and responsibilities. Together with your teammates you form the management team of The Blue Connection. Each team member has a specific role: Design/Purchasing Manager, Sales Manager, Supply Chain Manager or Finance Manager. All team members have their own responsibilities and can make their own decisions. However, as a great philosopher once said, 'Together is not alone'. Cooperation is the key to saving The Blue Connection from going under:

- *Design/Purchasing Manager.* The Design/Purchasing Manager is responsible for purchasing the components. They design the end product by choosing the right components for the right price. The Design/Purchasing Manager plays a crucial role in the game. By choosing the right components, the preferred circular strategy can be pursued.

- *Sales Manager.* The Sales Manager oversees product sales. They negotiate The Blue Connection's terms of delivery with the customers. It is particularly important to negotiate appropriate services and the levels of circularity. They also decide on revenue model(s) of The Blue Connection. The Sales Manager plays an extremely important role in the game and their bargaining can result in a high sales or subscription price. But only as long as The Blue Connection can live up to its promise.

- *Supply Chain Manager.* The Supply Chain Manager is the glue that holds the other roles together. By providing enough capacity and the right capabilities, the Supply Chain Manager plays a decisive role in the team. This role is responsible for managing the return flows in the right directions depending on the team's strategy.

- *Finance Manager.* The Finance Manager is responsible for managing the company's capital funding and cash flow. They negotiate the terms of lending with the banks, and ensure that The Blue Connection has sufficient cash flow and appropriate loans in place to meet its business needs. The Finance Manager plays a fundamental role in the game by having the right vendor lease programmes per customer for the best interest rates. A unique feature is the possibility to agree on an overall company circularity level with the bank that can impact your interest rate levels. Last but not least, the finance manager decides on the intensity of the buy-back programme per customer.

Strategy. Each team member can make decisions individually, but as a team you need a shared strategy to achieve the best results. For example, you don't want the Finance Manager to agree to higher vendor lease levels with the bank, while the Sales Manager is moving all to Direct Sales! So make sure to always discuss your decisions with each other.

Decisions. You will make many decisions during The Blue Connection. A trade-off is incorporated into every decision, so a decision will never only have positive effects, but negative ones too. The trick is to assess these consequences and to balance them. Should you reconsider any decisions during a given round, the decisions made in the previous round will then be reused.

Drive to become circular. The board has indicated that it wants the company to become more circular. In part this is because there are clear signals from the market that retail customers are finding additional value in buying from more circular suppliers. In addition, there is a trend in the market that banks are offering better lending conditions to companies achieving better degrees of circularity.

Scores. The objective of the game is for you and your team to achieve the best Return on Material (ROM). This KPI integrates your performance on circularity with your performance on profitability. ROM is defined as *profit per kilogram of used virgin material*.[2]

In Chapter 1 we spoke about *the lack of agreement about definitions* in the area of the circular economy. This highlights the importance of clarifying terminology whenever working with others in order to avoid confusion. In TBC's system you will find a lot of specific terminology. Some of it might be very clear or straightforward, other wordings might be less familiar to you. In those cases, don't guess nor make assumptions about what things could possibly mean. Like in real life, go out and ask for clarification. In this case, you can do that by clicking on the 💡 symbol or on the ⓘ symbol, which can be found next to many of the words on the TBC screens.

In Chapter 2 we spoke about the different circular strategies, based on the R-ladder and the Value Hill. We also highlighted that one of the elements for capturing a circular business model would be to create a mapping of the physical value chain in order to gain clarity on the movements of goods and the required supporting activities. At the beginning of the game, TBC has a straightforward linear set-up, as seen in Figure 6.3.

FIGURE 6.3 TBC's linear value chain

What's wrong with The Blue Connection?

A step-by-step approach to analyse the baseline

As you have seen so far, The Blue Connection is a company that's in big trouble. With your team you enter as the new board of managers with the objective to turn the financial results around and make the company profitable again. This process of turnaround would obviously start with getting a very clear view on the current situation, so that on the basis of your observations you will be in a position to define corrective actions to improve the situation.

EXERCISE 6.1

Analyse the initial situation of The Blue Connection

In the following pages, we present a step-by-step approach for the analysis phase. Besides getting a first view on what needs to be done to change things and become circular, you will also get to know the screens of the simulation, as well as the information you have at your disposal.

Referring back to the section 'Guided tour, web resources and business simulation game' at the beginning of the book, you should use the appropriate course code to enter into the system via the game portal. Initially, focus your efforts on analysing the information corresponding to your own role in the team (sales, design/purchasing, finance, supply chain). This would be valid for Steps 1–2, which you could do individually. Then, in Step 3 you bring your individual observations, conclusions and suggestions together with those of your fellow teammates, so that an integrated approach can be defined. Please note that the information you will find in the reports in the different screens represents the situation of one year of the company's performance.

The three steps as presented in this chapter will help you to establish a thorough understanding of the initial situation in which The Blue Connection finds itself. Please note that all steps can also be applied in exactly the same way after every single round of gameplay, with one important side remark: in the different rounds of gameplay TBC's value chain will no longer be linear, but will be moving to circular. This implies that in addition to the steps below, the elements of circularity will then also need to be analysed. More about that later on in Chapter 7.

Step 1: Create a map of the linear value chain infrastructure and flows

In order to get clarity on the initial linear situation that TBC finds itself in, you may now take a piece of paper, or an empty PowerPoint presentation and make a *network flow mapping* of the material flows of TBC.

FIGURE 6.4 Template TBC's value chain (network view)

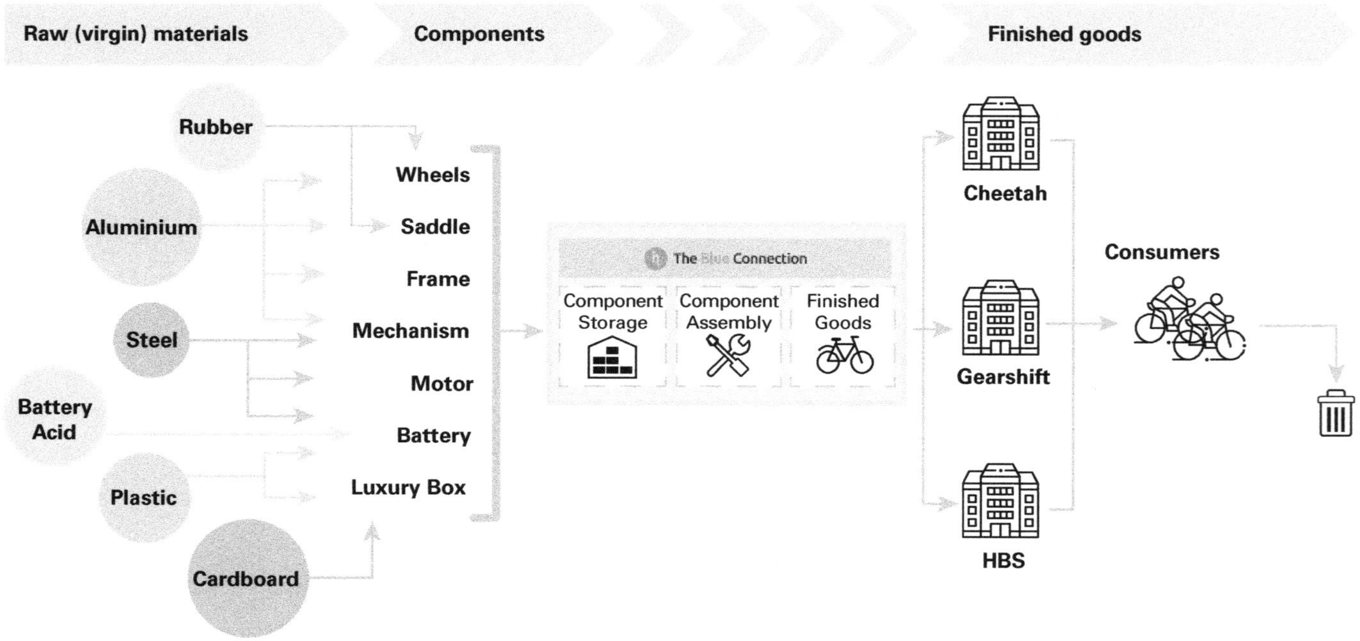

Your mapping should include the following elements:

- six materials, out of which the components are made by the suppliers;
- seven components as purchased from the suppliers by The Blue Connection;
- one final product, an e-Bike called Monsoon;
- three retail customers;
- consumers;
- landfill, in this case representing all of the possible destinations where bikes and/ or their components and/or waste materials may end up.

Your initial mapping should look something like the one in Figure 6.4, as done by Team SuperBike.

Step 2: Populate the mapping with relevant information from TBC's system

In Step 1 we have created the basic flowchart, showing the three different types of physical flows related to the company's linear value chain: flows of raw materials, flows of components and flows of finished goods. In Step 2, each of these three types of flows can now be analysed from three relevant, but very different, perspectives: the number of pieces flowing, the number of kilograms this represents per flow and the amount of money associated to each of these flows. Like in real life, you may need to combine information from different (functional) domains in the company's system in order to create the full view.

For Step 2 of the mapping, you will be mainly using the *basic information tab* as well as the *historical reports* in the domains of each of the functional roles. The information tab contains a lot of very detailed basic information about materials, products, prices and entities in TBC's value chain (see Figure 6.5).

In addition to the information tab, which contains basic information independent from the rounds of gameplay, the historical reports per functional role provide specific historical information about goods flow volumes, financial totals and so on (see Figure 6.6). Historical information contains those reports that change over time, in function of the decisions made by the management team. Since you're only at the beginning of the game, in Step 2 of the analysis you can focus on the reports of Round 0, which is the starting point of the simulation game experience.

To complement the mapping created in Step 1, you can now look into the following information about *pieces*, *kilograms* and *money* (it's advised to work on the basis of one-year totals):[3]

FIGURE 6.5 TBC screen: Information tab

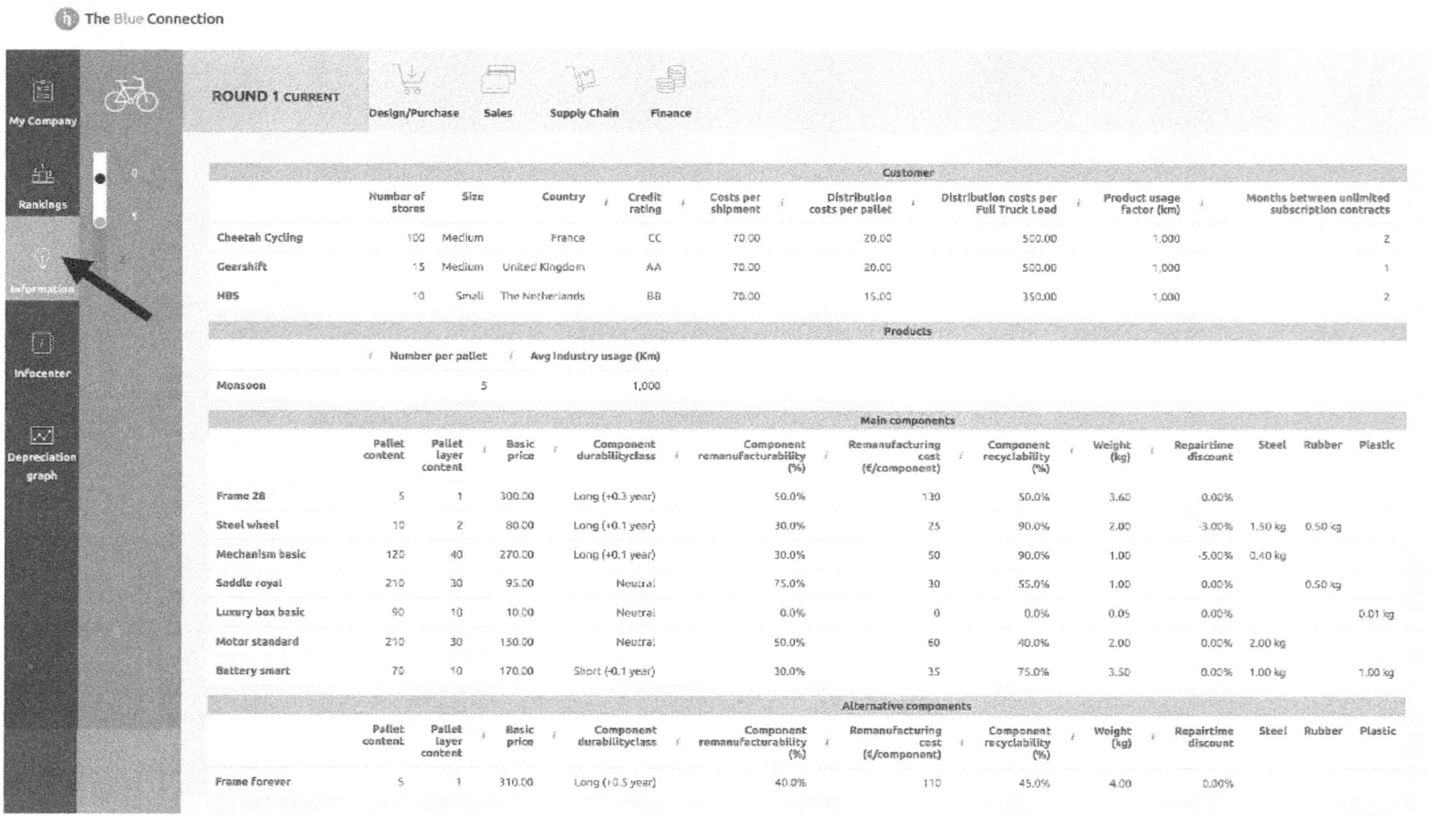

The Blue Connection

ROUND 1 CURRENT | Design/Purchase | Sales | Supply Chain | Finance

My Company
Rankings
Information
Infocenter
Depreciation graph

Customer

	Number of stores	Size	Country	Credit rating	Costs per shipment	Distribution costs per pallet	Distribution costs per Full Truck Load	Product usage factor (km)	Months between unlimited subscription contracts
Cheetah Cycling	100	Medium	France	CC	70.00	20.00	500.00	1,000	2
Geershift	15	Medium	United Kingdom	AA	70.00	20.00	500.00	1,000	1
HBS	10	Small	The Netherlands	BB	70.00	15.00	310.00	1,000	2

	Number per pallet	Avg Industry usage (Km)
Monsoon	5	1,000

Products

Main components

	Pallet content	Pallet layer content	Basic price	Component durability class	Component remanufacturability (%)	Remanufacturing cost (€/component)	Component recyclability (%)	Weight (kg)	Repairtime discount	Steel	Rubber	Plastic
Frame 2B	5	1	300.00	Long (>0.3 year)	50.0%	130	50.0%	3.60	0.00%			
Steel wheel	10	2	80.00	Long (>0.1 year)	30.0%	25	90.0%	2.00	-3.00%	1.50 kg	0.50 kg	
Mechanism basic	120	40	270.00	Long (>0.1 year)	30.0%	50	90.0%	1.00	-5.00%	0.40 kg		
Saddle royal	210	30	95.00	Neutral	75.0%	30	55.0%	1.00	0.00%		0.50 kg	
Luxury box basic	90	10	10.00	Neutral	0.0%	0	0.0%	0.05	0.00%			0.01 kg
Motor standard	210	30	150.00	Neutral	50.0%	60	40.0%	2.00	0.00%	2.00 kg		
Battery smart	70	10	170.00	Short (<0.1 year)	30.0%	35	75.0%	3.50	0.00%	1.00 kg		

Alternative components

	Pallet content	Pallet layer content	Basic price	Component durability class	Component remanufacturability (%)	Remanufacturing cost (€/component)	Component recyclability (%)	Weight (kg)	Repairtime discount	Steel	Rubber	Plastic
Frame Forever	5	1	310.00	Long (>0.5 year)	40.0%	110	45.0%	4.00	0.00%			

FIGURE 6.6 TBC screen: Historical reports per functional role

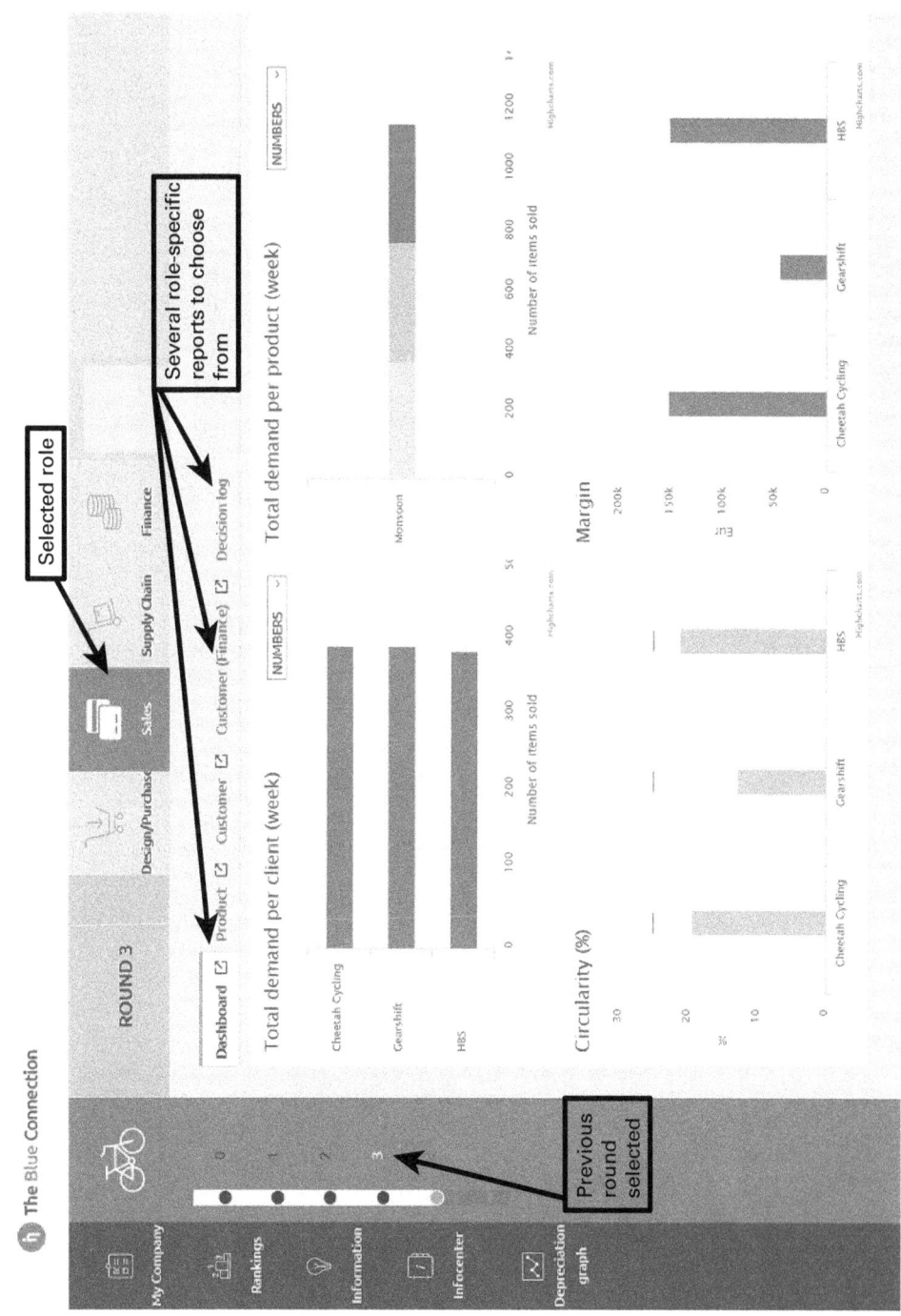

FIGURE 6.7 Mapping enriched with company data (example of small part of map)[4]

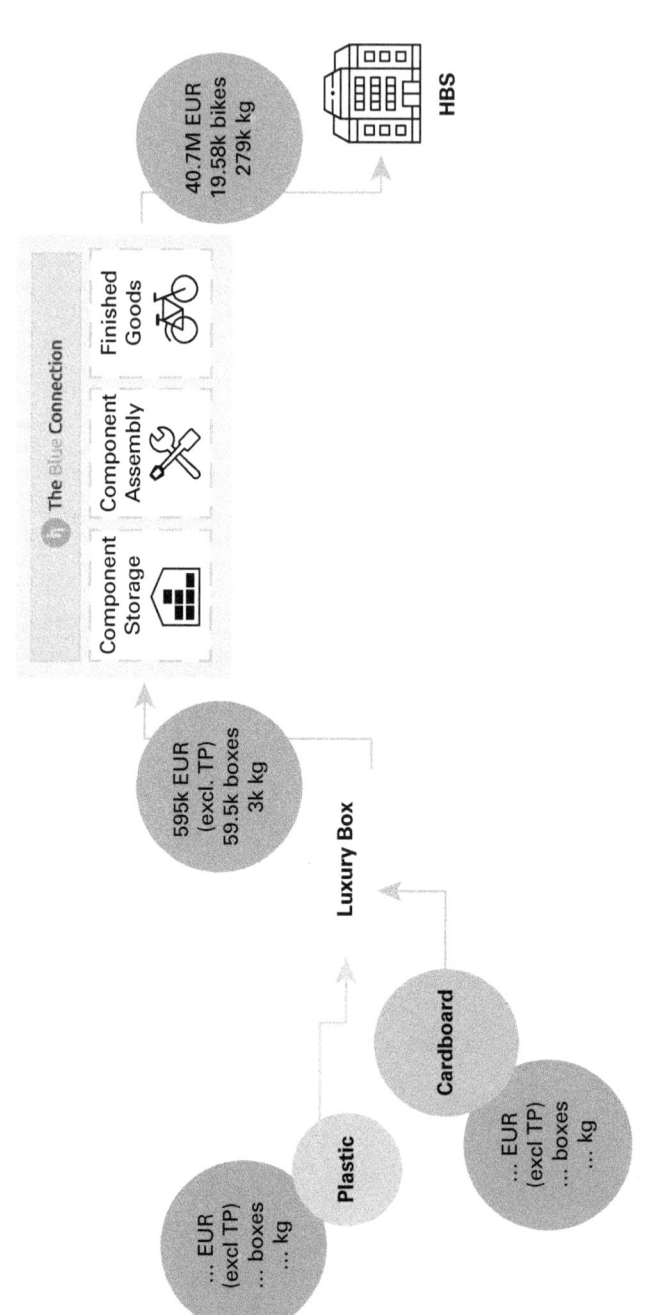

- *Finished goods.* Information can be found in the historical sales reports (the general sales dashboard and the various detailed reports, such as the '*Customer*' and the '*Customer (finance)*' report). Some additional information about the customers as well as the e-Bike can be found in the information tab.

- *Components.* Starting point is the number of bikes sold, which can then be translated into the amount of each of the components needed. Information can be found in the historical design/purchase reports (the general design/purchase dashboard and the various detailed reports, such as the '*Component*' and '*Supplier*' reports). Some additional information about the components can be found in the information tab.

- *Raw materials.* Starting point is the amount of components used, combined with information about the materials these components are made out of. Basic information about the components and the amounts of raw materials needed per component, as well as the basic prices per kilogram of raw material can be found in the information tab. This can then be combined with the quantities of the component flows as analysed in the previous step.

Your map should now be getting filled with information about the number of pieces, the amount of kilograms and the amounts of money flowing in TBC's initial linear value chain (Figure 6.7).

In addition, you may want to check out the historical reports in the Finance domain, where, in the Income Statement and the Financial Position overview, you can find what the major elements of revenue and costs are and the major elements on the balance sheet.

Step 3: Putting the various roles together – creating an integral view

Now bring your individual inputs, observations and suggestions together with those of your colleagues on your team. This will give you a complete and comprehensive insight into the overall performance of the company and potential causes for current losses and, particularly, the order of magnitude of the different flows in the value chain. Go through the map together and gain clarity on each of your observations and highlight, for example with a red colour, all items that catch your attention.

TBC gameplay: what you need to know

Your first analysis of the initial situation of the company has been done and you're almost ready to go, but before going to the company perspective of circularity applied to TBC's value chain, let's first take an additional look at TBC gameplay.

Normally, you would be participating in a game in which different teams from the same school, university or company play together in the same pool of gameplay. The exact configuration of the game, meaning which decisions can be taken in which round, has been decided upon by the course instructor, taking into consideration the exact learning objectives of the course in which the game is used.

There is a wide variety of possibilities for course set-ups. Sometimes the game is played 100 per cent face to face, with the active presence of the course instructor in terms of explaining concepts and being available to answer teams' questions. Sometimes the game is played 100 per cent online, with the instructor being available at given times to give feedback and/or clarify doubts. Also, more and more blended formats can be found. Again, the decision about how to set up a course using TBC is a choice by the course instructor depending on available time and the course's learning objectives and would normally be communicated to you prior to the start of the course or programme.

Whichever the format chosen, the sequence of activities is normally quite similar, pretty much following the learning cycle of Kolb as discussed previously in the Preface:

1 profound analysis by the team of the current situation;

2 decision making and implementation of decisions in the simulation;

3 closing of the round by the instructor in order to calculate results;

4 reflection on the results of the round just played, typically complemented by some exercises in order to 'conceptualize' the reflections;

5 back to Step 1, profound analysis, now for the next round.

Please note that there are certain parallels between the steps above and the steps normally performed according to frameworks of continuous improvement, such as CAPD (check-act-plan-do). The main, but important, difference lies in Step 4, in which explicit reflection takes place with the aim of analysing relationships between causes and effects, as well as the players' own actions. This step invites you to take a step back from the immersion in the gameplay and look at what has actually happened, from a distance so to speak. If well done, this should boost learning based on a much deeper understanding of the factors at play.

Depending on the exact size of the group of participants in a course, it is common for course instructors to request you to prepare your thoughts on the reflections and conceptualizations and send them in for feedback. Remember, it is in those reflections and the translation of them into new decision-making that the real learning takes place.

A few words on decision-making in the business simulation. For each of the roles, there are one or more different tabs each representing a different part of the

FIGURE 6.8 TBC screen: Negotiation window (example from sales role)

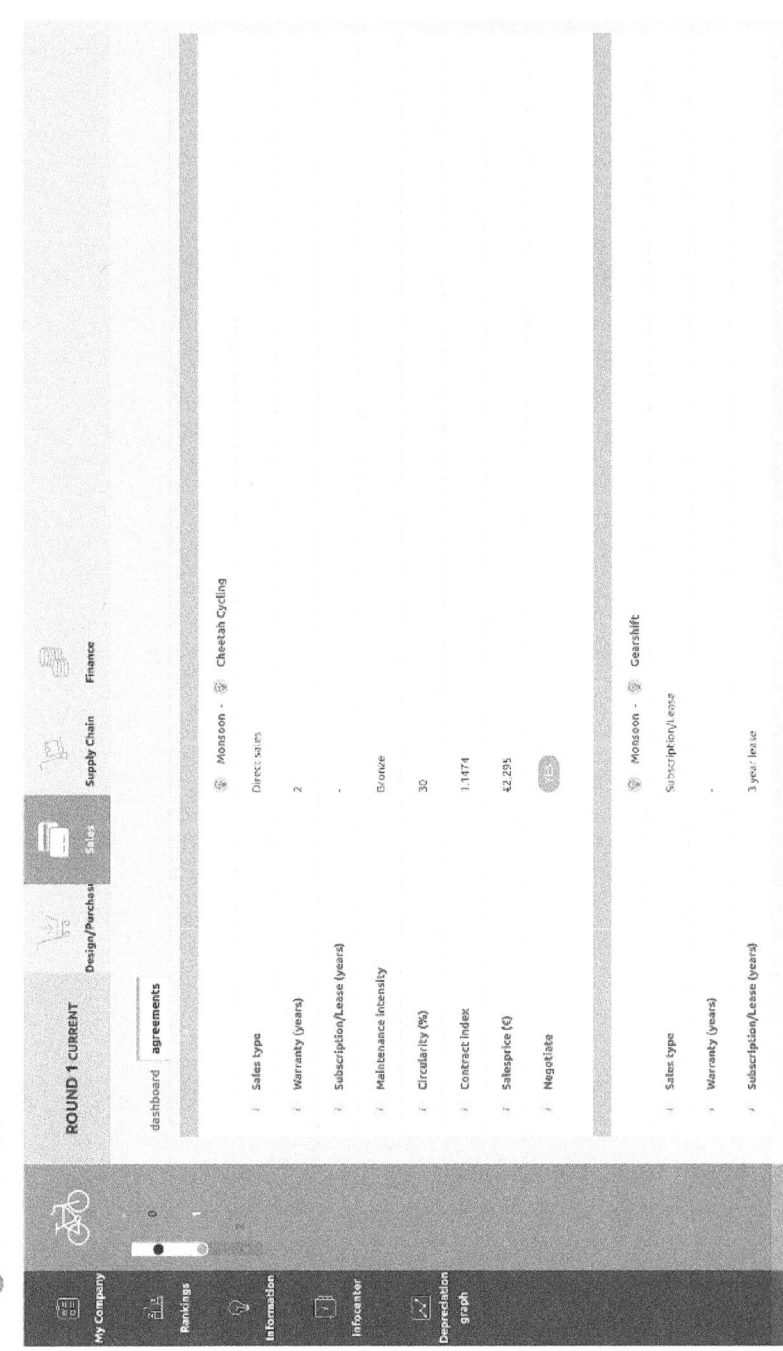

functional scope for which decisions need to be made, so in case you have more than one tab, please make sure you address the various decisions on each of the tabs corresponding to your role. Basically, on each of those tabs one or more parameters need to be defined, potentially changed and then saved by clicking on the 'save' button or 'deal' button, depending on the role. Decisions (parameter changes) that haven't been explicitly saved will not have been implemented, so please make sure to check carefully if indeed your decisions have been saved. Please note that in the following pages and chapters a number of screens from the game will be shown, but on some occasions in a slightly 'stylized' way. These screens are shown to illustrate relevant concepts, but they have been stylized in order to cater to the possibility of design changes which might take place on the real screens in the game.

In the roles of Sales and Finance, there are decisions which arise out of negotiations with retailers and banks, respectively. In Sales, negotiation takes place individually with each retailer. In order to start a negotiation, the corresponding Vice President only has to click the 'yes' button in the agreement screen of a particular retailer or bank in order to access the negotiation screen. In the negotiation screen, the negotiable contract parameters can be seen, as well as the *resulting final price*, in the case of negotiations with retail customers in Sales, or *resulting base interest rate*, in the case of negotiations with a bank in Finance (see Figure 6.8).

If the change of a certain contract parameter is considered, it can be changed in the corresponding field in the negotiation screen and then, by clicking on the 'calculate' button, the new price/interest rate will be shown, so that the difference in price becomes clear. If the new price is acceptable, clicking the 'deal' implements it.

Two more comments before we go to the real gameplay. First, be aware that in the case of all four of the roles, all decisions can be undone, changed, redone, etc, as many times as you want during the gameplay of one round. Those parameters that are set at the moment of closing a round for calculation are the ones that will effectively go into the calculation of the results of the round. Secondly, please note that if you play as part of a course in a school, university or company training, your course instructor will typically guide you during those rounds of gameplay and assist in defining the focus for each round. The exercises within each of the chapters will be of help. Like in real life, the company continues and decisions will have to be updated and made constantly, adjusting to previous results. Catherine McLaren, the Circular Turnaround Manager at The Blue Connection introduced to you before, will be giving you almost unlimited autonomy to take decisions. Of course, at some point in time, she will be back to ask you about the progress made.

Summary

CHALLENGE DAY 1, RIGHT AFTER FINISHING THE INITIAL ANALYSIS

'Oh, wow!' Sarah said, looking a bit concerned. 'This looks way more complex than I thought! And we have only looked at the current linear value chain yet... Imagine how complicated it will become once we start introducing circularity.'

'Don't worry, Sarah,' Peter responded, 'we'll surely get a grip on the situation as soon as we start playing, because then we will see the relation between our own decisions and our own results. At least we now know The Blue Connection in much more detail and we have a clearer view on the problems they are having. Just give it some time, you cannot expect to turn a company around in one day!'

'I agree,' Maria added, 'and what we should also do is what Aunt Joanna suggested. That we keep the points Peter and I looked at in our Project 'Circularity' at hand during gameplay. You know, all of those aspects of the company perspective, the leadership perspective and the perspective beyond the company boundary that we studied in detail before. In the end, those points will help us stay focused.'

'Sounds great, let's do that,' Matthew nodded in agreement. 'OK, on to Round 1, then,' said Sarah. 'Let's go Team SuperBike!'

EXERCISE 6.2
Reflect on the way of working as a team during gameplay

Reflect

As a team you have now done your first analysis of the situation and you have your first conclusions about the current state of the company and its linear value chain. Similar to Steps 1–3 followed in this chapter, the analysis and decision-making around most of the topics in the following chapters (particularly Chapter 7) will be recurring and to be repeated every round of gameplay, taking the results of the previous round into consideration while preparing decisions for the next round. Therefore, it is also important to reflect upfront how you will organize yourselves as a team during the gameplay, when normally some more time pressure is there as well. Take some time to do that now.

Notes

1 In the case you use the book for self-study, please refer to the section about 'Access to The Blue Connection' as part of 'Structure of the book'.

2 The indicator of ROM was developed by Inchainge, the company behind The Blue Connection business simulation. ROM is inspired by the WBCSD's 'value the loop' indicator, part of their CTI (see Chapter 4, Figure 4.6). Remember that *virgin material*, or *linear inflow*, was defined in Chapter 1 as newly created raw material and used as so-called feedstock into the production process and thus seen as an input to be minimized.

3 Populating the map with the numbers is fairly straightforward. The numbers you're looking for can either be found directly in the information tab or in the reports, as mentioned below, or they can be calculated on the basis of the information found. For example: the number of wheels per year is number of bikes per year * amount of wheels per bike. The amount of kilograms of wheels = number of wheels per year * weight per wheel. The amount of money per year spent on wheels = amount of wheels per year * basic price per wheel.

4 Please note that names and quantities in the diagram might be different in the version of TBC you will be using.

07

Mastering the company perspective of circularity

PROJECT 'CIRCULARITY', PHASE 2: SIMULATION CHALLENGE DAY 1, ROUND 1 IS ABOUT TO BEGIN!

FIGURE 7.1 Towards Round 1 of gameplay

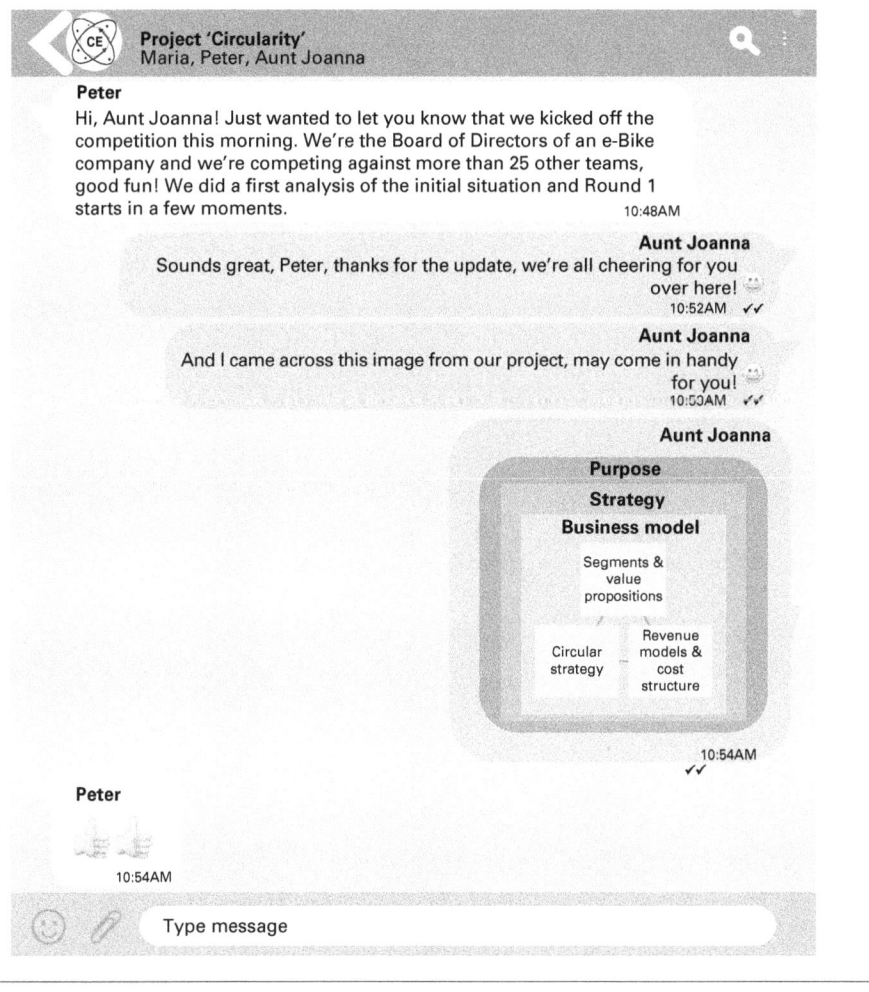

FIGURE 7.2   Topics from the company perspective of circularity applied to TBC

In this chapter we will go back to the main topics of Chapter 2: Exploring the company perspective of circularity, and we will directly apply those to The Blue Connection (TBC) so that you can get some real first-hand experience with the complexities involved. Rather than presenting extensive text here, we will do this through a number of practical exercises related to the gameplay.

Before diving into the details of elaborating specific circular business models, let's first look at the decision-making process in the game.

Decisions, inputs, installed base and decision support tools

Decisions

Like in a real company, in TBC decisions have to be made by the people who work there (you in this case!). And like in a real company, decisions are distributed over the various specialized functional departments. So each department has its own decisions to make and between the departments you have to manage how best to align the decisions in order to optimize the overall result you want to achieve.

In the basic version of TBC, Figure 7.3 shows the decisions to be made per department.

Inputs

Which inputs can you use for the decision making? Some of these sources of information you have seen already during the mapping exercise in the previous chapter: the information tab and the historical reports. To this we can add the decision log, especially if you have already played one or more rounds. The decision log can be found in the pages of the historical reports and in the log you can find the decisions made in past rounds.

Another input obviously is your own thinking: part of your task is to evaluate which circular business model you want to pursue and which decisions correspond to that business model. More about that in the following sections of the chapter.

The concept of 'installed base'

As you will see in gameplay, there is a very important concept related to the quantification of the circular business cases; this concept is often referred to as the 'installed base'. Other terms used in this context are 'pool' or 'pipeline'. For the sake of argument, here we will use installed base as the preferred term.

The installed base indicates how many products, bikes in the case of TBC, we have 'out there' in the market in a given moment. In any round of gameplay, you will always find TBC in a stable situation, in other words you will not have to worry about the transition period the company will have to go through until reaching a new stable situation. More about this transition will follow in the next section. So the installed base is the number of bikes out there in the market. This number is very relevant, because it is an input to a number of important calculations.

For example, if you would consider selling a maintenance service package together with the bike on the basis of one yearly service per bike, then the number of bikes sold per year is not enough for you to know how much maintenance service capacity you would need to put in place. Because unless specified differently, the maintenance service will be valid for the entire lifespan of the bike. In other words, you need sufficient capacity to service all of the bikes 'out there' with a service contract: the number of bikes per year sold with a maintenance package * average lifespan in years of a bike then gives you the total size of the installed base (Figure 7.4).

FIGURE 7.3 Decisions per role (TBC standard version)

	Sales	Purchasing	Finance	Supply Chain
1	• Circularity promise to retailer • Maintenance intensity • Warranty	• Product Design/supplier selection	• Circularity promise to bank	• Maintenance capacity
2			• Buy-back price	• Refurbishment bike age • Refurbishment bike capacity
3				• Recycle/remanufacture yes/no • RSP selection
4	• Lease or subscription		• Vendor lease contract	

Please note that it may be the case that your course instructor decides to deviate from this standard version or include additional decisions for one or more of the roles. Also, it may be that your instructor decides not to have all decisions active from the very beginning of the game, but that these are introduced gradually over the various rounds of gameplay.

FIGURE 7.4   The concept of installed base

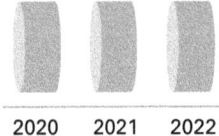

10,000 bikes sold per year, start of sales in 2020, average lifespan of a bike is 3 years installed base in 2022 = ... bikes?

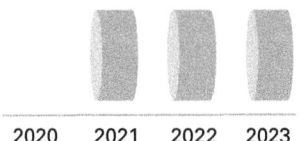

10,000 bikes sold per year, start of sales in 2020, average lifespan of a bike is 3 years, so bikes sold in 2020 are no longer 'active' in 2023 installed base in 2023 = ... bikes?

2020   2021   2022

2020   2021   2022   2023

The same concept of installed base is, for example, also valid in the case of considering offering a lease contract of a certain duration. In the case of TBC, such a lease contract will be financed 'off-balance': a so-called vendor lease agreement with a bank will have to be made. The question is of course how much vendor lease will have to be negotiated with the bank. Again, that depends on the size of the installed base. For example in the case of a three-year lease duration, the total installed base will be the amount of new bike lease contracts per year * the lease duration in years.

The concept of 'transition period'

Building further on the concept of installed base, you can imagine that in the moment when we decide to start with the introduction of something new we will need some time before that new implementation reaches a stable situation: first we have to go through a transition period. For example, if we introduce a three-year leasing scheme, then in the first year we will add a number of newly leased bikes into that scheme. In the second year, more bikes will enter and the same in the third year. In other words, during the first years, every year we will have a larger installed base. But then, in the fourth year, once again more new bikes will enter, but at the same time the lease contracts of year 1 will expire, so those bikes will disappear from the installed base and we will enter into the new stable situation.

Please note: although in TBC gameplay the reports in every round reflect one-year totals, **going to the next round is not the same as going to the next year!** In the game, going from one round to the next round means going from the 'old' stable situation to the 'new' stable situation. In other words, *the game opens again after the transition period has effectively already taken place.*

FIGURE 7.5   The concept of 'transition period'

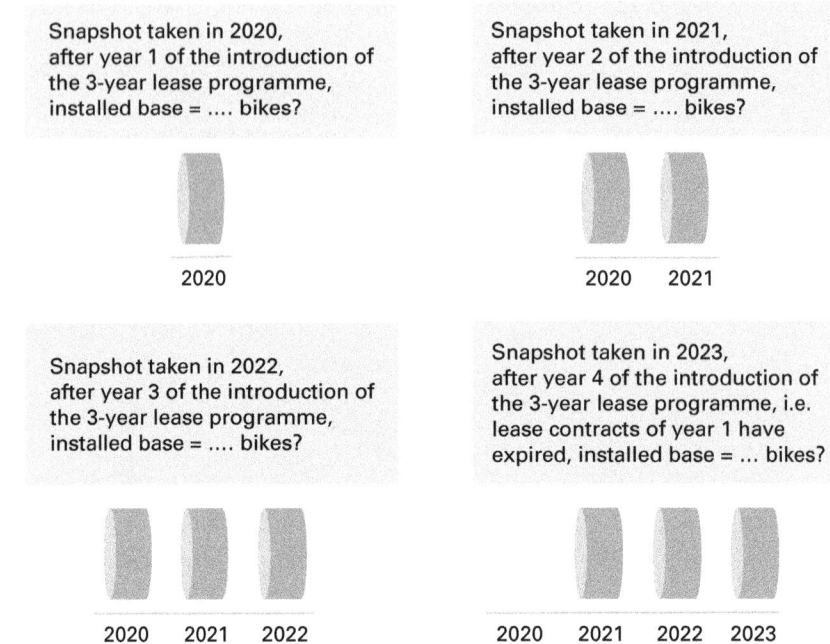

The transition period in all of its dimensions and complexities will be the main topic of Part Three of the book, so we will come back extensively to that once gameplay has finished. For the moment you don't have to worry about what happens during that period.

Decision support tool: the depreciation graph

Luckily for you, TBC has invested in a very useful decision support tool, called the *depreciation graph*. It can be found on the screen under the tab of the same name. The depreciation graph is in fact based on financial theory related to the circular economy (Steeman, 2017) in which it is argued that the economic logic of usage of a product, component or material depends ultimately on its value. At the moment of selling, a new product has a market value, which over time gradually decreases until at a certain moment in time the market value of its components is higher than the market value of the entire product. Economic logic then suggests that preference should be given to use of the components rather than still focusing on the entire product. A similar logic can be observed at some point later in time when the value of the materials is higher than the remaining value of the components (Figure 7.6).

FIGURE 7.6   Depreciation graph

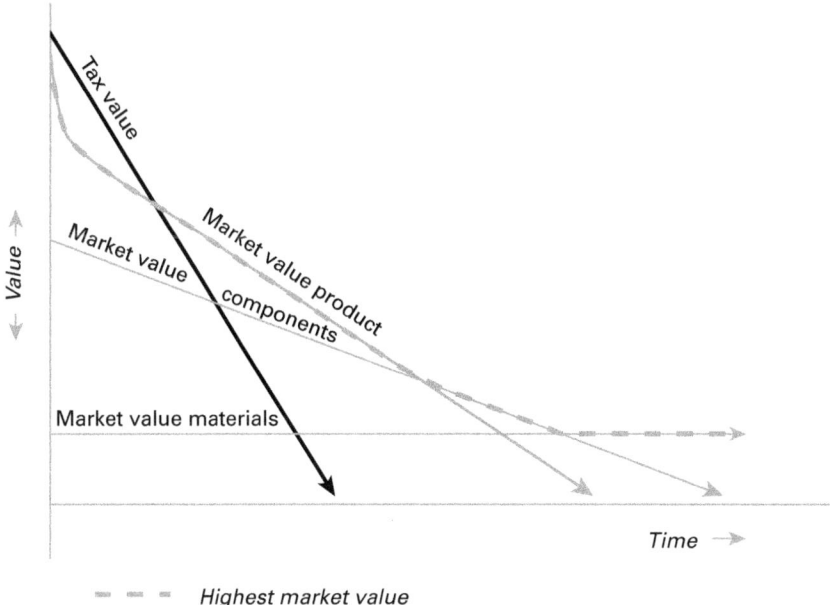

        ‑ ‑ ‑   *Highest market value*

SOURCE Steeman (2017)

As said, TBC has invested in a decision support tool based on the concept of the depreciation graph. This decision support tool is configured in such a way that when in TBC's system a parameter is changed that would have an impact on the information in the depreciation graph, the graph changes as a consequence. This change can then be analysed before a more informed final decision can be made.

EXERCISE 7.1
Using the depreciation graph

Develop

Develop an understanding of how the depreciation graph works. Preferably you do this with the entire team. First of all this will allow each team member to gain a deep understanding of how the depreciation graph works and secondly, doing the exercise together avoids different team members changing parameters at the same time that all have an impact on the same depreciation graph.

In the following steps, you are asked to implement a number of decisions for the sake of better understanding the depreciation graph. Don't worry too much about the changed decisions, these can all be undone without any penalty before you really start playing.

For example, choose one of your retailers and take a good look at the depreciation graph that corresponds to them. You may want to take a screenshot of the graph as a reference. Then ask the sales director of the team to go to the sales agreements page, click on the 'negotiate' button for the chosen retailer, change the 'maintenance intensity' from 'no maintenance' to 'gold' (which is the highest intensity programme), then click on 'calculate' and then on 'deal' (don't worry for the moment about the negotiation itself).

Now return to the depreciation graph that corresponds to the retailer and check it out. What has changed if you compare it with the initial one? Why has it changed? What does this tell you that can be useful during decision making?

Now go back to the sales agreement page, enter the negotiation, change the maintenance intensity back to 'no maintenance' and click 'calculate' and then 'deal' again. Now the settings are back to the initial ones.

You can apply the same logic for the following decisions (one by one and not all at the same time!): look at the depreciation graph, then implement the decision, then go back to the depreciation graph and analyse what has changed and try to understand why, then go back and undo the decision so that you're back to the initial situation:

- Sales (agreements tab): negotiate a five-year warranty with one of your retailers.

- Finance (buyback tab): implement a buyback price of €1,200.

- Design/purchasing (product design tab): change the frame from the standard frame to the alternative with the highest durability class.

After the analysis, make sure you put the parameters back into the initial values, unless you are already playing a round of gameplay, then you can obviously decide to leave the parameters as you want them for the coming round.

Hopefully, this exercise has given you a good understanding of how to use the depreciation graph decision support tool to your advantage during the gameplay. That now brings us back to the topics from Chapter 2, so let's put these topics into the practice of TBC.

Purpose

Chapter 2 started with a thorough elaboration of the topic of 'Purpose' as a powerful guiding principle for company strategy. Let's see how this would work out for The Blue Connection.

EXERCISE 7.2
Decide on a purpose statement for TBC

Decide

On the basis of your exploration of purpose statements in Chapter 2, now decide for yourself on a powerful purpose statement for The Blue Connection. Add your purpose statement to the template from Figure 7.7. Be prepared to present and discuss.

Strategy

Strategy was also discussed very briefly in Chapter 2 and it was defined as a plan related to the long term, containing the objectives a company wants to achieve, as well as the actions required to achieve those objectives. Although strategy in itself as a concept is of course not exclusively related to circularity, let's for the moment assume that we want circularity to be an explicit part of TBC's future strategy.

EXERCISE 7.3
Decide on strategic objectives related to circularity for TBC

Decide

Taking your purpose statement as the main starting point, now decide on a number of clear objectives towards circularity for The Blue Connection. Although there is no need yet to 'translate' those objectives into specific Key Performance Indicators and accompanying targets, please make sure that the objectives are clear enough to provide direction for actions to be defined later. Add your strategic objectives to the template from Figure 7.7. Be prepared to present and discuss.

On the basis of your purpose statement and the strategic objectives for circularity you have decided on, you should now be in the position to start elaborating the details for your circular business model. Figure 7.8 shows the template highlighting the elements we suggested for capturing a circular business model with all relevant details (see Figure 2.26 for a slightly more elaborated example).

In Exercises 7.4–7.11, you will subsequently touch upon the topics needed to fill the entire template from Figure 7.8. After finishing Exercise 7.11 you should then be in the position to present your entire strategic plan, combining the templates from Figures 7.7 and 7.8.

FIGURE 7.7 Template for capturing purpose, strategy and KPIs

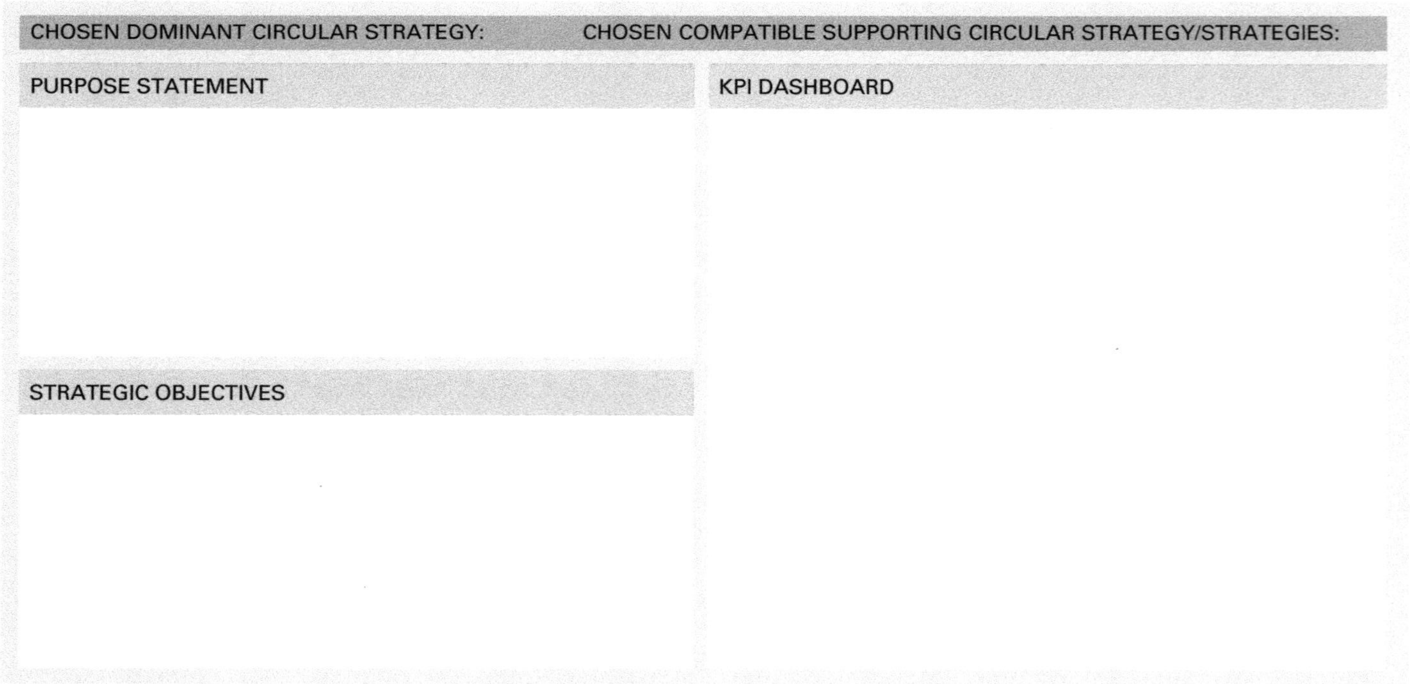

CHOSEN DOMINANT CIRCULAR STRATEGY:	CHOSEN COMPATIBLE SUPPORTING CIRCULAR STRATEGY/STRATEGIES:
PURPOSE STATEMENT	KPI DASHBOARD
STRATEGIC OBJECTIVES	

FIGURE 7.8 Items to be included for capturing a circular business model (empty template)

CHOSEN DOMINANT CIRCULAR STRATEGY:

CHOSEN COMPATIBLE SUPPORTING CIRCULAR STRATEGY/STRATEGIES:

BUSINESS MODEL OVERVIEW

MAPPING OF PHYSICAL FLOWS AND SUPPORTING ACTIVITIES

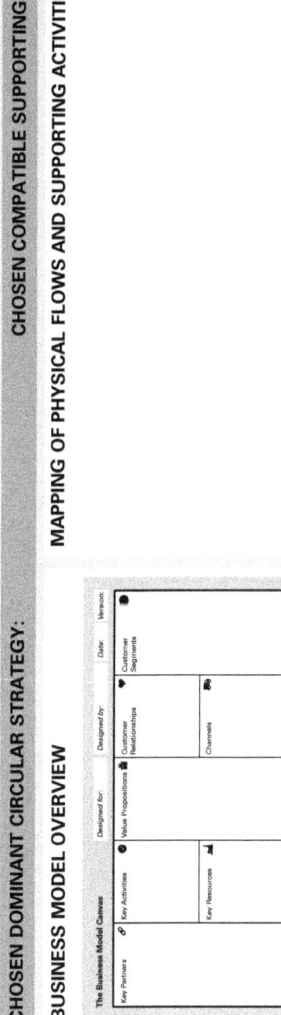

OVERVIEW OF REVENUE MODELS, MECHANISMS TO MONETIZE CIRCULARITY AND COSTS

REVENUE MODEL PER SEGMENT:

MECHANISMS TO MONETIZE CIRCULARITY:

- Segment 1:
- Segment 2:
- Segment 3:

NEWLY INTRODUCED COST ITEMS

NEWLY INTRODUCED SAVINGS

SOURCES USED:
ASSUMPTIONS MADE:

FIGURE 7.9   Circular strategies in TBC

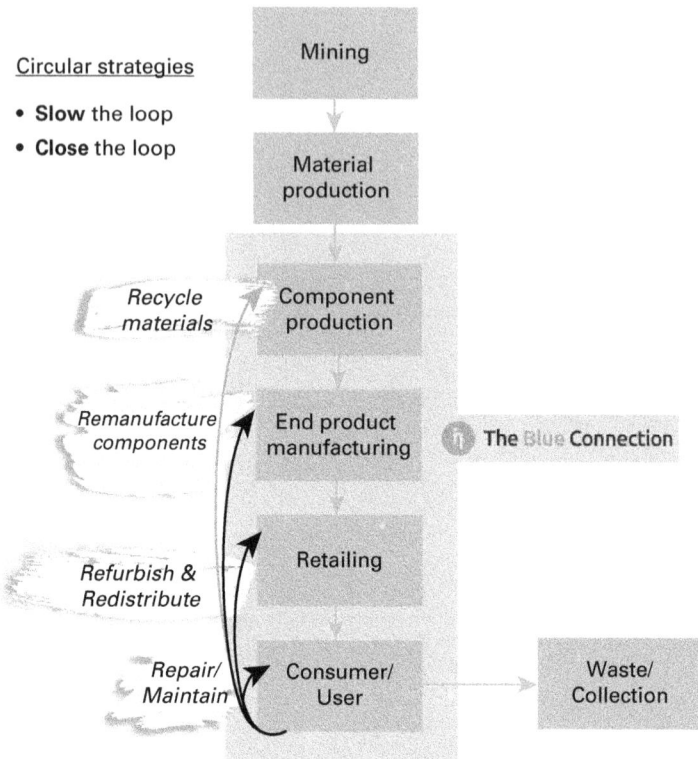

Please note that the template in Figure 7.8 captures the circular business model **of one dominant circular strategy**, plus the potentially compatible supporting circular strategies. If during gameplay you will be trying out different dominant circular strategies in subsequent rounds, either by your own choice or by indication of your course lecturer or trainer, then the template can be (re-)created once more for each dominant strategy.

In TBC the focus is on slow the loop and close the loop circular strategies (Stage 2 and Stage 3 as explained in Chapter 2): repair and maintain, refurbish and redistribute, remanufacture components and reuse, recycle materials. The basic circular strategy choices in TBC are shown in Figure 7.9.

Let's take a look at each of the areas in the template.

Business Model Canvas

Here you can add the standard Business Model Canvas, or any other (sustainability- or circularity-oriented) variation if you prefer.

EXERCISE 7.4
Develop a Business Model Canvas

Develop

On the basis of the chosen canvas or other business model template of your preference, develop a schematic overview of the circular business model, focusing on the dominant circular strategy and potentially supporting circular strategy or strategies you have chosen. Referring to the standard Business Model Canvas, you may include the revenue models in the definition of the value propositions. Add your business model to the template from Figure 7.8 and document any possible back-up materials to support your choices. Be prepared to present and discuss.

Circular strategies: mapping

Next in the template is the mapping of the physical goods flows and the corresponding supporting activities in the circular value chain, like it was done in Chapter 6 for the initial linear value chain of The Blue Connection.

EXERCISE 7.5
Develop a mapping of your circular strategy

Develop

The combined optional goods flows and supporting activities in the case of TBC can be seen in Figure 7.10 (please note that the diagram may include some flows that may not be very compatible).

On the basis of your chosen dominant circular strategy and the potential supporting circular strategies you are considering including, develop a mapping of the physical goods flows and the corresponding supporting activities in the circular value chain. Populate the mapping with numbers from the simulation (amounts in units, amounts in kilograms, amounts in money). You can use the basic information from the game, as well as the historical reports and the main assumptions underlying the simulation. Remember that you can also use the depreciation graph for assessing, for example, the number of bikes out there in the market, or the number of bikes coming back to you in an average year, for example due to the buyback price you implemented. Add your mapping to the template from Figure 7.8 and document any possible back-up materials to support your choices.

FIGURE 7.10   Possible physical flows and supporting activities in TBC

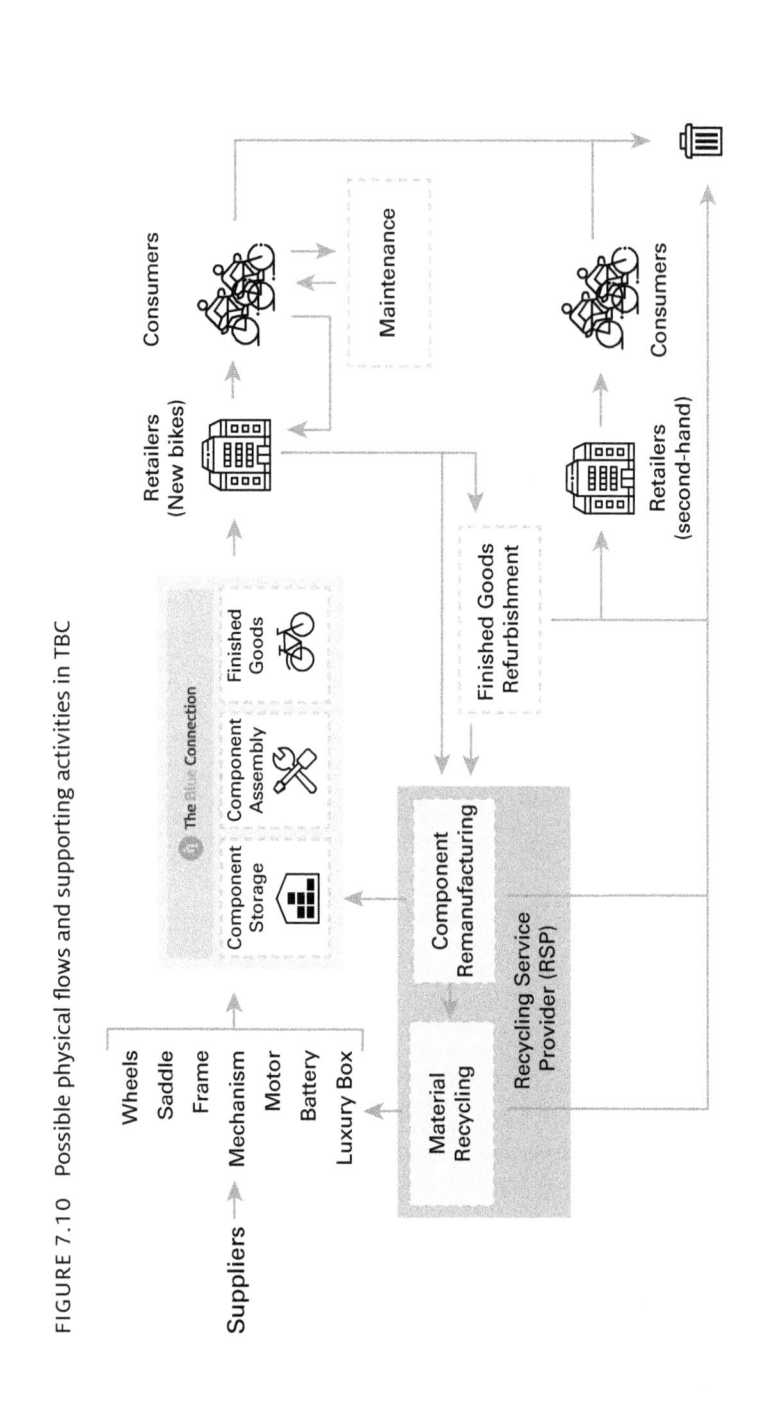

You can take this image as a basis for selecting the flows and activities which correspond to your chosen dominant circular strategy and any potential compatible supporting circular strategies.

Segments and revenue models

TBC has three different retailers as customers: Cheetah, Gearshift and HBS. In a way you could say that each of them can be seen as a representation of very different customer segments. So, the first thing to look into is to what extent they are in fact different in terms of consumers they deal with, preferences they may have for certain aspects of TBC's product or additional elements of the value proposition.

In terms of revenue models, the following options exist (some are compatible, some are not):

- Direct sales.
- Warranty, leading to additional revenue.
- Maintenance intensity (different packages), leading to additional revenue.
- Subscription (indefinite time period).[1]
- Lease (duration to be specified upfront).

EXERCISE 7.6
Analyse TBC's retail customers

Analyse

Go into the agreements tab in the Sales domain and find out more about your three retail customers. You can do this by first clicking on the lightbulb symbol next to the name of each of the customers. What do the descriptions tell you and how could you use this information to your benefit? Which differentiation in terms of value propositions can you foresee?

In the negotiation about the sales agreement, most contract terms are dealing with revenue models. With each retailer you negotiate the same items as part of the contract agreement, but the optimal value of these items can be very different between the different retailers, because they may have very different preferences. To what extent they are very happy or less so with a certain condition in the contract can be deduced from the price they are willing to pay, as explained in Chapter 6.

One by one, for each of the retailers, open up the negotiation and change one of the contract parameters, calculate the new sales price and evaluate how much the price has changed. Focus for the moment on the various revenue models, leaving the circularity promise (%) aside. We will deal with that separately afterwards.

You may do this a number of times with different values for the same parameter and then move on to another parameter. To which contract parameter is each retailer more sensitive or less sensitive? How are the retailers similar or different in this aspect – are they all equally sensitive to the same parameters or not? How can you explain the differences in sensitivities based on the description of the target audience of the different retailers? What does this imply for the value proposition you would offer to each of them? Which focus could you apply? Add your findings and subsequent choices to the template from Figure 7.8 and document any possible back-up materials to support your choices.

Mechanisms to monetize circularity: additional revenue

'Circularity premium'

The basic revenue models towards the retailers are in principle independent to circularity. On top of those revenue models, there are ways to effectively monetize the obtained circularity.[2] First of all, there are retailers and consumers who are willing to pay a certain premium on the basic price of a product if a certain degree of circularity can be demonstrated, similar to people willing to pay higher prices for Fairtrade products, bio-organic products and so on. TBC also has retailers as customers who are sensitive to circularity to some degree.

EXERCISE 7.7
Analyse TBC's retail customers' sensitivity to circularity

Analyse

Go into the agreements tab in the Sales domain and open the negotiation about the sales agreement. Now one by one for each of the retailers, change the circularity promise (%) and evaluate the sensitivity of each of the retailers towards circularity. How are the retailers similar or different in this aspect – are they all equally sensitive to circularity? What does this imply for the value proposition you would offer to each of them? Which focus could you apply? Add your findings and choices to the template in Figure 7.8 and document any back-up materials to support your choices.

Please note: if you don't deliver on your circularity promise, the corresponding retailer(s) will give you a (high) penalty for it, outweighing the extra revenue they were willing to pay you on the basis of the promise.

In a similar fashion, there can also be a circularity premium with banks, but since this is not an additional revenue but a discount, we will deal with this bank-related premium under the heading of cost savings later on.

Sales to the second-hand market

In addition to the circularity premium there are also other ways to monetize circularity. One way is to exploit the option of reselling refurbished bikes to the second-hand market. The financial potential of this option depends on a number of different factors and the depreciation graph plays an important role in the evaluation, as explained in the steps below:

1 First of all, you can only refurbish bikes if you can actually get them back from the market. This can be achieved through offering warranty or buyback options in the case of a direct sales model, or by working on the basis of subscription or leasing schemes, in which case the bikes remain the property of TBC and you get them back at the end of the lease contract period (lease) or at the end of the lifespan (subscription).

2 Secondly, how many bikes you effectively get back due to warranty and/or buyback depends on the quality of the bike (only broken bikes can apply for warranty) or on the amount of money offered for the buyback (the higher the amount, the more likely it is that consumers are interested in returning the bikes).

EXERCISE 7.8
Analyse monetization potential of reselling refurbished bikes
to the second-hand market

Analyse

For your chosen dominant circular strategy, analyse how much monetization potential you have for reselling refurbished bikes to the second-hand market by applying the two steps mentioned above. Please note that you may want to revisit Exercise 7.1 about the workings of the depreciation graph. Furthermore, you can use Figure 7.10 during your analysis, especially if you populate the chart with the corresponding volumes per each of the relevant goods flows. Add your findings and choices to the template in Figure 7.8 and document any back-up materials to support your choices.

Selling recycled materials back to the suppliers

A last option to monetize circularity is related to recycled materials, of course only in the case that you have effectively opted for recycling as your dominant circular strategy or as a supporting strategy. A number of factors play a role here, which should be analysed step by step (referring back also to the flow diagram in Figure 7.10):

1 First you need to analyse the size of the material flow that will ultimately reach your Recycling Service Provider (RSP) in order to be recycled. As you can observe in Figure 7.10, there are two possible material flows into your RSP: a direct flow of returned bikes from the market or a waste stream of unrefurbishable bikes or components coming out of the bike refurbishment activity. The parameter of *maximum refurbishment age* as set by the Supply Chain Manager defines until what age a returned bike will either first go to refurbishment, or go directly into the RSP. As we have seen before when discussing the monetization option of the second-hand market, the total size of the flow of returned bikes depends on the decisions made about warranty in combination with the bike's quality, any buyback option or leasing and/or subscription.

2 On the basis of the size of the flows coming into the RSP, it then depends on the decision of whether you want the recycling to be the main focus of the RSP or a secondary option only to be applied to the waste stream of the remanufacturing process. Your chosen dominant circular strategy should be leading in this, but specific component and material characteristics also play a role (remanufacturability of the components you use, recyclability of the materials that these components are made of). You can therefore decide component by component if you want your RSP to focus on remanufacturing or recycling.

3 Depending on the decisions you have made about the parameters mentioned in the previous steps, you will then need to analyse how many kilograms of effectively recycled materials you will have at the end and which can be sold back to the corresponding supplier.

EXERCISE 7.9
Analyse monetization potential of selling recycled materials back
to the suppliers

Analyse

Follow the three steps mentioned above and within the specific context of your chosen dominant circular strategy and analyse how much monetization potential you have for selling recycled materials back to your suppliers. Please note that you can use Figure 7.10 during your analysis, especially if you populate the chart with the corresponding volumes per each of the relevant goods flows. Add your findings and choices to the template in Figure 7.8 and document any back-up materials to support your choices.

Mechanisms to monetize circularity: savings potential

Savings in purchasing due to remanufacturing of components

There can also be a saving in purchasing which is not connected to the type of components purchased. If you have decided on remanufacturing as a dominant or supporting circular strategy, then those components that can be successfully remanufactured will flow back into TBC's own assembly process of new bikes; in other words, this quantity of components does not have to be purchased from external suppliers anymore, thus representing a saving.

Savings due to circularity premium with the bank

As we discussed in Chapter 2, more and more 'green financing' alternatives are appearing in the financial markets. Also TBC's bank is sensitive to sustainability-driven initiatives by its clients, meaning that it's willing to apply more attractive (read: lower) interest rates to their loans, based on the circularity percentage they promise.

Please note: if you don't deliver on your circularity promise, the bank will give you a penalty, outweighing the extra discount they were willing to allow you on the basis of your promise.

EXERCISE 7.10
Analyse potential savings

Analyse

For your chosen dominant circular strategy, analyse how much you could expect in terms of additional savings mentioned above. Please note that you can use Figure 7.10 during your analysis, especially if you populate the chart with the corresponding volumes per each of the relevant goods flows (particularly for analysing savings potential due to purchasing of remanufactured components). Add your findings and choices to the template in Figure 7.8 and document any back-up materials to support your choices.

Cost structure: newly introduced costs

Circularity is of course not only a potential source of additional revenue or monetization options – there are also costs and potential savings associated to it. Let's look at a number of these. Keep in mind that all depends on your chosen dominant circular strategy and any potential compatible supporting strategies you may have chosen to apply.

Maintenance

First of all, there is the potential extra cost of the maintenance activity. It has been TBC's choice to carry out this maintenance internally with staff. The amount of associated costs depends first of all on the chosen maintenance intensity, i.e. the amount of services per year per bike. As you remember, you can decide the maintenance intensity per customer, so they can be different from each other. Second, we need to know how much a bike is used per year on average. This number can be found in the information page. Third, we need to take the size of the installed base into consideration. Fourth, the maintenance activities take place during the entire lifespan of the bike, so we need to know that number as well. Then lastly, there is the average service time for one service, which is dependent on the type of components used in the bike (expressed through the 'repair discount time').

In the case that you have chosen the Silver or Gold maintenance schemes, you will also need to take the additional IoT (Internet of Things) costs into consideration. These two schemes work on a per-distance basis (one service per x kilometres), so a small device will be installed on each bike in order to be able to track the distance travelled, which adds a fixed cost to each bike in these cases.

Repair

The second potential additional cost is for repair activities. This is relevant in the case that the revenue models of lease and/or subscription have been chosen for particular customers. Since under lease and subscription schemes the bikes remain property of TBC, the company will also have to assume responsibility for keeping them in shape. Repair then refers to the activity of enabling that. TBC has decided to outsource this repair activity to an external company which invoices each repair service at a fixed price. This price can be reduced in case more durable or easier to repair components are used.

In the case of leasing, the repair services are obviously spanning the entire agreed lease contract duration. The expected number of repairs to be done on a yearly basis can be evaluated by using the depreciation graph. In the case of a subscription, there is a repair service taking place each time one subscription ends and another one starts. The overall lifespan of the bike then needs to be considered, as well as the average subscription duration and the time between subsequent subscription contracts. Due to the fact that the different retailers aim at different consumer segments with different profiles and preferences, the average subscription duration and time between subscriptions can vary between the retailers.

Additional costs due to warranty and/or buyback schemes

Another additional cost could be due to the introduction of a warranty programme and/or a buyback scheme. In both cases, money is offered to the consumers to return the bikes; however, where a buyback is free of conditions, warranty can only be used in the case of a bike being broken. Warranty is always a full refund, valued at the basic price of a bike (excluding the value of any additional services the customer may have paid for)[3] – the buyback price is a decision to be made.

Refurbishment cost

If the option of selling bikes into the second-hand market is chosen, then bikes coming back from the market will first need to be refurbished before they're considered good enough to be sold again. The estimation of the number of bikes coming back was already addressed previously. Take into consideration that not all bikes coming back from the market are in sufficiently good shape that they can effectively be refurbished. In that case they will either go to landfill or, in case you have selected and activated one, to an RSP.

RSP cost

In the case that you have selected an RSP and, importantly, that you have given instructions about what the RSP is supposed to do (per component, remanufacture and/or recycle), then you will have to take into consideration the cost of operations of the RSP.

Changes in paid interest rates due to changes in the vendor lease agreement

If changes are made to the leasing schemes, such as introducing it for the first time, or changing the length of the sold lease contracts, then the installed base of leased bikes changes and the vendor lease agreement with the bank will have to be adjusted accordingly. This will cause a change in the capital cost paid to the bank (interest costs).

Changes in purchasing cost due to changes in component choices

The Design/Purchasing Manager makes decisions about which components are to be purchased and used. Typically, the components will be fine-tuned to the chosen dominant circular strategy. Different components do not have the same price, so the total amount spent on purchasing of components may vary accordingly.

EXERCISE 7.11
Analyse costs

Analyse

For your chosen dominant circular strategy, analyse how much you could expect in terms of additional costs, evaluating each of the additional cost items mentioned above. Please note that you can use Figure 7.10 during your analysis, especially if you populate the chart with the corresponding volumes per each of the relevant goods flows. Add your findings and choices to the template in Figure 7.8 and document any back-up materials to support your choices.

Fine-tuning the chosen business model

After finishing Exercise 7.11 you should now have the template from Figure 7.8 completed, but before you prepare to present your overall strategic plan, let's do some checks and see where additional fine-tuning can still take place. In the previous exercises, we have taken a look at the individual elements of the circular business model you have chosen for TBC. This should already give you a fairly complete picture, but one thing we haven't really done is to take the point of view of the different functional roles and bring the individual elements together. Let's do that now and then prepare for presenting the final overall strategy.

EXERCISE 7.12
Analyse revenue model and cost structure

Analyse

The objective of this exercise is to get a rough picture of the lifetime net revenue per bike, so that we can see if our choices so far have been accurate or if they need to be adjusted. Analyse the following, separately for each one of your customers:

1   The 'gross lifetime revenue' per bike, in the case of direct sales, three-year lease, five-year lease, seven-year lease and unlimited subscription. You can find out through the negotiation screen for each of the customers.

2   Identify the main relevant cost components that go together with each of these revenue models, such as the buyback price, repairs, vendor lease loan interest and so on.

3 Now calculate the 'net lifetime revenue' by taking the gross lifetime revenue minus the main relevant corresponding cost components for each of the revenue models analysed. Draw the result into the template in Figure 7.11.

Even though you haven't gone to the tiniest level of detail, the graphic should give you a good and clear insight into the various revenue models and how they fit with each of the retail customers. Now put these insights together with your analysis from exercises 7.4–7.11 and adjust if and where necessary.

EXERCISE 7.13
Analyse installed lease base and vendor lease negotiated with the bank

Analyse

The objective of this exercise is to get a quick answer if the vendor lease agreement with the bank indeed covers TBC's needs. We also refer back to the section on the concept of installed base earlier in this chapter:

1 For each of the retail customers with a leasing agreement, define how large the installed base of bikes in the lease pool is (in the stable situation) by taking the yearly volume and the lease duration as inputs.

2 Check if the total installed base of all of the lease agreements, valued at the new price of a bike, is covered by the vendor lease agreement with the bank.

Now put these insights together with your analysis from exercises 7.4–7.11 and adjust if and where necessary.

FIGURE 7.11   Template for analysing revenue models and cost structures per retail customer

FIGURE 7.12   Template for maximum bike refurbishment age to the second-hand market

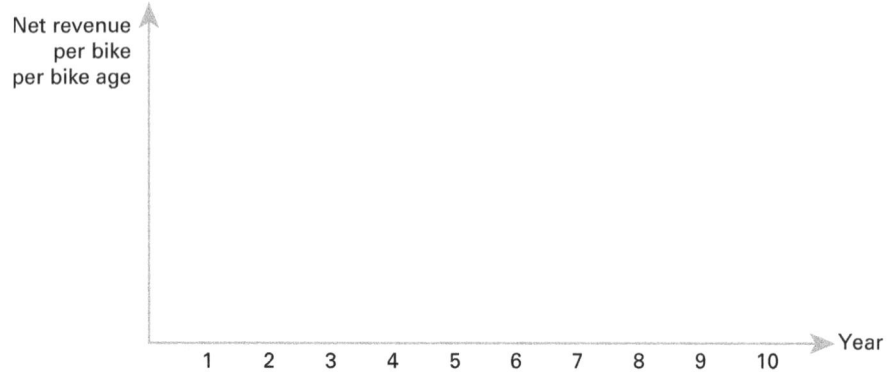

EXERCISE 7.14

Analyse maximum refurbishment age

Analyse

Please note: this exercise is particularly relevant if the chosen circular strategy includes bike refurbishment in order to sell to the second-hand market, potentially complemented by other compatible circular strategies. The objective of this exercise is to get a quick answer about what an appropriate maximum refurbishment age would be. For this purpose, it would be useful to elaborate two distinct (extreme) scenarios: one without refurbishing (i.e. maximum refurbishment set at zero) and one with a very high maximum refurbishment age, for example 10 years, and draw these into the graphic in Figure 7.12 as two separate lines, each representing the net revenue per bike per bike age:

1   Gross revenue: based on the depreciation graph, analyse the revenue value of the bike over its lifespan. Add any other potential revenue streams of recycled materials to this, in case you have applied those in your strategy.

2   Costs: based on the available information and for the number of bikes obtained back from the market, identify the main associated costs for refurbishing and remanufacturing and/or recycling, in case these have been applied as complementary strategies. If applicable, you may deduce any potential savings in purchasing due to the use of remanufactured materials.

3   Net revenue: per potential age of a bike, you can then calculate the net revenue per bike, taking the gross revenue minus the main relevant costs. You can draw your findings into the template in Figure 7.12.

Even though more cost components could be added to the equation, such as for example the costs for buyback, the above should already give you a clear insight into the break-even point associated with the maximum refurbishment age, being at some point between the zero years scenario and the 10 years scenario. Now put these insights together with your analysis from exercises 7.4–7.11 and adjust if and where necessary.

FIGURE 7.13   Template for analysing design principles per component

EXERCISE 7.15
Analyse trade-offs in design

Analyse

The objective of this exercise is to get a quick answer about appropriate application of design principles. You can do the analysis per component.

1   Component costs: what are the different options per component and how do they differ in purchase price?

2   Gross revenue per design principle: for each of the components, what extra revenue potential do they offer compared to the standard component?

3   Net revenue: per analysed component, you can then calculate the net revenue per design principle, taking the gross revenue minus the main relevant component costs. You can draw your findings into the template in Figure 7.13.

Even though more cost components could be added to the equation, the above should already give you a clear insight into the break-even point associated with the application of the different design principles to the different component and you should be in the position to decide where certain choices make more sense and where less. Now put these insights together with your analysis from exercises 7.4–7.11 and adjust if and where necessary.

On the basis of the work done in exercises 7.4–7.11, and the additional insights from exercises 7.12–7.15 you should now have a 'final' version of your strategic plan ready by combining templates 7.7 and 7.8, plus any supporting back-up materials you have prepared along the way.

EXERCISE 7.16

Present your strategic plans for TBC

Decide

Taking the templates from Figures 7.7 and 7.8 plus any supporting back-up materials as an input, decide on an approach for the presentation of your strategic plans for TBC. Prepare a presentation of maximum five minutes in which you convincingly expose your plans. Be ready to present and discuss.

Summary

SIMULATION CHALLENGE DAY 1, AFTER FINISHING ROUND 1

FIGURE 7.14   Towards Round 2

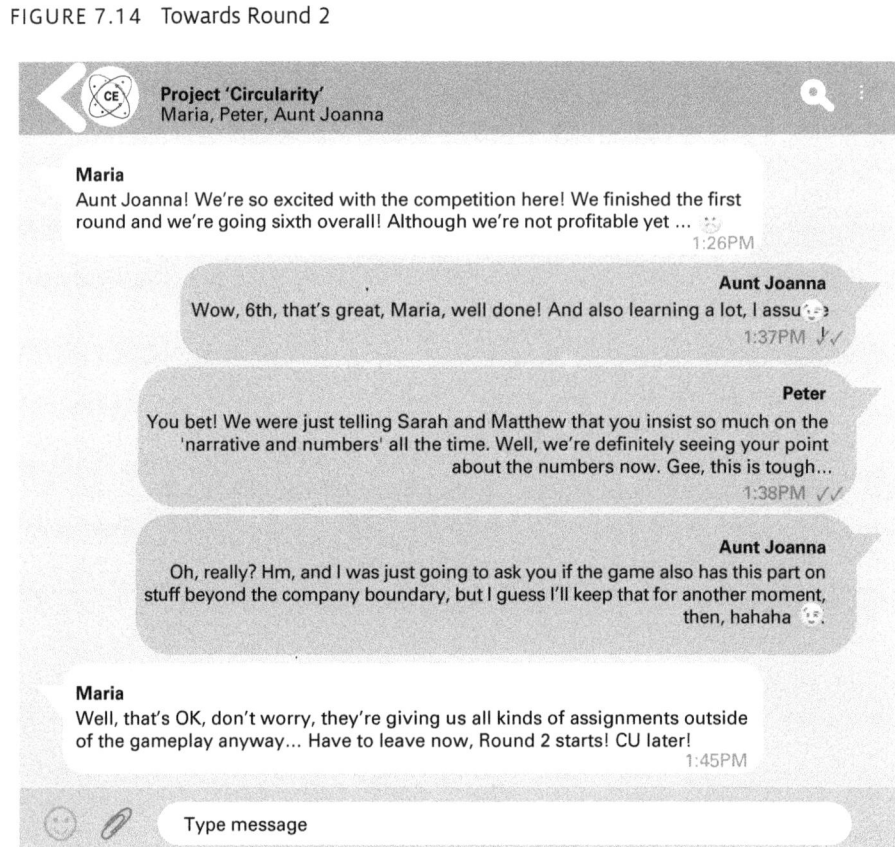

Notes

1 We would like to refer back to Chapter 2, in the section on Revenue models and cost structure, where we elaborated on the differences between subscription and lease.

2 Circularity, for example as expressed by the Circularity %, which we will deal with more extensively in Chapter 9 within the specific context of TBC.

3 The basic price of a bike can be found in the information page.

08

Mastering the perspective beyond the company boundary

FIGURE 8.1 On with the simulation challenge

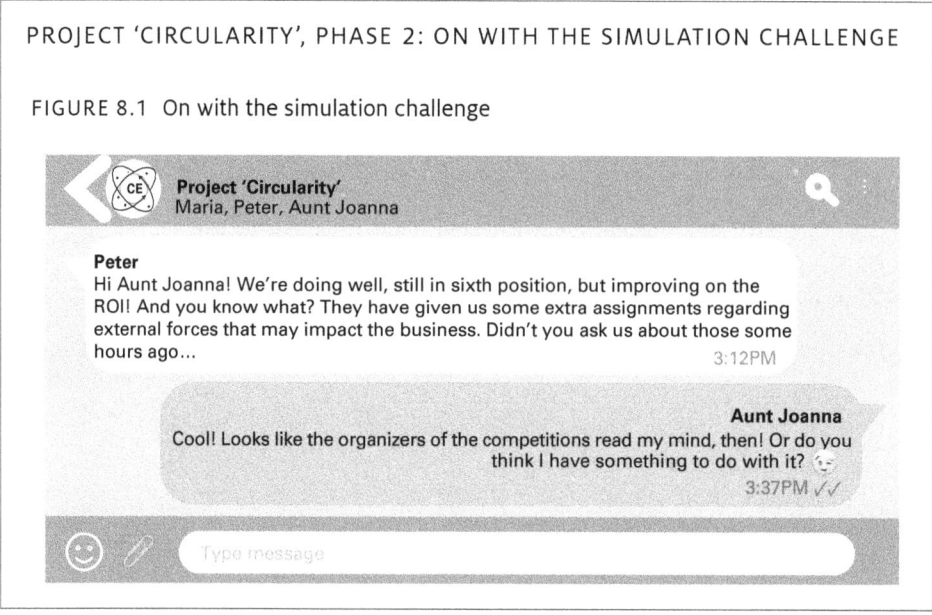

The exercises in this chapter contain the mini-cases that Maria referred to in her chat message to Aunt Joanna. They refer to most of the topics addressed in Chapter 3: legislation, interfirm collaboration and ecosystems. Don't let yourself be fooled by the limited number of pages in this chapter: most of it concerns brief descriptions of exercises, each of which requires some thorough thinking.

For all of the exercises you can take the completed template from Figure 7.8 that you filled out in the exercises in Chapter 7 as a point of reference. If you have made any changes to your circular strategy, revenue model(s) and/or cost structure since you did the exercises in Chapter 7, you may want to update the template so that it accurately reflects the current situation of TBC.

FIGURE 8.2 Topics from the perspective of circularity beyond the company boundary applied to TBC

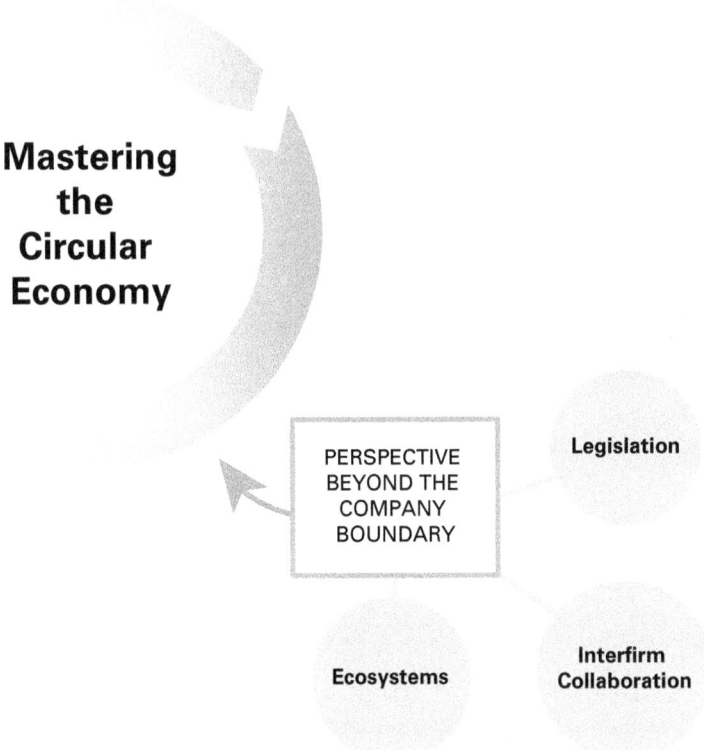

Legislation

The first mini-cases deal with the topic of legislation, from a number of different angles.

Mini-case: fiscal incentives to stimulate e-Bikes

EXERCISE 8.1

Legislation mini-case: fiscal incentives to stimulate e-Bikes

Analyse

The news gets out that governments are about to implement incentives to promote e-Bike use for home–work–home commuting. In the first instance, it is expected that these incentives will be mainly aimed at larger organizations (companies as well as government). For TBC, these organizations could represent a new customer segment in addition to the ones that already exist. There seem to be three options on the table, and it is not clear yet which will be the final chosen one: a subsidy that goes to the employer organization who thus would buy the e-Bikes for their employees at a discount (direct sales model); a tax advantage that goes to the employer organization who thus would lease the e-Bikes for their employees with a fiscal advantage (lease model); a lower VAT rate applied to commuter e-Bikes by the producer, e.g. to TBC, who would thus be able to sell or lease the bikes at a lower price or rate in the case of commuter e-Bikes:

1   Take the completed template from Figure 7.8 as a point of reference.

2   Analyse for the items in each of the boxes in the template if any changes can be expected due to each of the presented scenarios. What would the updated template ultimately look like if the scenario was effective (look at the new future stable situation, so please ignore the potential transition period)?

3   Which are the most important potential impacts you see?

4   Be prepared to present and discuss.

Mini-case: fiscal incentives for 'silver workers' and training of the unemployed

EXERCISE 8.2

Legislation mini-case: fiscal incentives for 'silver workers' and training of the unemployed

Analyse

The news gets out that governments are about to implement fiscal incentives or subsidies for the inclusion of so-called 'silver workers' (older generation workers), as well as for vocational training of people who have lost their jobs due to the emergence of new technologies.[1] Alternatively, governments speak about possible reduction of tax on labour. It is expected that labour-intensive businesses would benefit from such incentives, for example production companies, logistics companies and Recycling Service Providers (RSPs), ultimately leading to the creation of more jobs, but also to lower cost of labour for the aforementioned industries:

1   Take the completed template from Figure 7.8 as a point of reference.

2   Analyse for the items in each of the boxes in the template if any changes can be expected due to the presented scenario. What would the updated template ultimately look like if the scenario was effective (look at the new future stable situation, so please ignore the potential transition period)?

3   Which are the most important potential impacts you see?

4   Be prepared to present and discuss.

Mini-case: incentives to stimulate the use of environmentally friendly materials

---

EXERCISE 8.3

Legislation mini-case: incentives to stimulate the use of environmentally friendly materials

Analyse

The news gets out that governments are about to implement measures that would stimulate the use of more environmentally friendly materials. What is not clear yet is if these new measures will take the shape of penalties on the use of energy-intensive materials such as steel and aluminium, or on the use of fossil fuel-based materials such as plastic, or if they will take the shape of incentives to stimulate the use of alternative materials:

1 Take the completed template from Figure 7.8 as a point of reference.

2 Analyse for the items in each of the boxes in the template if any changes can be expected due to the presented scenario. What would the updated template ultimately look like if the scenario was effective (look at the new future stable situation, so please ignore the potential transition period)?

3 Which are the most important potential impacts you see?

4 Be prepared to present and discuss.

Mini-case: subsidies favouring repair of household articles

EXERCISE 8.4

Legislation mini-case: subsidies favouring repair of household articles

Analyse

The news gets out that more and more local governments are about to implement measures like the one that can be seen in the Austrian city of Graz (Graz Repariert, n.d.) where families get a yearly subsidy to be spent on repair of certain products, and where the city is stimulating the proliferation of the required repair infrastructure based on small-sized local businesses, thus favouring lifetime-extending strategies.

1 Take the completed template from Figure 7.8 as a point of reference.

2 Analyse for the items in each of the boxes in the template if any changes can be expected due to the presented scenario. What would the updated template ultimately look like if the scenario was effective (look at the new future stable situation, so please ignore the potential transition period)?

3 Which are the most important potential impacts you see?

4 Be prepared to present and discuss.

Mini-case: stimulating positive and reducing negative externalities

EXERCISE 8.5

Legislation mini-case: taxes or incentives on positive and negative externalities

Analyse

The news gets out that more and more governments are about to implement measures involving stimulating positive and reducing negative externalities (see Chapter 3, section on externalities).

1   Which positive and negative externalities could you think of in the case of TBC?

2   Take the completed template from Figure 7.8 as a point of reference.

3   Analyse for the items in each of the boxes in the template if any changes can be expected due to the presented scenario. What would the updated template ultimately look like if the scenario was effective (look at the new future stable situation, so please ignore the potential transition period)?

4   Which are the most important potential impacts you see?

5   Be prepared to present and discuss.

Mini-case: Extended Producer Liability (EPL)

EXERCISE 8.6

Legislation mini-case: Extended Producer Liability (EPL)

Analyse

The news gets out that more and more governments are about to implement legislation regarding Extended Producer Liability, implying that bikes with no value at the end of their service life can be returned by the owner to the original manufacturer:

1   Take the completed template from Figure 7.8 as a point of reference.

2   Analyse for the items in each of the boxes in the template if any changes can be expected due to the presented scenario. What would the updated template ultimately look like if the scenario was effective (look at the new future stable situation, so please ignore the potential transition period)?

3   Which are the most important potential impacts you see?

4   Be prepared to present and discuss.

Interfirm collaboration

Mini-case: analysing potential interfirm collaborations – beyond arm's-length buying-selling

---

EXERCISE 8.7

Interfirm collaboration mini-case: beyond arm's-length buying-selling

Analyse

From your perspective as a TBC board member, with which company/companies or financial institution(s) in the value chain would you look for close collaboration, beyond a simple buying/selling relationship?

1 Take the completed template from Figure 7.8 as a point of reference.

2 Which of the companies in the value chain would you prioritize in your drive to establish tighter collaborations?

3 Analyse for the items in each of the boxes in the template if any changes can be expected due to the presented scenarios. What would the updated template ultimately look like if the scenario was effective (look at the new future stable situation, so please ignore the potential transition period)?

4 In addition, for each collaboration you have identified, which concrete objectives would you want to achieve? Which concrete targets would you define between yourself and the potential partner(s)?

5 Be prepared to present and discuss.

Mini-case: analysing potential interfirm collaborations – data sharing and technology

---

EXERCISE 8.8

Interfirm collaboration mini-case: data sharing and technology

Analyse

More complex circular practices drive the need for better collaboration and data sharing among actors in a value chain. From your perspective as a TBC board member, how would you advise the company on the topic of Big Data, Open Source Circular Economy (see Chapter 3), Internet of Things, Blockchain and so on?

1 Take the completed template from Figure 7.8 as a point of reference.

2 Which parts of the value chain would see major impact(s) from these new technologies and which companies in the value chain would you prioritize in your drive to establish tighter collaborations?

3   Analyse for the items in each of the boxes in the template if any changes can be expected due to the presented scenarios. What would the updated template ultimately look like if the scenario was effective (look at the new future stable situation, so please ignore the potential transition period)?

4   In addition, for each collaboration you have identified, which concrete objectives would you want to achieve? Which concrete targets would you define between yourself and the potential partner(s)?

5   Be prepared to present and discuss.

Ecosystems

Mini-case: analysing ecosystem stakeholders

EXERCISE 8.9
Ecosystem mini-case: stakeholders

Analyse

From your perspective as a TBC board member, with which other entities/stakeholders beyond companies would you actively seek closer collaboration?

1   Take the completed template from Figure 7.8 as a point of reference.

2   Analyse for the items in each of the boxes in the template if any changes can be expected due to the presented scenarios. What would the updated template ultimately look like if the scenario was effective (look at the new future stable situation, so please ignore the potential transition period)?

3   In addition, for each collaboration you have identified, which concrete objectives would you want to achieve? Which concrete targets would you define between yourself and the potential partner(s)?

4   Be prepared to present and discuss.

Mini-case: from individualistic (corporate) thinking to we-thinking

EXERCISE 8.10
Ecosystem mini-case: towards we-thinking

Analyse

1   Take the identified stakeholders from Exercise 8.9 as a starting point.

2 Analyse to what extent TBC as a small/medium-sized enterprise could be the driving force for establishing and maintaining a spirit of 'we-thinking' among the stakeholders.

3 Be prepared to present and discuss.

Summary

FIGURE 8.3   Towards the final rounds

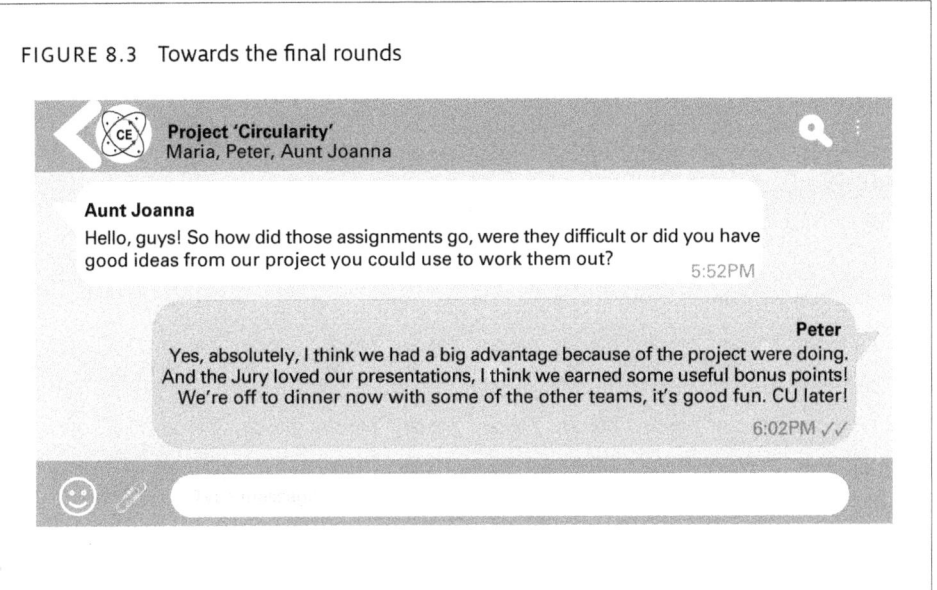

> **Project 'Circularity'**
> Maria, Peter, Aunt Joanna
>
> **Aunt Joanna**
> Hello, guys! So how did those assignments go, were they difficult or did you have good ideas from our project you could use to work them out?   5:52PM
>
> **Peter**
> Yes, absolutely, I think we had a big advantage because of the project were doing. And the Jury loved our presentations, I think we earned some useful bonus points! We're off to dinner now with some of the other teams, it's good fun. CU later!   6:02PM ✓✓

Note

1   Alluding to Stahel (2019), referenced in Chapter 3.

09

Mastering the leadership perspective of circularity

FIGURE 9.1   The challenge continues

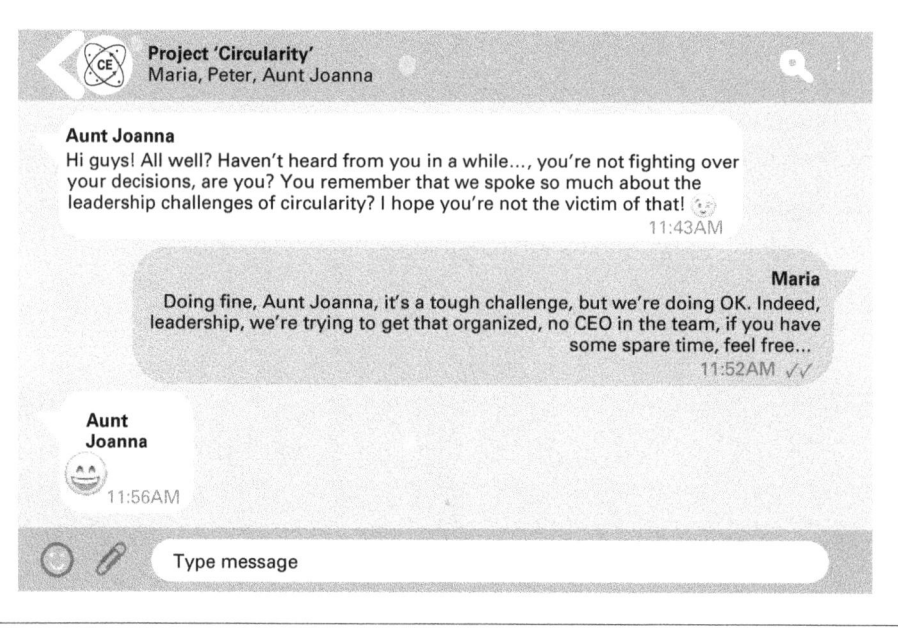

FIGURE 9.2   Topics from the leadership perspective of circularity applied to TBC

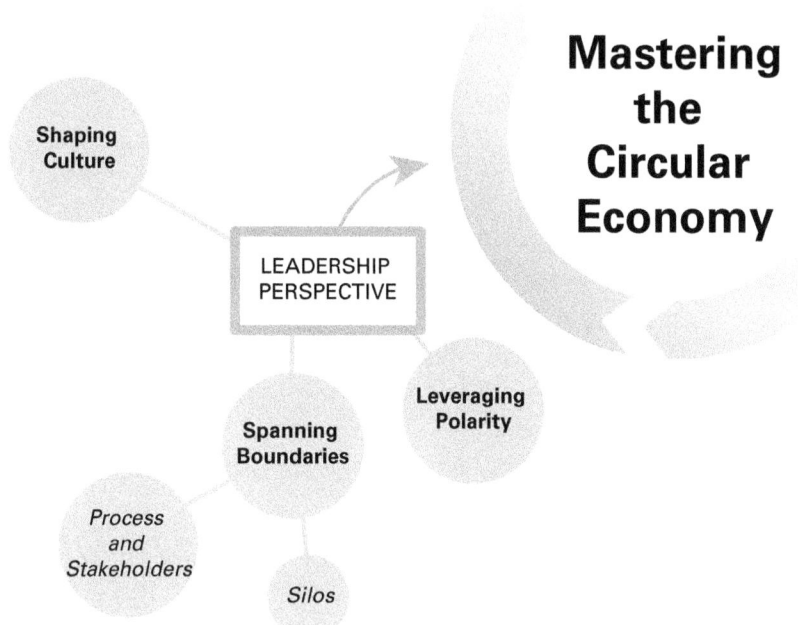

Leading by leveraging polarity: balanced objectives and scorecard(s)

As we have seen in Chapter 4, indicators and targets are used as a powerful instrument to influence people's behaviour and make them move in the desired direction. That's also why we cover the topic under the umbrella of the 'leadership dimension'. In order to understand where current company performance stands and to evaluate which corrective actions might be necessary so that instructions to collaborators can be given, clear Key Performance Indicators (KPIs) need to be established. Since many decisions are taken by functional experts, KPIs in companies are typically also determined per functional area. Whether that really is always the preferable and most desirable way of doing things will be touched upon later, but for now let's focus on those functional KPIs.

EXERCISE 9.1

Analyse KPIs per functional area and decide on how to use this information

Analyse

Building on what you developed in Chapter 7, take the purpose statement, the strategic circular objectives, the chosen dominant circular strategy and the selected revenue model(s) as a starting point and think of three meaningful KPIs for each of the four VPs: Sales, Design/Purchasing, Supply Chain and Finance (so 12 KPIs in total).

In addition, for the chosen KPIs per functional area, check by which role-specific decisions they are impacted. To what extent do these decisions cover the most important decisions of the corresponding functional role? Are there any gaps, i.e. important functional decisions not covered by the KPIs? If necessary, reconsider KPIs.

You can use the template from Figure 9.3.

Decide

Decide on a meaningful set of KPIs per role.

As mentioned briefly before, defining KPIs per functional area is no guarantee whatsoever for achieving effective cross-functional collaboration. It is therefore important to take this into consideration when designing the KPIs: they should be done in such a way that cross-functional alignment is secured in the best possible way. Now, to what extent do the functional KPIs as part of the global KPI dashboard as you have defined it, stimulate collaboration and alignment and make the company as a whole move in the right direction, rather than pushing functional experts each in a different direction?

EXERCISE 9.2

Analyse alignment between functional KPIs and decide on KPI dashboard

Analyse

For each of the KPIs in the list made in Exercise 9.1, check one by one if pursuing their objectives would be potentially going against one of the other KPIs in the list. This would be particularly important for different KPIs between the functional areas. If necessary, reconsider KPIs.

For each of the defined KPIs currently in your list, think of a target value.

Decide

Decide on the global KPI dashboard with three KPIs per functional role, including target setting for each of the defined KPIs.

Decide on how to use these KPIs and targets throughout gameplay. If necessary, update the template from Figure 9.3 with the changes made and then integrate it into the template from Figure 7.7 (Purpose-Strategy-KPIs).

If well-designed from a global context, the currently chosen KPIs should to a certain extent be reasonably well-aligned, and at least not be 'conflictive'. However, well-aligned could potentially be taken even a step further. As a complement to the purely functional KPIs, which can be used to 'judge' individual performance, it might be useful to think about some cross-functional KPIs as well: a small set of KPIs with the clear objective to actively stimulate internal coordination. Possibly, some of the KPIs just defined as functional KPIs already have such characteristics, but not necessarily (preferably not, because functional indicators should ideally be mainly related to decisions within that same functional area).

In TBC's overall circular dashboard, there is a central role for the Circular Transition Indicators (CTI), as discussed in Chapter 4, particularly focusing on the circular inflow and the circular outflow (Figure 9.4) as elements required to calculate the overall circularity percentage:

1 *% Inflow Circularity*: this indicator shows how circular the materials are that a company sources. It is defined as the circular inflow (non-virgin material) divided by the total inflow.

2 *% Outflow Circularity*: this indicator shows how circular the materials are that a company has 'produced'. It is defined as the circular outflow (recoverable outflow) divided by the total outflow.

3 *Circularity (%)*: the circularity % shows how circular the company is in terms of material circularity. It is defined as the average of the % inflow circularity and the % outflow circularity.

EXERCISE 9.3

Analyse relationship between the CTI and role-specific decisions

Analyse

Focusing on the KPIs of Circular Inflow % and Circular Outflow %, analyse by which decisions per role they are impacted. You can use the template in Figure 9.5.

Decide

Define and decide how these two cross-functional KPIs can be productively used by the management team when aligning throughout gameplay.

FIGURE 9.3 Template for KPIs per functional role

CHOSEN DOMINANT CIRCULAR STRATEGY:

CHOSEN COMPATIBLE SUPPORTING CIRCULAR STRATEGY/STRATEGIES:

DESIGN / PURCHASE

KPIs   Impacted by:

1.

2.

3.

SALES

KPIs   Impacted by:

1.

2.

3.

SUPPLY CHAIN MANAGEMENT

KPIs   Impacted by:

1.

2.

3.

FINANCE

KPIs   Impacted by:

1.

2.

3.

FIGURE 9.4 Circular inflow and circular outflow of TBC

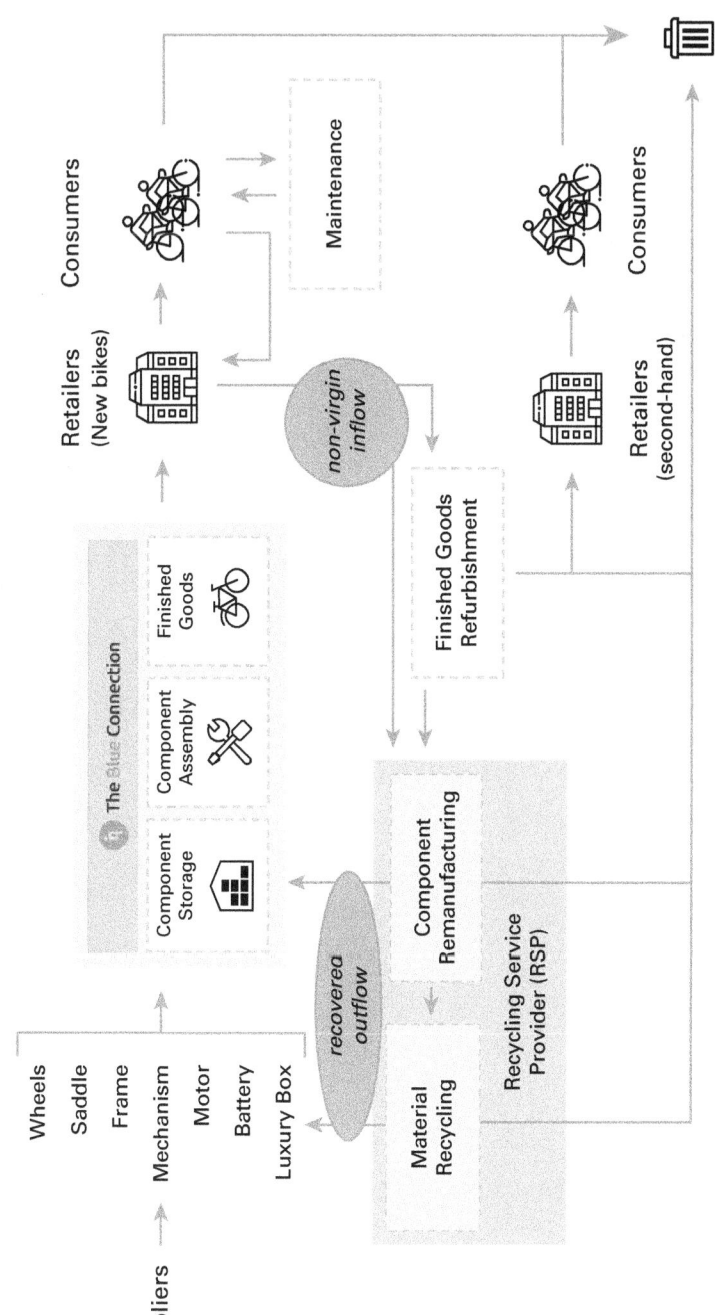

FIGURE 9.5 Analysing the CTI

CHOSEN DOMINANT CIRCULAR STRATEGY:	CHOSEN COMPATIBLE SUPPORTING CIRCULAR STRATEGY/STRATEGIES:
CIRCULAR INFLOW %, IMPACTED BY WHICH DECISIONS?	**CIRCULAR OUTFLOW %, IMPACTED BY WHICH DECISIONS?**
DESIGN / PURCHASING:	DESIGN / PURCHASING:
SALES:	SALES:
SCM:	SCM:
FINANCE:	FINANCE:

Leading by spanning boundaries: silos

Beyond purely measuring individual performance of the different roles, another reflection is useful at this stage. Each team member has assumed a different functional role in the game and by now you have some experience of how that works out during gameplay. The following reflections deal with the functional silos as introduced in Chapter 4.

EXERCISE 9.4
Analyse functional specialization and decide on actions

Analyse

To what extent has the functional specialization of having one person dedicated to each role had a positive impact in terms of causing a role-specific learning curve, enabling a better view and better individual judgement from a functional point of view within the silo?

To what extent has the functional specialization emphasized the functional silos in the team in a negative way, for example by creating tension if a person from one role tried to tell a person in another role which decisions to make? Or by creating more misunderstanding because of specific functional expertise that team members from another role were lacking?

Decide

Decide on how best to exploit the benefits of functional specialization while limiting the potential negative impact of silos in the team to a minimum.

Leading by shaping culture: organization and team dynamics

Measuring performance is a necessary first step for knowing where you are and for having a basis for deciding what needs to be done next. However, KPIs are not going to do all of the work. As soon as people start working together in achieving results, the people dimension of teams comes into play. Independent of each team member's functional role and responsibilities, we can speak then of team roles of individual team members.

The term 'team roles' refers to how individual people behave when put together in a team. For example, some people will be more likely to take the lead and push the team forward, others will perform as the 'glue' binding the individual team members together, whereas yet others will be searching relevant information and feeding that into the team. People's individual personalities and characters have a big impact on this aspect and the particular mix of a set of team members might be more or less balanced. Although there is plenty of academic debate about the topics, not necessarily with everyone always agreeing, the general idea is that the more balanced a team is in terms of team roles, the more likely it is that its performance will be better.

Obviously, there is then also another dimension related to personalities and characters, which together generate a more or less stable or explosive mix within a team. The concept of 'team dynamics' contemplates this by evaluating for example how good the atmosphere in the team is and the extent to which progress is made in the work at hand. In the following steps we are going to use two short and simple questionnaires as developed by Management Worlds, Inc. (reproduced with kind permission).

EXERCISE 9.5

Analyse task orientation of the team

Analyse

Using the template in Figure 9.6, assess your team's performance from the point of view of the 'TASK' at hand. Preferably, each team member should do this individually.

EXERCISE 9.6

Analyse team and relationship orientation of the team

Analyse

Using the template in Figure 9.7, assess your team's performance from the point of view of the 'TEAM dimension (RELATIONSHIPS)' in the team. Preferably, each team member should do this individually.

As an interesting extension of the reflection, individual team members might be challenged to complete the questionnaires more than once, each time reflecting a different moment (round) during the gameplay. In this way, the development over time can also be expressed and interpreted.

FIGURE 9.6   Template: analysing the 'TASK' dimension of leadership

TEAM: **DOMINANT STRATEGY:**   The Blue Connection

TEAM ASSESSMENT: TASKS

T 1:   *Do you have clear direction and objectives?*

          1   2   3   4   5   6   7

Goals and objectives are clearly   Goals and objectives are unclear.
understood and agreed on.   Few members feel ownership.

T 2:   *Do team members understand what each is to do?*

          1   2   3   4   5   6   7

Roles, responsibilities and assignments   Roles and responsibilities are unclear, unassigned.
are clear, accepted. There is a good division of labour.   Team not fully utilized.

T 3:   *How is the work organized and carried out?*

          1   2   3   4   5   6   7

Procedures for working together are   Work procedures are lacking or inefficient.
organized, efficient. Team is creative, flexible.   Team is rigid and does not experiment.

T 4:   *How well do you plan and control your project efforts?*

          1   2   3   4   5   6   7

Actions and decisions are planned
ahead, anticipating problems and alternatives.   Planning timeframe is limited and work is micro-managed.
Data is organized, balancing details with the big picture.   Data is scattered, unorganized, too detailed or too vague.

T 5:   *How do you come to decisions as a team?*

          1   2   3   4   5   6   7

Consensus is sought and tested.
An approach to decision making and problem   No agreed approach to decision making or problem solving.
exploration is set. Disagreements are explored.   Decisions are delayed, made by chance or default.

EXERCISE 9.7

*Analyse combined task, team and relationship orientations of the team and
decide on actions to improve team performance*

Analyse

Using the template in Figure 9.8, now express the outcomes from the two questionnaires in
one combined graphic, showing the individual assessments of the different team members.
*If the previous questionnaires have been filled out multiple times by each team member to
express development over time, this can also be incorporated into the graphic.*

Decide

What are the conclusions you and the team can derive from this? Based on your
observations as a team, what do you propose to do next?

FIGURE 9.7   Template: analysing the 'TEAM' dimension of leadership

TEAM:	DOMINANT STRATEGY:	The Blue Connection

TEAM ASSESSMENT: TEAM (RELATIONSHIPS)

R 1:   **What is the quality of participation in your team?**

1   2   3   4   5   6   7

All team members are involved and contribute views and ideas.   *Involvement is limited. A few members decide.*
Different opinions and views are listened to and valued.   *Some members are passive or even apathetic in*
providing views and ideas.

R 2:   **What is the degree of trust and openness between team members?**

1   2   3   4   5   6   7

Team members feel they can speak up and challenge each other.   *There is little trust among team members.*
Problems, conflicts, concerns are discussed openly and respectfully.   *Conflict is avoided.*
Communication is guarded, closed or diplomatically polite.

R 3:   **How is team leadership handled?**

1   2   3   4   5   6   7

Leadership is autocratic and direct.
Dominance by one or a few members.
Leadership is shared. All members participate and are influential.

R 4:   **To what extent are feelings important data?**

1   2   3   4   5   6   7

Feelings are valuable input,   *Feelings are hidden or ignored*
comfortably shared between team members.   *and not treated as useful information.*

R 5:   **Is your team having fun?**

1   2   3   4   5   6   7

Members feel good about working together. Success is   *Team members do not enjoy working together.*
celebrated and mistakes are learned from.   *Team is overly serious and celebration is minimized.*
Humour is energizing.

Leading by spanning boundaries: process and stakeholders

The process of cross-boundary alignment between the functional roles

In order to effectively align decisions, we need to span the boundaries between the different departments involved. As we have seen earlier on in this Chapter, as well as in Chapter 4, polarities might exist: potential 'conflicts' between departments because of differences in objectives, priorities and so on. The KPI dashboards you have developed should be of help in creating transparency in the existence of such potential polarities, but the transparency itself doesn't solve anything. In addition, you may consider looking at the decision-making process itself and seeing if a

FIGURE 9.8   Template: analysing the 'TASK' and 'TEAM' dimensions of leadership

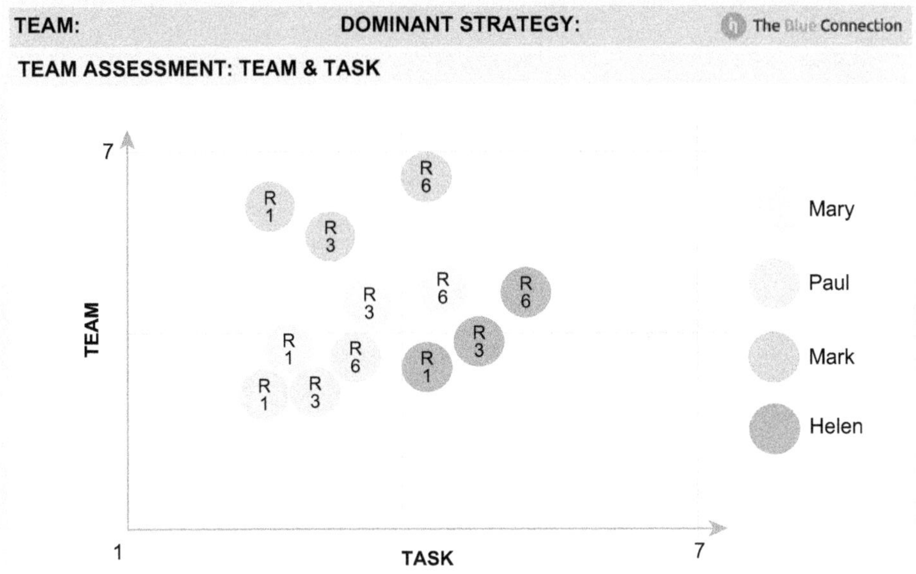

process can be implemented that facilitates better alignment. In Chapter 4, the example of the Sales and Operations Planning (S&OP) process from the (linear) supply chain world was given. Let's see if a similar logic can be applied in TBC's decision making.

EXERCISE 9.8
Developing an aligned decision-making process

Develop

Like Team SuperBike, use the template in Figure 9.9. It contains one column per functional area ('swimming lane diagram'). The team decided to use sticky notes to facilitate the activity. Figure 9.9 shows their diagram just after they started working on it.

Make a list of all the decisions per functional area which you have seen so far in the gameplay. You could write each decision on a separate sticky note. Out of all of these decisions create one global flowchart. In other words, for each decision, think of which other decisions provide an input to the decision. Please note that the flowchart doesn't necessarily have to go only in one direction: feedback loops are possible (some decisions have an iterative character rather than linear). Also, it could happen that you find

FIGURE 9.9   Template for development of decision-making process

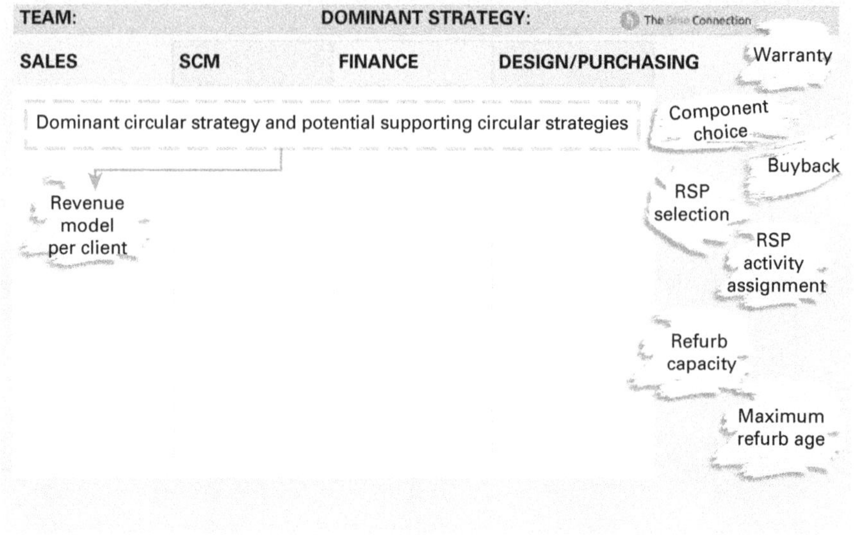

decisions that have no clear relationship to other decisions; that is, they do not require input from another decision, nor themselves provide an input to other decisions.

Decide

Now decide how you can implement the findings of the 'S&OP-inspired' flowchart in your team's decision making, the objective being to make the overall decision-making more efficient (faster) as well as more effective (better aligned and more well-informed decisions).

Stakeholders

In the specific setting of The Blue Connection, most of the internal stakeholders directly involved in what's going on in managing business and the (circular) flow of goods actually form part of the team participating in the simulation game. However, there is one other very important stakeholder we will have to address and to whom we haven't paid much attention since the beginning of this chapter: Catherine McLaren is back and she wants some answers!

Good reporting is an important and relevant skill to support effective stakeholder management. The way you inform others, what exactly you tell them and how you tell them, will create a starting point for the following steps in the process. It requires a healthy dose of empathy in order to understand what information your audience would be interested in, as well as a bit of creativity to make your report

FIGURE 9.10 Catherine McLaren is back!

attractive to look at as well as easy to understand. Be aware that the people who are going to look at your reporting are probably short on time, so they need to be able to quickly grasp your message. Also, be aware that you might not be there with them when they see it, so you might not have an opportunity to explain anything until they explicitly ask you to.

EXERCISE 9.9

Analyse what happened so far and create a reporting for the company's Circular Turnaround Manager

Analyse

Using the template below as developed by Team SuperBike, go back to the experiences of the rounds played so far and create a management report for Catherine McLaren.

Decide

Decide which elements to focus on and create the report. Make sure the report is accurate, to the point and self-explanatory.

FIGURE 9.11   Template: reporting for Catherine McLaren

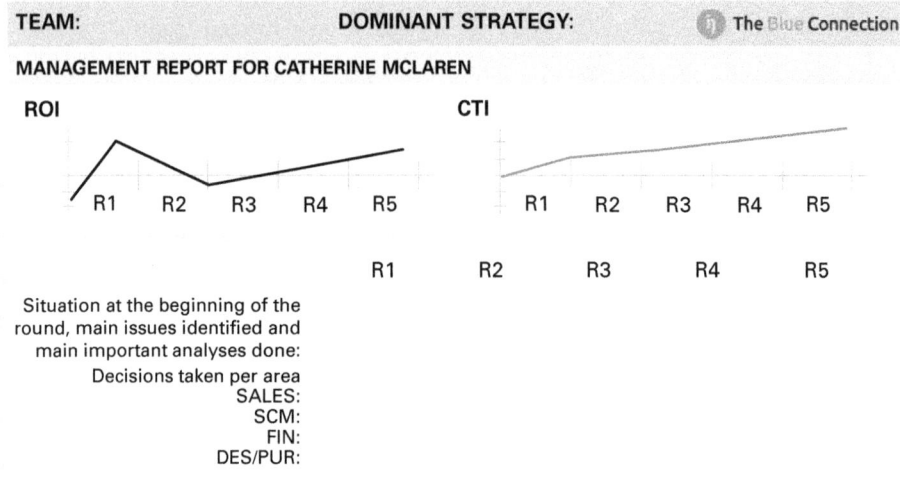

| TEAM: | DOMINANT STRATEGY: | The Blue Connection |

MANAGEMENT REPORT FOR CATHERINE MCLAREN

ROI

CTI

R1 R2 R3 R4 R5

R1 R2 R3 R4 R5

R1 R2 R3 R4 R5

Situation at the beginning of the
round, main issues identified and
main important analyses done:
Decisions taken per area
SALES:
SCM:
FIN:
DES/PUR:

OVERALL MESSAGE TO CATHERINE MCLAREN:

Summary

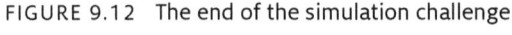

FIGURE 9.12   The end of the simulation challenge

Project 'Circularity'
Maria, Peter, Aunt Joanna

Maria
Hi Aunt J.! We just finished the competition and we're now waiting for the
final scores and ranking! I think we did quite well in the last Rounds, after we
got the leadership things straight, you know the KPIs and the decision-making
process. And they even made us present to the virtual Circular Turnaround
Manager, really cool!
                                                                    5:11PM

Aunt Joanna
Sounds good, Maria! What about you and Peter coming over to the office early
next week and you can present to a real-life CEO about your experiences... 😉 !
                                                                    5:23PM ✓✓

Peter
You can count on us, Aunt J., we have a lot to tell you! For example, how we
ran into ... oh, have to go now, they're going to announce the scores and the
winners of the competition! See you next week!
                                                                    5:27PM ✓✓

    Type message

In the next chapter we will end our journey of mastering the circular economy by going back for a moment to the topic of overall complexity due to the combination of the company perspective, the perspective beyond the company boundary and the leadership perspective and their many elements, and the corresponding need for alignment.

10

The Corporate Circular Imperative: narrative and numbers (3)

Wrapping up Phase 2 of Project 'Circularity'[1]

'Well, well, what an experience this has been!' said Aunt Joanna, welcoming Maria and Peter to her office. 'What about some delicious homemade apple pie to celebrate that you made it into the top three teams, I'm so proud of you!'

'Yeah, quite an experience, as you say, Aunt Joanna,' said Peter. 'Looking back, I don't think we knew what we were up to when we started the simulation challenge. In any case, it's been great fun with our team and with the other participants.'

'I agree,' said Maria, 'it was even more complex than I thought it would be, but it was absolutely worth it, even though we didn't win after all. I learned so much, and in just two days of participating in the challenge!'

'So, tell me, what did you learn exactly?' asked Aunt Joanna. 'We still have the flipcharts of our project here, so I'm curious to know how you experienced all of these topics during your gameplay.'

'First of all, we explored the company perspective of circularity and we spoke a lot about circular strategies, revenue models and costs,' Aunt Joanna continued, 'so how did you experience those in the game?'

EXERCISE 10.1
Reflection on mastering the company perspective of circularity

Reflect

What have been your learnings regarding the different theoretical concepts about circular strategies from Chapter 2 and their practical application in real-life situations as applied in Chapter 7? To what extent are the concepts clear and have you experienced the complexities involved? What would you do differently next time?

'That's really interesting, good observations, thank you,' Aunt Joanna said. 'OK, and after the company perspective, we looked at the perspective of circularity beyond the company boundary, and we spoke about legislation, ecosystems, education and so on. I remember that in one of your messages you told me that you were asked to prepare some assignments about those in the simulation challenge, so what did you pick up from those?'

EXERCISE 10.2

Reflection on mastering the perspective beyond the company boundary

Reflect

What have been your learnings regarding topics such as legislation, ecosystems and interfirm collaboration as dealt with in Chapter 3 and their practical application in real-life situations as applied in Chapter 8? To what extent are the concepts clear and have you experienced the complexities involved?

'Good thinking, guys, I'm really impressed,' Aunt Joanna said. 'That leaves us with the leadership perspective, in which we spoke extensively about KPI dashboards, team performance, the decision-making process and so on. How did you experience those in the game?'

EXERCISE 10.3

Reflection on mastering the leadership perspective of circularity

Reflect

What have been your learnings regarding KPI dashboards centred around circularity? How easy or difficult has it been to manage the decision-making process based on those KPIs?

How did you organize the decision-making process? To what extent was the sequence of decisions clear? To what extent has the process been efficient and was any time lost in discussions that were not strictly necessary?

What have been your learnings regarding your team's behaviour? To what extent did you share the same view with your teammates when analysing team behaviour? Why was that, do you think? What would you do differently now that you are aware of this?

'Wow, that's really wonderful, I see why you said you learned so much from the simulation game experience!' Aunt Joanna concluded. She paused for a moment. 'Alright, so let's try and tie all of this one step more firmly to our Project 'Circularity' then, and particularly to our storyline of *narrative and numbers*.'

'Maria, before you went on to play the game, you were completely convinced about the storyline we should apply, I mean the narrative in favour of circularity, I remember that clearly,' Aunt Joanna continued. 'You saw circularity as an unavoidable urgency and an obvious step for companies to take. But what about the numbers that should go together with that? Did the game give you any new insights into this?'

'Yes, Aunt Joanna, it did and it's all still very clear to me,' Maria responded. 'I'm still convinced about why companies should start going circular, but even more so, I think with our game we have demonstrated that a good degree of circularity goes very well together with good profitability. After all, we really improved a lot in our circularity and on top of that, we turned the company around and made it profitable again, scoring a very decent positive ROI. So, I rest my case, your honour!' she concluded with a big smile.

'Thanks, Maria, that's indeed very clear, I appreciate your enthusiasm and conviction about the path you choose,' said Aunt Joanna. 'And what about you Peter? Because I remember that before the gameplay started you still had quite some doubts. And if I'm not mistaken, your doubts were not so much about the reasons behind circularity, but more about whether profitability would be possible. I imagine that at least you have seen in the gameplay, as Maria just said, that circularity and profitability seem to go together well.'

'Well, what can I say, Aunt Joanna?' Peter started. 'First of all, I have been confirmed in my belief that the narrative for circularity is the easy part. I mean, if by "going circular", as Maria called it, companies can do something good for the planet, then who could possibly be against that? But although we did indeed reach profitability, in the game I've seen that achieving it is really not an easy task; there are so many things that need to be aligned. And also, in the virtual company in the game, we had only one product and three customers to deal with. And some customers were favourable to circularity, as was the bank. Is that really the case in real life? I know we have seen in the project so far that in some cases retailers, consumers and banks are favourable, but will it be soon enough?'

'In addition,' Peter continued, 'in the game we had a lot of information available and I wonder if a real company would have it available to them too. Also, everything you planned and implemented worked the way as intended, no surprises. On top of that, we didn't have to worry about the transition period between the initial situation and the new stable situation after implementation. In other words, the assumptions on the basis of which we made our decisions always worked out, because they came from the information in the game itself. I just wonder, in real life would a company have all of that available? And if not, where do the information and the assumptions come from? And which risks do you run if your assumptions prove to be wrong? So yes, we've proven that profitability and circularity can indeed go together, and I'm really happy that I've seen that, because as you said, I wasn't actually sure about that at all. But still, I have the feeling that there are so many other questions to be answered. Especially if you're an existing company starting from a linear value chain set-up, because then you have a complex and even risky transition ahead. That's of course very different from a circular startup.'

Final reflection on Part Two

'That's indeed a fair point you raise, Peter,' said Aunt Joanna. 'We haven't really taken a look at the assumptions, the implementation and the transition. But first, let's see if we can bring Phase 2 of our project to a productive end before we move on. You remember that before the gameplay I asked you to prepare me a pitch and at the time it was focused mainly on the narrative? Why don't we do that again, but now we include the numbers as well, based on your experience with the gameplay?'

EXERCISE 10.4

The narrative and numbers to support the Corporate Circular Imperative

Going back to the topics as covered in Part Two and visualized in Figure 10.1, reflect on the narrative for circularity from a company standpoint, but now also supported by your experience with the numbers in TBC gameplay: the Corporate Circular Imperative. Develop a convincing pitch of maximum 10 phrases that you yourself firmly believe in and that would also convince others to join you on the journey towards circularity.

'Good work, guys!' said Aunt Joanna. 'I like those pitches and I can see that we have indeed made good progress if I compare them to the ones you did before. I'm glad you got the invitation to participate in the simulation game challenge, because it did help in refining the narrative and the numbers.'

'But I would like to get back to what Peter mentioned some moments ago,' she continued, 'when he spoke about the assumptions, the information availability and the complexities of actually making the transition happen. I have the feeling that diving into the details of these topics will complete our picture.'

'Many of the topics covered in Phase 1 of our project were applied to your Blue Connection Challenge in Phase 2, so we can take these directly with us into Phase 3. But I think there were some other topics we addressed in Phase 1 and which were not touched on in the gameplay, for example education, innovation and change management and maybe some more, which we should bring back and deal with in Phase 3 of Project 'Circularity'.'

FIGURE 10.1   Overview of topics covered in Part Two: Mastering the circular economy

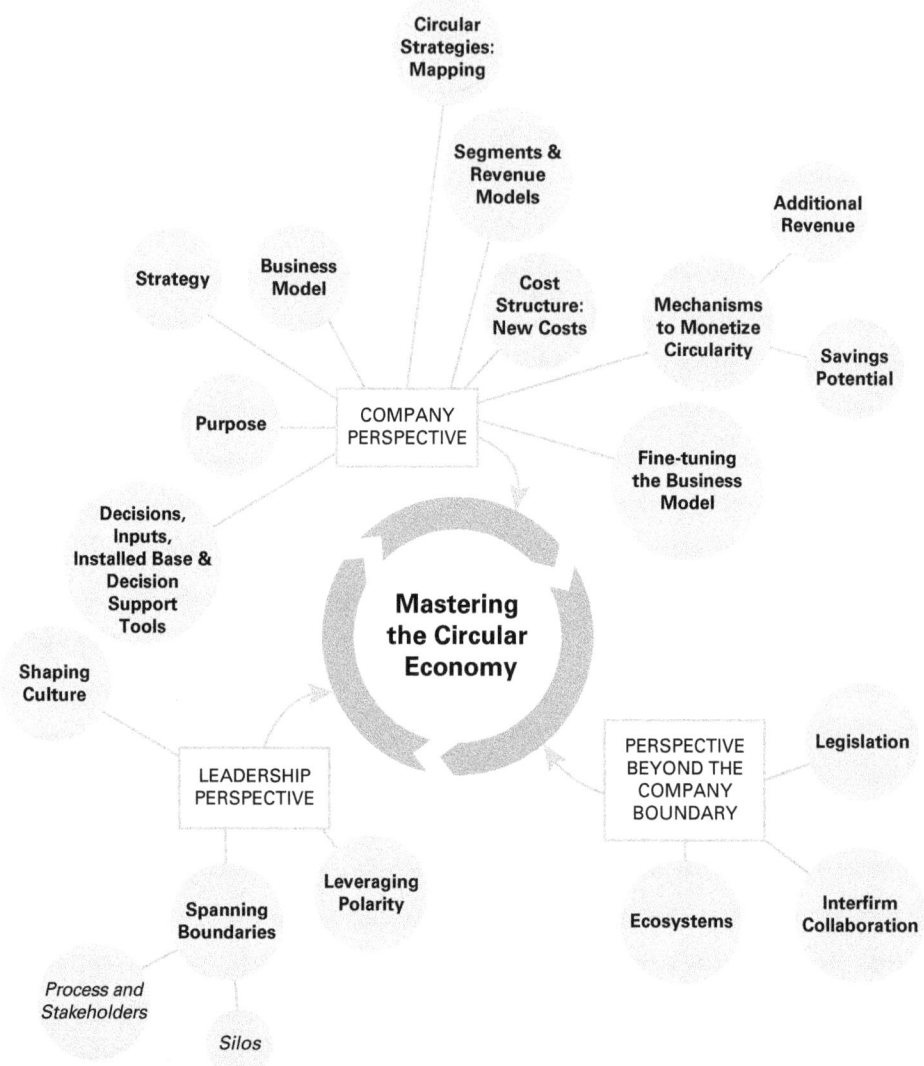

Note

1 This conversation builds on the WhatsApp exchange between Aunt Joanna, Maria and Peter during the simulation challenge (Chapters 6–9), as well as on their conversation at the end of Part One, Chapter 5.

PART THREE

Imagining the transformation from linear to circular value chains

Aunt Joanna's office: Project 'Circularity', kick-off of Phase 3

'So, guys,' Aunt Joanna said, 'in Phase 1 of Project 'Circularity' we started a general exploration of the many and diverse aspects of circularity, and then in Phase 2 you had the chance of directly applying many of those concepts in gameplay in The Blue Connection, focusing on mastering the aspects of running a relatively stable circular value chain.'

'Now in Phase 3, and building on what Peter was saying before,' she continued, 'we should "*imagine the transformation from a linear to a circular value chain*", so we will look beyond such a stable circular situation and imagine the required transformation in between the linear starting point and the circular solution. If you agree we can use your experience with The Blue Connection simulation game once again as a reference and we'll build on that, applying the company situation you know from the gameplay as a case study, so to speak, wherever possible using relevant data from the system to support our analysis.'

'As Peter said, and I think he has a fair point, the game represents a simplified situation; however, I do believe that it contains all of the relevant characteristics we need. And I think we should once again go back to the perspectives we have seen throughout the project: the company perspective, the perspective beyond the company boundary and the leadership perspective, and look at each of those from the specific point of view of "transformation from linear to circular". I'm sure that these three different perspectives applied to the transformation from linear to circular will give us critical insights into the concrete potential projects needed to actually make the transformation happen.'

Aunt Joanna wasn't finished yet: 'I'm convinced that a fair dose of your *imagination* will be required. This would be the same, by the way, for any board of directors of a real company contemplating potential roadmaps for the required transformation. But please note, as I've learned myself over the years, imagination is absolutely not the same as pure speculation. On the basis of imaginative ideas, very concrete scenarios and project plans can be developed and evaluated. Which is precisely what I would like you to work on. And I would like you to make sure that you don't develop your projects as independent and isolated initiatives, but to have your *plans for change integrated into your overall project plans, and not put together separately or in parallel. The challenge is to make change management part and parcel of the plans, and not an add-on that is managed independently.*'[1]

'And then the only other thing we will still need to do once you're done,' Aunt Joanna said with a smile, finishing exposing her plans about the coming steps, 'is to put all of these projects together in one big overview and this will then get us ready for the full story of narrative and numbers. What do you think?'

'No time to lose, let's get started,' said Maria. 'Come on, Peter, we have work to do!'

11

The transformation from linear to circular[2]

'Alright, Peter,' Maria said, 'so let's start with creating a clear starting point for looking at the transformation from linear to circular. During the gameplay we have mainly compared one steady state with another, but we didn't really have to worry about what happens in between those two steady states from one round in the game to another. And we have worked a lot on circularity so far, but I think we also need to imagine the linear starting point of The Blue Connection, because then we can really see the journey of transformation they would have ahead of themselves.'

'Good idea,' Peter responded. 'We already have the linear flow of materials of TBC, because we have seen that before. But then, following the logical flow of topics so far, we also need to discuss purpose, strategic objectives, KPIs and the linear business model. Let's start there, OK? I'll get some more flipcharts – will you get some coffee and tea?'

Visualizing the initial linear value chain: purpose, strategy, KPIs

In Part Two, Chapter 7, we worked on a purpose statement for TBC that would favour circularity and we also derived strategic objectives connected to this purpose. In Chapter 9 we then added meaningful KPIs to the picture. In order to be able to also look at these aspects from the perspective of transition and transformation, we need to establish a linear starting point for them. Using the template that we have used before in Chapter 7 as an inspiration, Team SuperBike has come up with their interpretation (Figure 11.1).

FIGURE 11.1 Template for capturing purpose, strategic objectives and KPIs

STRATEGY: *Linear – Team SuperBike*

PURPOSE STATEMENT

*We are a Dutch bicycle manufacturer with a passion for developing and
producing quality e-bicycles for a broad and international audience. Every day
we put our heart and soul into getting you from point A to B: the Dutch way! We
provide you with carefree cycling pleasure, optimal comfort, speed and safety.*

STRATEGIC OBJECTIVES

☐ Grow shareholder value
☐ Ensure financial sustainability
☐ Increase revenue
  • Expand sales to existing customers
  • Expand distribution volume
  • Introduce existing products into new markets
  • Improve service approach for new and existing customers
☐ Manage cost
  • Reduce cost by a certain amount annually
  • Streamline core business processes
  • To continually learn and adopt current best practices
☐ Have all TBC products meet standard of excellence guidelines
☐ Improve distributor and/or supplier relationships
☐ Promote company culture and values
☐ Improve the satisfaction of the employees

KPI DASHBOARD

KPI DASHBOARD

☐ **GLOBAL KPIs**
  • *Return on Investment (ROI)*
  • *On-Time-In-Full delivery service performance (OTIF)*

☐ **SALES**
  • *Total annual revenue achieved (EUR)*
  • *Increased market share (%)*

☐ **DESIGN / PURCHASING**
  • *Total expense in components (EUR versus budget)*
  • *Obtained discounts at suppliers (% versus budget)*

☐ **SUPPLY CHAIN MANAGEMENT**
  • *Amount of Finished Goods inventory (EUR versus budget)*
  • *Amount of Component inventory (EUR versus budget)*

☐ **FINANCE**
  • *Cash position (EUR)*
  • *Emergency loan (EUR)*

NOTE: functional KPIs are connected to individual bonuses

EXERCISE 11.1

Imagine purpose, strategic objectives and KPIs of the initial linear TBC

Imagine

Take a close look at what Team SuperBike has developed in terms of the purpose statement, strategic objectives and KPIs of The Blue Connection before it changed its course to become more circular, as expressed in Figure 11.1. On the basis of Team SuperBike's work, imagine what you think it could have been like. Make adjustments where you think it is appropriate.

Visualizing the initial linear value chain: Business Model Canvas

To be able to evaluate the potential impacts of the trends and developments we will look at, we need to create a clear view on the existing situation, the status quo. Based on the experience obtained with TBC during Part Two, we will assume that the ins and outs of TBC's initial linear value chain are known. But we haven't really looked at the overall initial business model of TBC. In order to establish a clear view on this, we go back to the concept of the Business Model Canvas, as introduced in Part One, Chapter 2.

EXERCISE 11.2

Imagine the linear business model of TBC

Imagine

Team SuperBike has gone to the website www.strategyzer.com to download a copy of the Business Model Canvas (everyone is allowed to do so, as long as you respect the exact Creative Commons licence conditions for its usage). You might also want to check out some of the other supporting resources for use of the canvas on the website.

Using sticky notes when creating the canvas, in order to be more flexible making adjustments, Team SuperBike has developed the following canvas, expressing the linear starting point of The Blue Connection. On the basis of Team SuperBike's work, imagine what you think the initial linear business model could have been like. Make adjustments where you think it is appropriate.

FIGURE 11.2 Template: linear Business Model Canvas Team SuperBike

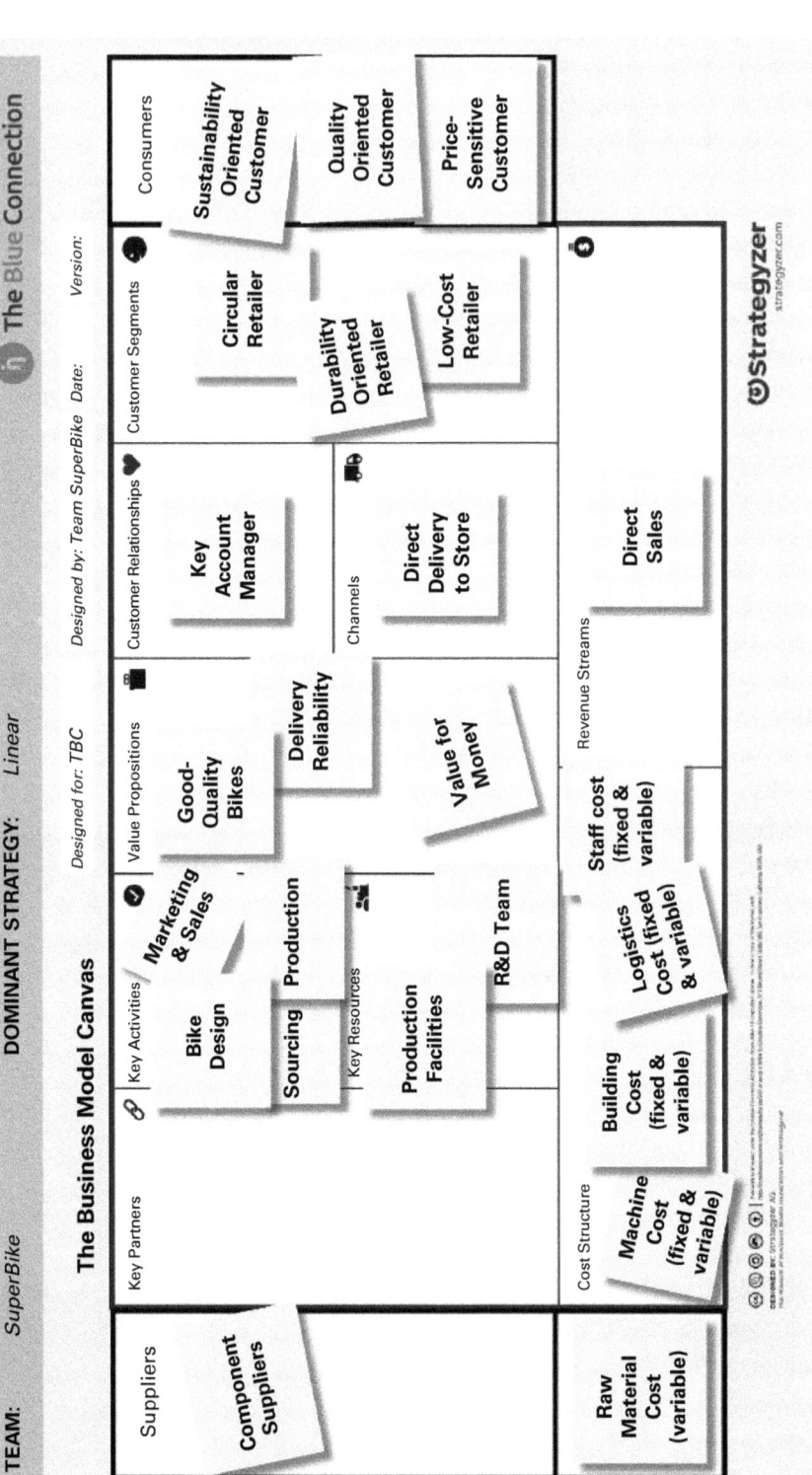

SOURCE Canvas template from Osterwalder and Pigneur (2010), www.strategyzer.com, with Team SuperBike amendments as well as elaboration of content

Please note that as kind of an experiment, Team SuperBike has decided to take the liberty of making some amendments to the standard canvas:

- Firstly, they have added a column called *consumers* on the right-hand side, in order to be able to clearly express the distinction between TBC's paying customers and the consumers who use TBC's bikes. Although the current market of TBC clearly is B2B (business to business), they feel the consumer cannot be left out of the business model since at the end of the day TBC produces consumer products. In order to avoid confusion, for example between value proposition towards customers and towards consumers, the extra column was added.

- Secondly, they have added a column on the left-hand side called *suppliers*, to be able to clearly express the distinction between key partners with whom a strategic relationship would be established and 'normal' arm's-length suppliers with whom there would be a more standard buying-selling relationship. They feel this would allow them to incorporate, for example, commodity suppliers from whom TBC might be buying a lot of money's worth of materials (i.e. important for the overall cost structure), but who would not be considered key partners, since commodities can be bought virtually anywhere. Accordingly, the box with cost structure has been extended to also cover the arm's-length suppliers.

- If you want, you can try out the amendments of Team SuperBike and see if they also work for you. If not, just move along with the original canvas.

Please note that when creating the canvas, you shouldn't only look at operational and supply chain aspects but consider all elements of the business. When developing the canvas, keep the following checks in mind:

- Are all elements on the 'what?' side of the canvas (segments, value propositions, channels, customer relations) supported by one or more elements on the 'how?' side (key activities, key resources, key partners, suppliers). If the answer is no, then there are two options: either you might have missed something, or you have discovered a gap in the coherence of the business model.

- Are all elements in the canvas strictly necessary? In other words, if you take a specific element away, does that really weaken the coherence of the business model? If you find something that is not so necessary, then you might have discovered something that is redundant, i.e. could be removed from the company without harming the strength of the business model.

Both checks can effectively be done in quite a 'mechanical' way, by simply going sticky note by sticky note and checking for each one at a time.

In Exercise 11.1 you have created your linear equivalent of the circular template created from the template from Figure 7.7 and based on the work of Team SuperBike. After finishing the Business Model Canvas, you now also have all the elements in place to create the linear equivalent of the circular template created from the template from Figure 7.8.

FIGURE 11.3   Template for capturing the linear business model of TBC

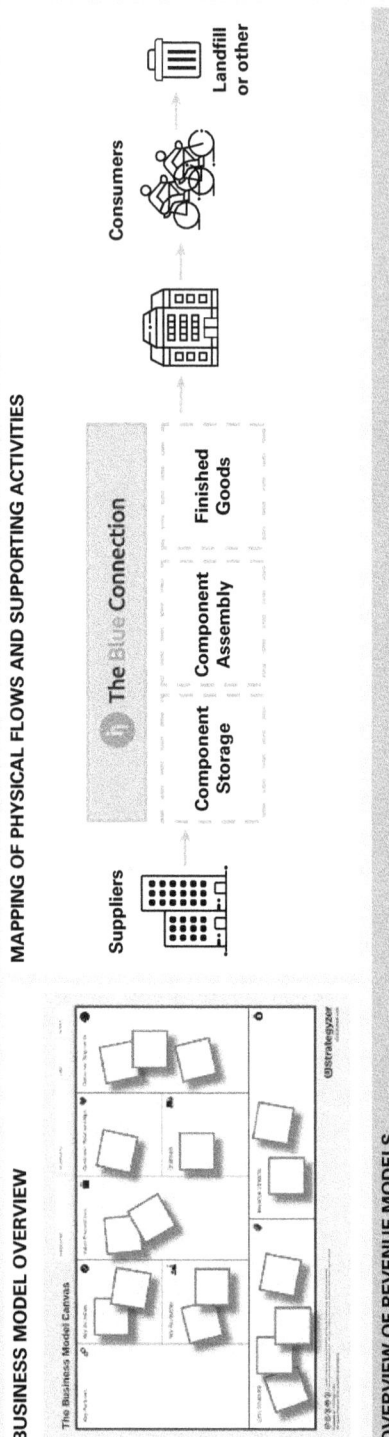

STRATEGY: *LINEAR*

BUSINESS MODEL OVERVIEW

MAPPING OF PHYSICAL FLOWS AND SUPPORTING ACTIVITIES

The Blue Connection

Suppliers

Component Storage

Component Assembly

Finished Goods

Consumers

Landfill or other

OVERVIEW OF REVENUE MODELS

MAIN COST COMPONENTS AND QUANTITIES

REVENUE MODEL PER SEGMENT:

SOURCES USED:
ASSUMPTIONS MADE:

FIGURE 11.4   Project charter template

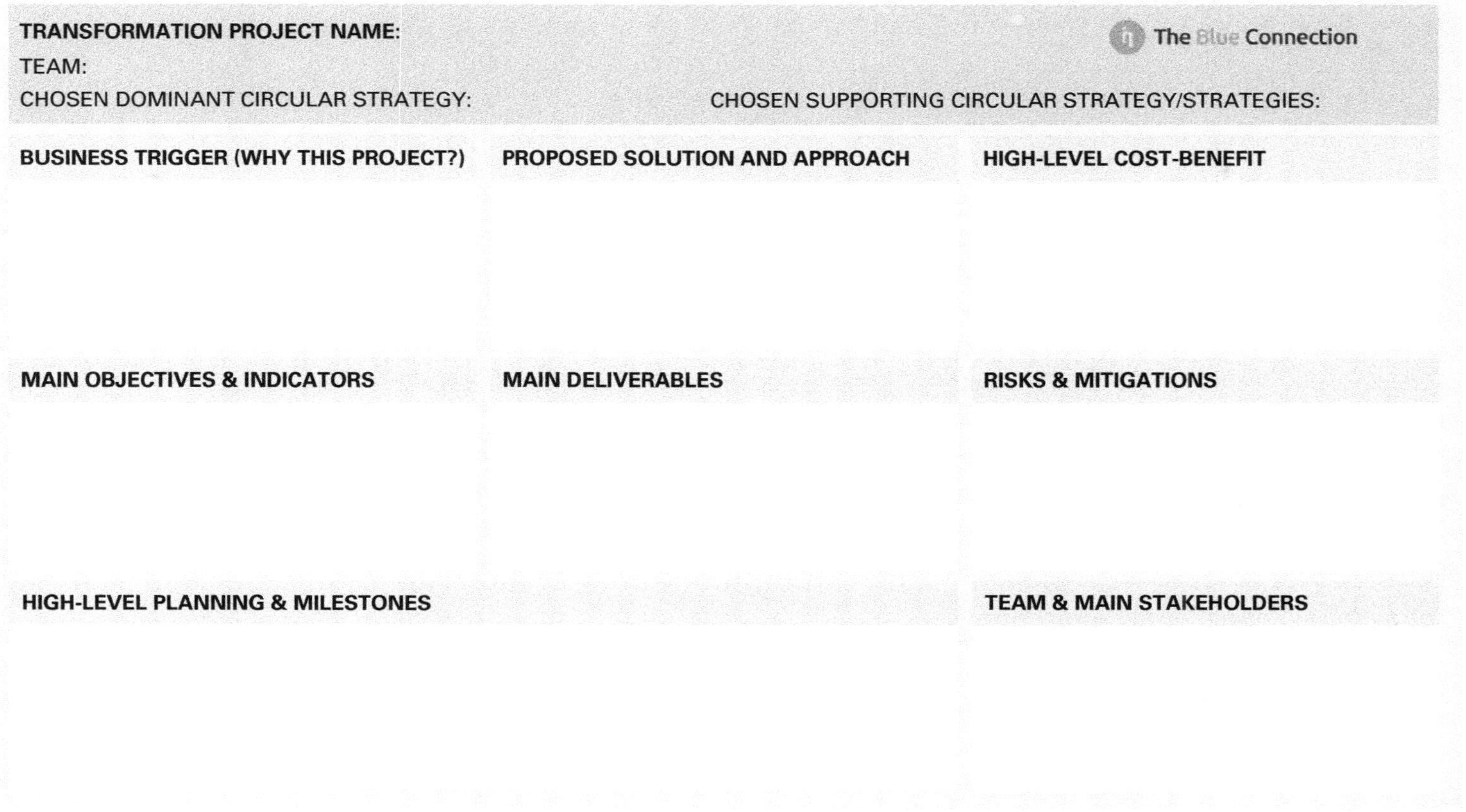

TRANSFORMATION PROJECT NAME:
TEAM:
CHOSEN DOMINANT CIRCULAR STRATEGY:
CHOSEN SUPPORTING CIRCULAR STRATEGY/STRATEGIES:

The Blue Connection

BUSINESS TRIGGER (WHY THIS PROJECT?)	PROPOSED SOLUTION AND APPROACH	HIGH-LEVEL COST-BENEFIT
MAIN OBJECTIVES & INDICATORS	MAIN DELIVERABLES	RISKS & MITIGATIONS
HIGH-LEVEL PLANNING & MILESTONES		TEAM & MAIN STAKEHOLDERS

EXERCISE 11.3

Capture the linear business model of TBC

Imagine

On the basis of the previous exercises, now put together all of your inputs and image the complete linear business model of TBC, based on Team SuperBike's work and any amendments/adjustments you have seen as appropriate. You can use the template from Figure 11.3.

Summary

'OK, so that was pretty quick,' Maria said. 'I think now we have a solid starting point for evaluating what the transformation from linear to circular would be like. As Aunt Joanna said, we now need to look at this transformation from each of the perspectives we have dealt with so far: the company perspective, the perspective beyond the company boundary and the leadership perspective. And she asked us to try and translate all the items we encounter to specific transformation projects based on the template she gave us. So I imagine that we will be using this template a lot in our coming activities.'[3]

'Will you get some water? Then I'll prepare the flipcharts'.

Notes

1 Quote from Ashkenas' 2013 article 'Change management needs to change'.
2 Please note: don't be put off-balance by the limited number of pages in this chapter. As you will see, there is a lot of thinking to be done, as well as a good number of projects to be elaborated.
3 See Figure 11.4 for the template.

12

Imagining the transformation from the company perspective[1]

'Here, Peter,' said Maria, 'take a look at the whiteboard. I've prepared an overview of the work Aunt Joanna asked us to do, so that we can keep track and make sure we cover everything.'

'Looks fine with me,' Peter responded. 'Aunt Joanna said she would be back with us towards the end of the afternoon, so let's get started with the first block of topics, then, which is about purpose and strategy and the business model.'

FIGURE 12.1   Making plans for the transition from linear to circular

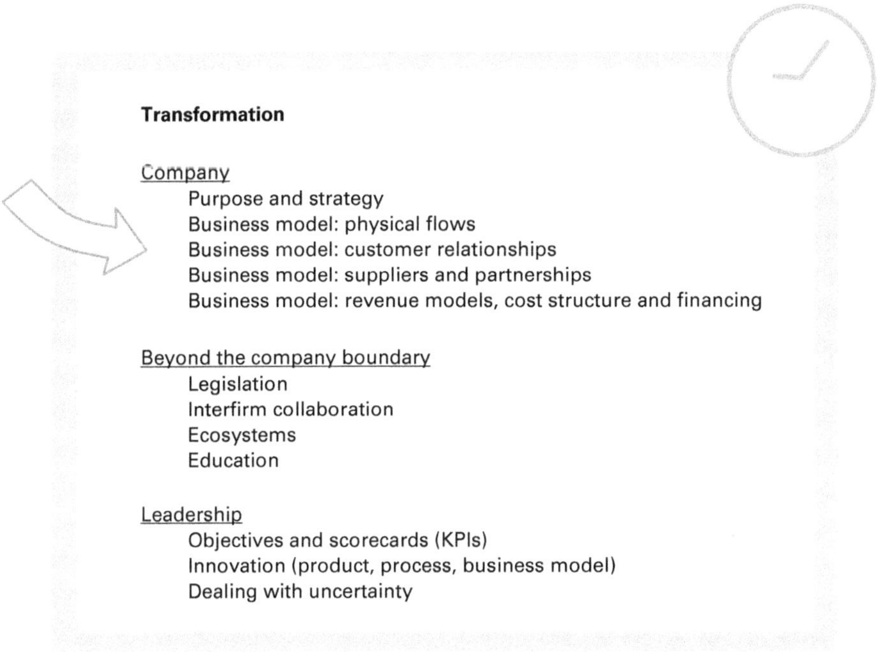

Transformation

Company
     Purpose and strategy
     Business model: physical flows
     Business model: customer relationships
     Business model: suppliers and partnerships
     Business model: revenue models, cost structure and financing

Beyond the company boundary
     Legislation
     Interfirm collaboration
     Ecosystems
     Education

Leadership
     Objectives and scorecards (KPIs)
     Innovation (product, process, business model)
     Dealing with uncertainty

FIGURE 12.2 Project charter template: purpose and strategy

TRANSFORMATION PROJECT NAME: PURPOSE AND STRATEGY
TEAM:

CHOSEN DOMINANT CIRCULAR STRATEGY:

CHOSEN SUPPORTING CIRCULAR STRATEGY/STRATEGIES:

The Blue Connection

BUSINESS TRIGGER (WHY THIS PROJECT?)

PROPOSED SOLUTION AND APPROACH

HIGH-LEVEL COST-BENEFIT

MAIN OBJECTIVES & INDICATORS

MAIN DELIVERABLES

RISKS & MITIGATIONS

HIGH-LEVEL PLANNING & MILESTONES

TEAM & MAIN STAKEHOLDERS

Imagine the transformation: purpose and strategy

Building on the exercises in Chapter 7, we will now zoom in on the transformation needed to achieve the transition from linear purpose and strategic objectives to circular ones.

EXERCISE 12.1

Imagine the transformation of purpose and strategic objectives

Imagine

1   Compare your final versions of templates 7.7 and 11.1, focusing for the moment on the purpose statements and the defined strategic objectives.
2   Imagine which steps the company should take in order to successfully implement the 'new' circular purpose statement and the accompanying strategic objectives. Think not only of how this process of formulating the new purpose statement and objectives would need to be organized in practice, but also particularly of how to get these accepted, diffused and effectively adopted among the relevant stakeholders (board, staff and so on).
3   In order to achieve the required changes, as identified in Step 2, develop a high-level project charter (see Figure 12.2, based on the template from Figure 11.4) and the supporting project management information in the Appendix, describing the transformation from the linear set-up to being prepared for the circular future.
4   Park your results for the moment.

Imagine the business model transformation: circular strategy

EXERCISE 12.2

Imagine the transformation of circular strategy: physical flows

Imagine

1   Compare your final versions of templates 7.8 and 11.3, focusing on the physical flows of products, components and materials and the activities involved.

2   Imagine which steps the company should take in order to successfully implement the transformation into the new circular network of physical flows and activities. Which new product, component and/or material flows will need to be managed and what would the implications be? Which new activities need to be introduced or developed, and what would be the operational, logistics and/or administrative implications of this?[2]

3   In order to achieve the required changes, as identified in Step 2, develop a high-level project charter (see Figure 12.3, based on the template from Figure 11.4) and the

supporting project management information in the Appendix, describing the transformation from the linear set-up to being prepared for the circular future.

4   Park your results for the moment.

If you want, you can repeat the above-mentioned steps 2–4 for each possible dominant circular strategy, combined with one or more compatible supporting strategies.

Imagine the business model transformation: customer relationships

EXERCISE 12.3

Imagine the transformation of circular strategy: customer relationships

Imagine

1   Compare your final versions of templates 7.8 and 11.3, focusing on the customer relationships in the canvas and the chosen revenue models per retail customer.

2   Imagine which steps the company should take in order to successfully implement the transformation into the new circular agreements per retail customer. What will the implications be for the strategic as well as day-to-day relationship and/or contracts with the retail customers, due to the introduction of circular strategies and new revenue models?

3   In order to achieve the required changes, as identified in Step 2, develop a high-level project charter (see Figure 12.4, based on the template from Figure 11.4) and the supporting project management information in the Appendix, describing the transformation from the linear set-up to being prepared for the circular future.

4   Park your results for the moment.

Imagine the business model transformation: suppliers and partnerships

EXERCISE 12.4

Imagine the transformation of circular strategy: suppliers and partnerships

Imagine

1   Compare your final versions of templates 7.8 and 11.3, now focusing on suppliers and partnerships in the canvas and the activities in the network of physical flows.

2 Imagine which steps the company should take in order to successfully implement the transformation into the new circular set-up. Think not only of which suppliers and/or partnerships may change, need to be replaced, or need to be introduced, but also about potential corresponding changes in contracts that need to be adjusted or terminated. Also consider any potentially required supplier selection processes, learning curves with existing or new suppliers and so on.[3]

3 In order to achieve the required changes, as identified in Step 2, develop a high-level project charter (see Figure 12.5, based on the template from Figure 11.4) and the supporting project management information in the Appendix, describing the transformation from the linear set-up to being prepared for the circular future.

4 Park your results for the moment.

Imagine the business model transformation: revenue models, cost structure and financing

EXERCISE 12.5
Imagine the transformation of circular strategy: revenue models, cost structure and financing

Imagine

1 Compare your final versions of templates 7.8 and 11.3, now focusing on changes in the financial flows, so revenue models, cost structure and corresponding changing requirements for financing.

2 Imagine which steps the company should take in order to successfully implement the transformation into the new circular set-up. For example, what kind of implications could there be for the way we will need to organize for proper invoicing, checking of payments, preventing and/or managing the risk of bad debtors and so on? What are the main expected changes in the cost structure in terms of fixed versus variable costs? What are the implications for our financing arrangements with the bank and other potential investors?

3 In order to achieve the required changes, as identified in Step 2, develop a high-level project charter (see Figure 12.6, based on the template from Figure 11.4) and the supporting project management information in the Appendix, describing the transformation from the linear set-up to being prepared for the circular future.

4 Park your results for the moment.

FIGURE 12.3　Project charter template: physical flows and activities

TRANSFORMATION PROJECT NAME: PHYSICAL FLOWS AND ACTIVITIES

🔵 The Blue Connection

TEAM:

CHOSEN DOMINANT CIRCULAR STRATEGY:

CHOSEN SUPPORTING CIRCULAR STRATEGY/STRATEGIES:

BUSINESS TRIGGER (WHY THIS PROJECT?)

PROPOSED SOLUTION AND APPROACH

HIGH-LEVEL COST-BENEFIT

MAIN OBJECTIVES & INDICATORS

MAIN DELIVERABLES

RISKS & MITIGATIONS

HIGH-LEVEL PLANNING & MILESTONES

TEAM & MAIN STAKEHOLDERS

FIGURE 12.4 Project charter template: customer relationships

TRANSFORMATION PROJECT NAME: CUSTOMER RELATIONSHIPS
TEAM:

🔵 The Blue Connection

CHOSEN DOMINANT CIRCULAR STRATEGY:

CHOSEN SUPPORTING CIRCULAR STRATEGY/STRATEGIES:

BUSINESS TRIGGER (WHY THIS PROJECT?)	PROPOSED SOLUTION AND APPROACH	HIGH-LEVEL COST-BENEFIT
MAIN OBJECTIVES & INDICATORS	MAIN DELIVERABLES	RISKS & MITIGATIONS
HIGH-LEVEL PLANNING & MILESTONES		TEAM & MAIN STAKEHOLDERS

FIGURE 12.5 Project charter template: suppliers and partnerships

TRANSFORMATION PROJECT NAME: SUPPLIERS AND PARTNERSHIPS

TEAM:

🔵 The Blue Connection

CHOSEN DOMINANT CIRCULAR STRATEGY:

CHOSEN SUPPORTING CIRCULAR STRATEGY/STRATEGIES:

BUSINESS TRIGGER (WHY THIS PROJECT?)	PROPOSED SOLUTION AND APPROACH	HIGH-LEVEL COST-BENEFIT
MAIN OBJECTIVES & INDICATORS	MAIN DELIVERABLES	RISKS & MITIGATIONS
HIGH-LEVEL PLANNING & MILESTONES		TEAM & MAIN STAKEHOLDERS

FIGURE 12.6   Project charter template: revenue models, cost structure and financing

TRANSFORMATION PROJECT NAME: REVENUE MODELS, COST STRUCTURE AND FINANCING
TEAM:
                                              The Blue Connection

CHOSEN DOMINANT CIRCULAR STRATEGY: CHOSEN SUPPORTING CIRCULAR STRATEGY/STRATEGIES:

BUSINESS TRIGGER (WHY THIS PROJECT?)	PROPOSED SOLUTION AND APPROACH	HIGH-LEVEL COST-BENEFIT
MAIN OBJECTIVES & INDICATORS	**MAIN DELIVERABLES**	**RISKS & MITIGATIONS**
HIGH-LEVEL PLANNING & MILESTONES		**TEAM & MAIN STAKEHOLDERS**

FIGURE 12.7   Making plans for the transition from linear to circular: company
perspective

Transformation

Company
✓ Purpose and strategy
✓ Business model: physical flows
✓ Business model: customer relationships
✓ Business model: suppliers and partnerships
✓ Business model: revenue models, cost structure and financing

Beyond the company boundary
Legislation
Interfirm collaboration
Ecosystems
Education

Leadership
Objectives and scorecards (KPIs)
Innovation (product, process, business model)
Dealing with uncertainty

Summary

'OK, good work, first part done!' said Peter, while putting checkmarks on the whiteboard. 'Let's move on directly, with the part beyond the company boundary.'

Notes

1 Please note: don't be put off-balance by the limited number of pages in this chapter. As you will see, there is a lot of thinking to be done, as well as a good number of projects to be elaborated.

2 Regarding administrative activities, you may need to think about activities related to maintenance and repair (contract management, contacting people for their maintenance service appointments, managing the IoT data in the case of the Silver and Gold maintenance packages and so on).

3 Regarding suppliers, you may not only focus on the more obvious suppliers related to physical material flows, but you may also need to think about any potential technology providers (IoT, Blockchain and so on).

13

Imagining the transformation from the perspective beyond the company boundary[1]

'Good, so we'll be looking into the transformation aspects related to legislation, interfirm collaboration, ecosystems and education,' said Maria. 'Are you ready to move on, Peter?'

FIGURE 13.1   Making plans for the transition from linear to circular: beyond the company boundary

Transformation

<u>Company</u>
    ✓ Purpose and strategy
    ✓ Business model: physical flows
    ✓ Business model: customer relationships
    ✓ Business model: suppliers and partnerships
    ✓ Business model: revenue models, cost structure and financing

<u>Beyond the company boundary</u>
    Legislation
    Interfirm collaboration
    Ecosystems
    Education

<u>Leadership</u>
    Objectives and scorecards (KPIs)
    Innovation (product, process, business model)
    Dealing with uncertainty

FIGURE 13.2   Circles of Concern, Influence and Control

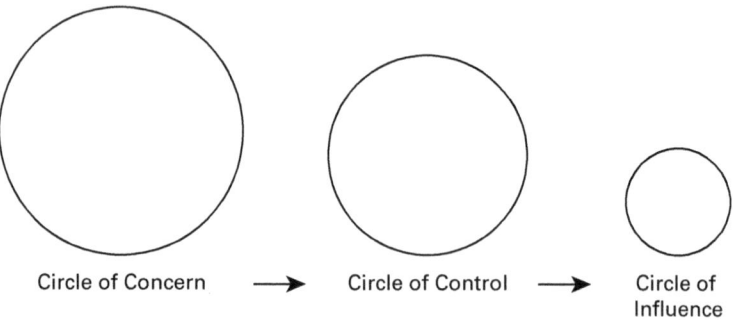

In this chapter, we are going to look in more detail at what could happen in the transition period from a linear to a circular economy in terms of the topics addressed in Chapter 3 (legislation, interfirm collaboration, ecosystems and education) and the corresponding what-if scenarios from Chapter 8. For all the exercises, you can use Figure 13.2 to describe the Circles of Concern, Influence and Control of the company. Important here is to figure out what it is that they can do within the transition period to adequately prepare for a circular economy.

Imagine the transformation: legislation

Look again at the legislation mini-cases in Chapter 8 focusing on fiscal incentives, stimulating the use of environmentally friendly materials and the reduction of negative externalities, subsidies in favour of repair and Extended Producer Liability. If needed, go back to Chapter 3 to look up the corresponding information. If a company only acts when the news comes out that governments are, for example, implementing fiscal incentives to promote sustainable behaviour or to enable the reskilling of people who have lost their jobs due to new technologies, then it might be too late to adequately react to this change. It is essential that companies look ahead to the future, even though it is not clear if the what-if scenarios will actually come true.

EXERCISE 13.1
Imagine the transformation from the legal dimension

Imagine

1   Look at the legal 'what-if' scenarios in Chapter 8 regarding fiscal incentives, the stimulation of environmentally friendly materials, taxing negative externalities, subsidies in favour of repair and Extended Producer Liability (Exercises 8.1–8.6).
2   Imagine what the company should do around, or change because of, these potential legal changes. How will they able to keep an eye on, and be prepared for, such potential future legal scenarios knowing that there is a fair degree of uncertainty

around them? In answering these questions, use Figure 13.2 to visualize the Circle of Concern, Circle of Influence and Circle of Control.

3   In order to effectively deal with the implications these changes may bring, as identified in Step 2, develop a high-level project charter (see Figure 13.3, based on the template from Figure 11.4) and the supporting project management information in the Appendix, describing the transformation from the initial linear set-up to being prepared for the circular future.

4   Park the results for the moment

Imagine the transformation: interfirm collaboration

As we mentioned in Chapter 3, multi-stakeholder interfirm collaboration is pertinent in implementing circularity, as it leads to transparency, technology transfer, organizational learning and the right partner connections necessary for clean technology and resource efficiency in a circular economy (Mishra et al, 2019). Essential for this type of collaboration is systems thinking, meaning that we look at the value chain as a whole in which all systems and every stakeholder are connected.

EXERCISE 13.2

Imagine the transformation from the dimension of interfirm collaboration

Imagine

1   Look at the interfirm collaboration exercise in Chapter 8 regarding potential collaboration partners in the value chain, beyond a simple buying/selling relationship (Exercise 8.7).

2   Imagine what the company should do in order to keep an eye on the potential collaboration partners and their developments in the value chain. How would you prepare the company to be ready when potential collaboration scenarios come to life, such as multi-stakeholder interfirm collaboration, corporate accelerators or sharing company data using Blockchain/implementing IoT/using Big Data to drive decision-making? In answering these questions, use Figure 13.2 to visualize the Circle of Concern, Circle of Influence and Circle of Control. Additionally, you can look up the Circle Economy (2020b) report 'Will you be my partner?' mentioned in Chapter 3 and of which an overview can be found in the Appendix ('Collaboration').

3   In order to effectively deal with the implications these changes may bring, as identified in Step 2, develop a high-level project charter (see Figure 13.4, based on the template from Figure 11.4) and the supporting project management information in the Appendix, describing the transformation from the initial linear set-up to being prepared for the circular future.

4   Park the results for the moment.

FIGURE 13.3   Project charter template: legislation

TRANSFORMATION PROJECT NAME: LEGISLATION		The Blue Connection
TEAM:		
CHOSEN DOMINANT CIRCULAR STRATEGY:	CHOSEN SUPPORTING CIRCULAR STRATEGY/STRATEGIES:	
BUSINESS TRIGGER (WHY THIS PROJECT?)	PROPOSED SOLUTION AND APPROACH	HIGH-LEVEL COST-BENEFIT
MAIN OBJECTIVES & INDICATORS	MAIN DELIVERABLES	RISKS & MITIGATIONS
HIGH-LEVEL PLANNING & MILESTONES		TEAM & MAIN STAKEHOLDERS

FIGURE 13.4 Project charter template: interfirm collaboration

TRANSFORMATION PROJECT NAME: INTERFIRM COLLABORATION
TEAM:

The Blue Connection

CHOSEN DOMINANT CIRCULAR STRATEGY:	CHOSEN SUPPORTING CIRCULAR STRATEGY/STRATEGIES:	
BUSINESS TRIGGER (WHY THIS PROJECT?)	**PROPOSED SOLUTION AND APPROACH**	**HIGH-LEVEL COST-BENEFIT**
MAIN OBJECTIVES & INDICATORS	**MAIN DELIVERABLES**	**RISKS & MITIGATIONS**
HIGH-LEVEL PLANNING & MILESTONES		**TEAM & MAIN STAKEHOLDERS**

Imagine the transformation: ecosystems

Within a circular ecosystem, collaborative innovation is essential, meaning that cross-sectoral and multidisciplinary collaboration is required to inspire innovative solutions (Bocken and Geradts, 2020). As mentioned in Chapter 3, this type of collaboration takes place to create a sustainable value proposition with narrowed, slowed and closed resource loops. Besides, this value creation is collaborative: ecosystems create more value as a whole than the sum of individual participants acting independently. It is therefore essential that businesses create these ecosystems to make a circular economy work.

EXERCISE 13.3
Imagine the transformation from the ecosystems dimension

Imagine

1 Look at the ecosystem exercise in Chapter 8, focusing on the ecosystem stakeholders and the shift from individualistic (corporate) thinking to we-thinking (Exercise 8.9).

2 Imagine what the company should do to adequately prepare for the shift to we-thinking and ecosystem collaboration – thus becoming more resilient – knowing that there is a fair degree of uncertainty around them, for example due to competition policies or a (virtual) Open Source Circular Economy. In answering these questions, use Figure 13.2 visualizing the Circle of Concern, Circle of Influence and Circle of Control. Besides, you can use the elements of a circular ecosystem (see Figure 3.3) to prepare for Step 3.

3 In order to effectively deal with the implications these changes may bring, as identified in Step 2, develop a high-level project charter (see Figure 13.5, based on the template from Figure 11.4) and the supporting project management information in the Appendix, describing the transformation from the initial linear set-up to being prepared for the circular future.

4 Park the results for the moment.

Imagine the transformation: education

As you already know from Chapter 3, the transition to a circular economy requires knowledge development, dissemination and innovation. If these are insufficient, this can impede the transition. Since structural cooperation between companies, knowledge institutions and governments is not yet guaranteed in a transition scenario, this

FIGURE 13.5 Project charter template: ecosystems

TRANSFORMATION PROJECT NAME: ECOSYSTEMS
TEAM:

CHOSEN DOMINANT CIRCULAR STRATEGY:

CHOSEN SUPPORTING CIRCULAR STRATEGY/STRATEGIES:

The Blue Connection

BUSINESS TRIGGER (WHY THIS PROJECT?)

PROPOSED SOLUTION AND APPROACH

HIGH-LEVEL COST-BENEFIT

MAIN OBJECTIVES & INDICATORS

MAIN DELIVERABLES

RISKS & MITIGATIONS

HIGH-LEVEL PLANNING & MILESTONES

TEAM & MAIN STAKEHOLDERS

raises the question of how a company goes from A to B: how can you organize knowledge development for a circular economy and how can the acquired knowledge be effectively marketed?

EXERCISE 13.4

Imagine the transformation from the education dimension

Imagine

1   Go back to the part on Education in Chapter 3 and review the content about a circular labour market, the needed competences, and the opportunities in education, skilling and reskilling. In addition, go back to Exercise 2.14 where you explored the dominant and compatible supporting circular strategies. Now, keep the TBC game in mind and their transformation from linear to circular.

2   Imagine what the company should do for each of the dominant circular strategies, to adequately prepare themselves and their employees in terms of education, knowing that there is a fair degree of uncertainty around them. Use the three types of competences identified in Chapter 3 (technical, valorization and transversal) to describe the educational preparation needed.

3   In order to effectively deal with the implications, as identified in Step 2, develop a high-level project charter (Figure 13.6), based on the template from Figure 11.4 and the supporting project management information in the Appendix, describing the transformation from the initial linear set-up to being prepared for the circular future.

4   Park the results for the moment.

FIGURE 13.6 Project charter template: education

TRANSFORMATION PROJECT NAME: EDUCATION		The Blue Connection
TEAM:		
CHOSEN DOMINANT CIRCULAR STRATEGY:	CHOSEN SUPPORTING CIRCULAR STRATEGY/STRATEGIES:	
BUSINESS TRIGGER (WHY THIS PROJECT?)	PROPOSED SOLUTION AND APPROACH	HIGH-LEVEL COST-BENEFIT
MAIN OBJECTIVES & INDICATORS	MAIN DELIVERABLES	RISKS & MITIGATIONS
HIGH-LEVEL PLANNING & MILESTONES		TEAM & MAIN STAKEHOLDERS

Summary

'Almost done, Maria,' Peter said. 'Two topics finished, one more to go.'

FIGURE 13.7   Making plans for the transition from linear to circular: beyond the company boundary (done)

Transformation

Company
  ✓ Purpose and strategy
  ✓ Business model: physical flows
  ✓ Business model: customer relationships
  ✓ Business model: suppliers and partnerships
  ✓ Business model: revenue models, cost structure and financing

Beyond the company boundary
  ✓ Legislation
  ✓ Interfirm collaboration
  ✓ Ecosystems
  ✓ Education

Leadership
  Objectives and scorecards (KPI´s)
  Innovation (product, process, business model)
  Dealing with uncertainty

Note

1   Please note: don't be put off-balance by the limited number of pages in this chapter. As you will see, there is a lot of thinking to be done, as well as a good number of projects to be elaborated.

14

Imagining the transformation from the leadership perspective[1]

'How are you progressing, Maria and Peter?' Aunt Joanna asked, peeking around the corner of the meeting room door. 'Do you think we can still get together at the end of the afternoon and you'll give me a briefing of where you are?'

'Hi, Aunt Joanna,' Maria responded, 'we're about to get started on the last items on the list and I think that we're ready then to give you the full story. Shall we say around 4:30 pm?'

'Sounds great!' said Aunt Joanna, and she was off again.

FIGURE 14.1 Making plans for the transition from linear to circular: leadership

Transformation

Company
- ✓ Purpose and strategy
- ✓ Business model: physical flows
- ✓ Business model: customer relationships
- ✓ Business model: suppliers and partnerships
- ✓ Business model: revenue models, cost structure and financing

Beyond the company boundary
- ✓ Legislation
- ✓ Interfirm collaboration
- ✓ Ecosystems
- ✓ Education

Leadership
- Objectives and scorecards (KPIs)
- Innovation (product, process, business model)
- Dealing with uncertainty

Building on the topics from Chapter 4 and some of the exercises from Chapter 9, we will now zoom in on the leadership aspects of the transformation from linear to circular.

Imagine the transformation: objectives and scorecards

EXERCISE 14.1
Imagine the transformation: KPIs

Imagine

1 Compare your final versions of templates 7.7 and 11.1, now focusing on the part of the KPIs.

2 Imagine which steps the company should take in order to successfully implement the 'new' circular KPIs. Think not only of the process of formulating the new KPIs, but particularly also of how to get these accepted, diffused and effectively adopted among the relevant stakeholders (board, staff and so on). You may even need to explicitly consider how to deal with the transformation of those KPIs if they were connected to individual employee bonus agreements.

3 In order to achieve the required changes, as identified in Step 2, develop a high-level project charter (see Figure 14.2, based on the template from Figure 11.4) and the supporting project management information in the Appendix, describing the transformation from the linear set-up to being prepared for the circular future.

4 Park your results for the moment.

Imagine the transformation: innovation

EXERCISE 14.2
Imagine the transformation: product innovation

Imagine

1 One of the areas the company could innovate in is product innovation, preparing for more circular products.

2 Imagine what the company should or could do in order to keep an eye on relevant technological developments and stimulate its capabilities in circular product innovation. Which changes would this imply to the initial linear way of doing business?

---

3 In order to achieve the required changes, as identified in Step 2, develop a high-level project charter (see Figure 14.3, based on the template from Figure 11.4) and the supporting project management information in the Appendix, describing the transformation from the linear set-up to being prepared for the circular future.

4 Park your results for the moment.

EXERCISE 14.3

Imagine the transformation: process innovation

Imagine

1 Another area the company could innovate in is process innovation, preparing for more circular production.

2 Imagine what the company should or could do in order to keep an eye on relevant technological developments and stimulate its capabilities in circular process innovation, making the internal production and logistics processes more circular. Which changes would this imply to the linear way of doing business?

3 In order to achieve the required changes, as identified in Step 2, develop a high-level project charter (see Figure 14.4, based on the template from Figure 11.4) and the supporting project management information in the Appendix, describing the transformation from the linear setup to being prepared for the circular future;

4 Park your results for the moment.

EXERCISE 14.4

Imagine the transformation: business model innovation

Imagine

1 Another one of the areas the company could innovate in is business model innovation, preparing for more circular business models and being at the forefront of new business model options.

2 Imagine what the company should or could do in order to stimulate its capabilities in circular business model innovation. Which changes would this imply to the linear way of doing business?

3 In order to achieve the required changes, as identified in Step 2, develop a high-level project charter (see Figure 14.5, based on the template from Figure 11.4) and the supporting project management information in the Appendix, describing the transformation from the linear set-up to being prepared for the circular future.

4   Park your results for the moment.

Imagine the transformation: dealing with uncertainty

Innovation, change and transformation lead to uncertainty. The journey from linear to circular is no exception. During TBC gameplay there were a number of elements given, for example through the available information, the depreciation graph or other implicit assumptions. One can obviously question if a company would always have these sources available and how they would deal with the resulting uncertainty. Let's look at some scenarios in which to assess the degree of uncertainty and potential mitigations.

EXERCISE 14.5
Imagine the transformation: market uncertainty

Imagine

1   During gameplay, market behaviour in terms of sales volumes and retail customer preferences were perfectly known.

2   Imagine which uncertainties could exist about market behaviour. Think particularly of sales volumes and retailers' and consumers' sensitivity to circularity. Taking the gameplay's situation as the 'neutral' starting point, add a positive and a negative scenario. What would be the implication of these two scenarios for the company? Imagine what the company could do in order to be prepared for dealing with the resulting uncertainty, or build in the required flexibility or resilience.

3   In order to be prepared for the uncertainty, as identified in Step 2, develop a high-level project charter (see Figure 14.6, based on the template from Figure 11.4) and the supporting project management information in the Appendix, describing the transformation from the linear set-up to being prepared for the circular future.

4   Park your results for the moment.

EXERCISE 14.6
Imagine the transformation: circularity strategy uncertainty

Imagine

1   During gameplay, consequences of the circular strategies were perfectly known and could be evaluated through the depreciation graph, for example the market response

to buyback prices or the rates of repairs in the leasing schemes. In practice, this information would most likely be unavailable, highly uncertain or even ambiguous, especially at the beginning of the transformation process.

2   Imagine which uncertainties could exist about these circular strategies. Think particularly of response to buyback prices in terms of the quantity of bikes expected to be returned per year, or the amount of repairs to be done per year as part of the leasing scheme. Taking the gameplay's situation as the 'neutral' starting point, add a positive and a negative scenario. What would be the implication of these two scenarios for the company? Imagine what the company could do in order to be prepared for dealing with the resulting uncertainty, or build in the required flexibility or resilience.

3   In order to be prepared for the uncertainty, as identified in Step 2, develop a high-level project charter (see Figure 14.7, based on the template from Figure 11.4) and the supporting project management information in the Appendix, describing the transformation from the linear set-up to being prepared for the circular future.

4   Park your results for the moment.

EXERCISE 14.7
Imagine the transformation: design choice uncertainty

Imagine

1   During gameplay, consequences of certain component design choices were perfectly known and could be evaluated through the depreciation graph, for example the choice for more durable components and their impact on the lifespan of the bike. In practice, this information would most likely be unavailable, highly uncertain or even ambiguous, especially at the beginning of the transformation process.

2   Imagine which uncertainties could exist about these design choices. Think particularly of lifespan impact on design choices. Taking the gameplay's situation as the 'neutral' starting point, add a positive and a negative scenario. What would be the implication of these two scenarios for the company? Imagine what the company could do in order to be prepared for dealing with the resulting uncertainty, or build in the required flexibility or resilience.

3   In order to be prepared for the uncertainty, as identified in Step 2, develop a high-level project charter (see Figure 14.8, based on the template from Figure 11.4) and the supporting project management information in the Appendix, describing the transformation from the linear set-up to being prepared for the circular future.

4   Park your results for the moment.

FIGURE 14.2   Project charter template: KPIs

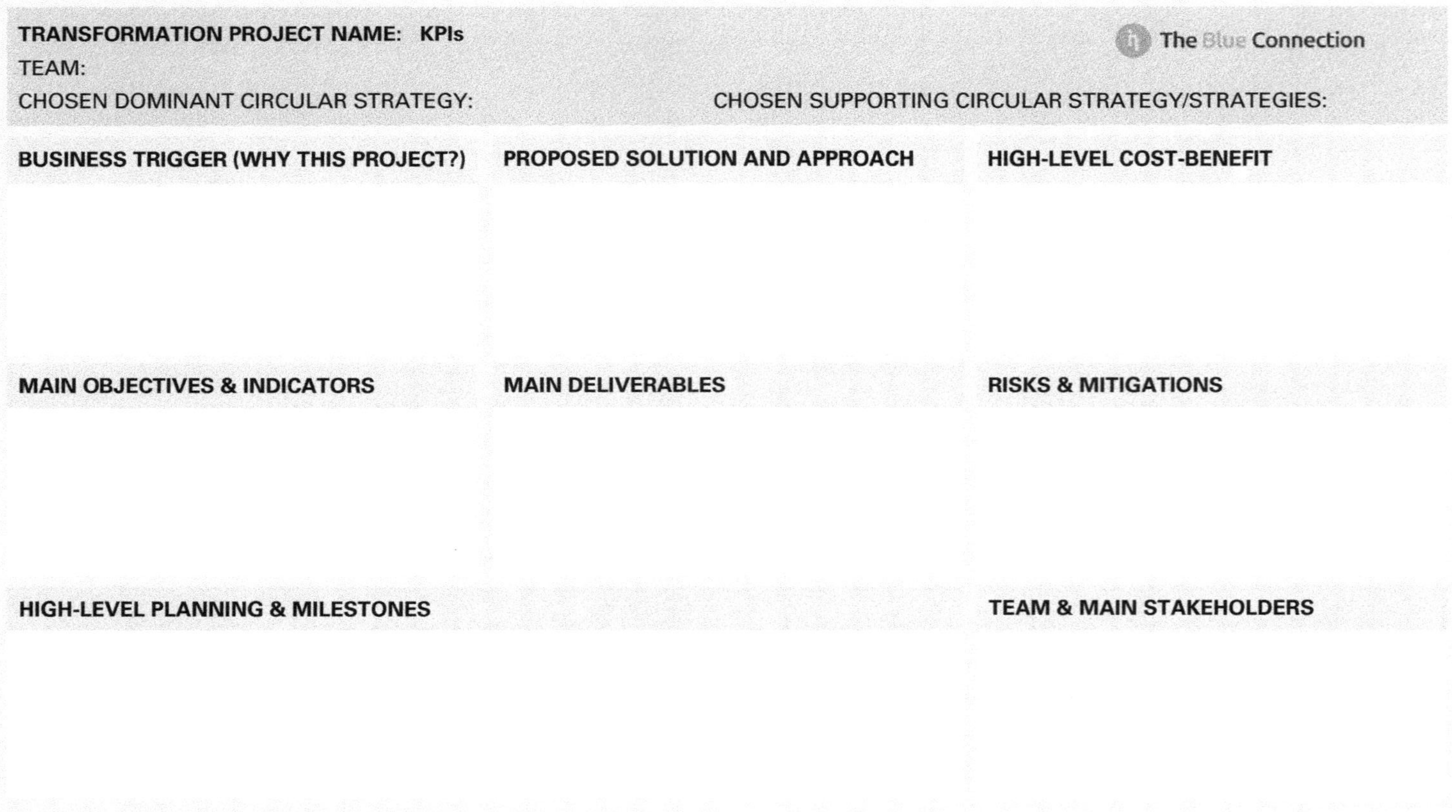

TRANSFORMATION PROJECT NAME: KPIs
TEAM:
CHOSEN DOMINANT CIRCULAR STRATEGY:

🔵 The Blue Connection

CHOSEN SUPPORTING CIRCULAR STRATEGY/STRATEGIES:

BUSINESS TRIGGER (WHY THIS PROJECT?)	PROPOSED SOLUTION AND APPROACH	HIGH-LEVEL COST-BENEFIT
MAIN OBJECTIVES & INDICATORS	MAIN DELIVERABLES	RISKS & MITIGATIONS
HIGH-LEVEL PLANNING & MILESTONES	TEAM & MAIN STAKEHOLDERS	

FIGURE 14.3   Project charter template: circular product innovation

TRANSFORMATION PROJECT NAME: PRODUCT INNOVATION

TEAM:

🔵 The Blue Connection

CHOSEN DOMINANT CIRCULAR STRATEGY

CHOSEN SUPPORTING CIRCULAR STRATEGY/STRATEGIES:

BUSINESS TRIGGER (WHY THIS PROJECT?)

PROPOSED SOLUTION AND APPROACH

HIGH-LEVEL COST-BENEFIT

MAIN OBJECTIVES & INDICATORS

MAIN DELIVERABLES

RISKS & MITIGATIONS

HIGH-LEVEL PLANNING & MILESTONES

TEAM & MAIN STAKEHOLDERS

FIGURE 14.4   Project charter template: circular process innovation

TRANSFORMATION PROJECT NAME: PROCESS INNOVATION
TEAM:

CHOSEN DOMINANT CIRCULAR STRATEGY: CHOSEN SUPPORTING CIRCULAR STRATEGY/STRATEGIES:

🔵 The Blue Connection

BUSINESS TRIGGER (WHY THIS PROJECT?)   **PROPOSED SOLUTION AND APPROACH**   **HIGH-LEVEL COST-BENEFIT**

MAIN OBJECTIVES & INDICATORS   **MAIN DELIVERABLES**   **RISKS & MITIGATIONS**

HIGH-LEVEL PLANNING & MILESTONES   **TEAM & MAIN STAKEHOLDERS**

FIGURE 14.5 Project charter template: business model innovation

TRANSFORMATION PROJECT NAME: BUSINESS MODEL INNOVATION		The Blue Connection
TEAM:		
CHOSEN DOMINANT CIRCULAR STRATEGY:	CHOSEN SUPPORTING CIRCULAR STRATEGY/STRATEGIES:	

BUSINESS TRIGGER (WHY THIS PROJECT?)	PROPOSED SOLUTION AND APPROACH	HIGH-LEVEL COST-BENEFIT

MAIN OBJECTIVES & INDICATORS	MAIN DELIVERABLES	RISKS & MITIGATIONS

HIGH-LEVEL PLANNING & MILESTONES		TEAM & MAIN STAKEHOLDERS

FIGURE 14.6 Project charter template: market uncertainty

TRANSFORMATION PROJECT NAME: **MARKET UNCERTAINTY**
TEAM:
CHOSEN DOMINANT CIRCULAR STRATEGY:

CHOSEN SUPPORTING CIRCULAR STRATEGY/STRATEGIES:

The Blue Connection

BUSINESS TRIGGER (WHY THIS PROJECT?)

PROPOSED SOLUTION AND APPROACH

HIGH-LEVEL COST-BENEFIT

MAIN OBJECTIVES & INDICATORS

MAIN DELIVERABLES

RISKS & MITIGATIONS

HIGH-LEVEL PLANNING & MILESTONES

TEAM & MAIN STAKEHOLDERS

FIGURE 14.7 Project charter template: circular strategy uncertainty

TRANSFORMATION PROJECT NAME: CIRCULAR STRATEGY UNCERTAINTY		The Blue Connection
TEAM:		
CHOSEN DOMINANT CIRCULAR STRATEGY:	CHOSEN SUPPORTING CIRCULAR STRATEGY/STRATEGIES:	
BUSINESS TRIGGER (WHY THIS PROJECT?)	PROPOSED SOLUTION AND APPROACH	HIGH-LEVEL COST-BENEFIT
MAIN OBJECTIVES & INDICATORS	MAIN DELIVERABLES	RISKS & MITIGATIONS
HIGH-LEVEL PLANNING & MILESTONES		TEAM & MAIN STAKEHOLDERS

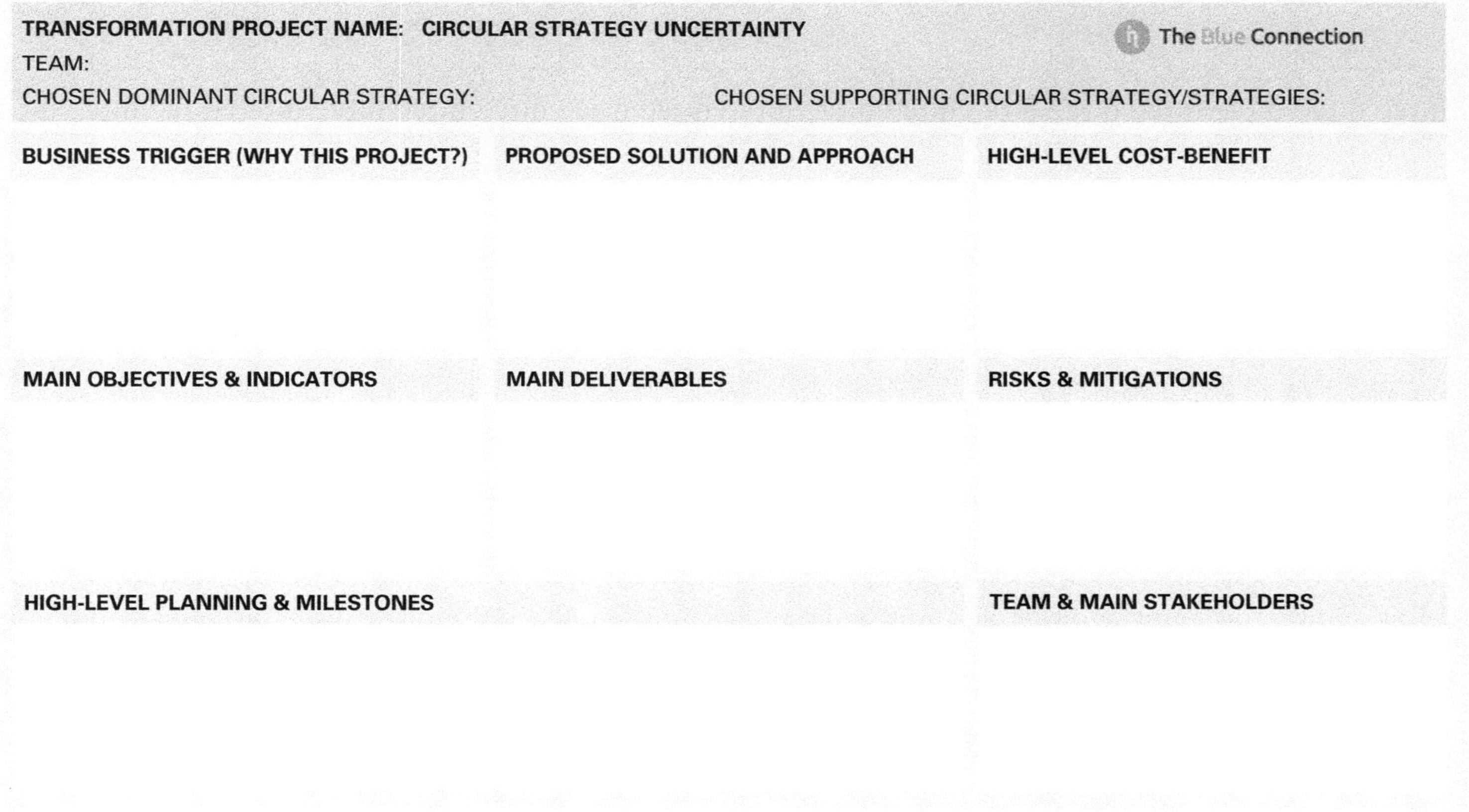

EXERCISE 14.8

Imagine the transformation: second-hand market value uncertainty

Imagine

1   During gameplay, the second-hand market value of the bikes was perfectly known and could be evaluated through the depreciation graph. In practice, this information would most likely be unavailable, highly uncertain or even ambiguous, especially at the beginning of the transformation process.

2   Imagine which uncertainties could exist about this second-hand market value. Taking the gameplay's situation as the 'neutral' starting point, add a positive and a negative scenario. What would be the implication of these two scenarios for the company? Imagine what the company could do in order to be prepared for dealing with the resulting uncertainty, or build in the required flexibility or resilience.

3   In order to be prepared for the uncertainty, as identified in Step 2, develop a high-level project charter (see Figure 14.9, based on the template from Figure 11.4) and the supporting project management information in the Appendix, describing the transformation from the linear set-up to being prepared for the circular future.

4   Park your results for the moment.

A few of the above-mentioned issues have to do with the depreciation graph. In the gameplay you have experienced how powerful an instrument it is for circular decision-making.

EXERCISE 14.9

Imagine the transformation: depreciation graph

Imagine

1   Evaluate the information you had available through the depreciation graph.

2   Imagine where this information would be available already in practice, where it could be found or how assumptions would need to be built in case there is no information available. How would the company need to deal with this?

3   Develop a high-level project charter for a project to create a reliable decision support tool like the depreciation graph (see Figure 14.10, based on the template from Figure 11.4) and the supporting project management information in the Appendix, describing the transformation from the linear set-up to being prepared for the circular future.

4   Park your results for the moment.

FIGURE 14.8 Project charter template: design choice uncertainty

TRANSFORMATION PROJECT NAME: DESIGN CHOICE UNCERTAINTY
TEAM:

The Blue Connection

CHOSEN DOMINANT CIRCULAR STRATEGY:

CHOSEN SUPPORTING CIRCULAR STRATEGY/STRATEGIES:

BUSINESS TRIGGER (WHY THIS PROJECT?)	PROPOSED SOLUTION AND APPROACH	HIGH-LEVEL COST-BENEFIT

MAIN OBJECTIVES & INDICATORS	MAIN DELIVERABLES	RISKS & MITIGATIONS

HIGH-LEVEL PLANNING & MILESTONES		TEAM & MAIN STAKEHOLDERS

FIGURE 14.9   Project charter template: second-hand market value uncertainty

TRANSFORMATION PROJECT NAME: SECOND-HAND MARKET VALUE UNCERTAINTY

TEAM:

🔵 The Blue Connection

CHOSEN DOMINANT CIRCULAR STRATEGY:

CHOSEN SUPPORTING CIRCULAR STRATEGY/STRATEGIES:

BUSINESS TRIGGER (WHY THIS PROJECT?)

PROPOSED SOLUTION AND APPROACH

HIGH-LEVEL COST-BENEFIT

MAIN OBJECTIVES & INDICATORS

MAIN DELIVERABLES

RISKS & MITIGATIONS

HIGH-LEVEL PLANNING & MILESTONES

TEAM & MAIN STAKEHOLDERS

FIGURE 14.10 Project charter template: depreciation graph

TRANSFORMATION PROJECT NAME: DEPRECIATION GRAPH
TEAM:

The Blue Connection

CHOSEN DOMINANT CIRCULAR STRATEGY:

CHOSEN SUPPORTING CIRCULAR STRATEGY/STRATEGIES:

BUSINESS TRIGGER (WHY THIS PROJECT?)	PROPOSED SOLUTION AND APPROACH	HIGH-LEVEL COST-BENEFIT
MAIN OBJECTIVES & INDICATORS	MAIN DELIVERABLES	RISKS & MITIGATIONS
HIGH-LEVEL PLANNING & MILESTONES		TEAM & MAIN STAKEHOLDERS

Imagine the transformation: change management

Although we will only put all of the project charters together in the next chapter, this may be a good moment to revisit the eight steps of change management as formulated by Kotter and listed in Chapter 4. These will come in handy when crafting the overall transformation approach.

Summary

> 'We're done, Maria!' said Peter, with a big and satisfied smile on his face. 'Let's call Aunt Joanna over here and we'll brief her on what we've done today, OK?'

FIGURE 14.11   Making plans for the transition from linear to circular: leadership (done)

Transformation

<u>Company</u>
  ✓ Purpose and strategy
  ✓ Business model: physical flows
  ✓ Business model: customer relationships
  ✓ Business model: suppliers and partnerships
  ✓ Business model: revenue models, cost structure and financing

<u>Beyond the company boundary</u>
  ✓ Legislation
  ✓ Interfirm collaboration
  ✓ Ecosystems
  ✓ Education

<u>Leadership</u>
  ✓ Objectives and scorecards (KPIs)
  ✓ Innovation (product, process, business model)
  ✓ Dealing with uncertainty

Note

1 Please note: don't be put off-balance by the limited number of pages in this chapter. As you will see, there is a lot of thinking to be done, as well as a good number of projects to be elaborated.

Conclusion: the Corporate Circular Imperative: narrative and numbers (4)

Wrapping up the journey of Project 'Circularity'

'That is indeed a great job, guys, what an extensive list of projects,' Aunt Joanna said. 'I'm not sure if I was prepared for this, but you certainly did answer my question about *what the strategic transformation from linear to circular could look like!*'

'Remember what I told you before? That the challenge is to make change management part and parcel of the plan, and not an add-on that is managed independently.[1] So, what we now need to do is to really take it one step further,' she continued, 'assigning some priorities to these many initiatives and develop a convincing, coherent and complete overall change management approach.'

EXERCISE 15.1
Imagine defining a strategic plan for the transformation from linear to circular: project heatmap

Imagine

Imagine you have to come up with a list of strategic priorities for TBC for the coming three to five years – what would it contain? Follow steps 1–3 and the corresponding templates below to formulate your answer.

Step 1: Go back to all of the actions, proposals and initiatives you listed in Chapters 12–14. Assume that all of the challenges to which they are related are real and relevant somehow at this moment. As a reminder, the following challenges have been dealt with:

- Company perspective of circularity:
  o purpose and strategic objectives;

- o physical flows;
- o customer relationships;
- o suppliers and partnerships;
- o revenue models, cost structure and financing.
- Perspective of circularity beyond the company boundary:
  - o legislation;
  - o interfirm collaboration;
  - o ecosystems;
  - o education.
- Leadership perspective of circularity:
  - o KPIs;
  - o product innovation;
  - o process innovation;
  - o business model innovation;
  - o market uncertainty;
  - o circularity strategy uncertainty;
  - o design choice uncertainty;
  - o second-hand market value uncertainty;
  - o depreciation graph.

Step 2: Using the heatmap template from Team SuperBike as shown in Figure 15.1, try to define priorities. The heatmap shows the identified projects 'scored' along two dimensions: impact/importance on the one hand (high to low) and required effort on the other hand (high to low). Take your time for positioning the individual projects well. Make sure to be able to defend your choices.

Step 3: On the basis of the heatmap, define where you would put the priorities, ranging from low impact/low effort to high impact/high effort. How many actions do you think you could reasonably put on the priority list for the coming three to five years (depending on the circular strategies chosen and the transition period these strategies imply)? How many of the actual resources would that require? Consider that TBC as a medium-sized company probably doesn't have a separate dedicated project department, meaning that the projects should be staffed either by people who have full-time tasks in parallel, or that external (expensive) resources would need to found and contracted. Using the template in Figure 15.2, try to assign a reasonable project timeline to your prioritized projects, ensuring that you get a feasible overall approach that would successfully transform the company from linear to circular.

FIGURE 15.1   Template: project heatmap

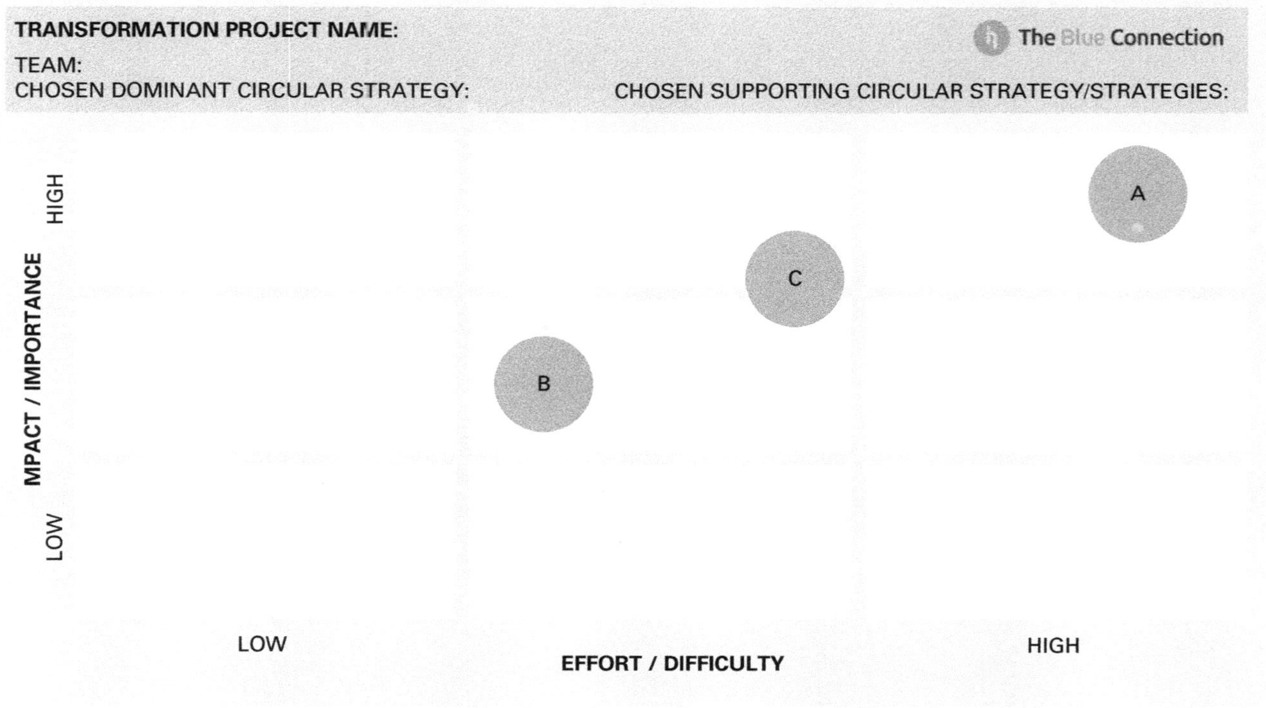

TRANSFORMATION PROJECT NAME:

h The Blue Connection

TEAM:

CHOSEN DOMINANT CIRCULAR STRATEGY:

CHOSEN SUPPORTING CIRCULAR STRATEGY/STRATEGIES:

A

C

B

HIGH

EFFORT / DIFFICULTY

LOW

HIGH

IMPACT / IMPORTANCE

LOW

FIGURE 15.2 Project timelines

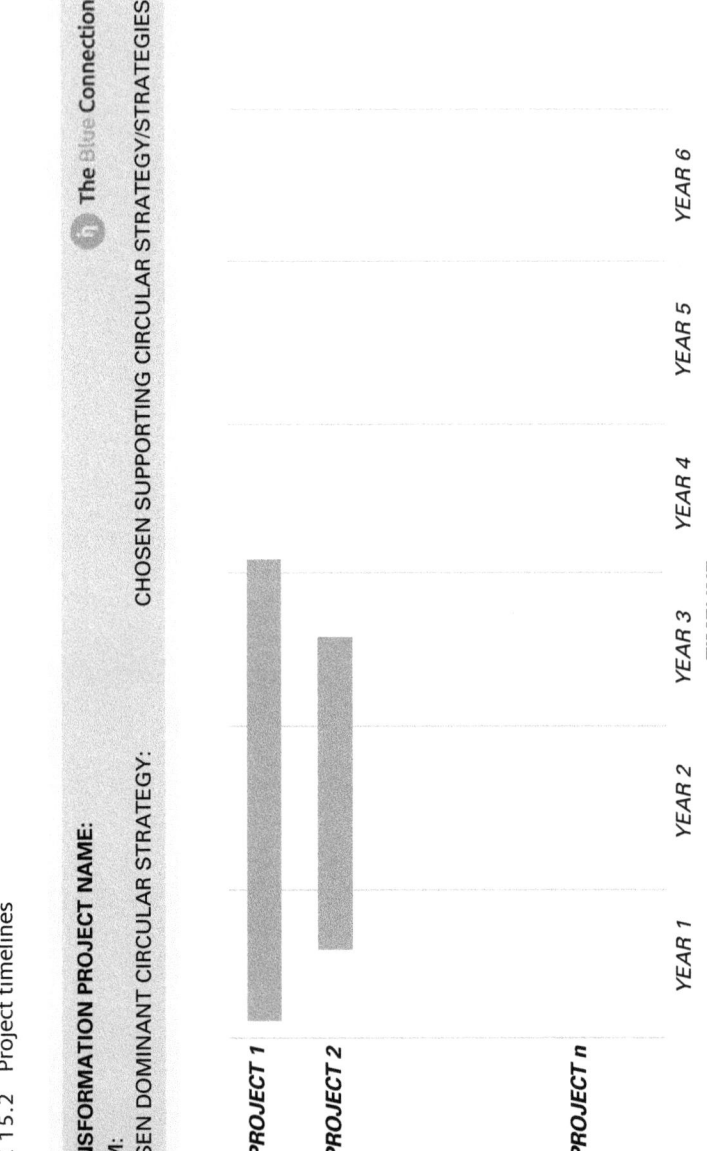

TRANSFORMATION PROJECT NAME:
TEAM:
CHOSEN DOMINANT CIRCULAR STRATEGY:

CHOSEN SUPPORTING CIRCULAR STRATEGY/STRATEGIES:

The Blue Connection

PROJECT 1

PROJECT 2

PROJECT n

YEAR 1   YEAR 2   YEAR 3   YEAR 4   YEAR 5   YEAR 6

TIMELINE

'Wow, it looks like we will have some work to do at Harrison Moore & Co – we may actually need to hire you,' said Aunt Joanna with a big smile. 'And I have some more questions for you.'

'But before I get to those, I'm curious to hear something else, now that we're getting to the end of the journey of our Project 'Circularity'. I just wanted to ask you about your experiences in the project. I remember that some time ago we spoke about the concepts of specific skills required for circularity and also of the T-shaped manager. So, what I'm curious to know about is how you would evaluate yourself on each of the elements in the chart, for example on a scale from 1–5. Would you consider yourselves to have what it takes to become Circular Turnaround Managers like the Catherine McLaren you told me about?'

EXERCISE 15.2
Imagine your own knowledge and skills to become Circular Turnaround Manager

Imagine

Take another good look at the diagram of the T-shaped supply chain manager in Figure 4.9, as well as the earlier exercise on circular competencies (Exercise 3.7). How would you score yourself now that you're getting near the end of the journey of exploring and mastering the circular economy and imagining the transformation from linear to circular?

'Hm, that sounds very good, guys,' said Aunt Joanna. 'As I said before, I may need to consider bringing you on board.'

'In any case, I really learned a lot from having you helping me out and I'm really happy that you've also learned a lot from the journey, by going through the experience, reflecting on what happened, conceptualizing the events and taking them further on in the journey. And be aware, the learning doesn't stop here. I would even argue that this is actually where the learning should really start to take off: you now have the basis and an outlook on where it might go. Now it's up to you to give that shape and form and define how to continue the learning process.'

'No, I'm serious, the learning doesn't stop here, it has merely begun. It's up to you to now define your own continuous circular value chain learning path and find what works best for you: self-study using books, linking into web resources such as sites of organizations and expert associations, subscribing to magazines and newsletters, following professionals' groups on social media such as in LinkedIn, finding mentors, reading general business and specific industry newspapers, doing project internships and so on. There is a wealth of possibilities for you to tap into.'

'And you know what, I actually think the same is valid for the company! I might even consider playing The Blue Connection with some key people from Harrison Moore & Co in order to have them co-create a discourse about circularity and get more people from within to buy into the topic. And Maria, I might even get some suppliers involved, like for example our plastics supplier.'

'In any case, you remember that some time ago we were discussing these blog-posts highlighting the supply chain manager's daily decathlon[2] and we said it was also very valid for circularity? It stated that "[...] managers need to be versatile, multi-skilled people, chameleonic in a way. A bit like the decathlon athlete, they need to perform well on a lot of different disciplines, not necessarily the best at each, but good enough to have a good shot at becoming the overall number 1 in the tournament." It seems to me from your conclusions that that's indeed a true statement equally valid for a Circular Turnaround Manager!'

'Summarizing, I'm glad to see that our Project 'Circularity' has provided you with the conditions in which you could actively do things and that it has aroused your curiosity. It seems to me that it has in a way invited you to ask many questions, that you have discovered new ideas and that you have felt the many exciting dimensions of circular value chain management, just like I have.'[3]

'So, congratulations on accompanying me on our journey along the different perspectives of circularity, from the company perspective, to the perspective beyond the company boundary down to the leadership perspective. I truly hope it's also been worth your while, and above all, that it has inspired you to move forward in this fascinating field of work. Challenges are numerous, and I'm convinced that lots of brain power will be needed in the future. We have dealt with many examples of such challenges along the way in our project, and for sure many more will appear

FIGURE 15.3   Aunt Joanna's beer coaster revisited

wherever you go. But with a solid way of working and a good attitude, you are hopefully well prepared for whatever will follow. Remember, it's not about who has all of the knowledge, it's about who knows how to ask the right questions.'

'Look what I have here,' she continued, pulling the beer coaster from the pocket of her jacket. 'It looks like we have indeed completed the phases I had in mind before we started!'

The Corporate Circular Imperative: narrative and numbers

'And that leaves me with the last and maybe even most important question of the project: what actually is the Corporate Circular Imperative? What's your "final" view on the narrative and the numbers? What would you suggest that we at Harrison Moore & Co do and why? Can you do me one more pitch each, just to let me know what your thoughts are at the end of the journey?'

'Well, Aunt Joanna,' Maria said firmly, 'Peter and I were actually prepared for your question and you know what we decided?'

'We decided,' Peter continued, 'that we would do this last pitch together. You know that Maria and I have been arguing a lot throughout the project. There have been quite some topics we seemed to disagree on.'

'Well, like we always do, really,' he added with a smile and a teasing look to Maria. 'In any case, we also found out that from the perspective of Harrison Moore & Co it didn't really matter if we disagreed or not on those many aspects of circularity, because we did seem to agree on the most fundamental one: circularity can in fact be a positive thing for the company. But let me not reveal everything before we even do the pitch.'

'Are you ready, Aunt Joanna?'.

EXERCISE 15.3
The narrative and numbers to support the Corporate Circular Imperative

Going back to the topics covered throughout the entire book, from the context of circularity all the way down to the three different perspectives that have been dealt with, add in your experience with The Blue Connection from Part Two of the book and the exercises about managing the transformation from linear to circular from Part Three. Now reflect one more time on the narrative and the numbers for circularity from a company standpoint: the Corporate Circular Imperative. Develop a convincing pitch of maximum five minutes that you yourself firmly believe in and that would also convince others to join you on the corporate journey towards circularity: why do it in the first place, what it would look like and how to make it happen.

FIGURE 15.4   The image of the journey of Project 'Circularity'

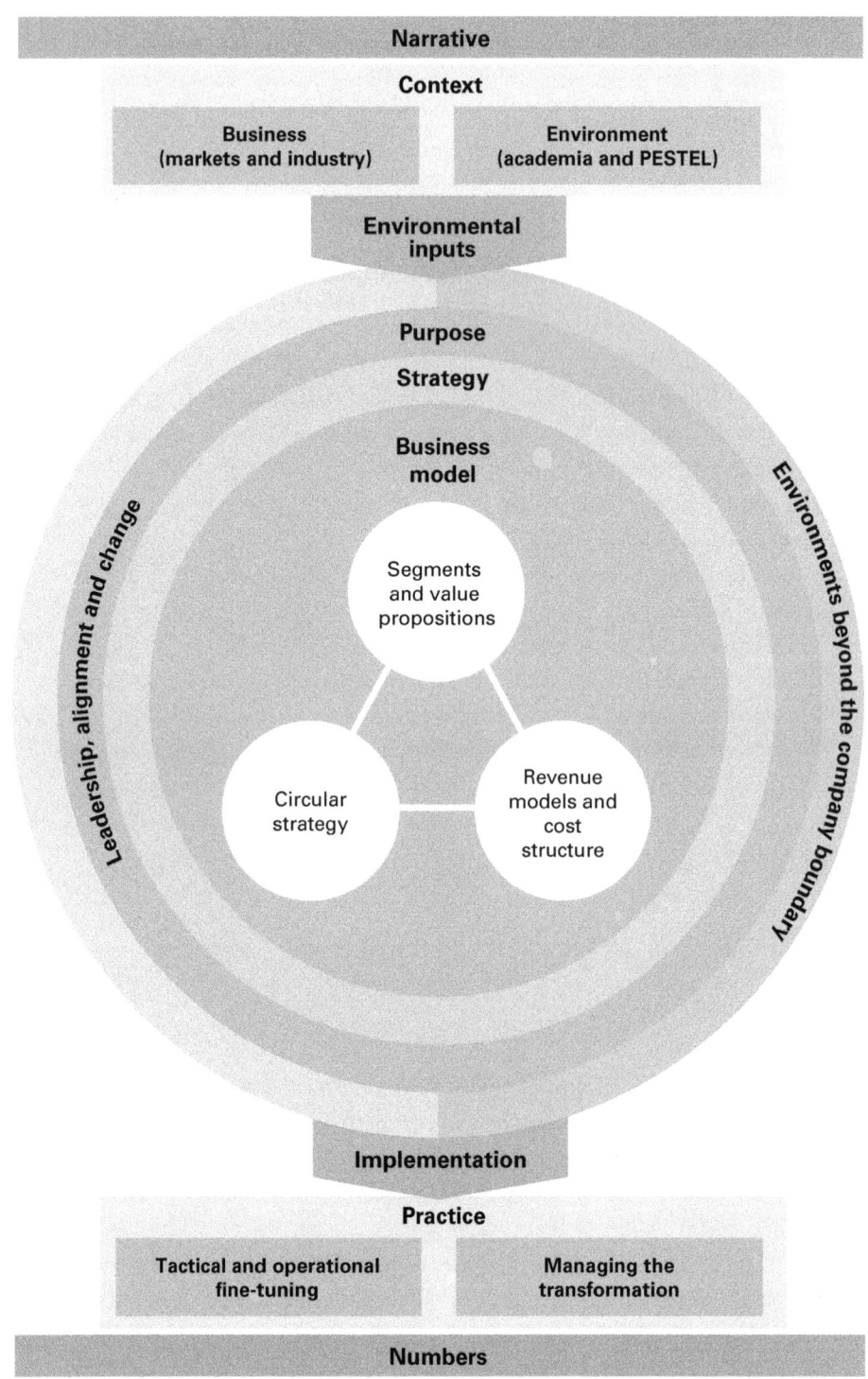

FIGURE 15.5 Maria and Peter's tile for Aunt Joanna: a phrase by Walter Stahel[4]

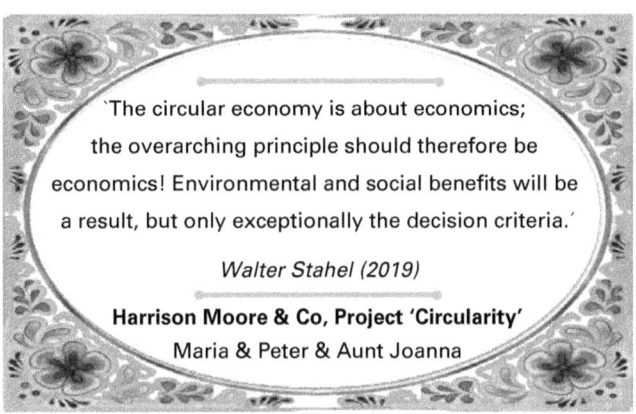

'The circular economy is about economics; the overarching principle should therefore be economics! Environmental and social benefits will be a result, but only exceptionally the decision criteria.'

Walter Stahel (2019)

Harrison Moore & Co, Project 'Circularity'
Maria & Peter & Aunt Joanna

'Absolutely fabulous, guys, great pitch!' said Aunt Joanna enthusiastically, when Maria and Peter had finished their presentation. 'Would you mind helping me prepare for my presentation here in the company once I have a date planned for that?'

'I really liked your image that captured the entire journey of Project 'Circularity', that one I'd like to use myself... If you allow me of course,' she added with a smile.

'And,' Aunt Joanna continued, 'I have to give it to you... your last slide was absolutely spot-on. I love the phrase and the way of presenting it as one of those tiles with expressions and sayings you can put on the wall. That was really well done!'

'Aunt Joanna,' Maria responded, 'Peter and I are so grateful you had us do this project with you, we had to give you a little gift to show our appreciation. In fact we had the tile we showed in the presentation made for you... here it is! And thank you so much again!'

'Now that will definitely inspire me! Thank you so much, guys! Let's find a place for it to hang on my wall right away! And I think we've all earned a drink – I invite you to please join me and we'll have some fun celebrating the end of our journey of Project 'Circularity'!'

'And maybe we can discuss what I read in an interesting article yesterday,' Aunt Joanna continued with a mysterious smile. 'It spoke about wicked problems, unintended consequences and the Midgely syndrome. What do you think? Would that maybe be our next project...?'[5]

Notes

1 Ashkenas (2013).
2 Weenk (2013b).
3 Alluding to the quote from Robinson and Aronica (2015) from the Preface of the book.
4 Stahel (2019), with kind permission of Mr. Walter Stahel.
5 E.g. Raworth (2017), Elkington (2020).

AFTERWORD

'Hi Aunt Joanna, how great to hear from you again!' Peter said after accepting the video group call where he found his aunt already waiting. Maria joined a few seconds later, saying 'Hi there, sorry I saw your call just now, how are you both doing?'

'Quite some news I wanted to tell you and Peter about,' Aunt Joanna said. 'As you know, after our project 'circularity', our company published an article about the research we did, our experiences with the circular business game and the conclusions we drew from the project. Also a state-of-the-art textbook has been published, called *Mastering the Circular Economy: A practical approach to the circular business model transformation*, which takes the same approach we took by first exploring, then mastering and in the end imagining the circular transition. It actually also integrates The Blue Connection!'

'I shared the article and the news about the book with some people in my network and it seems like it got around quite a bit! No other than Harald Friedl, the former CEO of 'Circle Economy', who is now one of the global leaders in bringing the circular transition forward with the COP 26 Climate Champions Team, reacted to me directly. Harald Friedl has spoken at conferences all around the world, is a thought leader in the field and an inspiration to many.'

'So what did he say, Aunt Joanna? I can't wait to hear about it,' Peter said impatiently.

'Actually,' Aunt Joanna continued, 'he wrote a very inspiring letter directed to the project team behind our project circularity, so to all of us! I was so flattered that I wanted to read it directly to you and see the reaction on your faces, which is why I video called you, so here we go:

Dear team from project 'circularity', it is all about creating change now. Creating the world we want to live in; the world we have somehow forgotten can exist – today. You are part of this journey, and have to be part. There are no more delays or excuses. Every one of us has to stand up, get in touch with themselves – and each other: because we do not need to do a little less bad, we need to do fundamentally better.

The circular economy is an amazingly powerful tool – to point us in the right direction. It is concrete and tangible, and drives powerful results. As always, it is not about the various definitions used but about the action taken. And to take this action we need leadership, courage and wisdom. This triangle can be our inspiration for action and change. It can fundamentally enrich the 3 Ps of people, planet and profit. As this does not tell us enough, how to look forward, take decisions and treat each other and the planet, the book *Mastering the Circular Economy* has been published at the right time to inspire more action. I really love the breadth of the topics covered and that the book takes a broad lens, also into the environmental and behavioural change needed to scale up circular action in the world. Education is key, and it reminds me of a quote one of my mentors used to say: "If we are educated enough, we can all put the hidden agendas on the table and take it from there" – when we master this, we can master real change and accelerate action. Thanks to all of you who are courageous enough to walk this path together.

Harald Friedl
COP 26 Climate Champions Team – Green Deal Circular Ambassador –
Member International Advisory Board @ Circle Economy

APPENDIX

Collaboration

As mentioned in Chapter 3, Circle Economy (2020b) identified nine steps for successful collaboration, including four collaboration types, fourteen roles and nine characteristics to identify suitable and attractive partners. Here, we will go deeper into the collaboration types, roles and the partner characteristics.

Collaboration types

Based on the current development stage in the circular value chain, Circle Economy (2020b) identified four types of multi-stakeholder collaboration. The types differ in focused effort, number and type of partners:

1 **Vertical networks**: these types of collaboration are aimed at working together with all parties involved in a value chain, from beginning (resource extraction) to end (resource recycling).

2 **Horizontal networks**: within this collaboration type the parties involved are located both inside and outside the value chain (e.g. knowledge institutions or governments). They work together to utilize existing circular networks (e.g. the operations of a packaging reuse system) or to develop new materials or technologies.

3 **One-to-one alliances**: here individual partners work together, either along or outside the value chain, to improve the circularity of processes within a value chain.

4 **Knowledge exchange**: this is an informal alignment and exchange of knowledge in favour of impact creation and industry-wide learning, with parties outside or along the value chain.

Fourteen roles

In Exercise 3.4 you have to explore the 14 roles in circular collaborations, identified by Circle Economy (2020b), to find out which role you would aspire to take on at your current or future job. The roles are listed in Table App 1, and serve as guidance in identifying which tasks should be fulfilled by partners internally, and where collaborative support is needed. They are important during the start, development or realization of a project. Besides, the relevance of the roles is influenced by three factors (product, company and circular strategy) and differ per project and business.

TABLE APP 1   Fourteen circular collaboration roles

ROLES IN THE PROJECT PHASE			OTHER ROLES	
Start	**Development**	**Realization**	**Collaboration**	**External**
Initiator *Idea-spreading; action-oriented role (e.g. developing new business models or starting an R&D project; or pressure-creator (e.g. demanding and provoking change).*	**Circularity expert** *Holds the knowledge on (technical) product level, circular innovations, challenges and (local) material flows.*	**Impact extender** *These can be found in competitors, following a pre-competitive approach, to promote circular innovations and gain a critical mass.*	**Mediator** *Connects parties in a value chain for one-to-one collaborations or to build circular ecosystems.*	**External educator** *Educates the public or players on an authority level on circularity to enable them to make informed choices and decisions.*
Financier *Directly or indirectly enables the financing of a circular innovation (in R&D, knowledge, collaboration or market).*	**Market expert** *Provides research, knowledge and advice in a market and industry context (e.g. legislation, usage scenarios, consumer behaviour).*	**Use-phase supporter** *Builds, operates or utilizes the circular value chain to extend the lifetime of a product.*	**Knowledge broker** *Creates learnings and research outcomes, manages collaborative processes, facilitates discussions and requires CE topics.*	**Enabler** *Has the political influence to co-create, push and steer the norms, legislation and markets towards the circular economy.*
Internal educator *The transfer and dissemination of knowledge on circularity within the business.*	**Piloter** *Develops and pilots circular innovations.*	**End-of-life supporter** *Collection, treatment and take-up of secondary raw materials aimed at creating a second life for end-of-life materials and products.*		**Promoter** *Establishes credibility and publicity to promote circular products.*

SOURCE Circle Economy, 2020b

If you need more information on these roles, or if you want specific examples, we suggest you look up the Circle Economy (2020b) report 'Will you be my partner?'

Nine partner characteristics

To select and evaluate the most suitable partners for the multi-stakeholder collaboration, Circle Economy (2020b) identified nine characteristics which partners (or the individuals in a potential partner organizations) should ideally fulfil. The characteristics are divided into specific ones for within a circular context, and general characteristics for every type of collaboration.

Specific circular economy partner characteristics:

1 **Strategic fit**: partners should align on vision, culture, market, context and circular strategy.

2 **Creativity**: partners should be open-minded and creative to be able to work on solutions for uncertain and complex issues in a circular economy.

3 **Open communication**: it is essential to share knowledge and challenges to realize shared progress and business advantages.

4 **Mission alignment**: partners should align on goals and mission as value is generated through synergy.

5 **Commitment**: all partners involved should be committed to create change and invest in favour of the transition to a circular economy.

Generic partner characteristics:

6 **Financial viability**: since without financial advantages for companies a circular economy is not viable, the financial viability of a partnership is essential.

7 **Complementarity**: all partners should perform and deliver the 14 roles to complement each other and to realize the required circular outcome.

8 **Reputation**: attracting well-known partners could legitimize the circular collaboration. Besides, it can lead to attracting other necessary partners as well.

9 **Trustworthiness**: as collaboration is key in the transition to the circular economy, the partners in a multi-stakeholder collaboration must be able to trust each other in terms of adhering to promises and putting those promises into action

Smart KPIs

A widely used concept in the context of KPI development is that of 'SMART' KPIs, alluding to the fact that the KPIs should be intelligently chosen. In addition, each letter of the word SMART represents a specific aspect to be taken into consideration. Although different explanations of each letter exist, the following ones typically work well:

- *S* = *Simple*: meaning for instance that the naming of the indicator, as well as the formula to calculate it should be clear and understandable to the users. If not, people might simply not trust the outcome, because they don't have a grip on the underlying concepts.

- *M* = *Measurable*: meaning that it should be possible to capture the concept in a number, a percentage or a value (e.g. yes-no). Since most things can be measured in some way or another, a second dimension of measurability should be considered, namely if it can be measured in a timely and cost-effective way. If a certain indicator should be tracked on a weekly basis but measuring and getting results takes more than two weeks of time, either because data is difficult to obtain, or because it requires a lot of work to get the reports done, or because the suppliers of the data take a relatively long time to make data available, then maybe another KPI should be considered.

- *A = Acceptable*: meaning that the audience for which the indicator is intended accepts it as being representative for what it is supposed to measure. If someone proposes to measure delivery performance based on the number of complaints received from customers, but a direct colleague is of the opinion that that would be measuring customer satisfaction rather than real delivery performance, then the proposed KPI would not be acceptable for both, and therefore not suitable, since at every publication of new results the discussion about its validity would start all over again.

- *R = Realistic*: meaning that the target value should be within reach. If not, it is very likely to only have demotivation as a result, instead of stimulating people to reach the objective.

- *T = Time-constrained*: meaning that there should be a deadline of some kind, otherwise people will lose interest, or they will say 'It's OK, we will reach it someday'.

Stages in the life of the team, motivation, communication

Stages in the life of the team

A second dimension to take into consideration is related to how long the team has been together and how well they have developed as a team. The famous psychological framework of Tuckman (1965) from the area of group dynamics describes this as a four-phase evolution – forming, storming, norming and performing – later on even complemented by an additional closing stage called adjourning, transforming and mourning. The basic thought behind the framework is that all groups go through the same stages of development, from a chaotic initial stage in which people are getting to know each other, profiling themselves and taking position within the group as a whole, to stages in which the group establishes its own internal rules and ways of working together and really starts performing.

It is very different if the challenging transformation from linear to circular is led by an already existing and solid team or if it needs to be done by a newly established task force who have maybe never worked together before. In order to highlight this phenomenon and drive home the point of the importance of team composition and team dynamics, many teachers and trainers involved in gameplay with The Blue Connection prefer to create mixed teams of people, who preferably have not worked together before in other team activities, thus opening up the possibility of reflecting on team performance. This topic is covered in Part Two of the book.

Motivation

The next aspect to take into consideration would be motivation, in this case of the individuals in the team. In a way it starts with whether team members have chosen to be in the team or not. If they haven't but they still like the team and/or the activity, they might end up happy. If they haven't chosen for themselves, but they don't like the task and/or the team, it will most likely have a negative impact on their behaviour, ultimately affecting team performance.

Libraries are full of books explaining many more aspects around the motivation of people. Let's highlight a few dimensions just in order to create some awareness and to enable useful reflection on the topic later on. An interesting angle is to look at intrinsic and extrinsic motivation. Intrinsic motivation comes from within the individual and represents a drive to learn new things, to meet new people, to deal with new challenges. Extrinsic motivation has to do with other people giving either rewards (positive) or punishment (negative) to the individual, thus causing an external motivation to do certain things.

There seems to be plenty of scientific evidence that intrinsic motivation is a much stronger driver for positive behaviour than extrinsic motivation. It can easily be observed in schools and universities: students who are there because they are genuinely interested in learning something new and useful have a much more positive mindset than those who are mainly there to get the diploma or because their parents told them to go. In companies this is not very different. Some team members are just there because they need a job to pay the bills and their boss told them to go to the meeting, whereas others might be driven by intrinsic motivations and come with a very positive mindset, ready to get things done. So in any team in any setting you might find one or both of these sources of motivation to be more or less present, with the potential of impacting the team's performance.

From the above it seems more reasonable then to try and have people on board in leading the transformation from linear to circular who are really firm believers in this way forward and who truly identify themselves with the purpose behind it. The organizational puzzle obviously is to try and find a match between those who are most motivated to lead the way and those who really have the required skills for the job.

Communication: questioning, listening, using common language

But there is yet another dimension to team performance, also very relevant, which is communication. There is a risk of this topic becoming very vague. We often hear in companies that communication is perceived to be insufficient and/or ineffective, but it's mostly much less clear what exactly that might mean and, more importantly, what can be done about it. For one thing, better communication doesn't necessarily mean talking more.

There is a simple and straightforward role play in communication and decision-making between sales and production that we often do in our company trainings.

Pairs of two people, each assuming a different role and having received a description of the hypothetical situation, are sent out for a meeting and must reach an agreement to solve the issue at hand. Obviously, the issue is potentially conflictive between the two roles. Afterwards there is a debrief of the activity in which potential solutions that have come up in the meeting are explored, but above all in which we try to put our finger on the key success factors of reaching an agreement. We've done this activity many times in trainings and in the debrief the same factors almost always appear as key success factors, for example and in random order:

- active listening, give explanations and ask for explanations;
- empathy and willingness to listen, attitude;
- clarity on expectations and ways of working;
- try to work based on facts, trying to avoid unsubstantiated opinions;
- try to establish a 'common language';
- willingness to solve the issue;
- contextualize, explore alternatives;
- come to the meeting prepared, with your homework done;
- try to avoid seeing questions as criticism towards a person;
- create an atmosphere that allows the challenging of assumptions;
- look for mutual interest, prepared to make compromises.

It is very interesting to see that this list has turned out very similar in all the times we have done this activity (and obviously without pushing or imposing any inputs). Apparently, most people intuitively and/or from personal experience know the key success factors to making such potentially conflictive conversations work, but apparently, we are very successful at failing to do it well. It seems to be another clear example of 'simple but not easy'. The mix of people, their backgrounds, skillsets, characters, personal situations, motivations, bosses, career perspectives, the stress of a particular day and so on, all play a role in making it work.

Project management concepts and tools

In Chapter 4, we referred to projects as a likely key methodology for achieving the transformation from linear to circular value chains. Below an overview can be found of the main important phases in the project lifecycle, as well as the key tools per project management area. For more details, the reader is referred to well-known project management approaches such as the ones from PMI® and Prince2®.

Project lifecycle and management areas

FIGURE APP 1   Phases in the lifecycle and management areas

PROJECT LIFECYCLE

PHASES IN THE LIFECYCLE AND MANAGEMENT AREAS

COMMUNICATION

Scope

Time

Cost

Quality

Team

Procurement

Risk

STAKEHOLDERS

INITIATION

PLANNING

EXECUTION

CONTROL & FOLLOW-UP

CLOSE-OUT

MANAGEMENT AREA: SCOPE

FIGURE APP 2   Scope

MANAGEMENT AREA:

SCOPE

KEY CONCEPTS:

o **Project Data Sheet (PDS) or Project Charter**
  ▪ Summary of main project characteristics per management area
o **Work Breakdown Structure (WBS)**
  ▪ A good WBS provides an excellent framework for elaborating the content of all of the other knowledge areas (the Swiss Army Knife of the Project Manager)

TOOLS:

o Mind Map

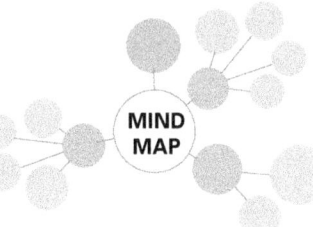

o Project Data Sheet

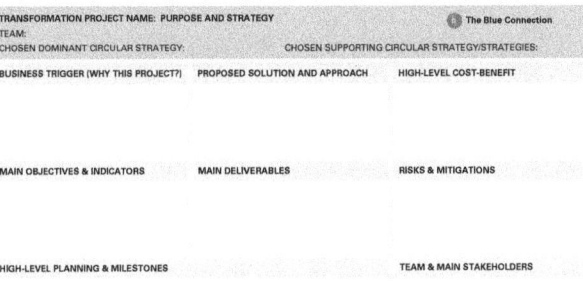

o Work Breakdown Structure

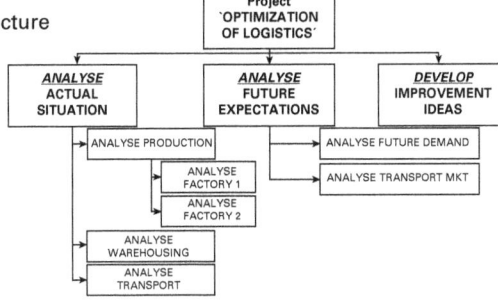

MANAGEMENT AREA: TIME

FIGURE APP 3   Time

MANAGEMENT AREA:

TIME

KEY CONCEPTS:
o Time management & planning
o Plan finish dates, milestones
o Set priorities
o Plan resources in time
o Identify potential bottlenecks
o Combine timing with required and available resources
o Identify the *critical path*

TOOLS:

o PDM (Precedence Diagram Method)

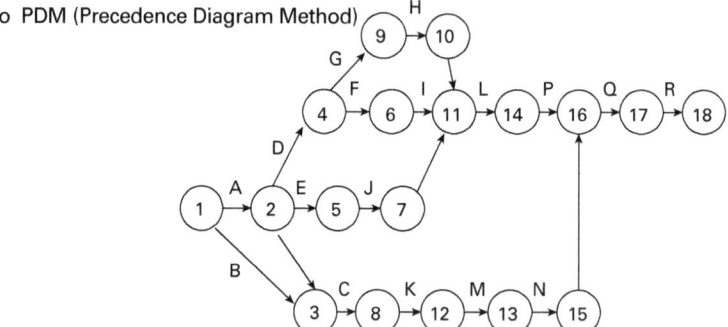

o PERT ('most likely time', 'optimistic time', and 'pessimistic time')

o GANTT chart and critical path

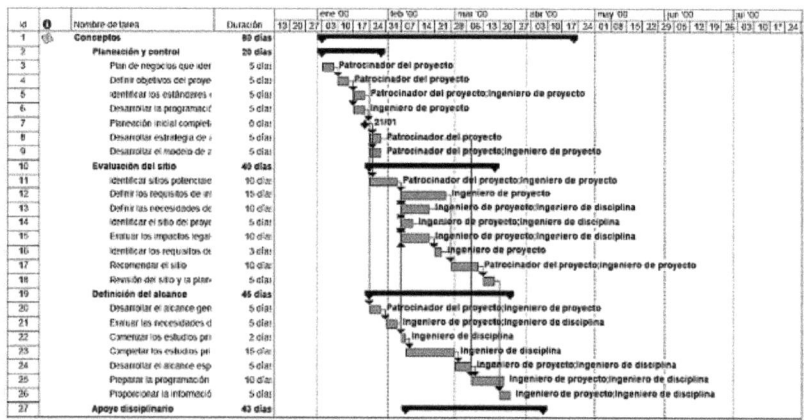

MANAGEMENT AREA: COST

FIGURE APP 4   Cost

MANAGEMENT AREA:

COST

KEY CONCEPTS:

o Cost estimation (rough, high-level estimation, e.g. in proposal phase)

o Budgeting (detailed planning, for execution & control phase)

o Cost control

o Financial evaluation

o Financial / cost components

■ Labour, material, external services, other (e.g. overhead)

■ Reservation 'unforeseen', margin (optional, if commercial)

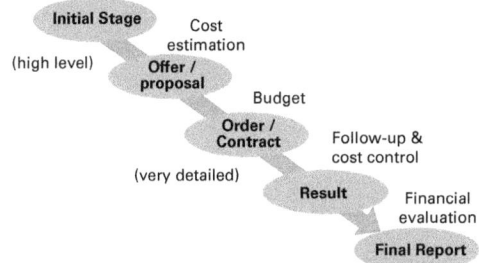

Initial Stage (high level)
Cost estimation
Offer / proposal
Budget
Order / Contract
(very detailed)
Follow-up & cost control
Result
Financial evaluation
Final Report

TOOLS:

o Cost estimation (high-level)

o Budget (detailed)

INCOME	JAN	FEB	MAR	APR	MAY	JUN	JUL	AUG
INCOME								
Bonus	$ 5.00	$ 5.50	$ 20.00	$ 5.00	$ 5.50	$ 20.00	$ 5.00	$ 5.50
Dividends and Capital G	$ 5.50	$ 10.00	$ 30.00	$ 5.50	$ 10.00	$ 30.00	$ 5.50	$ 10.00
Interest Income	$ 10.00	$ 20.00	$ 10.00	$ 10.00	$ 20.00	$ 10.00	$ 10.00	$ 20.00
Investment	$ 20.00	$ 30.00	$ 50.00	$ 20.00	$ 30.00	$ 50.00	$ 20.00	$ 30.00
Passive Income	$ 30.00	$ 10.00	$ 60.00	$ 30.00	$ 10.00	$ 60.00	$ 30.00	$ 10.00
Salaries/Wages	$ 10.00	$ 50.00	$ 5.00	$ 10.00	$ 50.00	$ 5.00	$ 10.00	$ 50.00
Reimbursement	$ 50.00	$ 60.00	$ 10.50	$ 50.00	$ 60.00	$ 10.50	$ 50.00	$ 60.00
Returned Purchases	$ 60.00	$ 5.00	$ 50.00	$ 60.00	$ 5.00	$ 50.00	$ 60.00	$ 5.00
Side Hustle Income	$ 5.00	$ 5.00	$ 60.00	$ 5.00	$ 5.00	$ 60.00	$ 5.00	$ 5.00
Other - Income	$ 10.50	$ 10.50	$ 5.00	$ 10.50	$ 10.50	$ 5.00	$ 10.50	$ 10.50
TOTAL INCOME	$ 206.00	$ 206.00	$ 300.50	$ 206.00	$ 206.00	$ 300.50	$ 206.00	$ 206.00
EXPENSES								
BILLS & UTILITIES								
Electricity	$ 1.00	$ 3.00	$ 4.00	$ 8.00	$ 5.50	$ 20.00	$ 5.50	$ 5.50
Garbage and Recycling	$ 2.00	$ 2.00	$ 5.00	$ 9.00	$ 10.00	$ 30.00	$ 5.50	$ 10.00
Heating	$ 3.00	$ 1.00	$ 6.00	$ 10.00	$ 20.00	$ 10.00	$ 10.00	$ 20.00
Internet	$ 4.00	$ 9.00	$ 7.00	$ 11.00	$ 30.00	$ 50.00	$ 20.00	$ 30.00
Landline Phone	$ 5.00	$ 8.00	$ 8.00	$ 1.00	$ 10.00	$ 60.00	$ 30.00	$ 10.00
Mobile Phones	$ 6.00	$ 7.00	$ 9.00	$ 2.00	$ 50.00	$ 5.00	$ 10.00	$ 50.00
Natural Gas	$ 7.00	$ 6.00	$ 10.00	$ 3.00	$ 60.00	$ 10.00	$ 50.00	$ 60.00
Rent	$ 8.00	$ 5.00	$ 1.00	$ 4.00	$ 5.00	$ 50.00	$ 60.00	$ 5.00
TV & Internet	$ 9.00	$ 4.00	$ 2.00	$ 5.00	$ 5.00	$ 60.00	$ 5.00	$ 5.00
Water and Sewer	$ 10.00	$ 3.00	$ 3.00	$ 6.00	$ 10.50	$ 5.50	$ 10.50	$ 10.50
Trash	$ 11.00	$ 2.00	$ 2.00	$ 7.00	$ 2.00	$ 2.00	$ 2.00	$ 2.00
Others - Bills & Utilities	$ 12.00	$ 1.00	$ 5.00	$ 8.00	$ 1.00	$ 1.00	$ 1.00	$ 1.00
Subtotal	$ 78.00	$ 51.00	$ 62.00	$ 74.00	$ 209.00	$ 303.50	$ 209.00	$ 209.00

o Follow-up (control)

MANAGEMENT AREA: QUALITY

FIGURE APP 5   Quality

MANAGEMENT AREA:

QUALITY

KEY CONCEPTS:
o Product quality vs process quality
o *'Must quality'*
  ▪ Formally agreed minimum level of quality
o *'Should quality'*
  ▪ Real expectation of the client: management of expectations & relationships
o *'Can quality'*
  ▪ What the team is capable of achieving

TOOLS:
o Quality-plan
o List criteria (SMART!), clear link to project objectives
o Order based on importance
o Which organization or team capabilities required?
o Identify criteria which require above-average attention
o Define control-instruments
o Link effects of non-quality to project contract

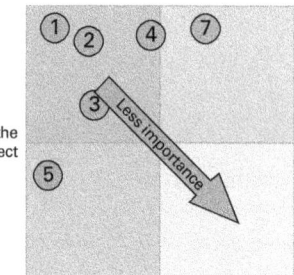

Nr	Quality-criterion	Norm	Control-instrument
1			
2			
3			
4			
5			
6			
7			
8			
..			
n			

MANAGEMENT AREA: TEAM

FIGURE APP 6   Team

MANAGEMENT AREA:

TEAM

KEY CONCEPTS:
- o Company organization vs project organization
- o Team composition & roles
- o Team development

TOOLS:
- o Role identification
- o Role-mapping (individual)
- o Role-mapping (team total)

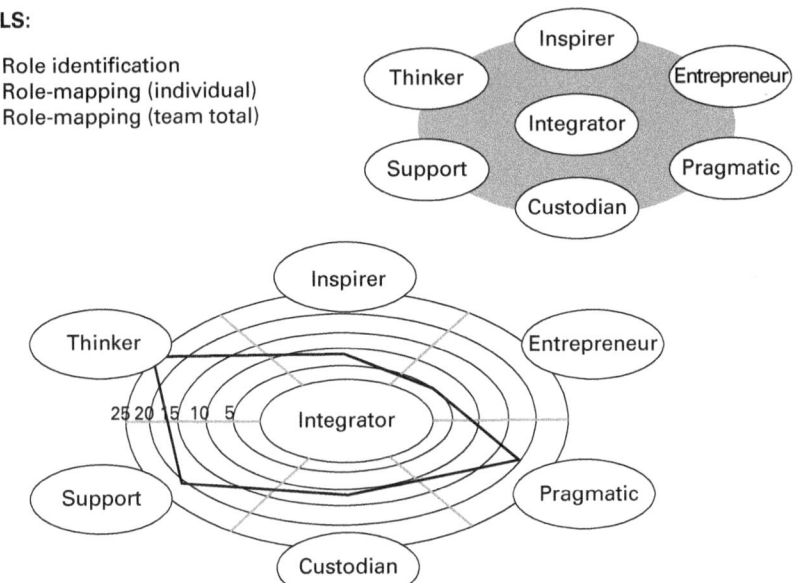

	Team member 1	Team member 2	Team member 3	...	Team member n	Total
INSPIRER	8	..	..	..	..	..
THINKER	25	..	..	..	..	..
ENTREPRENEUR	5	..	..	..	..	..
SUPPORT	21	..	..	..	..	..
PRAGMATIC	20	..	..	..	..	..
CUSTODIAN	11	..	..	..	..	..

MANAGEMENT AREA: PROCUREMENT

FIGURE APP 7   Procurement

MANAGEMENT AREA:

PROCUREMENT

KEY CONCEPTS:

o Buying in many cases multidisciplinary affair
o The strategic 'make or buy' decision
o Buying products vs buying services
o The buying process
  - Specify, define selection criteria, identification of candidates, invite, obtain offers, evaluate, select, negotiate, sign contract
  - Evaluation process might be different for different types of products / services

TOOLS:

o Supplier evaluation matrix
  o Criteria
  o Relative weight
  o Scores per supplier per criterion

Warehouse re-location IBERIA - Proposal Evaluation Scores

(scale 1 to 10, 1=very poor, 10=very good)

Item				LOCATION 1	LOCATION 2	LOCATION 3
A	Company Information	Total - Company Information		0,0	0,0	0,0
	0,0%		Rank	1	1	1
B	Solution - Location	Total - Location		7,8	6,0	7,0
	40,0%		Rank	1	3	2
C	Solution - Building	Total - Building		4,2	4,6	4,3
	30,0%		Rank	3	1	2
D	Implementation & timing	Total				
	20,0%					
E	Commercial					
	10,0%					
	Total Proposal Evaluation Score					
	100,0%					

Warehouse re-location IBERIA - Proposal Evaluation Scores

(scale 1 to 10, 1=very ...)

	A	B	C	D	E	F	G	H
Item						LOCATION 1	LOCATION 2	LOCATION 3
B	Solution - Location	1	Distance to factory as proxy for employee travel time	40%	8		8
	40,0%	2	Possibilities to reach by public transportation	5%	5	7	8
		3	Services in the area (restaurants etc)	2%	5	8	7
		4	Availability local labour	5%	8	9	8
		5	Logistics infrastructure of the area (reception)	10%	9	5	7
		6	Proximity to carriers	30%	7	9	8
		7	Connection to main roads	5%	9	7	9
		8					
		9					
				100%			
		Total - Location			7,8	6,0	7,0
		Rank			1	3	2
C	Solution - Building	1	Fit with company operation & growth perspectives - square meters - docks - possibility to divide zones (ambient, quarantine, etc) - possibility to place refrigerated storage - etc	40%	9	9	9
	30,0%	2	Sprinkler, fire extinguishing, internal walls	5%	7	7	7
		3	Main electrical installation warehouse	5%	1	8	1
		4	Main electrical installations hall & office	6%	1	9	1
		5	Telephone & data connections	1%	1	1	1
		6	Anti-burglary system	1%	1	5	5
		7	Heating & cooling offices	2%	5	1	1
		8	Temperature-control warehouse	15%	1	1	1

H ◄ ► H \ Geographical overview / Evaluation - summary \ Evaluation - details / Details per location /

MANAGEMENT AREA: RISK

FIGURE APP 8   Risk

MANAGEMENT AREA:

RISK

KEY CONCEPTS:
o Deal with insecurity and/or unpredictability
o Minimize probability and/or impact
o Define appropriate measures
   ▪ Risk-prevention
   ▪ Early-warning systems
   ▪ Impact minimization

TOOLS:

o Risk analysis & control
o SWOT

Description	Probability	Impact	Response-time	Risk-value	Ranking
Hardware problem	2	4	1	8	4
Software issue	3	4	2	24	3
Network issue	4	4	3	48	1
Electricity issue	3	4	4	48	1
...					

MANAGEMENT AREA: COMMUNICATION

FIGURE APP 9   Communication

MANAGEMENT AREA:

COMMUNICATION

KEY CONCEPTS:
o Internal vs external communication
o Supporting function or key success factor?
o Inform, sell, challenge, ask, influence, stimulate, mobilize, etc

TOOLS:

o (Internal) information matrix
o (External) communication plan

	Project owner	Project leader	Project team members	Project secretary		
Project contract	Sign-off	Create	Create	Create Distribute Archive		
Decision documents	Sign-off	Create	Create	Create Distribute Archive		
Progress reports	For info	Sign-off	Create	Create Distribute Archive		
Action lists	-	Sign-off	For info	Create Distribute Archive		
...						

Target group	Objective of communication	Types of messages	Media types	Frequency of communication	Responsible
Group Board of Directors	Inform, influence	Project status reports, stakeholder opinions	Personal meetings, email	Whenever necessary, at least once per week	Managing Director
Scientific board	Ask opinion, ask input, obtain green light	Investigation status report, research issues,research planning	Personal meetings, email	At least once a month	Project leader
Local inhabitants	Influence opinion	Project status, project risks	Local media (TV, radio, internet), meetings	...	Communication dept
Regional government	...	...	...	...	...
...	...	...	...	...	...

MANAGEMENT AREA: STAKEHOLDERS

FIGURE APP 10   Stakeholders

MANAGEMENT AREA:

STAKEHOLDERS

KEY CONCEPTS:

o Identification of key stakeholders
o Identification of attitude of key stakeholders
  towards the project
  ▪ Positive, negative, neutral
o Identification of strength of relationship
  towards the stakeholder
  ▪ Strong, neutral, weak
o Identify associated opportunities and risks
  (coalition forming, influencing)
o Link to risk plan and to communication plan

TOOLS:

o Force-field analysis (stakeholder mapping)
o Link to risk & mitigation plan
o Link to communication plan

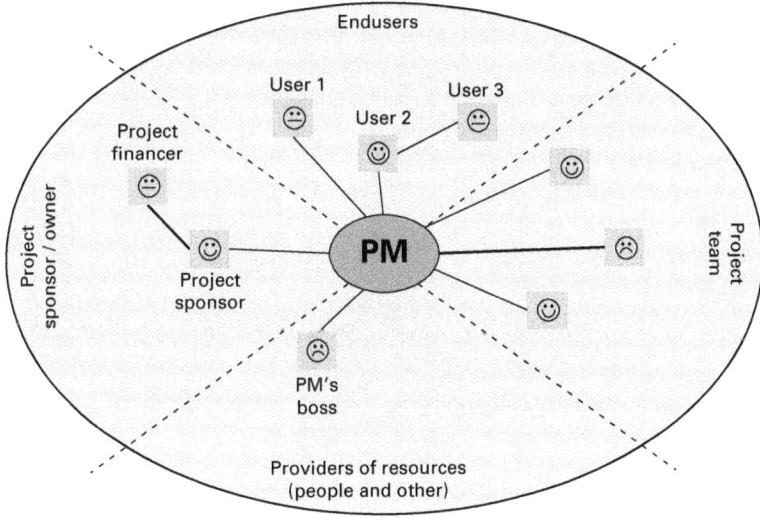

BIBLIOGRAPHY

ABN Amro (2018) *Waarom nieuw kopen als het anders kan?* insights.abnamro.nl/2018/01/waarom-nieuw-kopen-als-het-anders-kan/ (archived at https://perma.cc/6RJW-N96W)

Accenture (2018a) Make your wise pivot to the new, www.accenture.com/gb-en/insights/consulting/wise-pivot (archived at https://perma.cc/WNL8-JLB2)

Accenture (2018b) Circular Advantage: Innovative business models and technologies that create value, EU-Indonesia Business Dialogue, Jakarta, 25 October 2018

Accenture (2018c) To Affinity and Beyond: From me to we, the rise of the purpose-led brand, www.accenture.com/t20181205t121039z__w__/us-en/_acnmedia/thought-leadership-assets/pdf/accenture-competitiveagility-gcpr-pov.pdf (archived at https://perma.cc/72W2-TPLD)

Achterberg, E, Hinfelaar, J and Bocken, N (2016) Master circular business with the Value Hill, *Circle Economy*, www.circle-economy.com/resources/master-circular-business-with-the-value-hill (archived at https://perma.cc/LND5-S8P9)

Antikainen, M and Valkokari, K (2016) A framework for sustainable business model innovation, *Technology Innovation Management Review*, 6 (7), pp 5–12

APICS (n.d.) Supply Chain Operations Reference (SCOR) model, www.apics.org/apics-for-business/frameworks/scor (archived at https://perma.cc/Z892-DZGK)

Ashkenas, R (2013) Change management needs to change, *Harvard Business Review*, April, hbr.org/2013/04/change-management-needs-to-cha.html (archived at https://perma.cc/6AEK-26TN)

Ashkenas, R (2015) Jack Welch's approach to breaking down silos still works, *Harvard Business Review*, September 9, hbr.org/2015/09/jack-welchs-approach-to-breaking-down-silos-still-works (archived at https://perma.cc/S3B4-UYMF)

Backes, C (2017) *Law for A Circular Economy*, Eleven International Publishing, Den Haag

Bakker, C et al (2015) *Products That Last, Productontwerpen voor circulaire businessmodellen*, TUDelft (in Dutch)

Baldassarre, B et al (2020) Implementing sustainable design theory in business practice: a call to action, *Journal of Cleaner Production*, 273

B Corporation (n.d.) The B Corp Certification, bcorporation.net/certification (archived at https://perma.cc/PDX3-WM6R)

Bebchuk, L A and Tallarita, R (2020) The illusory promise of stakeholder governance, *Cornell Law Review*, December, papers.ssrn.com/sol3/papers.cfm?abstract_id=3544978 (archived at https://perma.cc/KH2V-JRKC)

Belbin, R M (2010) *Team Roles at Work*, 2nd edition, Routledge, New York

Benyus, J (1997) *Biomimicry: Innovation inspired by nature,* William Morrow

Bernick, L (2019) Can sustainable companies get a lower cost of capital? www.greenbiz.com/article/can-sustainable-companies-get-lower-cost-capital (archived at https://perma.cc/2UV5-968U)

Beschorner, T and Hajduk, T (2017) Creating shared value: a fundamental critique, in *Creating Shared Value: Concepts, experience, criticism*, ed J Weiland, Springer, pp 27–37

BlackRock (2018) Larry Fink's 2018 letter to CEOs: A Sense of Purpose, www.blackrock.com/corporate/investor-relations/2018-larry-fink-ceo-letter (archived at https://perma.cc/E92X-D6B2)

BlackRock (2019) Larry Fink's 2019 letter to CEOs: Profit & Purpose, www.blackrock.com/americas-offshore/2019-larry-fink-ceo-letter (archived at https://perma.cc/ER89-LWBX)

BlackRock (2020) Investment Stewardship Annual Report, www.blackrock.com/corporate/literature/publication/blk-annual-stewardship-report-2020.pdf (archived at https://perma.cc/4NQ6-Y6Z6)

Blank, S (2013) Why the lean startup changes everything, *Harvard Business Review*, May

Blomsma, F and Brennan, G (2017) The emergence of Circular Economy: a new framing around prolonging resource productivity, *Journal of Industrial Ecology*, 21 (3)

Bocken, N and Boons, F (2017) Designing sustainable business models: expanding boundaries to create positive value, 18th European Roundtable on Sustainable Consumption and production Conference (ERSCP 2017)

Bocken, N and Geradts, T (2020) Barriers and drivers to sustainable business model innovation: organization design and dynamic capabilities, *Long Range Planning*, 53

Bocken, N and Snihur, Y (2020) Lean startup and the business model: experimenting for novelty and impact, *Long Range Planning*, 53

Bocken, N, Schuit, C and Kraaijenhagen, C (2018) Experimenting with a circular business model: Lessons from eight cases, *Environmental Innovation and Societal Transitions*, 28, pp 79–95

Bocken, N et al (2016) Product design and business model strategies for a circular economy, *Journal of Industrial and Production Engineering*, 33 (5), pp 308–20

Bocken, N et al (2019) A review and evaluation of circular business model innovation tools, *Sustainability*, 11, p 2210

Boudry, M (2020) Overbevolking? Straks zijn we met steeds minder, column, *NRC*, www.nrc.nl/nieuws/2020/09/04/overbevolking-straks-zijn-we-met-steeds-minder-a4010852 (archived at https://perma.cc/5V6P-2Z7V) (in Dutch)

Boulding, K E (1966) The economics of the coming Spaceship Earth, essay

Bradford, A (2020) *The Brussels Effect: How the European Union rules the world*, Oxford University Press

Braungart, M and McDonough, W (2002) *Cradle to Cradle: Remaking the way we make things*, North Point Press, New York

BRT (2019) Business Roundtable redefines the purpose of a corporation to promote 'an economy that serves all Americans', www.businessroundtable.org/business-roundtable-redefines-the-purpose-of-a-corporation-to-promote-an-economy-that-serves-all-americans (archived at https://perma.cc/JQZ8-97GS)

BSDC (2017) Better business, better world, Business and Sustainable Development Commission

Business Insider (2009) The 10 most-respected global warming skeptics, www.businessinsider.com/the-ten-most-important-climate-change-skeptics-2009-7 (archived at https://perma.cc/4SG3-TANZ)

Business Insider (2018) Trump says he thinks the Earth will cool back down, denying his own administration's climate change report, www.businessinsider.nl/trump-climate-change-back-on-own-denies-government-report-2018-11 (archived at https://perma.cc/TGC9-6EQV)

Campbell, D H (2011) What great companies know about culture, *Harvard Business Review*, 14 December, hbr.org/2011/12/what-great-companies-know-abou (archived at https://perma.cc/ZB49-K2VW)

Capital Institute (n.d.) Thought Leadership, capitalinstitute.org/thought-pieces/ (archived at https://perma.cc/A7TN-YSEE)

CGRi (2020) Circularity Gap Report, www.circularity-gap.world/2020 (archived at https://perma.cc/3HCD-VGN3)

Christopher, M (2016) *Logistics and Supply Chain Management*, 5th edition, Pearson Education, Harlow

Chua, J (2018) Circularity: sustainable fashion's Holy Grail or greenwashing? www.businessoffashion.com/articles/professional/circular-economy-the-holy-grail-of-sustainable-fashion (archived at https://perma.cc/79D4-LTGD)

Chua, J (2020) Is recycled polyester green or greenwashing? *Common Objective*, www.commonobjective.co/article/is-recycled-polyester-green-or-greenwashing (archived at https://perma.cc/G54M-CJBE)

Circle Economy (n.d.) About us, www.circle-economy.com/about (archived at https://perma.cc/C4VD-H35A)

Circle Economy (2020a) Jobs & skills in the circular economy: state of play and future pathways, www.circle-economy.com/resources/jobs-skills-in-the-circular-economy-state-of-play-and-future-pathways (archived at https://perma.cc/GWU2-2WH7)

Circle Economy (2020b) Will you be my partner? www.circle-economy.com/resources/will-you-be-my-partner-collaborations-in-the-circular-economy (archived at https://perma.cc/C7KT-GMMX)

Circulab (n.d.) Circular Canvas: The tool to design regenerative business models, circulab.com/toolbox-circular-economy/circular-canvas-regenerative-business-models/ (archived at https://perma.cc/9NHV-JG29)

Circular Flanders and VITO (2020) Veerkracht enquête circulaire ondernemingen, vito.be/sites/vito.be/files/resultaten_veerkracht-enquete_vito_vlaanderen_circulair.pdf (archived at https://perma.cc/EX9A-GSCX)

Cirkellab (2015) How long will it last? http://cirkellab.nl/wp-content/uploads/2015/08/ResourcesInfographic.jpg (archived at https://perma.cc/76KT-4N6U)

Club of Rome (1972) The limits to growth, clubofrome.org/publication/the-limits-to-growth/ (archived at https://perma.cc/VE2V-BVR7)

Club of Rome (2019) Nations should declare a planetary emergency says Club of Rome, www.clubofrome.org/2019/09/24/nations-should-declare-a-planetary-emergency-says-club-of-rome (archived at https://perma.cc/SGA8-59TT)

Condemi, A, Cucchiella, F and Schettini, D (2019) Circular economy and e-waste: an opportunity from RFID TAGs, *Applied Sciences*, 9, p 3422

Cordon, C (2020) How omnichannel can inspire a circular revolution, blogpost, www.supplychainmovement.com/how-omnichannel-can-inspire-a-circular-revolution (archived at https://perma.cc/3PZA-V2BE)

Covey, S R (2020) *The 7 Habits of Highly Effective People*, 30th anniversary edition, Simon & Schuster, New York City

Cranfield University (2014) Combining profit and purpose: our work with Coca-Cola Enterprises, www.cranfield.ac.uk/som/case-studies/coca-cola-enterprises-combining-profit-and-purpose (archived at https://perma.cc/NJV3-9KXZ)

Crawford, F and Mathews, R (2003) *The Myth of Excellence: Why great companies never try to be the best at everything*, Random House

Culey, S (2019) *Transition Point: From steam to the singularity*, Matador, UK

de Bono, E (1999) *Six Thinking Hats,* revised and updated edition, Back Bay Books

de Los Reyes, G et al (2017) Beyond the 'Win-win': creating shared value requires ethical frameworks, *California Management Review*, **59** (2), pp 142–67

De Wit, B and Meyer, R (1994) A discussion on strategy process paradigms, in *Strategy: Process, content, context*, West Publishing Company, St. Paul, MN, USA

Deloitte (2019) The Deloitte Global Millennial Survey 2019: Societal discord and technological transformation create a 'generation disrupted', www2.deloitte.com/content/dam/Deloitte/global/Documents/About-Deloitte/deloitte-2019-millennial-survey.pdf (archived at https://perma.cc/N7QE-AQYD)

Departement Omgeving (n.d.) Wat is een Green Deal? omgeving.vlaanderen.be/wat-is-een-green-deal (archived at https://perma.cc/4GXD-MTVD)

DeSmet, B (2018) *Supply Chain Strategy and Financial Metrics: The supply chain triangle of service, cost and cash*, Kogan Page, London

Doctorow, C (2019) Wework, Uber, Lyft, Netflix, Bird, Amazon: late-stage capitalism is all about money-losing predatory pricing aimed at creating monopolies, boingboing.net/2019/09/26/gresham-v-godwin.html (archived at https://perma.cc/7XAN-AJRE)

Dougherty, J and Gray, C (2006) *Sales & Operations Planning: Best practices, lessons learned from worldwide companies*, Partners for Excellence

Douma, S, Dooms, E and Van Oijen, A (2020) *Ondernemingsstrategie*, 8th edition, Noordhoff, Groningen (in Dutch)

Drucker, P (2004) What makes Executives effective? *Harvard Business Review*, June

Dunlap, R E (2013) Climate change skepticism and denial: an introduction, *American Behavioral Scientist,* **57** (6)

EC (n.d.) Waste from electrical and electronic equipment (WEEE), https://ec.europa.eu/environment/topics/waste-and-recycling/waste-electrical-and-electronic-equipment-weee_en (archived at https://perma.cc/D33J-JKSM)

Eccles, R and Klimenko, S (2019) The investor revolution: shareholders are getting serious about sustainability, *Harvard Business Review*, May–June

Ecovadis (n.d.) Business Sustainability Risk and Performance Index 2020, resources.ecovadis.com/sustainability-impact/ecovadis-index-2020 (archived at https://perma.cc/E946-UJ37)

EEA (2020) Countries which adopted a national resource efficiency or circular economy strategy or action plan, www.eea.europa.eu/data-and-maps/figures/countries-which-adopted-a-national (archived at https://perma.cc/5GTX-XTPY)

EEC (1975) Waste Framework Directive (75/442/EEC), eur-lex.europa.eu/legal-content/EN/TXT/?uri=CELEX:31975L0442 (archived at https://perma.cc/8UP4-KH6L)

Elkington, J (1997) *Cannibals with Forks: The triple bottom line of 21st century business*, Capstone, Chichester

Elkington, J (2014) Towards the sustainable corporation: win-win-win business strategies for sustainable development, *California Management Review*, 36 (2)

Elkington, J (2017a) Saving the planet from ecological disaster is a \$12 trillion opportunity, *Harvard Business Review*, May, https://hbr.org/2017/05/saving-the-planet-from-ecological-disaster-is-a-12-trillion-opportunity (archived at https://perma.cc/38SG-7ER3)

Elkington, J (2017b) The 6 ways business leaders talk about sustainability, *Harvard Business Review*, October, hbr.org/2017/10/the-6-ways-business-leaders-talk-about-sustainability (archived at https://perma.cc/2VKQ-LD7Z)

Elkington, J (2018) 25 years ago I coined the phrase 'Triple Bottom Line': here's why it's time to rethink it, *Harvard Business Review*, hbr.org/2018/06/25-years-ago-i-coined-the-phrase-triple-bottom-line-heres-why-im-giving-up-on-it (archived at https://perma.cc/W7C5-MTLU)

Elkington, J (2020) *Green Swans: The coming boom in regenerative capitalism*, Fast Company Press

Emerson, J (2000) The Blended Value Framework, www.blendedvalue.org/framework (archived at https://perma.cc/H2JD-74KP)

EMF (n.d. a) Mission and vision, Ellen Macarthur Foundation, www.ellenmacarthurfoundation.org/our-story/mission (archived at https://perma.cc/83HD-C994)

EMF (n.d. b) Circularity indicators - MCI, www.ellenmacarthurfoundation.org/assets/downloads/insight/Circularity-Indicators_MCI-Product-Level-Dynamic-Modelling-Tool_May2015.xlsx (archived at https://perma.cc/5CQ8-H8U7)

EMF (n.d. c) The circular economy in detail, www.ellenmacarthurfoundation.org/explore/the-circular-economy-in-detail (archived at https://perma.cc/V7HT-WEZ6)

EMF (n.d. d) Circulytics – measuring circularity, https://www.ellenmacarthurfoundation.org/resources/apply/circulytics-measuring-circularity (archived at https://perma.cc/DF9E-JMVS)

EMF (2012) Towards the circular economy: economic and business rationale for an accelerated transition, www.ellenmacarthurfoundation.org/assets/downloads/TCE_Ellen-MacArthur-Foundation_9-Dec-2015.pdf (archived at https://perma.cc/D7RU-QLQS)

EMF (2015) Delivering the circular economy: a toolkit for policy makers, www.ellenmacarthurfoundation.org/publications/delivering-the-circular-economy-a-toolkit-for-policymakers (archived at https://perma.cc/H2PK-MWEK)

EMF (2016a) Business Model Canvas worksheet, www.ellenmacarthurfoundation.org/assets/design/Business_Model_Canvas_Final.pdf (archived at https://perma.cc/QB2F-HNW3)

EMF (2016b) Intelligent assets: unlocking the circular economy potential, www.ellenmacarthurfoundation.org/publications/intelligent-assets (archived at https://perma.cc/EAN5-G2XS)

EMF (2020) Financing the circular economy, www.ellenmacarthurfoundation.org/assets/
downloads/Financing-the-circular-economy.pdf (archived at https://perma.cc/
N8SW-LCN5)

EPCA/AMS (2019) Individual sustainability leadership: identifying the key characteristics,
competences, benefits, barriers and enablers, Antwerp Management School, offer,
antwerpmanagementschool.be/en/en/download-briefing-epca (archived at https://perma.
cc/TL8F-9VDG)

Esposito, M, Tse, T and Soufani, K (2018) Introducing a circular economy: new thinking
with new managerial and policy implications, *California Management Review*, 60 (3),
pp 5–19

Etzkowitz, H and Leydesdorff, L (1995) The triple helix – university-industry-government
relations: a laboratory for knowledge based economic development, *EASTT Review*,
14 (1), pp 14–19

EU (2006) Commission implementing regulation (EU) 2016/1245, eur-lex.europa.eu/
legal-content/EN/TXT/PDF/?uri=CELEX:32016R1245&from=EN (archived at https://
perma.cc/8D8X-3PMA)

EU (2014a) Attitudes of Europeans towards waste management and resource efficiency,
ec.europa.eu/commfrontoffice/publicopinion/flash/fl_388_en.pdf (archived at https://
perma.cc/GD3T-9HNW)

EU (2014b) Ecodesign your future: how ecodesign can help the environment by making
products smarter, op.europa.eu/en/publication-detail/-/publication/4d42d597-4f92-4498-
8e1d-857cc157e6db/language-en/format-PDF (archived at https://perma.cc/86QX-2VU4)

EU (2016) Regulatory barriers for the Circular Economy, ec.europa.eu/growth/content/
regulatory-barriers-circular-economy-lessons-ten-case-studies_en (archived at https://
perma.cc/5KLC-9JYR)

EU (2019) A European Green Deal: striving to be the first climate-neutral continent,
ec.europa.eu/info/strategy/priorities-2019-2024/european-green-deal_en (archived at
https://perma.cc/J3JU-RT72)

EU (2020) EU Circular Economy Action Plan: a new Circular Economy action plan for a
cleaner and more competitive Europe, ec.europa.eu/environment/circular-economy/
index_en.htm (archived at https://perma.cc/X8Q6-S64K)

European Commission (2020) Open data and the Circular Economy, www.
europeandataportal.eu/nl/highlights/open-data-and-circular-economy (archived at https://
perma.cc/3696-EFR7)

European Standards (n.d.) British Standards, www.en-standard.eu/bs-standards/ (archived at
https://perma.cc/YTF6-XNLB)

EuroVAT (n.d.) Sweden introduces a reduced VAT rate on repairs and home services in order
to manage consumption and help refugees, www.eurovat.com/vat-news-20161010-
Sweden-introduces-reduced-VAT.htm (archived at https://perma.cc/GU2B-MXUV)

Evans, S et al (2017) Business Model Innovation for sustainability: towards a unified
perspective for creation of sustainable business models, *Business Strategy and the
Environment*, 26, pp 597–608

Ex'tax (n.d.) The Ex'tax Project, ex-tax.com/#about_us (archived at https://perma.cc/
MS7A-3STR)

Flapper, S D P (1995) One-way or reusable distribution items?, Working Paper, Eindhoven University of Technology, research.tue.nl/files/4425561/436114.pdf (archived at https://perma.cc/RQ97-56GH)

Flapper, S D P and de Ron, A J (ed) (1999) *Re-use:*international working seminar : proceedings, 2nd, 1–3 March, 1999, Eindhoven University of Technology, Eindhoven

Fleischmann, M et al (1997) Quantitative models for reverse logistics: a review, *European Journal of Operational Research*, **103** (1)

Freeman, R E (1984) *Strategic Management: A stakeholder approach*, Pitman, Boston

Freeman, R E and Parmar, B L (2017) Managing for stakeholders and the purpose of business, *Technical Note*, University of Virginia Darden Business Publishing

Friedman, M (1970) The social responsibility of business is to increase its profits, *The New York Times Magazine*, 13 September

FSC (n.d.) Forest management certification, fsc.org/en/forest-management-certification (archived at https://perma.cc/DS6P-35LZ)

Fuller, B (1969) *Operating Manual for Spaceship Earth*, Lars Muller Publishing

Gassmann, O, Frankenberger, K and Csik, M (2014) *The Business Model Navigator: 55 models that will revolutionize your business*, FT Publishing

Gattorna, J (2015) *Dynamic Supply Chains: How to design, build and manage people-centric value networks*, 3rd edition, Pearson Education, Harlow

Geissdoerfer, M et al (2017) The Circular Economy – a new sustainability paradigm? *Journal of Cleaner Production*, **143**

Geissdoerfer, M et al (2018) Business models and supply chains for the circular economy, *Journal of Cleaner Production*, **190**

Global Footprint (n.d.) Earth Overshoot Day, www.overshootday.org/ (archived at https://perma.cc/W9T7-RKQL)

Głuszek, E (2018) CSR Maturity Model – theoretical framework, conference paper for the conference 'Positive management and leadership in socially responsible organisations', at Toruń, Poland, February

Gooch J (2011) Virgin Material, in *Encyclopedic Dictionary of Polymers*, ed J W Gooch, Springer, New York, NY

Govindarajan, V (2010) Innovation is not creativity, *Harvard Business Review*, August, hbr.org/2010/08/innovation-is-not-creativity.html (archived at https://perma.cc/EJT5-ABZB)

Graz Repariert (n.d.) Grazer Reparaturförderung, grazrepariert.at/grazer-reparaturfoerderung/ (archived at https://perma.cc/48J4-USHR)

Greenhouse Gas Protocol (n.d.) We set the standards to measure and manage emissions, ghgprotocol.org/ (archived at https://perma.cc/5A7H-4CKN)

Gregson, N, et al (2015) Interrogating the circular economy: the moral economy of resource recovery in the EU, *Economy and Society*, **44** (2), pp 218–43

Griffith, E (2020) Airbnb was like a family, until the layoffs started, *New York Times*, www.nytimes.com/2020/07/17/technology/airbnb-coronavirus-layoffs-.html (archived at https://perma.cc/C4K3-NQL6)

Guardian (2013) Is incineration holding back recycling?, www.theguardian.com/environment/2013/aug/29/incineration-recycling-europe-debate-trash (archived at https://perma.cc/WKU8-8QYF)

Guardian (2019) Donald Trump reportedly wants to purchase Greenland from Denmark, www.theguardian.com/us-news/2019/aug/15/donald-trump-greenland-purchase-denmark (archived at https://perma.cc/D2CF-B3XQ)

Guardian (2020) Unilever plans to remove oil-based ingredients from all cleaning products, www.theguardian.com/business/2020/sep/02/unilever-plans-to-remove-oil-based-ingredients-from-all-cleaning-products (archived at https://perma.cc/CH3P-XYU5)

Guest, D (1991) The hunt is on for the Renaissance Man of computing, *The Independent*, 17 September

Gupta S et al (2019) Circular economy and big data analytics: A stakeholder perspective, *Technological Forecasting and Social Change*, **144**, pp 466–74

Hammer, M (2001) The super-efficient company, *Harvard Business Review*, September

Hansen, M T and von Oetinger, B (2001) Introducing T-shaped managers: knowledge management's next generation, *Harvard Business Review*, March

Hansen, M T and Birkinshaw, J (2007) The innovation value chain, *Harvard Business Review*, June

Hart, S L and Milstein, M R (2003) Creating sustainable value, *Academy of Management Executive*, **17** (2), pp 56–69

Hax, A (1990) Defining the concept of strategy, *Planning Review*, May–June

Heineman, B W (2011) Steve Jobs and the purpose of the corporation, *Harvard Business Review*, hbr.org/2011/10/steve-jobs-and-the-purpose-of (archived at https://perma.cc/QE95-RVUK)

Heinrich, M and Lang, W (2019) Materials passports – best practices, Technische Universität München in association with BAMB, www.bamb2020.eu/wp-content/uploads/2019/02/BAMB_MaterialsPassports_BestPractice.pdf (archived at https://perma.cc/ZX4T-5MJG)

Helbling, T (2010) What are externalities? www.imf.org/external/pubs/ft/fandd/2010/12/pdf/basics.pdf (archived at https://perma.cc/P9T9-YTSW)

Henzen, R (2019) *De kleine circulaire economie voor Dummies*, BBNC Uitgevers, Amersfoort (in Dutch)

Het Groene Brein (n.d.) Barriers in current policy and legislation? https://hetgroenebrein.nl/ (archived at https://perma.cc/XN4G TAU8)

Hollender, J (2010) Greenwashing is only getting worse, *Greenbiz*, www.greenbiz.com/article/greenwashing-only-getting-worse (archived at https://perma.cc/43CH-89G7)

Homrich, A S et al (2018) The circular economy umbrella: trends and gaps on integrating pathways, *Journal of Cleaner Production*, **175**, 525–43

Hopkinson, P et al (2018) Managing a complex circular economy business model: opportunities and challenges, *California Management Review*, **60** (3), pp 71–94

Hughes, R, Colarelli Beatty, K and Dinwoodie, D (2014) *Becoming a Strategic Leader: Your role in your organization's enduring success*, 2nd edition, Jossey-Bass, San Francisco

HumanProgress (2020) The Simon Abundance Index 2020, www.humanprogress.org/the-simon-abundance-index-2020/ (archived at https://perma.cc/9TLA-A82T)

Hurst, A (2014) *Welcome* to the purpose economy, *Fast Company*, www.fastcompany.com/3028410/welcome-to-the-purpose-economy (archived at https://perma.cc/A5NJ-CAEK)

IBM (2020) The rise of the sustainable enterprise: using digital tech to respond to the environmental imperative, IBM Institute for Business Value

IIRC (2013a) Capitals, Background paper for <IR>, International Integrated Reporting Council

IIRC (2013b) The International <IR> Framework, International Integrated Reporting Council

Iles, J (2018) Which country is leading the circular economy shift? *Medium*, medium.com/circulatenews/which-country-is-leading-the-circular-economy-shift-3670467db4bb (archived at https://perma.cc/JP5L-CMKT)

IRTC (2020) Material criticality: an overview for decision makers, International Round Table on Materials Criticality, irtc.info/wp-content/uploads/2020/05/IRTC-Brochure-2.pdf (archived at https://perma.cc/SCS4-7AS4)

ISO (n.d.) ISO 14000 family: environmental management, www.iso.org/iso-14001-environmental-management.html (archived at https://perma.cc/FV7D-TACW)

Janssens, L and Kuppens, T (2018) De professional van de toekomst in de circulaire economie, www.uhasselt.be/Documents/ORA/ORA_cleantech_rapport.pdf (archived at https://perma.cc/6NYC-NEDW) (in Dutch)

Johnson, M, Christensen, C and Kagermann, H (2008) Reinventing your business model, *Harvard Business Review*, December

Jonker, J, Stegeman, H and Faber, N (2018) CE. Denkbeelden, ontwikkelingen en business modellen, Whitepaper (in Dutch)

Jonker, J et al (2018) *Circulair Organiseren. Werkboek voor het ontwikkelen van een circulair business model*, www.circulairebusinessmodellen.nl (archived at https://perma.cc/4YDB-36RF) (in Dutch)

Joyce, A and Paquin, R (2016) The triple layered business model canvas: a tool to design more sustainable business models, *Journal of Cleaner Production*, **135**, pp 1474–86

Joustra, D J, De Jong, E and Engelaer, F (2013) Guided choices towards a circular business model, *C2CBIZZ*, http://www.opai.eu/uploads/Guided_Choices_towards_a_Circular_Business_Model_pdf11.pdf (archived at https://perma.cc/7CHB-T7QH)

JWMI (2015) What is the role of a leader? Jack Welch Management Institute, *YouTube*, www.youtube.com/watch?v=ojkOs8Gatsg (archived at https://perma.cc/YT48-BJ37)

Kaplan, R S and Norton, D P (1992) The balanced scorecard: measures that drive performance, *Harvard Business Review*, Jan–Feb

Keurmerk Refurbished (n.d.) Zorgeloos refurbished, van duur naar duurzaam, www.keurmerk-refurbished.nl/ (archived at https://perma.cc/HM27-QVJN) (in Dutch)

Kirchherr, J, Reike, D and Hekkert, M (2017) Conceptualizing the circular economy: an analysis of 144 definitions, *Resources, Conservation & Recycling*, **127**, pp 221–32

Kolb, D (2015) *Experiential Learning: Experience as the source of learning and development*, 2nd edition, Pearson Education, Upper Saddle River, NJ

Korhonen, J, Honkasalo and A, Seppälä, J (2018) Circular economy: the concept and its limitations, *Ecological Economics*, **143**, pp 37–46

Koster, H R (2014) *Essays on Sustainable Supply Management*, CentER, Center for Economic Research

Kotler, P and Keller, K L (2015) *Marketing Management,* Global Edition, Pearson Education, Harlow

Kotter, J (n.d.) The 8-step process for leading change, www.kotterinc.com/8-steps-process-for-leading-change/ (archived at https://perma.cc/5Z9E-2Y8Z)

KPN (2017) Circular Manifesto and Appendix, www.overons.kpn/content/downloads/news/2017-10-11-Circular-Manifesto-and-Appendix-TEMPLATE-V1.0.pdf (archived at https://perma.cc/R22P-MXMN)

Kraaijenbrink, J (2015) *The Strategy Handbook*, Effectual Strategy Press, Doetinchem

Kramer, M and Pfitzer, M (2016) The ecosystem of shared value, *Harvard Business Review*, October

Kuik, S S, Nagalingam, S V, Amer, Y (2011) Sustainable supply chain for collaborative manufacturing, *Journal of Manufacturing Technology Management*, 22 (8), pp 984–1001

Kurpjuweit, S and Wagner, S (2020) Startup supplier programs: a new model for managing corporate-startup partnerships, *California Management Review*, 62 (3)

Lacy, P and Rutqvist, J (2017) *Waste to Wealth: The circular economy advantage*, Palgrave Macmillan, London

Lacy, P, Long, J and Spindler, W (2020) *The Circular Economy Handbook: Realizing the circular advantage*, Palgrave Macmillan, London

Lansink, A (n.d.) De man van de ladder, www.adlansink.nl/voorbeeld-pagina/de-man-van-de-ladder/ (archived at https://perma.cc/NW2Z-DQTF) (in Dutch)

Lawrence, A and Weber, J (2017) *Business and Society: Stakeholders, ethics, public policy*, 15th edition, McGraw Hill, NY

LinkedIn & Imperative (2016) Purpose at work: the largest global study on the role of purpose in the workforce, business.linkedin.com/content/dam/me/business/en-us/talent-solutions/resources/pdfs/purpose-at-work-global-report.pdf (archived at https://perma.cc/BR4Z-QGS3)

Lofvers, M (2020) The sustainability slog, blogpost, www.supplychainmovement.com/the-sustainability-slog (archived at https://perma.cc/9F4D-L8G9)

LPI (n.d.) Living Planet Index, www.livingplanetindex.org/ (archived at https://perma.cc/25M7-EL4W)

Lyle, J (1996) *Regenerative Design for Sustainable Development and Design for Human Ecosystems*, Wiley

Magretta, J (2002) Why business models matter, *Harvard Business Review*, 80, pp 86–92

Malthus, T (1798) An essay on the principle of population, in digital form, *Electronic Scholarly Publishing Project*, http://www.esp.org/books/malthus/population/malthus.pdf (archived at https://perma.cc/DU75-2GGC)

Markides, C (1997) Strategic Innovation, *Sloan Management Review*, Spring

Maurya, A (2012) Why Lean Canvas vs Business Model Canvas?, blogpost, blog.leanstack.com/why-lean-canvas-vs-business-model-canvas-af62c0f250f0 (archived at https://perma.cc/UVT8-E9UD)

McKinnon, A (1995a) Logistics and the environment, *Logistics Europe*, June

McKinnon, A (1995b) Reducing the impact, *Logistics Europe*, August

McKinsey & Company (2019) Artificial intelligence and the circular economy: AI as a tool to accelerate the transition, www.mckinsey.com/business-functions/sustainability/

our-insights/artificial-intelligence-and-the-circular-economy-ai-as-a-tool-to-accelerate-the-transition (archived at https://perma.cc/W6EX-RU3X)

Mestre, A and Cooper, T (2017) Circular product design: a multiple loops life cycle design approach for the circular economy, *The Design Journal*, **20** (1), pp 1620–35

Mikulka, J (2018) The secret of the great American fracking bubble, *Desmog*, www.desmogblog.com/2018/04/18/finances-great-american-fracking-bubble, (archived at https://perma.cc/9TCR-9NEB)

Milieu Centraal (n.d.) Afval scheiden: cijfers en kilo's, www.milieucentraal.nl/minder-afval/afval-scheiden-cijfers-en-kilos/ (archived at https://perma.cc/NE9K-CTZM)

Millennium Ecosystem Assessment (2005) *Ecosystems and Human Well-being: Synthesis*, Island Press, Washington, DC

Mintzberg, H (1991) Learning 1, Planning 0: Reply to Igor Ansoff, *Strategic Management Journal*

Mintzberg, H (2015) *Rebalancing Society. Radical renewal beyond left, right and center*, Berrett-Koehler Publishers, Oakland

Mintzberg, H and Waters, J (1985) Of strategies, deliberate and emergent, *Strategic Management Journal*, July–September

Mishra, J L, Chiwenga, K D and Ali, K (2019) Collaboration as an enabler for circular economy: a case study of a developing country, *Management Decision*

Moore, J F (1993) Predators and prey: a new ecology of competition, *Harvard Business Review*, hbr.org/1993/05/predators-and-prey-a-new-ecology-of-competition (archived at https://perma.cc/7NAG-VA7J)

Moreau, H et al (2020) Dockless e-scooter: a green solution for mobility? Comparative case study between dockless e-scooters, displaced transport, and personal e-scooters, *Sustainability*, **12**

Morgan Stanley (n.d.) Plastic waste resolution, www.morganstanley.com/Themes/plastic-pollution-resolution (archived at https://perma.cc/XW43-XWM5)

Muirhead, S (2016) How open source can accelerate the circular economy shift, *P2P Foundation*, blog.p2pfoundation.net/open-source-can-accelerate-circular-economy-shift/2016/06/03?cn-reloaded=1 (archived at https://perma.cc/2FZ7-QCPY)

Murray, A, Skene, K and Haynes, K (2017) The circular economy: an interdisciplinary exploration of the concept and application in a global context, *Journal of Business Ethics*, **140**, pp 369–80

Nederlandse Brouwers (n.d.) Bruine Nederlandse Retourfles (BNR), www.nederlandsebrouwers.nl/biersector/duurzaamheid-en-ketenbeheer/verpakkingen/statiegeld-retourflessen/ (archived at https://perma.cc/CS8N-QWE7) (in Dutch)

Neessen, P (2020) Closing the Loop: Intrapreneurship and circular purchasing, PhD thesis, October 2020

Nobre, G and Tavares, E (2020) Assessing the role of Big Data and the Internet of Things on the transition to circular economy: Part I, *Johnson Matthey Technology Review*, **64** (1), pp 19–31

NRC (2020a) De aandeelhouder blijft het belangrijkste voor Amerikaanse bedrijven, www.nrc.nl/nieuws/2020/09/16/de-aandeelhouder-blijft-het-belangrijkste-voor-amerikaanse-bedrijven-a4012361 (archived at https://perma.cc/3AGQ-T2WK) (in Dutch)

NRC (2020b) 'Mijn soort mensen is nooit tevreden. Nooit.' Interview with Frank Slootman (CEO of Snowflake), www.nrc.nl/nieuws/2020/09/19/mijn-soort-mensen-is-nooit-tevreden-a4012769 (archived at https://perma.cc/X5G6-BF3P) (in Dutch)

OECD (n.d.) Extended producer responsibility, http://www.oecd.org/env/tools-evaluation/extendedproducerresponsibility.htm (archived at https://perma.cc/S5GU-LYLH)

OECD (2012) Recommendations of the Council on Principles for Public Governance of Public-Private Partnerships, OECD

Osterwalder, A and Pigneur Y (2010) *Business Model Generation: A handbook for visionaries, game changers, and challengers*, John Wiley and Sons, Hoboken. The Business Model Canvas diagram is licensed under Creative Commons Attribution-Share alike 3.0 (creativecommons.org/licenses/by-sa/3.0/ (archived at https://perma.cc/Q3R5-VAL2))

Osterwalder, A et al (2014) *Value Proposition Design: How to create products and services customers want*, John Wiley and Sons, Hoboken

Osterwalder, A et al (2020) *The Invincible Company*, Wiley

Padilla-Rivera, A, Russo-Garrido, S and Merveille, N (2020) Addressing the social aspects of a circular economy: a systematic literature review, *Sustainability*, **12** (7912): doi:10.3390/su12197912

Pauli, G (2017) *The Blue Economy 3.0: The marriage of science, innovation and entrepreneurship creates a new business model that transforms society*, Xlibris, Australia

Perez, H D (2013) *Supply Chain Roadmap: Aligning supply chain with business strategy*, CreateSpace Independent Publishing Platform

Phadnis, S et al (2013) Educating supply chain professionals to work in global virtual teams, Working Paper, CSCMP Educators Conference

Phillips, R A et al (2019) Stakeholder Theory, in *The Cambridge Handbook of Stakeholder Theory*, Oxford University Press, pp 1–16

Piketty, T (2017) *Capital In the Twenty-First Century*, Harvard University Press

Pieroni, M, McAloone, T and Pigosso, D (2020) From theory to practice: systematizing and testing business model archetypes for circular economy, *Resources, Conservation & Recycling*, **162**, 105029

Poelmans, S (2020) *Paradoxes of Leadership: Neuroscience-based leadership in the information age*, Pelckmans uitgevers – KCC

Porcelijn, B (n.d) Mijn verborgen impact, mijnverborgenimpact.nl/ (archived at https://perma.cc/VF9B-E67T) (in Dutch)

Porter, M E (1980) *Competitive Strategy: Techniques for analyzing industries and competitors*, Free Press, New York

Porter, M and Kramer, M (2006) Strategy and society: the link between competitive advantage and corporate social responsibility, *Harvard Business Review*

Porter, M E and Kramer, M R (2011) Creating Shared Value, *Harvard Business Review*, October

Potting, Hanemaaijer (2018) CE. Systeem en nulmeting

Rabello, J, Bernus, P and Romero, D (2015) Innovation ecosystems: a collaborative networks perspective, Conference Paper, PRO-VE 2015, Risks and Resilience of Collaborative Networks, pp 323–36

Rau, T and Oberhuber, S (2016) *Material Matters: het alternatief voor onze roofbouwmaatschappij*, Bertram + de Leeuw Uitgevers, Haarlem (in Dutch)

Raworth, K (2017) *Doughnut Economics: Seven ways to think like a 21st-century economist*, Random House, London

Reike, D, Vermeulen, W and Witjes, S (2018) The circular economy: new or refurbished as CE 3.0? Exploring controversies in the conceptualization of the circular economy through a focus on history and resource value retention options, *Resources, Conservation and Recycling,* **135**, www.sciencedirect.com/science/article/pii/S0921344917302756 (archived at https://perma.cc/2X59-N6ZW)

Reuter M A, Schaik van A and Ballester, M (2018) Limits of the circular economy:
Fairphone modular design pushing the limits, *World of Metallurgy – Erzmetall,* **2** (71), pp 68–79

Rigby, D, Sutherland, J and Takeuchi, H (2016) Embracing agile, *Harvard Business Review,* May

Rli (2015) Circulaire economie: van wens naar uitvoering, www.rli.nl/sites/default/files/rli028-1_wtk_advies_circ_eco_interactief_2.pdf (archived at https://perma.cc/7NL5-9NSQ) (in Dutch)

Robinson, K and Aronica, L (2015) *Creative Schools: Revolutionizing education from the ground up*, Penguin Random House

Rood, T and Kishna, M (2019), *Outline of the Circular Economy*, PBL Netherlands Environmental Assessment Agency, The Hague

Rosling, H and Härgestam, F (2020) *How I Learned to Understand the World: A memoir*, Flatiron Books

Rosling, H et al (2018) *Factfulness: Ten reasons we're wrong about the world – and why things are better than you think*, Sceptre, UK

Rothwell, R (1994) Towards the fifth-generation innovation process, *International Marketing Review,* **11** (1)

Rushton, A, Croucher, P and Baker, P (2017) *Handbook of Logistics and Distribution Management: Understanding the supply chain*, 6th edition, Kogan Page, London

SASB (n.d.) Financial Materiality Maps, www.sasb.org/standards-overview/materiality-map/ (archived at https://perma.cc/NNN2-DP88)

Sawhney, M, Wolcott, R and Arroniz, I (2006) The 12 different ways for companies to innovate, *MIT Sloan Management Review,* **47** (3)

SBA (2012) Do economic or industry factors affect business survival?, US Small Business Association, www.sba.gov/sites/default/files/Business-Survival.pdf (archived at https://perma.cc/G4CC-LH84)

SB Insight (n.d.) Sustainable Brand Index, www.sb-index.com/ (archived at https://perma.cc/88BB-79GE)

Schippers, M, Rook, L and Van de Velde, S (2011) Team supply chain management decisions. Curvilinear effects of reflexivity and regulatory focus, Working Paper, Erasmus University / Rotterdam School of Management. Abstract to be found on discovery.rsm.nl/articles/detail/47-crisis-performance-predictability-in-supply-chains/ (archived at https://perma.cc/T7BS-NS3Y)

Schumpeter, J (1942) *Capitalism, socialism and democracy*

Schwab, K (2016) *The Fourth Industrial Revolution*, World Economic Forum, Coligny/ Geneva

SDG Compass (n.d.) The guide for business action on the SDGs, sdgcompass.org/ wp-content/uploads/2016/05/019104_SDG_Compass_Guide_2015_v29.pdf (archived at https://perma.cc/FNN6-RZHW)

Sehnem, S et al (2018) Circular economy: benefits, impacts and overlapping, *Supply Chain Management: An International Journal*, 24 (6), pp 784–804

Sihvonen, S and Ritola, T (2015) Conceptualizing ReX for aggregating end-of-life strategies in product development, *Procedia CIRP*, 29, pp 639–44

Simchi-Levi et al (2009) *Designing and Managing the Supply Chain: Concepts, strategies and case studies*, 3rd edition, McGraw-Hill, New York

Sinek, S (2009) *Start with Why: How great leaders inspire everyone to take action*, Penguin Books Ltd

Singularity University (n.d.) Global grand challenges, su.org/about/global-grand-challenges/ (archived at https://perma.cc/58C7-C8VB)

SP Global (n.d.) Dow Jones Sustainability World Index, www.spglobal.com/spdji/en/indices/ equity/dow-jones-sustainability-world-index/ (archived at https://perma.cc/N5XM-VDK6)

Stahel, W R (2013) Policy for material efficiency – sustainable taxation as a departure from the throwaway society, *Philosophical Transactions of the Royal Society A, 371*, http://dx. doi.org/10.1098/rsta.2011.0567 (archived at https://perma.cc/H2EJ-TGDK)

Stahel, W R (2019) *The Circular Economy: A user's guide*, Routledge, Oxon

Stahl, R (2009) Sales and operations planning: simpler, better and more needed than ever, *Foresight*, 14, http://rastahl.fatcow.com/-Final%20Summer%20Column%20.pdf (archived at https://perma.cc/YA3F-C5BW)

Steeman, M (2017) Viewpoint: supply chain finance in the circular economy, SCF Academy, http://scfacademy.org/briefing/viewpoint-supply-chain-finance-in-the-circular-economy/ (archived at https://perma.cc/M5SX-WGV6)

Steffen, W et al (2015) The trajectory of the Anthropocene: the great acceleration, *The Anthropocene Review*, March

Steward, R, Bey, N and Boks C (2016) Exploration of the barriers to implementing different types of sustainability approaches, *Procedia CIRP*, 48, pp 22–27

Stock, J (1992) Reverse Logistics: white paper, Council of Logistics Management, Oak Brook, IL

Stockholm Resilience (2015) New planetary dashboard shows increasing human impact, stockholmresilience.org/research/research-news/2015-01-15-new-planetary-dashboard-shows-increasing-human-impact.html (archived at https://perma.cc/8NDA-U5VV)

Suurmond, R, Wynstra, F and Dul, J (2020) Unraveling the dimensions of supplier involvement and their effects on NPD performance: a meta-analysis, *Journal of Supply Chain Management*, 56 (3)

Takacs, F, Stechow, R and Frankenberger, K (2020) Circular Ecosystems: Business model innovation for the circular economy, White Paper of the Institute of Management & Strategy, University of St. Gallen

Teece, D (2010) Business models, business strategy and innovation, *Long Range Planning*, **43**, pp 172–94

Thierry, M et al (1995) Strategic issues in product recovery management, *California Management Review*, **37** (2), pp 114–35

Toffel, M W (2003) The growing strategic importance of end-of-life product management, *California Management Review*, **45** (3), Spring

Treacy, M and Wiersema, F (1995) *Discipline of Market Leaders: Choose your customers, narrow your focus, dominate your market*, Ingram Publishers

Tuckman, B (1965) Developmental sequence in small groups, *Psychological Bulletin*, **63** (6)

UMIO (2020), A circular economy approach, umio-prime.nl/finding-opportunity-in-crisis/ (archived at https://perma.cc/U5NB-PYT6)

UN (n.d.) Making global goals local business, www.unglobalcompact.org/sdgs (archived at https://perma.cc/M7DU-MVUN)

UN (2020) *The SDG Partnership Guidebook*, sdgs.un.org/publications/sdg-partnership-guidebook-24566 (archived at https://perma.cc/5NFR-X5HD)

UNDP (2020) National Circular Economy Strategy and Action Plan, www.kh.undp.org/content/cambodia/en/home/presscenter/speeches/2020/national-circular-economy-strategy-and-action-plan.html (archived at https://perma.cc/LS4A-NL2Y)

UNFCCC (n.d.) What is the Paris Agreement? unfccc.int/process-and-meetings/the-paris-agreement/what-is-the-paris-agreement (archived at https://perma.cc/SY2J-WJ8A)

Unilever (n.d) Sustainable living: together we can change the way the world does business, www.unilever.com/sustainable-living/ (archived at https://perma.cc/9M9C-BK3J)

United Nations Foundation (2019) The sustainable development goals in 2019: People, planet, prosperity in focus, unfoundation.org/blog/post/the-sustainable-development-goals-in-2019-people-planet-prosperity-in-focus/ (archived at https://perma.cc/8DKJ-ACQC)

UN IRP (2018) Redefining value: the manufacturing revolution. Remanufacturing, refurbishment, repair and direct reuse in the circular economy, Report of the International Resource Panel, United Nations Environment Program, Nairobi, Kenya.

Upward, A and Jones, P (2016) An ontology for strongly sustainable business models: defining an enterprise framework compatible with natural and social science, *Organization and Environment*, pp 1–27, core.ac.uk/download/pdf/54849742.pdf (archived at https://perma.cc/7BT6-VUWX)

USGBC (n.d.) LEED rating system, www.usgbc.org/leed (archived at https://perma.cc/D43P-J23C)

Vaccaro, A and Kusyk, S (2011) *The Trial of Business Ethics, Technical Note*, IESE Business School publishing

Van Poppel, J (2020) Waarom bijna geen enkele circulaire 'oplossing' echt duurzaam is, *De Correspondent*, decorrespondent.nl/11912/waarom-bijna-geen-enkele-circulaire-oplossing-echt-duurzaam-is/725922652312-76dacf90 (archived at https://perma.cc/3KPB-QC43) (in Dutch)

Vegter, D, van Hillegersberg, J and Olthaar, M (2020) Supply chains in circular business models: process and performance objectives, *Resources, Conservation & Recycling*, **162**, 105046

Velter, M et al (2020) Sustainable business model innovation: the role of boundary work for multi-stakeholder alignment, *Journal of Cleaner Production*, 247

Vermeulen, W, Reike, D and Witjes, S (2018) Circular Economy 3.0. Solving confusion around new conceptions of circularity by synthesizing and reorganizing the 3R's concept into a 10R hierarchy, *Renewable Matter Think Tank*, 27

Visser, W (2014) *CSR 2.0: Transforming corporate sustainability and responsibility*, Springer

Visser, W and Kymal, C (2014) Creating integrated value: beyond CSR and CSV to CIV, Kaleidoscope Futures Paper Series, No. 3, http://www.waynevisser.com/papers/creating-integrated-value-civ (archived at https://perma.cc/BB9H-TCN9)

Visser, W (2017a) Integrated value: what it is, what it's not and why it's important, *Huffpost*, 30 September, www.huffpost.com/entry/integrated-value-what-it-is-what-its-not-and-why_b_59cffdc3e4b0f58902e5ccbf (archived at https://perma.cc/VM5C-X5X9)

Visser, W (2017b) *World Guide to Sustainable Enterprise, vol 1-4*, Greenleaf Publishing, Sheffield, UK

Vollset S E et al (2020) Fertility, mortality, migration, and population scenarios for 195 countries and territories from 2017 to 2100: a forecasting analysis for the Global Burden of Disease Study, *The Lancet*, 14 July, 2020, www.thelancet.com/article/S0140-6736(20)30677-2/fulltext (archived at https://perma.cc/JHH4-5REX)

Wallace, T (2009) S&OP 101, www.rastahlcompany.com/10101.html (archived at https://perma.cc/NM29-2EHG)

Wang, N et al (2019) The circular economy and carbon footprint: a systematic accounting for typical coal-fuelled power industrial parks, *Journal of Cleaner Production*, 229 (20)

WBSCD (n.d. a) WBCSD Vision 2050, www.wbcsd.org/Overview/About-us/Vision-2050-Refresh/Resources/WBCSD-Vision-2050 (archived at https://perma.cc/JWV7-8F6G)

WBCSD (n.d. b) Redefining Value, www.wbcsd.org/Programs/Redefining-Value (archived at https://perma.cc/2BK4-2WHY)

WBCSD (2018) Circular metrics, landscape analysis, docs.wbcsd.org/2018/06/Circular_Metrics-Landscape_analysis.pdf (archived at https://perma.cc/Z8JP-ZECZ)

WBCSD (2020a) Circularity transition indicators v1.0, www.wbcsd.org/Programs/Circular-Economy/Factor-10/Metrics-Measurement/Resources/Circular-Transition-Indicators-V1.0-Metrics-for-business-by-business (archived at https://perma.cc/JS3G-DEPZ)

WBCSD (2020b) Measuring stakeholder capitalism: towards common metrics and consistent reporting of sustainable value creation, http://www3.weforum.org/docs/WEF_IBC_Measuring_Stakeholder_Capitalism_Report_2020.pdf (archived at https://perma.cc/6LSG-3X4A)

Webster, K (2017) *The Circular Economy: A wealth of flows*, 2nd edition, Ellen MacArthur Foundation Publishing, Cowes, Isle of Wight

Weenk, E (2013a) *The Perfect Pass: What the manager can learn from the football trainer*, QuSL/Libros de Cabecera, Barcelona

Weenk, E (2013b) The supply chain manager's daily decathlon, SupplyChainMovement.com. Published between March and June 2013 as a series of six blogposts, www.supplychainmovement.com/the-supply-chain-managers-daily-decathlon-part-1-of-6/ (archived at https://perma.cc/Z5SX-MZHM)

Weenk, E (2019) *Mastering the Supply Chain: Principles, practice and real-life applications*, London, Kogan Page

Weetman, C (2020) *A Circular Economy Handbook for Business and Supply Chains: Repair, remake, redesign, rethink*, Kogan Page, London

WEF (n.d.) What is systems change? http://reports.weforum.org/schwab-foundation-beyond-organizational-scale/explaining-systems-change/?doing_wp_cron=1604853045.21142101 28784179687500 (archived at https://perma.cc/NY8N-GTF2)

WEF (2019) Davos Manifesto 2020: The universal purpose of a company in the Fourth Industrial Revolution, www.weforum.org/agenda/2019/12/davos-manifesto-2020-the-universal-purpose-of-a-company-in-the-fourth-industrial-revolution/ (archived at https://perma.cc/H2PG-9CAT)

WEF (2020a) To build a resilient world, we must go circular: here's how to do it, www.weforum.org/agenda/2020/07/to-build-resilience-to-future-pandemics-and-climate-change-we-must-go-circular/ (archived at https://perma.cc/JZR2-L8NU)

WEF (2020b) *Global Risks Report 2020*, World Economic Forum, www.weforum.org/reports/the-global-risks-report-2020 (archived at https://perma.cc/YS7D-7789)

WEF (2020c) Measuring stakeholder capitalism: towards common metrics and consistent reporting of sustainable value creation, http://www3.weforum.org/docs/WEF_IBC_Measuring_Stakeholder_Capitalism_Report_2020.pdf (archived at https://perma.cc/PFC4-4QHZ)

Weiblein, T and Chesbrough, H W (2015) Engaging with startups to enhance corporate innovation, *California Management Review*, 57 (2), pp 66–90

Wijkman, A and Skanberg, K (2020) The circular economy and benefits for society, a study report at the request of the Club of Rome with support from the MAVA Foundation, clubofrome.org/wp-content/uploads/2020/03/The-Circular-Economy-and-Benefits-for-Society.pdf (archived at https://perma.cc/T9BT-ZRBE)

Wilms, F (2020) Wat je moet weten over de 2 leiderschapsstijlen, blogpost, managementcursussen.com/twee-leiderschapsstijlen/ (archived at https://perma.cc/F7AV-995M) (in Dutch)

World Bank (2018) *What a Waste 2.0 : A global snapshot of solid waste management to 2050*, openknowledge.worldbank.org/handle/10986/30317 (archived at https://perma.cc/C9HL-WD4T)

WRAP (2015) Employment and the circular economy: Job creation in a more resource efficient Britain, http://www.wrap.org.uk/sites/files/wrap/Employment%20and%20the%20circular%20economy%20summary.pdf (archived at https://perma.cc/CT97-T8CJ)

INDEX

Italics denote information within a figure.

CPSIA information can be obtained
at www.ICGtesting.com
Printed in the USA
BVHW022040240421
605734BV00005B/3